Cuban Music from A to Z

Cuban Music from A to Z

Helio Orovio

Duke University Press

Durham 2004

For a wide variety of genres
of Cuban music,
visit: www.tumimusic.com

Printed in the United States
of America on acid-free paper ∞
Designed by Mary Mendell
Typeset in Quadraat by Tseng
Information Systems, Inc.
Library of Congress Cataloging-
in-Publication Data appear on the
last printed page of this book.

Consulting editor, Mo Fini. Translated from the
Spanish by Ricardo Bardo Portilla and Lucy Davies
and revised by Sue Steward.
Illustrations by Bobby Carcassés.
All photographs, with the exception of those
credited to Mo Fini and that of Helio Orovio
on page 156, were provided courtesy of the
Museo Nacional de la Música, Havana.

Contents

Preface

This reference work began life over twenty years ago. The idea was developed at the Institute of Ethnology and Folklore at the Cuban Academy of Sciences, and began as a list of composers, songwriters, musical interpreters, groups, genres, instruments, musical institutions, and other relevant classifications. I added to my own musical knowledge that of researchers, respondents, and journalists, as well as information found in catalogues, songbooks, press clippings, and many other diverse sources. I even made use of those sugary interviews published in the 1940s magazines *Bohemia* and *Carteles*. This initial research was followed by the indexing of records, a project that, after two years, resulted in an extensive catalogue. Finally the writing of the entries began, an enterprise that has required constant input, revisions, and corrections, right up to the present day.

As I wanted to avoid the common transgression of planning, researching, and writing from a library or desk in Havana only, I also traveled around the island so as to emphasize those other cities of specific cultural importance. Music is a complete entity in itself, involving highly technical elaboration, irrespective of time and space, whether it is the playing of a symphony or the fervent, rhythmic beating of a drum. Throughout Cuba, experts in all fields of music helped greatly, and it is impossible to mention every individual who provided assistance. Suffice it to say, I thank all of you for your help and your invaluable and permanent contribution to Cuban culture.

This is the first work in which the music of Cuba and its musicians appear in a reference format. Researchers, academics, musicians, teachers, art workers, and fans now have at their disposal a long-sought text to consult. I have included a wide range of composers, interpreters, groups, and institutions. My criteria were always based on the subject's worthwhile contribution, and every effort was made to avoid turning this reference into a "phone book." Undoubtedly, there have been mistakes and omissions (unavoidable in this type of work); readers and specialists will be able to point them out so that they can be corrected in subsequent editions. As Percy A. Scholes has written in his prologue to *The Dictionary of Music*: "There are many young stars appearing at every moment on the horizon but even the most clear-sighted of prophets could not distinguish between those who will ascend higher and illuminate the world, and those who will quickly pale to extinction."

This work is, above all else, a tribute to Cuban music and its musicians, many of them unknown, who have brought Cuban music to the entire world.

—Helio Orovio

Acknowledgments

for additions, updates, and corrections for future editions are welcome and should be sent to

Mo Fini
Tumi Music Ltd.
8/9 New Bond Street Place
Bath, BA1 1BH, U.K.
T (44) (0) 1224 464736
F (44) (0) 1225 444870
mofini@tumimusic.com

Thanks to Carmen Valdés, a profoundly analytical teacher, who revised all the entries, making important amendments and additions; to the maestro Vicente González Rubiera ("Guyún"), who worked with the original entries, enriching them notably and providing musicological analysis, as did Rosendo Ruiz Jr.; to María Anonieta Henríquez and the *compañeros* of the National Museum of Music under the direction of Rogelio Marínez Furé, notable researcher of African cultural elements in America; to the *compañeros* of the music department of the José Martí National Library and especially to the department's director, Teresita Alonso; to the musicologist María Teresa Linares; to Alberto Muguercia for examining the path of the Cuban *son*; to the young researcher Zoila Gómez; to Ezequiel Rodríguez, enthusiastic performer of Cuba's popular music; to Jorge Antonio González, a specialist in Cuban theatrical music; to the well-informed Oscar Luis López; to the Guantánamo musician Rafael Iniciarte; to the poet and folklorist Miguel Barnet; to Luis Grau, performer of the Cuban *trova*; to Raúl Martínez Rodríguez, untiring researcher; to the musicologist Cristóbal Díaz Ayala; to the *compañeros* of the music section of the Writers and Artists Union of Cuba; to researcher José Piñero; and to Blanquita Portuondo, secretary of the music section of the Writers and Artists Union of Cuba, whose efforts reinforce the union's true collaborative nature.

The erudite work of Fernando Ortiz was of fundamental help in creating the entries on musical instruments. Raul A. Fernandez, Katherine J. Hagedorn, Robin Moore, and Sue Steward assisted greatly in the preparation of the English-language edition of this volume. The publisher, author, and translators are grateful for their technical and editorial insight.

Every effort was made to make this new edition of *Cuban Music from A to Z* as comprehensive as possible. Almost certainly, however, there are worthy musicians who are not featured here. Any suggestions

Introduction

A Brief Outline of Cuban Music

The roots of Cuban music lie in the fusion of Spanish and African cultural elements. Very little is known of the music of the aboriginal Indo-Cubans, whose *aríetos* (festivals) were conducted to the accompaniment of maracas, horns, flutes, and drums. These indigenous groups were destroyed by genocidal settlers, and their music was lost to history.

The Afro-Spanish heritage, on the other hand, helped establish a rich and transcendent Cuban musical expression whose beauty and authenticity are now admired throughout the entire world. The fusion of Spanish and African influences, contrary to popular belief, didn't have to wait for America's discovery to take place; already in Spain, there had been a centuries-long interaction between artistic forms from the African continent and those generated with vitality and extraordinary color in the Peninsula. The first blacks came to Cuba on Columbus's own ships, and from 1510 onward, with the conquest of Cuba led by Diego Velázquez, Africans were brought to the island in successive migratory waves as slaves for manual labor. Soon, music of Yoruba, Congo, Carabalí, and Arará origin would resonate in the island alongside the ballads and dances of Hispanic origin, beginning what Fernando Ortiz refers to as *transculturación*. The pulsating string and the vibrating drum, along with Andalusian or Canarian song, melted together in the Antillean earth.

In a process that evolved alongside the remarkable development and growth of the island's sugar and coffee plantations and peaked at the end of the eighteenth century, a new indigenous music took shape, enriched by elements of Italian song and of African-French music, which was brought by refugees who were fleeing the Haitian revolution. The quadrille, which evolved into the Cuban *danzón*, *son*, *clave*, *guajira*, *habanera*, rumba, and conga, are all genres that encapsulate the Cuban spirit. In the classical sphere, the island saw the birth of Miguel Velázquez in the sixteenth century and Esteban Salas in the eighteenth century, both learned musicians in the European tradition.

The nineteenth century produced a great flowering of Cuban music. Manuel Saumell, followed by Ignacio Cervantes and others, began what might be called *musical nationalism*. In 1879, Miguel Faílde created the first *danzón*, "Las Alturas de Simpson" (Simpson Heights), which opened the door to other innovative contributions. Genres like the *danzón* and the *son* were melded through the works of Raimundo Valenzuela and others and came to be epitomized in 1910 by the song "El bombín de Barreto," by José Urfé. The *son* made its way down from the mountains of the province of Oriente to such cities as Guantánamo, Santiago de Cuba, and Manzanillo, and later spread throughout the island. Finally, the essence of traditional Cuban song (*canción*) was set in the voices and guitars of the troubadours of Santiago de Cuba, led by Pepe Sánchez, Sindo Garay, and others.

At the beginning of the twentieth century, the Municipal Band of Havana and similar institutions in other cities and provinces helped to disseminate a universal repertoire across the island, thereby helping to promote the development of national composers. Guillermo Tomás, Eduardo Sánchez de Fuentes, and Jorge Ánckermann updated the Cuban sound. The work of the pianist Ernesto Lecuona soon became universally popular. In 1922, the Havana Symphonic Orchestra was founded under the direction of Gonzalo Roig; two years later, the Havana Philharmonic Orchestra emerged, under Pedro Sanyuán. Soon thereafter Amadeo Roldán, along with Alejandro García Caturla, began incorporating the basic elements of Afro-Hispanic Cuban folklore into symphonic music. All subsequent national musical expression in this area had as its primeval source the admirable work of these two outstanding figures, who pointed the way to the future by fusing the island's music with the most advanced universal trends.

In the 1940s, in the arena of *música culta* (classical music), the Grupo de Renovación Musical strove to establish technical and expressive excellence. In popular and dance music, great rhythms emerged — rhythms such as the mambo, created by Israel and Orestes López and made popular by the Orquesta de Arcaño, and the *cha-cha-chá*, invented by Enrique Jorrín. These were undeniably rooted in the *son*, which had been popular since the 1920s, not only with the general populace but also with the middle class. Jorrín's innovative rhythm inspired new musical trends, both within Cuba and abroad.

Figures of equal importance in other genres included the guitarist and composer Leo Brouwer. Brouwer forged a movement of new Cuban identity, in which folklore and popular music were entwined with the best of universal musical culture to create an art form that, in its historical significance and high achievements, matched the political importance of the Cuban revolution. Similarly, the *nueva trova* (new song) movement included notable soloists and groups, as well as brilliant and creative composers, who, like the folkloric and popular music groups, moved Cuban music forward. At the Concurso Long–Thibaud in Paris the young pianist Jorge Luis Prats was honored for his interpretation of Rachmaninov's Concerto no. 1, and Ernesto Lecuona performed his *danzas* to great acclaim at the García Lorca Theater in Havana.

The 1980s brought further innovations from established and recognized composers of classical music, who employed fresh perspectives. Choral music was performed all over the island, and light instrumental music was also popular among audiences. On the popular music scene, groups and soloists began creating music in nontraditional ways, with new and experimental forms that now appeared alongside the more traditional *son*. *Bolero* gained a new flavor, and song writing in general was pushed beyond its former frontiers. Meanwhile, Cuban folk music, representing the different Cuban origins, continued its strong tradition. And with the fusion of rumba and conga with jazz and rock, *timba* was born, as performed by such groups as Irakere, Opus 13, Afrocuba, Charanga Habanera, and José Luis Cortés's NG La Banda.

In the 1990s, we saw these various forms of musical expression developing and intermixing even further. In the postmodern age, we can listen and dance to old and new forms—*trova, canción, son,* salsa, rumba, *danzón,* bolero, *timba*—all co-existing together. Thus, Cuba, the Island of Music, has entered the twenty-first century, sharing its sound and musical flavor with the world, just as it has done in past centuries, and winning the favor and fervor of listeners from all latitudes.

Abbreviations

AE   Author's Edition
BN   Biblioteca Nacional (National Library), Havana
CF   Carl Fischer, New York
CNC   Consejo Nacional de Cultura (National Council for Culture)
CTC   Central de Trabajadores de Cuba (Cuban Workers' Association)
EGREM   Empresa de Grabaciones y Ediciones Musicales (Musical Editions and Imprints Firm), Havana and Santiago
ICAIC   Instituto Cubano del Arte y la Industria Cinematográficos (Cuban Institute for Movie-Making, Art, and Industry), Havana
ICR   Instituto Cubano de Radiodifusión (Cuban Broadcasting Institute), Havana
ICRT   Instituto Cubano de Radio y Televisión (Cuban Institute of Radio and Television), Havana
IIM   Instituto Interamericano de Musicología (Inter-American Institute of Musicology), Montevideo
MS   Maurice Senart, Paris
NM   *New Music*, San Francisco
RM   *Revista Musicalia*, Havana
RS   *Revista Social*, Havana

Organizational Structure of the Entries

The main entries for each musician or musical item have been placed alphabetically under the name most commonly used for that musician or musical item. However, to aid the reader in finding entries, cross-references for alternate names and terms, and occasionally for Spanish-language terms and their English-language equivalents, have also been used.

When a work has started a whole new style, a brief note on that work has been placed in the style's entry; when a musician has created an institution or orchestra, a cross-reference to the institution or orchestra has been included. Such a system has prevented lengthy descriptions of institutions or orchestras within the listings for artists, thus attemtping to maintain a better equilibrium in each entry.

It was not always possible to give entries of equal length to subjects of equal importance, since the amount of information available on each subject varies.

A number of archival resources have been used in the preparation of the images for this book, including the National Museum of Music (Havana), the music department at the José Martí National Library, the Cuban Ministry of Culture (Havana), and back issues of the magazine *Bohemia*, as well as the personal files of Dulcila Cañizares and Oscar Luis López.

Cuban Music from A to Z

A

Abakuá, música. Originating in the African region of the Calabar (Nigeria), Abakuá, or Ñáñigo, groups arose in Cuba during the early part of the nineteenth century in Havana and Matanzas. The groups were originally established as mutual aid or support societies according to a religious and cultural structure called a *cabildo*. The Abakuá dance is performed by an *íreme*, or ancestor spirit, a predominant force in the Ñáñigo fiestas. Instruments used in the dance include drums (*bonkó enchemiyá, obiapá, kuchiyeremá, binkomé*), cowbells (*ekón*), two percussive sticks (*itónes*), and rattles (*erikundí*), as well as secret ceremonial instruments like the *ekué*, whose sound is produced using friction. Fiestas, or *plantes*, take place in a special *fambá* room, as well as during processions at which the *íreme* dancers and others join in a musical chorus. "The Abakuá recount legends (*enkames*) in the African Efik language, stories of the origins of their people told during the long ceremonies. The narrator, who is a member of the hierarchy, alternates a sung chorus with another member to the accompaniment of a sacred drum" (Linares, *Viejos cantos afrocubanos*).

abebe. A fan made of dried palm-tree leaves, lined with luxurious fabrics and ornamented with shells, colored beads, peacock feathers, bells, and other symbols allusive to the female *orishas* (deities) (Ortiz, *Los instrumentos de la música afrocubana*, 2:302).

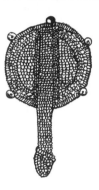

Abreu, Charles. Composer and pianist. Born 29 February 1919, Marianao. Studied at the Havana Municipal Conservatory. In Cuba, Abreu worked as an accompanist in theaters, nightspots, and on the radio, and he also sang in various groups. In 1948 he toured Haiti, Curação, Puerto Rico, Aruba, Venezuela, Peru, and Mexico, and later traveled to Spain, Italy, and France. In 1962 he moved to the United States, where he continued to work as a pianist and arranger and also formed his own group. His best-known songs include "Te necesito," "Cariño mío," "Seran tus pa'ca," and the waltz "La vida mía."

Acosta, Idelfonso. Guitarist. Born 24 January 1939, Matanzas. As a child, Acosta studied violin with Cándido Faílde and later studied trumpet with Rafael Somavilla and Dagoberto Hernández Piloto. He is a self-taught guitarist but also studied with Isaac Nicola. In 1960 he began to give concerts, performing throughout Cuba and also touring abroad. He composed guitar pieces and transcribed works by other composers. He is the author of "Quinteto para dos musicaturas cubanas," which won the Chamber Music Prize in 1974 in the FAR's 26th of July Contests; and "Homenaje al 26," a symphonic poem for chorus and orchestra. He teaches guitar at the School of Professional Achievement in Matanzas and is president of the Provincial Committee of the Writers and Artists Union of Cuba (UNEAC).

Acosta, Leonardo. Saxophonist, musicologist, writer. Born 25 August 1933, Havana. Studied saxophone with José Raphel and José Pérez; harmony and orchestration with Federico Smith; and orchestration, composition, and musical form with Leo Brouwer. Acosta has played in jazz bands such as Havana Melody, Cubamar, Rey Díaz, Calvet, and Loquibambia Swing, as well as with Julio Gutiérrez, Armando Romeu, Rafael Somavilla, and with the Banda Gigante de Benny Moré and Aldemaro Romero (Venezuela). He formed his own jazz quartet with Frank Emilio, Papito Hernández, and Walfredo de los Reyes. In 1970 he formed the Grupo de Experimentación Sonora of the ICAIC (Cuban Institute for Movie-Making, Art, and Industry). He has written incidental music for the cinema and has worked as a journalist for various newspapers. He is the author of *Paisajes del hombre* (short stories, 1967), *Martí, La América precolombina y la conquista española* (1974), *El barroco de indias y otros ensayos* (1984), *Música y épica en la novela de Alejo Carpentier* (1981), *Música y descolonización* (1982), *Del tambor al sintetizador* (1983), *Elige tú que canto yo* (1993), *Novela policial y medios masivos* (1988), and *El sueño del samurai* (poetry, 1993), as well as of an unedited volume, "Descarga cubana." He has organized conferences at universities and cultural centers in New York, Caracas, Bogotá, and Havana and has published articles in various magazines in Cuba and abroad. His most recent book, *Cubano Be, Cubano Bop: One Hundred Years of Jazz in Cuba*, was published in 2003 by the Smithsonian Institution Press.

Adams, Salvador. Guitarist and composer. Born 6 August 1894, Santiago de Cuba; died 21 January 1971. A great friend of Miguel Matamoros. Around 1920 Adams formed a trio with Che Toronto and Rufino Ibarra. In 1952 he composed *Estudios*, for the guitar. In 1962 he directed Los Trovadores Santiagueros in the first festival of popular music in the Amadeo Roldán Theater. In Santiago, he brought together singers and experts in traditional music. He is the composer of "Altiva es la palma" (*criolla*), "Ma causa celos" and "Sublime ilusión" (*boleros*), and "Gitana negra" and "El jilguero."

afro. A genre of popular song that developed out of the Cuban blackface theater in the nineteenth century. It reached its peak of popularity in the 1930s, during the heyday of an artistic movement known as *afrocubanismo. Afros* sometimes present black themes in a stereotypical, derogatory fashion; in other cases they are excellent artistic portrayals of black, working-class Cubans. Some of the most famous *afro* songs include "Ogguere," by Gilberto Valdez, "Drume Negrita," by Ernesto Grenet, and "Bruca Manigua" by Arsenio Rodríguez.

Afrocuba, Grupo. Founded in 1977, the ensemble integrates Cuban musical roots with contemporary elements, including jazz, to produce unique and original music. The original band was formed by Nicolás Reinoso (director and saxophone), with José Carlos Acosta and Fernando Acosta (saxophones), René Luis Toledo (guitar), Ernán López-Nussa (piano), Roberto García (trumpet), Angel Luis López (guitar, bass), Tony Valdés (drums), Mario Luis Pino (percussion), and Anselmo Febles (vocalist and percussion). It won First Prize in the Fifth Musical Contest of the Writers and Artists Union of Cuba in 1978. Later, new instrumentalists joined the band, first directed by Ernán López-Nussa and later by Roberto García.

afrocubana, música. Genre of music with origins in the Afro-Cuban religious cults whose musical rituals include elements of African and Catholic expression. Africans who arrived in Cuba from Nigeria (such as the Yoruba or Lucumí) and from the Congo (the Bantu) brought with them their gods and an intact set of magical beliefs. Their *orishas*, or deities, were the motivation for such commercial songs as "Babalú," an invocation to the god of small pox and other contagious diseases (equivalent to the Catholic saint Lazarus), which was performed by Margarita Lecuona and popularized by Miguelito Valdés. The well-known salsa singer Celia Cruz, together with Merceditas Valdés, recorded invocations to such *orishas* as Babalú Ayé and Chango on the 1950s LP *Santero*, as well as on *Homenaje a los Santos* with Tito Puente. More recently, many artists have performed popular pieces dedicated to other deities, including songs such as "Oggere" by Gilberto Valdés, "Lacho" by Facundo Rivero, and "Facundo" by Eliseo Grenet. "A Santa Bárbara" by Celina (González) and Reutilio Domínguez is a true classic of this type. The piano piece by Ernesto Lecuona "La comparsa" also has an Afro-Cuban element, as does the concert music of

Amadeo Roldán and Alejandro García Caturla. Popular music and dance styles such as rumba, conga, and mambo also contain important Afro-Cuban elements. In jazz, this element can be seen in the work of Mario Bauzá with Machito's Afro-Cubans and in the work of the *conguero* Chano Pozo, who worked with Dizzy Gillespie. Salsa music also has a strong Afro-Cuban content.

Afro-Cuban All Stars. Formed in 1995 and directed by Juan de Marcos González, the Afro-Cuban All Stars were the backbone of the *Buena Vista Social Club* album, which won a Grammy Award in 2000. The original members of the band were Puntillita, Felix Baloy, Omara Portuondo, Lino Borges, Fernando Alvarez, Teresa Garcia Caturla, Barbarito Torres, Changuito, Tata Guines, Ibrahim Ferrer, and Cachaito, among others.

Afro-Cuban jazz. The Afro-Cuban jazz movement resulted from the fusion of Afro-Cuban percussion instruments, folkloric songs, and traditional rhythms with the harmonies, improvisational styles, and ensemble formats characteristic of jazz. The roots of the style date back to the nineteenth and early twentieth centuries, reflecting the common origins of jazz and Cuban music in influences from Africa. The movement propelled a repertoire for marching bands, wind orchestras, and other ensembles. Scott Joplin and Jelly Roll Morton, for instance, included *tresillos, cinquillos, habanera* rhythms, and other Latin elements in their compositions. Other early jazz artists were influenced by Caribbean music as well because of the close contact between New Orleans and many nearby port cities. In the 1920s and 1930s, *jazzbands* that began to experiment with the incorporation of local percussion into their ensembles—including La Orquesta Hermanos Palau, La Orquesta Hermanos Castro, and La Orquesta Riverside—formed in Havana and elsewhere in Cuba. At the same time, these and other groups began to imitate the instrumentation and orchestrational formats established by U.S. big bands. In the United States, Duke Ellington's collaborations with Puerto Rican trombonist and composer Juan Tizol were an important precursor to the Latin jazz movement, as were compositions by Cuban Alberto Socarrás and other Caribbean immigrants. The Afro-Cuban jazz movement achieved widespread acclaim only in the late 1940s. Central figures from this period include composer and arranger Mario Bauzá, band leaders Dizzie Gillespie and Stan Kenton, and percussionist Luciano "Chano" Pozo. The orchestras of Bauzá and Gillespie especially are among the first to have prominently featured a variety of Afro-Cuban traditional rhythms and instruments in their arrangements. Other seminal artists following in the footsteps of the Bauzá/Gillespie generation include Tito Puente, Mongo Santamaría, and Cal Tjader. In more recent decades, Afro-Cuban and Latin jazz has become one of the most vital avenues of experimentation and development among jazz artists internationally.

Afrokán, Pello el. *See* Izquierdo, Pedro.

agogo. Small liturgical bells of various shapes and sizes, used to conjure up the saints in Yoruba cults. The word "*agogo*" is Yoruban, meaning "bell." The Obatalá *agogo*, called an *adyá*, is a long, conical bell of a silver color with a curved handle. The Ochún *agogo* is made of brass, copper, or any yellow metal. It has no special shape and is generally a standard manual bell. The Olókum *agogo* has a wooden handle a little more than a *jeme*, or six inches, long. On its upper end there is a enclosed conical metal rattle, about five centimeters long, fixed to the handle at its circular base. Inside, there is something that, when shaken, rattles faintly. The Egún *agogo*, which represents the spirit of the ancestors, is made of an iron rod, about a half-meter long, to which three round metal bells with no clappers are successively fixed; these are struck with a small bar. The Oddúa *agogo* consists of a handle one *jeme* long, at whose ends there are two truncated conical bells that sound freely and simultaneously. The Babalú Ayé *orisha* of

the Lucumí is associated with wooden *agogos* (Ortiz, *Los instrumentos de la música afrocubana*, 2:281–93).

Agramonte, Eduardo. Soldier, doctor, musician. Died 8 March 1872, Camagüey. Studied music in Camagüey. In the Cuban War of Independence, in 1868, Agramonte joined the Mambí army and fought in many battles. He created the *toques militares*, the bugle call of the liberating army. He fell in combat in San José del Chorillo in the province of Camagüey.

Agramonte, Emilio. Pianist and singing teacher. Born 28 November 1844, Camagüey; died 31 December 1918, Havana. Brother of Eduardo and cousin of Ignacio Agramonte. In 1865 Emilio Agramonte received a degree in law in Spain, where he also studied music, and then continued his musical studies in Italy and France. In 1893 he founded a school of opera and oratorio in New York, where for fifteen years he directed the Gounod Society. In 1902, when the Cuban Republic was established, he returned home and opened the Chaminade Choral Society in Havana. He was a professor at the Havana Municipal Academy of Music.

Aguabella, Francisco. Percussionist. Born 1925, Matanzas; died (?). Began his career singing and playing the congas with rumba and folkloric ensembles in Matanzas and Havana. In the 1950s Aguabella joined the dance company of Katherine Dunham and moved to the United States, where he played in many Cuban dance bands and Afro-Cuban jazz bands. In Los Angeles and San Francisco he has played the congas and *batá* drums on many recordings and at concerts and jazz festivals. He has worked with Pérez Prado, Tito Puente, Cal Tjader, Mongo Santamaría, Al Mckibbon, Dizzy Gillespie, Eddie Palmieri, and also with Peggy Lee.

Aguado, Ana. Soprano. Born 3 May 1866, Cienfuegos; died 6 May 1921, Havana. In 1889 Aguado went to the United States, where she became a soloist in New York's Church of Saint Francis Xavier. Along with José Martí, she took part in many festivals, with the aim of accumulating funds for the liberation of Cuba. She also performed in Spain. When the War of Independence ended in 1898, she returned to Cuba, where she taught music.

Agüero, Elisa. Singer. Born in Camagüey; died (?). Between 1870 and 1880 Agüero interpreted lyrical songs and performed on tours in Mexico and Spain.

Agüero, Gaspar. Teacher of melody and piano. Born 15 February 1873, Camagüey; died 18 May 1951, Havana. With a Ph.D. in musical pedagogy, in 1893 Agüero became a music teacher with the Dependents' Association. He was also a director of choral and orchestral groups. Agüero published various musicological texts and collaborated in the research of Fernando Ortiz. In 1902 he began teaching at the National Conservatory. In 1915 he took a senior teaching post in the Normal School for Teachers in Havana. He was a member of Cuba's National Academy of Arts and Letters and of the Economic Society of Friends of the Country.

Agüero, Oliverio. Teacher of music. Born 1844, Camagüey; died 1923, Havana. Professor at the Institute of Secondary Education in Camagüey. Agüero studied music in Germany and England and provided musical guidance to many young musicians.

Aguilar, Grupo Campesino de. Directed by the laud player Alejandro Aguilar, who was born Pedro Betancourt on 21 April 1906. The ensemble played the entire range of *punto guajiro* and gave concerts all over Cuba until it disbanded in 1970.

Aguilera, Ripoll, Ana M. Teacher and researcher of Cuban music. Born 1903, Holguín; died 25 July 1972. Studied piano with Rosa Betancourt. Author of *Cancionero infantil de hispanoamerica* (1960). Aguilera organized conferences and wrote articles on Cuban music.

Ajo, José Oriundo de Buenaventura. Musician, maker and tuner of organs. Born in Holguín. In 1914 Ajo founded the musical group Ciudad de Paris, in which he played timbales, having taught himself the mechanics of the instrument. As an organist, he instituted a number of fiestas throughout Cuba and recorded various popular dance pieces. The arrangements he used for the organ were written by Horacio Olivera. Ajo's sons continued his organ-making work: Arnaldo made them and Alcideds tuned them. The third son, Arquímedes, directed the traditional music group Hermanos Ajo y Su Organo Oriental (The Ajo brothers and their Eastern organ), which was the subject of a documentary made by the Cuban Institute for Movie-Making, Art, and Industry.

akpwón. A solo singer in the music of Yoruba origin. The soloist sings a phrase, nearly always high pitched, that is answered by a chorus; this pattern is then repeated a number of times.

Alarcón, Salvador. Musical director and composer. Born 30 January 1931, Bayamo. Has studied music with Rafael Cabrera and has also worked under the directorship of Felix Guerrero, Manuel Duchesne Cuzán, and Leo Brouwer. Since 1959 Alarcón has directed several musical groups for whom he has written choral and instrumental works.

Alarcón, Tomás. Music teacher and director of popular music groups; composer of dances and Cuban airs. Born in early eighteenth century, Havana; died 1795. Renowned in Havana at the end of the eighteenth century, Alarcon excelled as a violinist, playing with his left hand; he had lost the use of his right hand due to a fight.

Alas del Casino, Carlos. Singer. Born 1914, Guanabacoa; died 8 May 1993, Miami. Beginning in the 1940s, Alas del Casino performed traditional Cuban music, in particular the *guajira*. In the 1960s he performed on various Cuban radio stations and toured Latin America, later moving to the United States.

Alba Marina. *See* Fernández, Alba Marina.

Albuerne, Fernando. Singer. Born 28 October 1920, Sagua de Tánamo. A graduate in agricultural engineering from Havana University, Albuerne went on to work in soap production. In 1941 he performed on Radio Cadena and became one of the station's exclusive artists until 1954, also appearing in theaters, cabaret shows, and on television. Albuerne recorded a large selection of Cuban and Mexican songs. In 1947 he toured various countries in Latin America and in 1953 made appearances in Madrid, Lisbon, and Paris. In 1960 he moved to Caracas, Venezuela, and later lived in Tampa, Florida.

Alday, Ángel. Composer, singer, guitarist. Born 19 July 1914, Santiago de Cuba; died 1995, Havana. Between 1922 and 1926 Alday lived in Jamaica with his parents. On returning to Cuba, he lived in Havana, where he worked as a troubadour for Cadena Roja radio. He was a member of several trios including El Caribe, El Habana, and Servando Díaz, and he later formed the Trío Cuba, which toured virtually every country in Central and South America. He is the author of such boleros as "No te pido mucho," "Caribe soy," "Como tú nadie," and "Al comprender," and of the *guarachas* "Tic tac" and "Chiquita."

Alea, María Matilde. Teacher and composer. Born 6 March 1918, Camajuaní. Lived in Pinar del Río, where she began studying music with her mother, María Teresa Fernández. Later, in Havana, Alea studied in the Conservatorio Orbón and worked under the tutelage of Professor Oscar Lorié. She taught music and became a teacher in the Alejandro García Caturla Conservatory. She wrote many instructional pieces for the piano. Some of her best-known works include Three preludes for clarinet and piano (1975), Music for violoncello and piano (1975), *Cabildo*, for two pianos (1978), Three miniatures for oboe piano (1983), and Cuban rhythmic miniatures.

Alemán, José. Double bassist, violinist, flutist, pianist, musical director; composer of religious and dance music. Born 22 December 1846, Guanabacoa; died 25 February 1924, Santiago de las Vegas. Studied music with the teacher Pedro Ilvarez. Alemán later played with various orchestras and led small religious music groups in churches in Havana. He played in the orchestra of the Havana Cathedral alongside the best musicians of the time. In 1870 he went to live in Santiago de las Vegas and played the double bass in the Juan de Dios Alfonso Orchestra. In 1972 he formed his own orchestra, which performed for many years. Aleman was also a tailor and worked in Santiago de las Vegas.

Alemán, Orquesta. A so-called *orquesta típica* (wind orchestra) created in 1878 by the double bass player José Alemán in Santiago de las Vegas. In addition to José Alemán, the orchestra included Alejo Carrillo (cornet), Pedro Espinosa (trombone), Leobino Zayas (ophiclenic), Julián Allende (first clarinet), Ramón

Alemán (second clarinet), Elías Fuentes (first violin), Juan Tomás Alemán (second violin), Aniceto Rodríguez (timbales), and Quirino Sastre (*güiro*). The band traveled to Tampa, Florida, in 1920 and performed in several dance halls. When José Alemán died in 1924, his son Ramón became the director and new musicians joined the orchestra: David Pérez (cornet), Manuel J. Hernández (trombone), Rogelio Valdés (ophiclenic), Guillermo Arteaga (second clarinet), José Valdés Alemán (second violin), Rafael Campos (timbales), and Enrique Murgas (*güiro*). The orchestra split up in the 1930s.

Alén, Alberto. Musicologist and cellist. Born 21 November 1948, Havana. Studied music at the Alejandro García Caturla Conservatory, the Amadeo Roldán Conservatory, and at the Higher Institute of Art, where he graduated in 1982 with a degree in musicology. Alén worked as a cellist in the Pequeña Orquesta Sinfonica, the Orchestra of the Grand Theater in Havana, and in several orchestras affiliated with Cuban radio and television stations. He has given classes and conferences in Cuba, Mexico, and Algeria. He taught at the Higher Institute of Art and was a researcher at the Center for Research and Development of Cuban Music and an adviser for musical programs on Cuban television. In 1986 he was awarded the Musicological Prize by the Casa de las Américas for his book *Diagnosticar la musicalidad*. His other written works include *Perspectivas de la investigación musical actual* (1976), *La forma de las formas musicales* (1981), and *La génesis del espacio musical* (1986).

Alén, Andrés. Pianist. Born 7 October 1950, Havana. Studied at the National School of Art and later was a student of L. N. Vlasenko at the Tchaikovsky Academy, in Moscow, where he graduated in 1976. Alén has performed throughout Cuba and has toured the Soviet Union, Poland, Czechoslovakia, Germany, and India. He taught piano in the National School of Art and is an arranger of popular music. He has recorded with EGREM and is a member of the group Perspectiva.

Alén, Olavo. Musicologist. Born 23 December 1947, Havana. Studied piano at the National School of Art and later became the director of music at the National School of Modern Dance. Alén was also an adviser in the Ministerial Department of Support for the Arts. He studied at the Institute of Musicology at Humboldt University in Berlin, graduating in 1977. In 1979 he received a doctorate with honors. In 1975 and 1980 he took part in international conventions in Germany, Czechoslovakia, the Soviet Union, Hungary, and Iraq and was invited to participate in the Chopin Concurso in Poland. In 1981 he taught at the Center for Musical Research and Documentation in Mexico. He has published *Combinaciones instrumentales y vocales de Cuba* (1973), *Géneros de la musica cubana* (1976), *Tumba fracesa* (1977), and *Generos musicales de Cuba: De lo afro a la salsa* (1992), and other articles and essays in Cuban publications. He was a teacher in the Higher Institute of Art and the director of the Center for Research and Development of Cuban Music.

Alfaro, Xiomara. Singer. Born 11 May 1930, Havana. Began his career performing in the musical *Batamú*, at the Martí Theater in Havana, directed by Obdulio Morales. Later Alfaro sang in the casts of Havana's most significant cabarets, including those at the Sans Souci, Tropicana, and Monmartre. He also appeared on radio, television, and in other theatre productions. Later, he toured the world and appeared in the film *Mambo* alongside Silvana Mangano and Vittorio Gassman. He has recorded many songs, Cuban and otherwise. He lives in the United States, where he continues to perform.

Alfonso, Adolfo. Singer of *punto guajiro*. Born 1925, Melena del Sur. Began his career by interpreting Cuban *decimas* on children's radio programs. Alfonso later performed with the Casita Criolla, a group of politically motivated improvisationists who toured Cuba. He also performed on several radio stations, including Cadena Azul, Mil Diez, CMQ, and Union Radio. He was a member of the Cantores de Ariguanabo. In 1962 he joined Justo Vega, with whom he had worked on the folkloric television show *Palmas y cañas*. He toured various Latin American countries and many cities in Europe and Africa, interpreting *guajiras*.

Alfonso, Ariel. Composer. Born 1950, Pinar del Rio. Worked in the Poder Popular of his home region and won prizes for his compositions in national competitions and festivals. One of Alfonso's songs won him First Prize in the Festival of Dresden in Germany. His compositions include "Ven y abrázame,"

"Invitación a una montaña lejana," and "Así llega la canción."

Alfonso, Carlos. Composer, arranger, bass player. Born 10 August 1949, Havana. Studied with the teachers Juan Elosegui, Leopoldina Núñez, Federico Smith, and Leo Brouwer. Alfonso directed the quartet Tema IV and, after 1978, the group Síntesis, with whom he has toured widely abroad. He is the author of various songs and instrumental pieces, and he has done considerable work on Afro-Cuban songs together with the *akpwón* Lázaro Ross.

Alfonso, Gerardo. Composer and troubadour. Born 1 November 1958, Guanabacoa. During the early 1980s Alfonso sang his own songs and played guitar. He has since performed in theaters and cultural centers and toured abroad. He is the author of "Sabanas blancas," among other works.

Alfonso, Juan Carlos. Pianist, composer, director. Born 30 March 1963, Bejucal. Studied at the Alejandro García Caturla Conservatory and later at the Ignacio Cervantes School. Alfonso studied harmony and orchestration with Armando Romeu. He was a pianist in several popular groups, including Supersón, Colonial, and Orquesta Revé. He has written numerous successful dance songs (*sones*), including "Yo sé que tú sabes que yo sé," "La boda en bicicleta," "No me cojan para eso," "Más viejo que ayer," "El chico Suchel," "Más rollo que película," "Ritmo Dan Den," and the salsa ballads "Amame con tu experiencia" and "Mi cuerpo." In 1988 he formed the group Dan Den and has since performed with them on radio and television and at live shows and dances throughout Cuba, as well as in Mexico, Colombia, and Europe.

Alfonso, Juan de Dios. Clarinetist, composer, orchestra director. Born 1825, San José de las Lajas; died 1877, Guanabacoa. Moved to Havana when he was nineteen years old. In Havana, Alfonso formed the *orquesta típica* La Flor de Cuba, which became very popular with dancers in the second half of the nineteenth century. He composed and arranged *contradanzas* and *danzas*, including "Ay! Manuelita," "La Bella María," and "Suelta el peso," as well as *canciones* and *guarachas*. In 1869, during a period of conflict over Cuban independence from Spain, his orchestra was playing at the Villanueva Theater in Havana when Spanish volunteer military recruits savagely attacked the theatergoers. *See also* (La) Flor de Cuba, Orquesta.

Alfonso, Octavio ("Tata"). Flutist, composer, orchestra director. Born 1881, Havana; died 1963. Performed with the Antonio María Romeu Orchestra, and later went on to organize his own *charanga francesa*, which played in Havana and the surrounding areas between 1912 and 1946. Alfonso was the first person to combine *guaguancó* songs and carnival effects with *danzón*. His *danzón* compositions include "El volumen de Carlota," "Cabo de la guardia," "Tata Coñengue," "Catuca," "El 20 de mayo," and "El triunfo de Aldabó." He also performed variations of troubadour songs. He perfected the interpretative style of flute-playing used in *danzón*.

Alfonso, Orquesta de Tata. A *charanga* group that was very popular in Cuba at the beginning of the twentieth century. The flute player Octavio Alfonso, known as "Tata," was its director. At the peak of its fame, the orchestra's members were Jesus López (piano), Pablo Bequé (double bass), Bruno Quijano (violin), Ulpiano Díaz (timbales), Abelardo Valdés (*güiro*), and Tata Alfonso (flute).

Alhambra Theater. Founded in Havana in 1900, it was the venue that pioneered Cuban *bufo* (comic) theater. *Zarzuelas*, musicals, and comedies were all presented there for the first time. Many singers, including Blanca Becerra, Luz Gil, Blanca Vázquez, Hortensia López, and the unrivaled Arquímides Pous and Ramón Espígul, performed there. Manuel Mauri was its first musical director, replaced by Jorge Ánckermann in 1911. Many of Ánckermann's famous *zarzuelas*, such as *La casita criolla*, *La isla de las cotorras*, and *La danza de los millones* were performed there. The most prolific librettists working at the Alhambra were Federico Villoch and Gustavo and Francisco Robreño. The building had an enormous artistic and psychological importance, but it collapsed in 1935.

Aliamen, Orquesta. *Charanga* band formed in Santa Clara in 1964. Miguel René Pinto, Silvio Vergara, and Tomás Muñoz have all directed this band, which has its own *son* repertoire and a distinctive way of playing *son*. It was the first orchestra of its kind to use the electric guitar and other electronic instruments. The band has played on television, at musical festivals, and at fiestas, and has recorded many LPs. It has toured extensively abroad.

Almanza, Enriqueta. Pianist and arranger. Born 15 July 1934, Havana; died 11 August 1996. She began her career on RHC Cadena Azul radio in 1948 as an accompanist and went on to work in television, radio, theater, and cabaret. Almanza created children's music and music for ballet and theater. She lived in Europe between 1955 and 1957 (in Spain, Italy, France, Switzerland, and Germany), and in 1965 joined the Music Hall of Cuba, with whom she traveled to France, Poland, Germany, and the Soviet Union. She subsequently worked in Latin America as an accompanist to various soloists. She was a musical consultant for Cuban television.

Almeida, Juan. Composer. Born 17 February 1927, Havana. Studied at the National Academy of Arts and Letters. At the age of fourteen Almeida composed his first pieces, but his true composing life began in 1959. He participated in the Moncada barracks assault and as part of the "Granma" expedition, alongside Fidel Castro. He would later become a member of the Political Bureau of the Communist Party of Cuba. Among his best-known pieces are "La Lupe," "Carita de ángel," "Compréndeme te pido," "No podrás ser feliz," "Un beso de recuerdo," "Este camino largo," "Decide tú," "Mejor diciembre," "Los recuerdos vividos," "No me olvides amor," "Es soledad," "Déjame mirarte," "Es mejor concluir," "Yo no te olvido," "Tiempo ausente," "Hablo a tu corazón," "Fue anoche," "A Santiago," "Que le pasa a esa mujer," "Dame un traguito," and "Este son homenaje."

Almenares, Ángel. Guitarist and composer. Born 14 May 1902, Santiago de Cuba; died 1981. Studied music at the Academy of Fine Arts with Ramón Figueroa. In 1919 Almenares played timbales in an *orquesta típica*. Later, he became an excellent guitarist; he is remembered as one of the most notable guitar accompanists of *trova cubana*. He played in a duo with José Sierra and, later, with Bebó Garay, as well as with various *trova* ensembles. He was a founder of the *casa-café* of Virilio Palais in Santiago, which became the center of *trova santiaguera* (Santiago-style *trova*). He composed the boleros "Ya te olvidé" and "¿Por que me engañaste?"

Almendra, Orquesta. *Charanga* band formed in Havana by the composer and double bass player Abelardo Valdés in 1940. Its first musicians were Gustavo Sorís (piano), Abelardo Valdés (double bass), Domingo Franco (violin), José Fajardo (flute), and Evaristo Martínez (timbales). Later, José Piedra (piano), Miguel O'Farrill (flute), Rafael Blanco Suazo (conga), and Dominica Verges (vocalist) all joined the band, whose repertoire included *danzón*, bolero, *guaracha*, and *pasodoble*. The ensemble split up in 1960.

Alonso, Arturo. Composer, guitarist, saxophonist, teacher. Born 9 March 1922, Ciego de Avila. Lived in Cabaiguán as a child and later became a tobacco worker in local factories. Alonso studied guitar and worked in several duos, trios, and septets. He studied music with Eduardo Egües and became a saxophonist with the Music Band of Cabaiguán. He also taught melody, theory, and guitar. In 1978 he founded the Cabaiguán Municipal Chorus. He is the author of the boleros "Espero tu carta," "Cumple tu misión," "Alma impura," "Un canto a Cabaiguán," "Frente a la verdad," "Sancti-Spiritus," and "Mi dulce serenata," of the *guajira-cha* "Voy a hablar con tu papá," and of the *danzón* "Su majestad el danzón." He was president of the Society of Authors and Composers of Sancti Spiritus.

Alonso, María Conchita. Singer and actress. Born in Cienfuegos, (?). Lived in Caracas, Venezuela, as a child with her parents, and from there began her career as a singer in the ballad style. She was also influenced by rock music. Alonso has recorded and performed in concert in many countries and has appeared in films made in North and South America, as well as on television.

Alonso, Pachito. Pianist and musical director. Born 6 January 1955, Santiago de Cuba. A 1980 graduate in piano from the National School of Art, Alonso directed the group Los Egresados. In 1983 he joined his father's group, Los Pachucos, as keyboard player and director. When his father (Pacho Alonso) died, he remained director and renamed the group Los

Kini-Kini. He has toured widely abroad and composed many modern songs in the *sonero* style known as *pilón*.

Alonso, Pacho. Singer. Born 22 August 1928, Santiago de Cuba; died 27 August 1982, Havana. Took part as a singer in school groups in the old Coliseo Theater in Santiago de Cuba and studied teaching at the Santiaguera Normal School. Alonso sang on the local Cadena Oriental radio station. In 1946 he traveled to Havana, where he met pianist Bebo Valdés and guitarist and singer José Antonio Méndez, who introduced him to the radio station Mil Diez. In 1951, back in Santiago, he joined the dance band of Mariano Mercerón, playing alongside Fernando Alvarez and Benny Moré. He formed his own band in 1954 and performed with them in Havana and eastern Cuba. In 1958 he moved to the capital with his group Los Bocucos and played at dances in the leading nightspots and on radio and television. In 1962 he traveled to France, Czechoslovakia, and the Soviet Union. In Moscow, Los Bocucos broke with tradition by being the first band to play popular music in the Tchaikovsky Room. In 1969 Alonso performed in Spain and France, and in 1970 he traveled to Panama. In 1972 he toured extensively in Europe, and in 1978 he toured Spain. Alonso popularized the style known as *upa-upa* and created a personal style of bolero and oriental *son*, which brought him many hit records. In his later years, he renamed his group Los Pachucos.

Alqueza, Matías. Choir director, musician, printer. Born mid–eighteenth century, Santiago de Cuba; died 8 January 1819. A multi-instrumentalist who also possessed a good singing voice, Alqueza formed a choir in 1795 at the Santa Lucia Church in Santiago. He played cello in the Santiago de Cuba Cathedral under the directorship of Esteban Salas and later directed the choir there. He was for many years the only printer in Santiago de Cuba.

Álvarez, Adalberto. Composer, pianist, bassoonist, singer, orchestral arranger. Born 22 November 1948, Havana. Moved with his family to Camagüey when he was three. Beginning in 1966 he studied bassoon at the National School of Art. Álvarez became a music teacher at the Provincial School of Music in Camagüey and then director of the group Avance

Infantil. In the 1980s he founded and directed the group Son 14 in Santiago de Cuba and subsequently has written many popular boleros, *sones*, and *guarachas* which have made new advances in the areas of harmony and orchestration. His compositions include "Realidad y solución," "Sobre un tema triste," "Que me quieres," "Por un besito mi amor," "Son sentimental" (for trumpet), "Son de Adalberto," "A Bayamo en coche," "Son de la madrugada," "Agua que cae del cielo," "Esperando a María," "Que tú quieres que te den," "Dale como es," and "El toca toca." Today he directs the group Adalberto Alvarez y Su Son, with which he has traveled widely.

Tomás Casademunt

Álvarez, Calixto. Composer, pianist, organist. Born 15 March 1938, Santa Isabel de las Lajas. Studied music in Santa Clara and in the United States. From 1967 to 1971 Álvarez studied in Poland with Dobrowolski, Kotonski, and others. Back in Cuba, he came under the influence of Federico Smith and Leo Brouwer. He has also written incidental music for the theater. His works include "Sonatina," "Quinteto de viento," "Torus per contrabasso," "Poker," and "Música" (orchestral); as well as "Stripofumios and varsiflorios" (orchestral); Trio op. 13, no. 72; Canto cardinal for contralto, percussion, and piano; Theme and six variations for piano; and Canon. He was a musical adviser to CMBF radio.

Álvarez, Carlos. Composer. Born 2 March 1945, Havana. Studied music at the National School of Art from 1962 to 1968 and was a pupil of Roberto Ondina and Emigdio Mayo (flute), Federico Smith (composing), and José Ardévol and Roberto Valdés Arnau (conducting). Álvarez's incidental music for theater and cinema has brought him many awards. He was a member of the Advisory Board for Cuban radio and television. His compositions include "Despedida a un guerrillero" (for voice and piano), "Ser," "Pueblo invencible," "Sobre piedras," and "Grabados."

Álvarez, David. Composer, singer, guitarist. Born 12 March 1972. Sang with Pedro Luis Ferrer and in 1994 formed his own band, Juego de Manos. Álvarez has achieved international recognition as one of the best singer-songwriters of his time.

Álvarez, Fernando. Singer. Born 4 November 1928, Santiago de Cuba. Began his career as a vocalist in 1947 in Santiago de Cuba as a member of the Armonía Tropical Orquesta, the Hermanos Giro Orquesta, and Mariano Mercerón Orquesta. In 1953 Álvarez moved to Havana and joined the Banda Gigante di Benny Moré. From there, he moved to the group Casino. He has performed as a soloist on many recordings. Álvarez has appeared on radio and television, in theater, and in nightclub shows. He has traveled widely in Latin America.

Álvarez, Lisette. Singer. Born in Lima, Peru. Daughter of singers Olga Chorens and Tony Álvarez. Born accidentally in South America while her parents were on tour there, Álvarez lived in Havana from an early age and began her career there as a child singer. When her parents moved to Puerto Rico, she continued her singing career there as an adult, later moving to Miami. Álvarez has built a successful career in Latin America as an interpreter of romantic songs influenced by the ballad. She has written many hit songs, and six of her thirty records became Gold Records. She lives in Miami with her husband, the Cuban salsa musician Willie Chirino.

Álvarez, Mario. Composer and pianist. Born 1911, Güines; died 25 June 1970, Havana. Received a law degree from Havana University. Álvarez lived in Havana in the 1930s; in the 1940s, he went to Mexico City as a pianist with Ernesto Lecuona and decided to stay. Among his best-known bolero compositions are "Vuélveme a querer," "Sabor de engaño," "Tu no mereces," "Temor sublime," "Luna de plata," "Ansias," "Rumbo perdido," "Aprende a olvidar," "Estas mintiendo," "Y eres culpable," and "No esperes."

Álvarez, Paulina. Singer. Born 29 June 1912, Cienfuegos; died 22 July 1965, Havana. Began singing at parties and school functions at the age of nine. In 1926, when her family moved to Havana, Álvarez continued singing. In 1929, she was the first woman to sing *danzonete*, a new variation of *danzón* created by Aniceto Díaz. By way of the new medium of Cuban radio in the 1930s, she became a professional singer and sang with different orchestras, beginning with La Elegante in 1931. In 1938 she formed her own group, which met with tremendous success. She was known as the "Empress of Danzonete." In 1939 she performed at a concert in the Auditorium Theater, which was the first time a dance orchestra had played in such a select venue. She continued to sing a repertoire of different genres of popular music with her own orchestra and with other groups.

Álvarez, René. Singer. Born 16 June 1918, San Antonio de los Baños; died 23 June 1997, Havana. Interpreter of boleros and *sones*. Álvarez began singing as a child in his neighborhood, known as El Rincón. In 1932, he moved to Havana. He sang with many groups, including Gloria de Cuba, Carabina de Ases, and the group directed by Arsenio Rodríguez, as well as with the dance bands Godínez and Melodías del 40, and with the group Chapottin y Sus Estrellas. He went on to form his own band, Astros, which had its own radio program and performed at dances.

Álvarez Mera, Manolo. Tenor. Born 1925, Havana; died 16 October 1986, New York. After studying voice, in 1943 Álvarez performed in Ernesto Lecuona's work *La Plaza de la Catedral*, directed by the composer. He sang in the same work for the radio stations RHC Cadena Azul and CMQ. In 1947 he went to New York, where he appeared in *Violins over Broadway*, under the auspices of Billy Rose. That show ran for two years. In 1950 Álvarez moved to Rio de Janeiro and performed in São Paulo and on various Brazilian radio stations, and later in Argentina, Chile, and Uruguay. On his return to the United States, he appeared on the television show *The Colgate Comedy Hour* with Eddie Cantor and in the Hotel Flamingo floorshow in Las Vegas with Freddie Martin. In 1954 he sang in a concert in Pasadena under the direction of David Rose, and at the Hollywood Bowl with the conductor Miklos Rozza. He appeared in shows at the Waldorf Astoria in New York, at the Edgewater Beach Hotel in Chicago, and at the Mapes Hotel in Reno, Nevada. He took the lead role in the production *The Spanish Fantasy Show*, which toured America, and he sang on the NBC television program *Saturday Night Review, Coast to Coast*. In Cuba, he performed on television and in the theater and released several records, as well as singing in shows at the Tropicana and Hotel Capri. He is considered to have been one of the best Latin tenors.

Álvarez Otero, Reynol. Orchestra director and guitarist. Born 28 July 1922, Matanzas. Began studying music in Matanzas with Raúl Valdés and Gustavo Lamothe. Álvarez later studied guitar with Carlos Moré, piano with Tomasa Angulo, and harmony with Gonzalez Lahirigoyen. Beginning in 1949 he was a cellist with the Chamber Orchestra of Matanzas, which he later conducted. He taught guitar in the Provincial School of Art in Matanzas. He also conducted the Matanzas Symphony Orchestra.

Álvarez Ríos, María. Composer, pianist, teacher. Born 5 June 1919, Tuinucú. Studied music from an early age and went on to Havana University and later the University of Michigan, where she obtained a doctorate in music. Álvarez traveled to various countries and dedicated her talents to children's music, but she also composed music for the theater and for the poems of Nicolás Guillén. Among her compositions are "Abrázame amor," "Anda di, corazón," "La rosa y el ruiseñor," "Cómo me duele," the *Sonata Yoruba*, and a concerto for piano and orchestra. In 1980 she received a graduate degree in musical composition from the Higher Institute of Art in Havana.

Alvariño, Margot. Singer. Born 1912, Havana; died 1 May 1993, Miami. Began her artistic career with Ernesto Lecuona and later became an exclusive artist of the RHC Cadena Azul radio station. Alvariño performed in the theater and cinema and lived for many years in Cienfuegos. She also played guitar accompaniment. She sang mostly in the style known as *pregón* and was known as "the Queen of Pregón."

Amador, Efraín. Guitarist, composer, teacher. Born 15 June 1947, Morón. Studied at the Amadeo Roldán Conservatory with Isaac Nicola; graduated in 1970 from the National School of Art. In 1981 Amador completed a bachelor's degree in music at the Higher Institute of Art. He was tutored by Leo Brouwer and Alirio Díaz. He gave recitals and concerts in Cuba and other countries. Amador wrote the following works for guitar: Study for the left hand (1976), "Suite para un cacique" (1972), "Canto Latinoafricano" (1977), "Fantasía del son" (1981), "Fantasía guajira" (guitar and piano, 1983). He has edited two volumes of his writings and is currently a guitar teacher in the Higher Institute of Art. He writes for choral and chamber groups.

Amat, Francisco L. ("Pancho"). *Tres* player, composer, arranger. Born 22 April 1950, Güira de Melena. A self-taught musician who was influenced by the *tres* player Lucumí and the percussionist Sixto Sotolongo, Amat has played in several groups in his hometown. He graduated in chemistry and physics from the Higher Pedagogical Institute. In 1971 he joined the group Manguaré and became its director. He studied formally at the Ignacio Cervantes Conservatory, under the guidance of Frank Fernández. He has scored music for the cinema and is the author of the *sones* "Por un camino seguro," "Razones para cantar," "Para hacerte un regalo," and "El gallo pinto." He has played as a soloist on various records and has traveled outside of Cuba. He is the *tres* player with Adalberto Alvarez y Su Son, but he works primarily as a soloist.

América, Orquesta. *Charanga* band formed by Ninón Mondéjar in 1942. The ensemble played on radio and at dances. It was the first orchestra to play *cha-cha-chá* and in 1953 became famous with the initial popularization of *cha-cha-chá* in Cuba. The original members of the band were: Ninón Mondéjar (director); Alex Sosa (piano); Enrique Jorrín, Antonio Sánchez, and Félix Guerra (violins); Juan Ramos (flute); Augusto García (timbales); Gustavo Tamayo (*güiro*); and Jacinto Montes (double bass). The group traveled to Mexico, then to the Dominican Republic, and then to Vienna in 1959, and also performed in the Soviet Union, Finland, France, and Spain. It recorded several LPs and singles and appeared in six films. Recently, Manolo Cauto and Jorge Machado have been directors.

Amézaga, Froilán. Guitarist. Born 11 May 1925, Matanzas. Began his musical activities in Matanzas and in 1944 moved to Havana, where he later played in various musical groups. Amézaga worked as a guitar accompanist to such singers as Elena Burke, with whom he traveled abroad. He has participated in many recording projects and has appeared at different nightclubs. He developed a personal style of accompaniment, especially with songs in the *fílin* genre, which other guitarists have imitated.

Anacaona, Orquesta. Created in 1932 by eight sisters from the Castro family: Argimira (drums), Xiomara (trumpet), Concepción (saxophone), Caridad (double bass), Ada (trumpet, violin, *tres*), Olga (saxophone, clarinet, flute, maracas), Alicia (saxophone, clarinet, double bass), and Ondina (trumpet). Hortensia Palacio and Graciela Pérez (vocalists) were also members of the band. The sisters were all students and were also taking music classes, but a students' strike against President Gerardo Machado caused the president to close down their college, and they were forced out of school. They began assembling to play and from there founded the band. Orquesta Anacaona has traveled to Colombia, Venezuela, Puerto Rico, Mexico, Panama, the United States, and France. It currently performs under the auspices of the Ministry of Culture and the conductor is Georgina Aguirre.

anakué. Also spelled *anukué*. A metal rattle used in Arará ceremonies that is made up of two long cones, united at their vertices and filled with small stones,

seeds, or pellets (Ortiz, *Los instrumentos de la música afrocubana*, 2:324).

Ánckermann, Carlos. Teacher, composer, violinist, clarinetist. Born 10 March 1829, Palma de Mallorca, Spain; died 17 February 1909, Havana. Father of two notable musicians, Jorge and Fernando. Carlos Ánckermann came to Havana at the age of eighteen, where he played clarinet in the well-known Military Band. He was a violinist in the orchestra of the Tacón Theater and taught at the Hubert de Blanck Conservatory. He recorded with Federico Edelmann. He wrote a Grand mass for four voices and other works, including *zarzuelas*.

Ánckermann, Fernando. Double bass player and composer. Born 5 September 1890, Havana; died 24 December 1933. Began his musical studies with his father Carlos (double bass) and his brother Jorge (melody, theory, piano, harmony). Although Fernando played the piano in various groups, his main instrument was the double bass, which he played in the orchestras of the Payret, National, and Alhambra theaters. He played first double bass in the Havana Symphony Orchestra. He became a professor at the Jones de Castro Conservatory. His compositions include the *danzones* "La Rosa de la China," "La niña bonita," "Los cuatro gatos," "Papaíto," "Aguántate Santiago," "Las travesuras de Venus"; the waltzes "Diamela," "Consuelo," and "Un velorio de santo"; the bolero "El pensamiento"; and the dance "No me olvides."

Ánckermann, Jorge. Pianist, composer, orchestra director. Born 22 March 1877, Havana; died 3 February 1941. Began his musical studies with his father at the age of eight. By the age of ten, Jorge was able to take the place of Antonio Gonzalez in conducting a trio. In 1892 Ánckermann went to Mexico as musical director for a group of clowns led by Narciso Lopez, and they toured Mexico and California. He lived for some years in Mexico City, working as a music teacher, and on his return to Cuba he became musical director at some of the city's most important theaters. He produced *zarzuela* scores, revues, and comic sketches, and he wrote *sones, criollas, claves, boleros, guarachas,* rumbas, and *danzónes.* He is considered the creator of the *guajira.* The greatest venue for his works was the Alhambra Theater, where *La isla de las cotorras, La casita criolla,* and other notable scores were performed. He was responsible for great changes in Cuban theater music through his formation of an enlarged *orquesta típica.* Among his most popular works are "El quitrín," "Flor de Yumurí," "Un bolero en la noche," "El arroyo que murmura," "Oye mi clave," and various *danzones.*

Andraca, Antonio. Clarinetist, teacher, orchestra director. Born 8 July 1888, Matanzas; died 11 September 1971, Havana. Began as a clarinet player in the Banda de Bomberos in Matanzas and later joined the *orquesta típica* of Miguel Faílde. Andraca moved to Havana and became solo clarinetist in the Municipal Band and worked in several theater orchestras. In 1922 he helped found the Havana Symphony Orchestra and later became its president. From there, he was appointed director of the Banda de la Marina. He worked as a teacher of musical theory and melody at the Havana Municipal Conservatory and taught clarinet in the Guillermo Tomas Conservatory in Guanabacoa.

Angulo, Héctor. Composer. Born 3 September 1932, Santa Clara. Began his musical studies in Santa Clara and continued them in Havana. Angulo studied architecture at Havana University until the fourth year. In 1959 he received a grant to study at the Manhattan School of Music in New York. He returned to Cuba in 1964, where he studied with Leo Brouwer. His works include the Trio for flute, violin, and piano; Sonata for eleven instruments; Quartet for strings; Variations for a string orchestra; Poem for six instruments; Soneras (homage to the bongó); Son and sonata for piano; and Two canciones (from texts by Nicolás Guillén); as well as "Poemas africanos"; *Ibeyi Añá* (an opera for chamber group); "Cantos yoruba de Cuba" (for guitar); and Toque for piano and Cuban percussion. He combines modern methods of composing with traditional Cuban folklore. He is a musical adviser for the National Puppet Theater.

Anido, Alberto. Composer, writer, painter. Born 10 May 1938, Santa Clara. A self-taught musician and composer, many of Anido's songs have received awards at various national festivals. He took First Prize in the National Theater Festival for Children and Youth for his piece "Margarita en el país de las maravillas." He has written stories, theater pieces, poetry, criticism, and is also a journalist. He is the author of the songs "Calla tú," "Al verme solo cruzar entre la gente," "En la montaña hay un niño que no duerme," "Para siempre venir (to Che Guevara)," and of a work for piano, chorus, and orchestra, "La ciudad de los puentes." He also performs on CMHW radio in Santa Clara.

Anido, Freyda. Pianist. Born 15 January 1943, Santa Clara. Sister of the composer Alberto Anido. Freyda Anido studied piano with Gloria Villar de Franco, Dolores Anido, and Margo Rojas, and at the Ignacio Cervantes Conservatory in Havana. She is known for her work as a piano accompanist and pianist in the Santa Clara Symphony Orchestra and has given concerts in Havana and the area around Santa Clara.

Ansa, Carlos. Pianist and orchestra director. Born 16 December 1915, Havana. Worked for many years as a piano accompanist. Ansa played with various orchestras, most notably that of Alfredo Brito, with whom he worked for almost twenty years. He became a pianist for CMQ radio in 1944 and later became its orchestra director. He has written music for children and done considerable work as an arranger.

Antomarchi, Juan Antonio ("Coto"). *Tres* player. Born 24 November 1964, Havana. Has played in the Orquesta Revé and the groups Avance Juvenil, Conjunto Chapotin, Albit Rodríguez, Jovenes Clasicos del Son, and El Muso y Su Orquesta. He is currently the director of his own band, Coto y Su Eco del Caribe.

Antúnez, Esteban. Guitarist and orchestra director. Born 15 May 1920, Manzanillo; died 6 April 1979, Portland, Oregon. Lived in Santiago de Cuba during his childhood, and in 1934 moved to Havana. Antúnez worked as a guitarist/accompanist and played in recitals. He later directed orchestras and performed on the radio and in the theater. In 1958 he went to Mexico City and then moved to the United States, where he completed his musical studies and became a teacher.

Aparicio, Evaristo. Author and interpreter of Cuban folkloric music. Born 28 January 1925, Havana; died 1985. Began as a percussionist playing in Afro-Cuban rumba bands and in dance groups. Aparicio founded Los Papacuncún in 1970. He is the author of "Cañonazos," "Amor de nylon," "Xiomara," "Bola de humo," "Sarará," "Por la ventana," and other rumbas and *guarachas*.

Aquino, Rafael. Baritone. Born 5 August 1931, Havana. Has appeared on television and in the theater. Aquino took part in numerous operas and operettas and performed across the country. He was a soloist in the Cuban National Opera.

Aragón, Jorge. Pianist and arranger. Born 5 October 1950, Havana. Studied at the Amadeo Roldán Conservatory. In 1971 Aragón joined the orchestra of the Cuban Institute of Radio and Television, where he remained until 1981. He worked for two years in the Orquesta Cubana de Música Moderna, and in 1984 became the keyboard player, arranger, and director of the group led by singer Pablo Milanés. He has also worked as a pianist and accompanist with several other groups and singers. He has written music for the cinema and television, and has toured Brazil, Ecuador, Mexico, the Soviet Union, Poland, the United States, Argentina, Uruguay, Spain, Puerto Rico, Panama, Nicaragua, Peru, Germany, Romania, Hungary, Czechoslovakia, and Bulgaria. He is an adviser to the director of music at the Cuban Institute of Radio and Television.

Aragon, Orquesta. *Charanga* band created by the double bass player Orestes Aragón in Cienfuegos in 1939. The orchestra began playing in its hometown and later performed all around Cuba. After settling in Havana, it became very popular. It is known for playing mainly *cha-cha-chá*. It has performed on radio and television and has recorded many LPs. The orchestra has traveled to Panama, Venezuela, Guatemala, Puerto Rico, the United States, France, Poland, the German Democratic Republic, Japan, and some other countries. During the peak of its popularity, its musicians were: Rafael Lay (violin, vocalist, director), José Palma (piano), José Beltrán (double bass), Celso Valdés and Dagoberto González (violins), Tomás Valdés (cello), José An-

tono Olmos and Rafael Bacallao (vocalists), Richard Egües (flute), Orestes Varona (timbales), Francisco Arboláez (*güiro*), and Guido Sarría (conga). Rafael Lay Jr. is the conductor.

Aragú, Domingo. Percussionist. Born 4 August 1910, San Juan de los Yeras. Began his studies at a very young age and continued them in Cienfuegos with Pedro Gracés. In 1933 Aragú moved to Havana, where he joined the philharmonic orchestra and the army's staff band. Although almost entirely self-taught as a percussionist, he trained other percussionists at the Havana Municipal Conservatory, the Garcia Caturla Conservatory, the National School of Art, and the Higher Institute of Art. He played kettledrums in the Havana Municipal Band and for various groups that performed on local radio. He is the author of the manual *Instrumentos cubanos de percusión*. He also helped found the National Symphony Orchestra and has received much praise from conductors who have been invited to work with this group of musicians. He is a Professor of Merit at the Higher Institute of Art.

Aragú, Luis. Percussionist. Born 17 May 1934, Havana. Son of Domingo Aragú, with whom he studied. Luis later studied in the Higher Institute of Art. He began his professional career as a percussionist in 1960 with the National Symphony Orchestra. He has also worked with other musical groups and recorded classical music as well as contemporary. He has toured widely abroad.

Arango, José Doroteo. Harpist. Born in Camagüey; died at the beginning of the twentieth century in Havana. Known as "Pachencho." Arango played tuba in the Havana Municipal Band. Up until the final years of his life he ran the last *charanga* group in Havana to retain the harp, an instrument that was subsequently replaced by the piano.

Arango, Secundino. Violinist, cellist, pianist, organist. Born at the end of the eighteenth century in Havana; died 15 December 1842. Arango was a pupil of Ramón Menéndez. Later he became an organist in the Church of La Merced. He also taught piano. He composed many dances and *guarachas*, including "La viuda de Plácido," and also composed religious music, motets, and salves. In his final years he was organist at the San Francisco Convent in Guanabacoa.

Aranzola, Pedro. Author of popular works. Born 21 June 1917, Nueva Paz. Moved to Havana in 1933. Aranzola's compositions include "El paso de Encarnación," "Charlas del momento," "Los problemas de Atilana," and "Sin clave y bongó no hay son," which was popularized by the Orquesta Aragón; as well as the *sones* "Sacando palo" and "Puntéame bien el tres."

Arará drums. Generally played in sets of three, with a cowbell. The hollow-sounding body of the largest drum is beaten with two sticks. The drums are tuned by adjusting the tension of the drumhead. On the end opposite the drumhead is an opening through which a smaller cylinder is inserted to serve as a stand. When played, they are leaned against a bench or a forked pole. The body of the instrument is decorated with geometrical drawings and carvings. They are currently found in the Arará *cabildos* (Afro-Cuban societies) in the province of Matanzas.

Arcaño, Antonio. Flutist and orchestra director. Born 29 December 1911, Havana; died 28 June 1994. During his childhood, Arcaño lived in Regla and Guanabacoa, outside Havana. He studied music with Armando Romeu, director of the Banda de Regla, and with him learned the cornet and the clarinet. He later studied flute with his cousin José Antonio Díaz, for whom he subsequently substituted in cabarets and at dances. He joined the *charanga* orchestra of Armando Valdespí; then the Orquesta Gris, directed by Armando Valdés Torres; and then the Orquesta Las Maravillas del Siglo under the auspices of singer Fernando Collazo. By 1937, he had founded

Tomás Casademunt

his own group, Arcaño y Sus Maravillas. The group performed on the radio and on television, on the *Show del Mediodia* on CMQ, and also performed extensively across Cuba. Arcaño's band made many popular records. In 1944 he modified his *charanga* format by forming a bigger group called Radiofonica, with an ensuing change in sound and greater interpretation of arrangements. The group boasted "an ace on every instrument" and included the López brothers—Orestes on piano and Israel ("Cachao") on double bass. In 1938, during their time in the band, the López brothers composed the *danzón* variation called "Mambo," which provided the template for the global success of that dance in the following decade. In 1958 Arcaño played his last dance. He subsequently worked with the Cuban Workers' Alliance as a music teacher and cultural activist, until 1966 when he moved to the Popular Music Seminary. As a flute player, he produced a strong, high-quality sound and unique improvisations to the *montunos* of the *danzón* form.

Arcaño y Sus Maravillas, Orquesta. *Charanga* band created in Havana in 1937 by the flute player Antonio Arcaño together with Elizarde Aroche (violin), Raúl Valdés (violin), Israel López (double bass), Jesús López (piano), Ulpiano Díaz (timbales), and Oscar Pelegrín (*güiro*). In 1944 it became a radio orchestra and began performing on Mil Diez. At that time, the musicians were: Elio Valdés, Salvador Muñoz, Fausto Muñoz, Enrique Jorrín, Félix Reina (violins), Miguel Valdés (viola), Juan Pérez and Juan Rodríguez (cellos), Jesús López (piano), Israel López (double bass), Ulpiano Díaz (timbales), Julio Pedroso (*güiro*), Eliseo Martínez (conga), and Antonio Arcaño (flute). It was the first *charanga* band to use conga drums. Arcaño y Sus Maravillas made significant contributions to the development of Cuban dance music: Arcaño was one of the first to write *danzón* compositions that demonstrated the influence of the *son*, a tendency that proved extremely influential and eventually contributed to the development of the *cha-cha-chá*.

Arcos, Pilar. Singer and actress. Born 6 June 1893, Havana; died 10 January 1989, Los Angeles, California. Arcos began her musical studies in Cuba and continued them in Spain, where she also became involved in theater. Later, she lived in the United States, where she sang at the Columbus Circle Theater of New York under the direction of Manolo Noriega. Arcos made many recordings of Spanish and Latin American songs. She toured in Puerto Rico, Mexico, and Spain. In Havana, she sang at the Martí Theater with Amadeo Vives. She is remembered as an excellent actress and a notable singer, especially in the interpretation of "variety songs."

Ardévol, José. Composer, teacher, orchestra director. Born 13 March 1911, Barcelona, Spain; died 10 January 1981, Havana. José's father, Fernando Ardévol, a naturalized Cuban, was his first music teacher. He later studied orchestra direction with Hermann Scherchen. In 1930 Ardévol moved to Havana, where he performed in concerts and gave conferences. In 1934 he founded the Havana Chamber Orchestra, which he directed for eighteen years. In 1936 he entered the Havana Municipal Conservatory as a teacher. Two years later, he replaced Amadeo Roldán as teacher of composition and orchestration. He advised the Grupo de Renovación Musical, formed in 1942, and many promising young composers were brought together to study with him. He is the author of many critical texts and of the historical work *La música* (1969), among others published both in Cuba and abroad. He composed more than one hundred pieces of symphonic music, chamber music, ballet, choral works, and solo pieces. Included in his works are: Concerto no. 2 for six stringed instruments; Nine small pieces; Chamber music for six string instruments; Concerto for piano, wind, and percussion; Quartet no. 2; Music for small orchestra; and Music for guitar and small orchestra; along with three complete symphonies, two symphonic movements, several quartets, six sonatas for *tres* guitar, three piano sonatas, and three piano studies. He is also the author of *La victoria*

de Playa Girón, *Burla de Don Pedro a caballo*, and *Che Comandante* (all three cantatas); *Tres ricercari*; *Tríptico sinfónico*; *Tríptico sinfónico de Santiago*; *Tríptico sinfónico de Pinar del Río*; *Versos sencillos*; and *Forma*, a ballet. His work began with an early period of impressionism, after which he favored atonal music and then neoclassicism and neonationalism; he subsequently moved toward postserialist styles, all the while composing in a sober, concise, clear, and balanced style. His music drew on his Spanish heritage but also incorporated both Cuban and other international elements. He was a musical director of the National Council for Culture, the president of the Music Association of the Writers and Artists Union of Cuba, and the dean of the faculty of music of the Higher Institute of Art.

Ardois, Dolores. Teacher and harp player. Born at the end of the nineteenth century in Havana; died in the middle of the twentieth century. Sister of the harpist Margarita Ardois. Dolores Ardois gave concerts in Cuba and abroad and became very well known.

Ardois, Margarita. Teacher and harpist. Born at the end of the nineteenth century in Havana; died in the middle of the twentieth century. Margarita's musical studies began at the Madrid Conservatory, where she won First Prize in Melody at the age of ten. Her harp teacher was Vicenta Torma. Later, she completed her studies with her sister Dolores. She was a notable player and teacher who also gave concerts in Cuba.

areíto. A term used to describe the religious, musical, and dance expression of the indigenous peoples of Cuba at the time of the Spanish conquest. None of their songs or rhythms were recorded by the Spanish conquistadors, whose chroniclers wrote about the Indians only generally, without focusing on their ceremonies. The Spanish introduced the Indians to Christianity, though few adopted the religion, primarily because of the terrible suffering they endured under the rule of the invaders. The roots of their music have been lost along with the culture. Later, Cuban music would be made up of songs and dances of Spanish origin, which were then mixed with African elements. The African influence was brought in by the slaves who replaced the by then extinct indigenous Cubans. An *areíto* sung to the Virgin Mary is mentioned in one archival source, but nothing about it was recorded in detail. We can acquire some idea of the music of the indigenous Cubans by studying the music of the Arawak peoples of South American origin, who had expanded throughout the Antilles before the advent of the Spanish. We know of certain instruments that they used: the *mahohuacán*, a drum; the *guano*, a bone flute; and rattles. The musicologist Fernández de Oviedo has researched some of their dances, finding that the men and women would join together and hold hands after having chosen a *tequina* (leader), who could be either a man or a woman. The *tequina* then guided the others through the dance, stepping back and forth while singing in a low voice. The dancers responded by taking the same steps and answering the *tequina*'s song on a higher note. (Gonzalo Fernández de Oviedo, *Historia general y natural de las Indias*, 1851–55.)

Argenter, Mario. Teacher, orchestra director, cellist. Born 14 November 1911, Matanzas. Argenter studied music with his aunt and also with Agustín Martín, who, starting in 1924, taught him quite rigorously on the cello. In 1936 he joined a small dance orchestra in Matanzas under the direction of Justo Ojanguren, and in 1949 formed a chamber music group, popularizing this style of music in the town. Beginning in 1962 he was at the forefront of both the Symphony Orchestra and the Provincial Music School in Matanzas. In addition to his musical activities, he also worked in the electronics trade.

Arias, Pedro. Baritone. Born 17 August 1940, Havana. Studied with Mariano Meléndez, Manuel Llinás, and Fernández Vila. Arias later worked under the guidance of Ramón Calzadilla, Zoila Gálvez, Kiril Krastev, and Liliana Yablenska. He also had a position in the choir of the Lyric Theater and sang as a soloist there in 1961 in the musical drama *La tempestad by Chapí*. He was a member of the Lyric Theater Company from its founding in 1962. He performed in operas, musical dramas, and concerts at theaters and concert halls all over Cuba. He has also organized and produced lyrical musical events and worked as an artistic director.

Ariza, Hilario. *Tres* player and composer. Born 25 November 1911, Matanzas. Ariza began playing in Ha-

vana in Septeto Terry and later in the septets Hatuey, Lira Matancera, Típico Habanero, and Nacional. He is the author of "Kun Kun Kun" (*son*), "El mambito" (mambo), and "Dejen bailar al loco" (*guaracha*).

Arizti, Cecilia. Composer and pianist. Born 28 October 1856, Havana; died 30 June 1930. Studied with her father, Fernando Arizti, and with Nicolás Ruiz Espadero, and subsequently gave concerts in Cuba and America. Cecilia Arizti was a teacher in the Peyrellade Conservatory. Her works include "Trío," "Improntu en fa menor," "Vals lento," "Romanza," "Noctuno," "Capricho," as well as other piano pieces, waltzes, mazurkas, and *canciones*.

Arizti, Fernando. Teacher and pianist. Born 1828, Havana; died 23 April 1888. Arizti studied music with Agustín Cascantes, Enea Elía, and Juan F. Edelmann, then moved to Paris where he completed his musical education with Frédéric Kalkbrenner in 1842. He later played in Madrid, Spain, with fellow Cuban Pablo Desvernine. He returned to Havana in 1848 to concentrate on teaching, with great success. His pupils included Nicolás Ruiz Espadero and Angelina Sicouret and his daughter Cecilia. His compositions include Fantasy for piano and Melody for violin.

Arjona, Catalino. Violinist. Born 1895, Bayamo; died 1945. Studied music with his father José Arjona, who played the ophicleide and the violin. Catalino played in different orchestras and later performed in Havana and in eastern Cuba.

Armenteros, Alfredo ("Chocolate"). Trumpet player. Born 4 April 1928, Ranchuelo. Initially a member of the ensemble led by Arsenio Rodríguez, Armenteros later joined Benny Moré's La Banda Gigante as lead trumpet and musical director. He settled in New York, where he joined the orchestra Machito y Sus Afrocubanos. Later, in 1979, he joined the record label SAR and toured various countries. He also played with the group Sonora Matancera.

Armiñan, Pablo. Troubadour. Born 17 August 1895, Santiago de Cuba. Joined up with the duo of Luis Felipe Portes and Pepe Sánchez. Armiñan later played guitar and sang with Manuelico Delgado,

José Figarola, Pepe Priol, Bebé Garay, and Pepe Banderas. He traveled around Latin America with Juan Limonta and in 1919 returned with Sindo Garay to Havana, where they formed a duo. He directed and recorded with the Conjunto Típico Oriental. Armiñan also played in duos with Angel Almenares, Valeriano Daugherti, and Rufino Ibarra. He was a member of the Ronda Lírica Oriental and author of the *sones* "Alma loca," "Perdí en amores," "Berta," and the *guaracha* "Me voy de verbena."

Arnaz, Desiderio ("Desi"). Singer and author. Born 2 March 1917, Santiago de Cuba; died 2 December 1986, San Diego, California. Moved when he was young to Miami, Florida, where he began to sing Cuban music in the dock cafés. Arnaz went on to sing, accompanied on the guitar, in hotels. He later became a vocalist with Xavier Cugat's band, which was popular throughout North America. In 1949 he formed his own band, with whom he popularized the conga dance. He married the American comedienne Lucille Ball and they became a professional artistic couple, appearing together on the television show *I Love Lucy*, which became incredibly popular among American audiences in the 1950s and 1960s. Arnaz appeared in countless films and also became involved in the business side of American entertainment, but he always maintained a certain level of quality in his work.

Aroche, Alberto. Singer. Born 1902, Santiago de Cuba; died 30 November 1968, Havana. Formed a duo with Siro Rodríguez. In 1930 Aroche moved to Havana and joined the band of Neno González. He later joined a number of *charanga*-style orchestras, such as those of Belisario López, José Antonio Díaz, and Cheo Belén Puig. He was an outstanding interpreter of the *danzonete*. For several years, Aroche was director of the Aroche Quartet, and during the 1960s he joined the Tanda de Guaracheros, supported by the National Council for Culture.

Arriaza, Ana. Choral director. Born in Santiago de Cuba. A student of Dulce Maria Serret, Arriana later joined the Santiago Choral Society. In 1964 she directed the Holguín Choral Society, touring Cuba and making records with them. In Nicaragua, she directed a large choir in a performance of "Canto General," by the poet Pablo Neruda.

Arrondo, Juan. Composer. Born 14 May 1914, Regla; died 16 August 1979, Guanabacoa. Lived in Guanabacoa from the age of two. Throughout the 1940s Arrondo became popular through songs such as "Qué pena me da," "Más daño me hizo tu amor," "Como lo soñó Martí," "Fiebre de tí," "Mi juramento," "Vamos a jugar a la verdad," and "Desde aceras opuestas." His later pieces, such as "Si en un final" and "Esa que está allí," were also generally popular. As a tribute to the time he spent as a member of a *son* sextet, a Cuban song competition carries his name.

Arteaga, Francisco. Composer. Born at the beginning of the nineteenth century in Havana. Very notable in his time, Arteaga gained popularity between 1825 and 1830 for his *contradanzas, danzas,* and *criollo* rhythms, which comprised the dance music of Havana in the 1800s.

Asencio, Gonzalo ("Tio Tom"). Author of rumbas. Born 5 April 1919, Havana; died 10 February 1991. Began singing, playing, and dancing the rumba in the fiestas of Cayo Hueso in Atarés and in other neighborhoods in Havana, where he later lived. From the age of fifteen, Asencio wrote incredible *guaguancós*, among them the popular "Me regaña el corazón," "Los cubanos son rareza," "Changó va vení," "Una chambelona," "Dónde están los cubanos," "Consuélate como yo," "Mal de yerba," "Tierra brava," "Este es mi país," "Rumbearemos y cantaremos," "Bombón," and "Se ha vuelto mi corazón un violín." He combined beautiful lyrics with an amazing melodic and rhythmic imagination. His themes varied from love to social and political issues and to the idea of friendship in the urban world. A self-taught musician and composer, he was particularly skilled at improvisation.

assongué. A type of rattle with a cylindrical body that is closed at both ends by conical covers (Ortiz,

Los instrumentos de la música afrocubana, 2:320). It is used in music of Arará origin, which is played in ritual ceremonies in the provinces of Matanzas and Havana.

atcheré. Also spelled *acheré*. Like the *agogó*, this maraca is used by the Lucumí to "call" the deities in their ritual ceremonies. Only one is used, and it is sometimes rattled close to the ear of the practitioner (*santero*) to connect him more directly with the *orishas*. When it is shaken, the seeds or small stones inside rattle. There are special *atcherés* for the deities Eleguá, Changó, Ogún, Ochosí, Inle, Agayu, Orishaoko, Ogué, Obba, Yemayá, Oyá, and Yegguá. Traditional *atcherés* were long, narrow maracas; today, they are usually made with handles, which are usually ornamented with stringed beads representing the ritual colors of the respective saint and also with paintings which are usually geometrical (Ortiz, *Los instrumentos de la música afrocubana*, 2:81). In Brazil, ritual instruments of African origin are similar to the *atcheré* of Cuba.

Averoff, Carlos. Saxophonist. Born 6 December 1947, Matanzas. Lived in Havana since he was a child and studied at the Amadeo Roldán Conservatory with the teachers Arturo Bonachea (saxophone) and Alfredo Portela (flute). In 1966 Averoff joined the group Sonorama, and the following year he joined the orchestra of the Cuban Institute of Radio and Television. Between 1968 and 1970 he was a member of the staff band of the army and afterward joined the band of the Escuela Interarmas. In 1971 he became a member of the Grupo de Experimentación Sonora of the Writers and Artists Union of Cuba. Then, in 1973, Averoff moved on to the Orquesta Cubana de Música Moderna, which featured the core members of the Afro-Cuban jazz band

Irakere. He left Irakere to play with NG La Banda, made one solo record, and taught saxophone at the Higher Institute of Art, moving to the United States in 1997.

Avilés, Danilo. Composer and clarinetist. Born 5 May 1948, Holguín. Studied composition with Argeliers León and then attended the National School of Art, where he worked with José Ardévol and José Loyola in the Higher Institute of Art. Avilés's works include "Mujer nueva," "Dibujos," "Esa sangre en las calles de Santiago" (for soprano and orchestral group), "Siento un bombo mamita" (for symphony orchestra), Three small poems for voice and piano, and Variations for string quartet. He also composed music for children, vocal works, and incidental and chamber music. He was a clarinetist in the Orquesta de Teatro y Danza. He now lives abroad.

Avilés, Jesús. Clarinetist. Born 1866, Holguín; died 1928. Avilés came from a family of musicians and was playing the clarinet by the age of fourteen. In 1886 he was treble clarinet player for the Volunteers' Regiment's band in Holguín. In 1895 he joined the Liberation Army, where he organized the Banda Invasora, which accompanied Antonio Maceo. He finished the war as a great musician.

Avilés, Manuel. Composer and orchestra director. Born 2 February 1864, Holguín; died (?). A well-known figure in Holguín, where he worked as a tailor. Avilés studied music from an early age with the Spanish maestro Magín Torres, and by the age of nineteen he was already writing popular pieces. He took part in the War of Independence, reaching the level of second lieutenant in the liberating army. For many years, he was the director of the Orquesta Avilés, which was formed by his fourteen children. The group still survives with descendents of the original members. Avilés wrote hymns, *contradanzas*, and *danzas* and composed a very Cuban *cocoyé*, distinct from the Spanish version scored by Juan Casamitjana.

Avilés, Orquesta. The oldest band known in Cuba. Founded by Manuel Avilés in 1882 with relatives and other musicians in Holguín, Oriente Province. Some members of the band fought in the war against Spain. It was originally a wind orchestra, then changed to a *charanga*, and finally, during the 1920s, it remodeled itself as a *jazzband*. In 1956 it traveled to Venezuela. The orchestra has always remained in Oriente Province, and has traveled from time to time to Havana. At present, the musicians are Avilés's descendents, playing traditional and contemporary music.

Ayoub, Nelson. Bass singer. Born 10 November 1944, Santiago de Cuba. Lived in Havana since he was a child and studied at the Havana Municipal Conservatory. Ayoub then extended his vocal knowledge by studying with Francisco Fernández Dominicis and Zoila Gálvez. He interpreted operatic arias, *zarzuelas*, and Cuban and Latin American songs. He performed in the Soviet Union, Germany, Bulgaria, Romania, Czechoslovakia, and Poland, and is now a member of the Cuban National Opera.

Ayué, Gualfredo ("Nene"). Composer and guitarist. Born 25 June 1905, Camagüey; died 12 October 1959, Havana. Worked mostly in the trio form, first with Alberto Aroche and Joaquín García, and later as part of the Trío Garcia, which he founded with Justa and Ana María García. Auyé's long-term work was as an accompanying guitarist, but he also composed troubadour songs.

Azpiazu, Eusebio. Organist and pianist. Born 1817, Oyarzun, Spain; died 1870, Havana. On his arrival in Cuba, Azpiazu gained the position of organist at the Cienfuegos Parochial Church. In 1858 he moved to Havana to play organ in the convent of San Agustín. He also taught piano, and composed for piano and orchestral groups.

Azpiazu, Justo. Composer and orchestra director. Born 23 January 1893, Cienfuegos; died 20 January 1943, Havana. Always known as "Don" Azpiazu. He founded an orchestra in Havana in the mid-1920s that performed at the Casino Nacional. In 1930 he went to New York, working in nightclubs and theaters. Azpiazu introduced Cuban dance music to New York in 1931, when his full orchestra, including singers and dancers, performed there. The singer Antonio Machin performed "El Manisero" with the orchestra, which became remarkably successful all over the world. In 1932 Azpiazu performed at the Cabaña Cubana in Paris, with Machín as vocalist and Alicia Parlá as dancer. Later, he traveled to Spain, after which he returned to Cuba and then to New York. His compositions include "Por tus ojos negros" (*habanera*). Azpiazu also directed the band that accompanied the Argentine tango singer Carlos Gardel in the film *Esperáme*, which was first shown in Paris. He also performed in other films. His group recorded with RCA Victor.

B

Bacallao, Juana. Singer and musical entertainer. Born 26 May 1925, Havana. Family name is Amelia Martínez. Bacallao came from a humble background and, as a child, worked as a maid. In the late 1940s she appeared in a show at the Martí Theater produced by Obdulio Morales, and she subsequently performed in Venezuela, New York, and Las Vegas, and toured in Santo Domingo. She returned to Cuba in the 1950s with an original act that combined singing, dancing, mimicry, and comedy. In Cuba, she took leading roles in theater shows and performed at nightspots and cabarets like the Riviera, the Parisién, the Caribe, the Tropicana, and the Capri. She has also traveled in North America, Italy, and Mexico.

Badía, Enma. Pianist and teacher. Born 13 June 1915, Havana; died 1960. Studied piano initially with Juan Molinari and harmony with Rosich in Spain, where she was also a member of the choral society Catalá de Barcelona. Badia finished her piano studies with Isabelle Vengerona and Carl Friedberg in New York and graduated in 1934 from the Institute of Musical Art at the Juilliard School. She gave many piano recitals in different cities in Europe and the United States. In 1938 she founded the Musical Institute in Havana and became a full-time teacher. In the last year of her life, she taught at the Alejandro García Caturla Conservatory.

Ballagas, Patricio. Composer and guitarist. Born 17 March 1879, Camagüey; died 15 February 1920, Havana. Performer of the traditional *trova*. Ballagas is well known today for having written his songs in 4/4 time in a period when the convention was 2/4. His songs are decidedly rhythmic but do not make use of rubato time. His greatest invention was the use of the "double text," where the melody is superimposed over the lead vocal, which then becomes the second voice. He introduced *contracanto* (or *contrapunto*) into the Cuban troubador (*trova*) form, in which the second voice changes from being intricately connected with the first voice to being a melodic and harmonic musical expression with its

own identity. Ballagas formed the Cuarteto Nano with Bienvenido León, Tirso Díaz, and Ramón León, and worked as a duo with Alejandro Montalván until his death in 1920. His most famous piece is "Timidez," made famous in 1914, but he is also remembered for "Te ví como las flores," "Nena," "No quiero verte," and "El trovador."

Baloy, Félix. Singer. Born 1943, Havana. Vocalist with various groups, including Chapottín y Sus Estrellas, Revé, and Adalberto Álvarez y Su Son. Baloy interpreted *son* within the style of *guaguancó*. He was a member of the Afro-Cuban All Stars, which won a Grammy in 1998 for the recording *Buena Vista Social Club*. His first solo album with the Afro-Cuban All Stars was released in 2000 by Tumi Music. His latest band is called *Félix Baloy y Su Son*.

Mo Fini

Banda Municipal de La Habana. *See* Havana Municipal Band.

Banderas, José. Composer and guitarist. Born 19 March 1891, Santiago de Cuba; died 19 April 1967. An outstanding interpreter of troubadour music (*trova*), along with Gabriel Rubio, Juan Limonta, and José Figarola. Banderas suffered from nervous disorders from childhood and spent time in the psychiatric hospital in Mazorra, where treatment improved his condition. He also worked as a carpenter. He taught the extraordinary guitar player Guyún (Vicente González Rubiera). His song compositions include "Boca roja," "La sirena," "Volvió mi corazón," "Sabrás que por ti," "La cima," and "María."

bandurria. An instrument brought to Cuba by the Spanish, played as an accompaniment to *guajiro* music. The strings—formerly three but now usually twelve, tuned in pairs—are plucked with a plectrum.

The *bandurria* is similar to the *laúd* and, like it, has been adapted by Cuban musicians and artisans during a process of transculturation.

Bantú, música. Folkloric musical expression that originated with the Bantú-speaking ethnic groups from the Congo who were brought to Cuba during the colonial period. Bantú musical groups are known as *paleros*. They play three drums with straight staves, glued together in the form of an inverted cone and covered with a leather skin, which is nailed to the top of the open conical shape. The *paleros* hit these drums with sticks (*palos*) made from metal or hard wood. The old original Bantú groups played a *kinfuiti* drum and three large *yuka* drums (Argeliers León, *Música folklórica cubana*, 37–40). These Bantú drums are still played in Cuba during conga sessions and street processions. One of these festivals is the *macuta*, in which Bantús perform songs that feature alternating chorus and solo parts—a characteristic of African music.

Baquero, Aldo. Composer. Born 10 July 1931, Havana. Studied music with his mother and then took up the piano at the Municipal Conservatory. From 1969 Baquero was the national director of music on Cuban radio. In 1996 he joined the Writers and Artists Union of Cuba, where he was placed in charge of the Peña del Bolero. He is the author of "Si me dieran a escoger," "Eres en todo momento," "Piénsalo y decide tú," "Te imagino en la distancia," and "Soy tu historia."

Barberis, Carmelina. Interpreter of the *punto* and *música campesina*. Born 8 August 1938, Havana. Barberis's greatest work was in radio and television. Her voice is one of the most characteristic of *música guajira*.

Baro, Rolando. Composer, instrumentalist, pianist. Born 26 April 1932, Havana. After playing piano in various groups, Baro joined the group Casino in the 1950s. He is the author of numerous boleros, including "Esta canción de amor." His most important musical contribution was as an instrumentalist of popular Cuban music.

Barreiro, Hugo. Baritone. Born 13 August 1944, Güira de Melena. Studied at the Ignacio Cervantes Conservatory in Havana and later at the Higher Institute of Art. From singing popular music, Barreiro moved on to lyric opera in 1979, when he performed in *La Traviata*. He later took other leading roles in opera and in Cuban *zarzuelas*. He also has performed a great repertoire of traditional Cuban songs. He has appeared on television and in the theater and has toured in Cuba and abroad, singing with local symphony orchestras. Barreiro has undertaken research into the Cuban vocal repertoire, its methodology, and the technical ability required for each song. He is a professor at the Higher Institute of Art.

Barreto, Guillermo. Percussionist. Born 11 August 1929, Havana; died 1991. Barreto was a drummer with Obdulio Morales and Los Hermanos Martínez, and then became a member of the orchestra at the Tropicana, where he remained for many years. He also worked in the Sans Souci cabaret and on Channel 4 television. He accompanied many American performers when they performed in Havana, playing with the Tommy Dorsey Band, accompanying Nat King Cole on drums, and recording with Johnny Richards and the Chico O'Farrill Band. He sometimes played percussion in Benny Moré's band. In 1959 he founded the Quinteto Cubano de Música Moderna with Frank Emilio, from which he moved to the Orquesta Cubana de Música Moderna and the instrumental group Los Amigos. He also performed with the National Symphony Orchestra.

Barreto, Julián. Flute and violin. Born 16 February 1879, Havana; died 1964. Studied flute with Rafael Rojas and later violin with Juan Torroella. Barreto became a violin teacher in the Municipal Academy of Havana and was also a member of the Municipal Band. In 1926 he performed popular Cuban music in Spain and France, and on his return to Cuba, he founded a music academy in the Havana suburb of La Víbora. He played violin in various orchestras, primarily those under the direction of the famous Enrique Peña. One of Barreto's hats inspired José Urfé to compose the *danzón* "El bombín de Barreto."

Barreto, Justi. Composer and percussionist. Born 14 November 1923, Havana. Began as a singer and player of rumba and conga in the suburbs of Havana. In 1946 Barreto composed the *guarachas* "El pollo," "El tramposo," and "Qué tarde será." A year later, he joined the orchestra Casino de la Playa as a *bongó* player. He traveled to Mexico City, where he appeared in theaters and in the films *Rayito de luna, Al son del mambo, Los pecados de Laura, En cada puerto un amor,* and *Callejera,* in which he sang, danced, and played Afro-Cuban percussion. In Mexico City, he also recorded his own songs, "Rabo y oreja," "Dulce Veracruz," and "Enójate." He returned to Cuba in 1951 and found success with the songs "Encantado de la vida," "Monterrey," "O felicidad," "Adiós ya me voy," "España," and "Batanga no. 2." In 1952 he moved to New York, where he made famous the songs "La isla del encanto," "Qué bonito es Puerto Rico," and "Déjame en paz," and recorded an LP entitled *Santería.* In 1954 he presented his work *Yényere cumá buenas noches* at the Tropicana cabaret. His career as a composer and interpreter of Cuban music has continued to blossom.

Barrios, Maria Eugenia. Soprano. Born 16 December 1940, Havana. Studied voice with Carmelina Santana and music with Gonzalo Roig. In 1972 Barrios graduated from the Tchaikovsky Academy in Moscow and has subsequently performed throughout Cuba and abroad. She is a soloist in the Cuban National Opera, which is known for its repertoire of operas and *zarzuelas.*

Barrios, Renée. Singer. Born in Havana. Studied music in the Havana Municipal Conservatory. Barrios worked as a piano accompanist until 1957, when he formed a successful duo with Nelia. In 1960 he began to perform as a soloist and toured America while living in Puerto Rico. His work is mostly in the *fílin* style of music.

Barroso, Abelardo. Singer. Born 21 September 1905, Havana; died 27 September 1972. Began as an interpreter of songs and *sones* with the Sexteto Habanero and later joined other groups and *orquestas típicas* as an interpreter of *danzonete.* Barroso was the leader of Charanga López Barroso. In the early 1950s he joined the Orquesta Sensación, with whom he recorded many records.

Barrueco, Manuel. Guitarist. Born 1952, Santiago de Cuba. Began his musical studies at the age of eight with the teacher Manuel Puig in the Provincial Conservatory of Oriente. In 1967 Barrueco moved to the United States to study at the Peabody Conservatory of Music in Baltimore. Today, he is an established concert performer and has recorded significant classical music albums featuring his transcriptions of Mozart and Bach. He is a member of the faculty at the Peabody Conservatory.

Baserva Soler, Rafael. Pianist, orchestra director, composer. Born 4 July 1936, Santiago de Cuba. At the age of thirteen Baserva graduated in piano from the Provinical Conservatory of Oriente. Later, he continued his studies in New York, with Edward Stewerman. He has performed in Havana and Santiago de Cuba and was a soloist in the Havana Philharmonic Orchestra. He has played piano on radio and television and also in nightclubs and has toured various Latin American countries. In 1960 he moved to the United States, where he has performed with his own group at Carnegie Hall, Town Hall, and at the Manhattan Center, all in New York City, as well as in other North American cities. Baserva is the author of the *guarachas* "Pancha Caridad," "Cualquier cosa," and "Fina Bacalao."

batá drums. Musically, these are the most important of the Afro-Cuban drums. They are played in sets of three: the *okónkolo,* the smallest; the *itótele,* a medium-sized drum; and the *iyá,* the largest of the three. The word "*batá*" is Yoruba for "drum." These drums are used in the religious ceremonies practiced in Cuba by the Lucumí or Yoruba and their Creole descendants (Ortiz, *Los instrumentos de la música afrocubana,* 4:205, 310). The *okónkolo* has a high-

pitched sound; the *itótele*, a medium-pitched sound, and the *iyá*, the lead drum, has a deep, low sound. The drums are cylindrical, with a narrowing at one-third of their length. Each has two drumheads, one slightly smaller than the other, and the drums are held horizontally so that the drumheads can be hit with both hands. A leather strap is generally attached to each of the *iyá* drums, and bells and cowbells, called *chaworo*, are usually strung from the strap. (León, *Del canto y el tiempo*, 45).

Batet, Elisa ("Lily"). Composer and guitarist. Born 23 February 1916, Havana. Studied piano and guitar with the teacher Clara Romero. In 1938 Batet formed a voice and guitar duo with Margot Blanco; they performed on the radio, and in theaters and cultural centers in the United States, Mexico, and Canada. Batet is the author of "Alma de roca," "Sueño navideño," and other songs. She has lived for many years in the United States, where she operates a guitar school.

Bautista, Ileana. Pianist. Born in Havana. In 1962 Bautista began studying at the National School of Art and later continued her studies at the Tchaikovsky Academy in Kiev. She has taught piano. Her repertoire includes symphonic works and chamber music. She has given concerts in Cuba and Europe.

Bauzá, Mario. Trumpet player, saxophonist, composer, arranger. Born 4 April 1911, Havana; died 12 July 1993, New York. Moved to New York at an early age and began his musical education, which was primarily autodidactic. Bauzá practiced the trumpet by studying the recordings of Phil Napoleón and Red Nichols. He also frequented jazz clubs. In 1931 he played in the band of Noble Sissle and the following year moved over to play with Chick Webb, alongside trumpeter Dizzy Gillespie and singer Ella Fitzgerald. He later joined the band of Cab Calloway, where he experimented mixing jazz with Cuban rhythms in original arrangements. Although he left Cuba at an early age, he remained deeply entrenched in its music all through his life. In 1940 he joined the singer and percussionist Machito to organize an orchestra, which they called the Afro-Cubans. Bauzá played lead trumpet and worked with Cuban pianist Rene Hernandez as arranger. He always attempted to conserve the Cuban essence in his arrangements while mixing it with jazz harmonies. He was undoubtedly the father of Afro-Cuban jazz.

Bavastro Cassard, Ernesto. Flutist. Born 1838, Oriente; died 1887. Took part in the War of Independence. Bavastro was president of the Cuban Delegation in Kingston, Jamaica. He played the flute in concerts abroad, with the aim of gaining funds for the independence of Cuba.

Bayard, Luis. Flutist. Born, 21 August 1948, Santiago de Cuba. Began his studies at the García Caturla and Amadeo Roldán Conservatories in Havana and continued at the National School of Art, then at the Weimar Academy in Germany, where he graduated in 1974. Bayard performed as a soloist, in chamber music groups, with the National Symphony Orchestra, and with the orchestra of Camagüey, introducing new works by Cuban and foreign contemporary composers. He was also a flute teacher in the Higher Institute of Art.

Becker, Remberto. Composer of boleros, *sones*, and *guarachas*. Born 4 February 1910, Havana. Worked as a painter and decorator, and was also a boxer. In 1943 Becker formed the Becker Quartet with Orlando Vallejo, Carlos Querol, and Elías Castillo, and with Carlos "Patato" Valdés on percussion. He is the author of the boleros "Llegaron las golondrinas" and "Qué belleza de mujer"; the bolero-mambo "De ti enamorado"; the *guajira* "Mi linda casita"; the *guarachas* "A toda Cuba le gusta," "Bailadores," and "Como cambian los tiempos"; and the *son* "Aquí nacen los soneros"; as well as other popular pieces.

bembé. An informal festival celebrated for the enjoyment of the Yoruba *orishas*, to the accompaniment of specialized *bembé* drums. A Bantú term, the *bembé* has its origins in Nigeria, where it was originally performed for Ochún, the river deity. The drums for this festival are of varying sizes and are played in threes and fours. Traditionally made from palm trunks, they are more recently made from mango or avocado wood and are topped with a single, nailed drumhead. The drums are tuned by applying heat.

Bencomo, Fernando. Trumpet player. Born 22 March 1916, Ciego de Avila. Bencomo moved with his family to Remedios, where he began his musical studies with Agustín Jiménez Crespo, Abelardo Cuevas, Everardo González Lahirigoyen, and Tomás Pérez. He became an accomplished trumpeter and played for a while with the Remedios Music Band. In 1934 Bencomo moved to Havana, where he became a member of the philharmonic orchestra under the leadership of Amadeo Roldán. He played the horn in ensembles on radio and television and also in operas. He was a member of the Havana Wind Quintet. He has played with orchestras in Mexico, Caracas, London, Paris, and Brussels. Since the founding of the National Symphony Orchestra in 1960, he has been one of its soloists. He is a teacher at the Amadeo Roldán Conservatory and the Music School of the ENA.

Bergaza, Felo. Pianist and composer. Born 26 August 1916, Trinidad; died 1969, Havana. Began studying music as a child. Evidence of Bergaza's musical talent could be seen in his performances in theater, radio, and television. He is the author of "Si tú me lo dijeras," "Por eso tienes la culpa," "Extraño amor," "Me parece increíble," "De eso nada," "Di por qué," "Seguiré sin soñar," "Cabildo Senseribó," and "Evanecile." He played for many years with the pianist Juan Bruno Tarraza, performing a number of pieces for four hands.

Berroa, Catalina. Pianist, composer, teacher. Born 28 February 1849, Trinidad; died 23 November 1911. Played guitar, violin, harp, various wind instruments, and piano, and was the composer of *sones*, *guarachas*, hymns, and religious music, including masses and salves. Berroa's most famous work is *La Trinitaria*. In Trinidad, she ran a music school, where she educated many young students, including her cousin Lico Jiménez. She was organist at the San Fransisco de Asís Church and organist and choral director of the Church of La Santísima Trinidad, both in Trinidad. She also formed a trio with Manuel Jiménez (violin) and Ana Luisa Vivano (piano) in which she played the cello. She was also a violinist in the orchestra of the Teatro Brunet.

Berroa, Jorge. Composer. Born 13 December 1938, Havana. After his musical studies at the Amadeo Roldán Conservatory, Berroa began composing such works as "Un hombre ha pasado," for soprano and piano; "Miguel Matamoros In Memoriam," for soprano, instrumental group, and recorded music; "Décimas contemporáneas," for soprano; "Lamento," "Shake dramático," for actor, soprano, and instrumental group; "Lo antiguo y lo moderno," for soprano and recorded music; Concerto, for piano and instrumental group; "Proporciones para explicar la muerte de Ana" (with text by Guillén), for baritone; *El son de la discusión* (a children's opera); as well as harmonized folk songs. He has also composed music for the theater and the cinema. Berrora was the director of music at Havana University and currently works at EGREM.

Betancourt, Joaquín. Violinist, composer, orchestrator, orchestra director. Born 27 May 1952, Camagüey. Studied violin at the National School of Art. Betancourt was a violinist in the Camagüey Symphony Orchestra and also played in popular music bands. He taught at several educational institutions. He has directed the groups Opus 13 and Isaac Delgado, as well as many studio recordings, and has received many awards. His compositions range from popular dance music to concertos. His most notable contribution has been as an orchestrator.

Betancourt, Jorge Luis. Orchestra and choral director. Born 1940, Camagüey. Began studying music with his family when he was eight years old and later attended the Rafols Conservatory of Camagüey and the Alejandro García Caturla Conservatory. Betancourt is a multi-instrumentalist and also studied conducting between 1967 and 1968 at the Leningrad Academy of Music. He has worked as conductor of the band of the Revolutionary Armed Forces (FAR) and of the chorus of Camagüey, and as guest conductor of the National Symphony Orchestra, the youth orchestra of Bulgaria, and the children's orchestra of the Leningrad Academy. He is currently conductor of the Camagüey Symphony Orchestra.

Betancourt, José Mercedes. Violinist, teacher, orchestra conductor. Born in Camagüey at the end of the eighteenth century; died in 1866. Specialized in composing *contradanzas*. Betancourt was a notable violin player and conducted various orchestras in Camagüey and Havana. He published a collection of musical pieces called *Ecos del Tínima*.

Betancourt, Justo. Singer. Born 6 December 1940, Matanzas. Began singing *guaguancó* as a child in Matanzas and later joined the group Club, with whom he recorded his first single. In 1964 Betancourt moved to New York, where he performed with the salsa orchestras led by Orlando Marín, Johny Pacheco, Eddie Palmieri, and Sonora Matancera (with whom he worked for five years). He developed a career as a soloist and recorded with different bands, most notably the Fania All Stars. He is a respected interpreter of *son*, *guaracha*, *rumba*, and salsa.

binkomé. Also *biankomé*. An Abakuá drum. It produces only one beat, which Ortiz describes as harsh and open, rendered by playing the drum with the tip of the forefinger (Ortiz, *Los instrumentos de la música afrocubana*, 4:25). It is the last in the trio of Abakuá drums called *enkómo*, which also includes the *opiapá* and *kuchí-yeremá* drums.

Blanca, Augusto. Composer, singer, guitarist. Born 24 July 1945, Banes. Graduated in the plastic arts from the Taller School in Santiago de Cuba. Blanca worked as a producer in the Conjunto Dramático de Oriente. He also gave recitals, singing and playing guitar, and performed such pieces as "Don Juan de los palotes," "Doña Pulcra, la carabina de Ambrosio," "El caracol," "Canción para no ser cantada," "Postal infantil," "Esquema de la impotencia," "Esquema del anonimato," and "Naturaleza muerta." Blanca took part in the third political song festival in Berlin and also visited the Soviet Union. He lives in Santiago de Cuba.

Blanck, Hubert de. Professor, composer, pianist. Born 11 June 1856, Utrecht, Holland; died 28 November 1932, Havana. Studied in the Lieja Academy

in Belgium and later toured Europe and America. In 1882 Blanck traveled for the first time to Cuba and returned the following year to live. In 1885 he founded the conservatory that bore his name (which was later renamed the National Conservatory). He was an active participant in the Cuban independence struggles and in patriotic festivals. At the end of the War of Independence, he returned to Cuba. His most significant compositions are "Capricho cubano," Concerto, Suite for chamber group, Quintet for piano and strings, and the operas *Patria*, *Actea*, and *Icaona*, as well as operettas, pieces for voice and piano, and hymns.

Blanck, Margot de. Pianist. Born 1903, Havana. Daughter of Hubert de Blanck and Pilar Martín. Margot de Blanck was a student at the National Conservatory, directed by her father. At the age of fifteen she began a concert career. She played several times at Carnegie Hall in New York and in other American cities. She also performed numerous times in Europe and Latin America and in Cuba. She taught piano, and has lived for many years outside of Cuba.

Blanck, Olga de. Composer, pianist, guitarist, arranger. Born 11 May 1916, Havana. Daughter of Hubert de Blanck and Pilar Martín. Olga de Blanck performed many piano and guitar concerts of popular Cuban music. In 1938 she traveled to the United States and Mexico to study music. In Havana she performed in the musical comedies *Vivimos hoy*, *Hotel Tropical*, and *Cuento de Navidad*. She was appointed deputy director of the National Conservatory in 1945, and in 1955 she became director. Of her many compositions, "Mi guitarra guajira," "Homenaje a la danza," and "Pentasílabo" have each won the National Prize in the Cuban Song Competition. More recently, she has done arrangements for piano, guitar, and voice. She worked at the National Council for Culture and is a specialist in children's music.

Blanco, Juan. Composer. Born 29 June 1919, El Mariel. Studied at the Municipal Conservatory of Havana. Blanco's music was first noticed in the 1950s. His first pieces, such as "Tríptico coral," "Cantata de la paz," "Elegía," "Divertimento," and Quintet for wood and cello, conveyed a nationalistic theme. He was the first Cuban to experiment in the arena of electronic, spatial, and random performance mixed with dance music, in such works as "Ensemble V," "Texturas," "Episodio," "Contrapunto espacial," "Erotofonías," and Studies for recorded group. He has written music for the ballet, cinema, and for open-air shows. He was musical director of the National Council for Culture for a number of years.

Blanco Leonard, Julio. Author. Born 16 February 1909, Havana; died 17 January 1982. An actor and dancer in various theater companies. Blanco composed excellent lyrics for pieces such as "Conciencia fría" (music by Rafael Ortiz), "Buscando la melodía," "La clave misteriosa," "Maleficio," "Ya ta'cansá," and "Sombra terrible" (music by Obdulio Morales). Blanco sang as a duo with Marcelino Guerra. He also composed both lyrics and music for many other pieces, including "Luna bruja," "Hoy sé más," "Mambo del amor," "Consuélame," and "Oyá, diosa y fe." For a few years, he directed the Trío Romántico.

Blez, Emiliano. Composer, guitarist, interpreter of troubadour (*trova*) songs. Born 11 October 1879, Santiago de Cuba; died 23 May 1973. A disciple of Pepe Sánchez, Blez became involved in the transcription of historical works on the verge of being lost to future generations. Early in the twentieth century he formed a duo in Santiago de Cuba with Sindo Garay, and a subsequent duo with Eduardo Dorilla Reyes. He joined the Quinteto de Trovadores Santiagueros together with Pepe Sánchez, Pepe Figarola, Bernabé Ferrer, and Luis Felipe Portes. Among his compositions are the boleros "Idilio," "Corazón de fuego," "Si al olvido me lanzas," and "Besada por el mar."

bocú. Drum used in the *comparsas* (street processions) typical of the eastern provinces in Santiago de Cuba. It has its origins in the Congo music complex ("*bocú*," in the Kikongo language, means "drum"). The body of the drum, open on one end, is made of staves held tightly together by iron hoops. Its single leather drumhead is affixed to the drum by nets. The drum is tempered by fire and is played only with the hands. The player, or *bocusero*, carries the drum on his left side, and it hangs from his neck by a strap. The body is long and narrow and in the shape of a truncated cone, and the leather is tensed by nails, as in the *candela* (fire) drums that are typical of the Congo peoples. Traditional *bocús* are approximately 1.10 meters long, with a diameter of 30 centimeters on the upper end, to which the leather is affixed, and of 20 centimeters on the lower end (Ortiz, *Los instrumentos de la música afrocubana*, 3:378). The *bocú* makes a high-pitched sound. Sometimes a small *bocú* is played with the larger *bocú*, and the smaller serves an improvisational function similar to that of a *quinto* in a rumba group. In the congas of Oriente, as many as twenty *bocús* can be played at once, along with congas, snare drums, cowbells, and Chinese clarinets. According to Ortiz, they have been heard in the ritual music of *espiritismo cruzado*—the calling down of the spirits of deceased relatives—in the province of Oriente.

(Los) Bocucos. Band created in Santiago de Cuba, 1958. At the beginning, Pacho Alonso was the director, but Roberto Correa, trumpeter, composer, and arranger, replaced him when Alonso decided to create his own band in the late 1960s. Correa is still the conductor of the band, which also includes Nilo Valle, Pedro J. Crespo, and Emilio Solá (trumpets);

Delfín Rodríguez (piano); Rolando Gómez (electric bass); Miguel Bridón (guitar); Jesús Pérez (batá drums); Manuel Cobas (conga); and Ibrahím Ferrer, Carlos Querol, and Albis Roca (vocalists). They play popular dance music, mainly son, with a distinctively rhythmic style. This band plays on radio and television and at popular festivals, and has recorded many LPs.

Bola de Nieve. See Villa, Ignacio ("Bola de Nieve").

bolero. A song and dance form quite different from its Spanish counterpart, the bolero was created during the final third of the nineteenth century within the traditional trova style of Santiago de Cuba. Without a doubt, the bolero is the first widely influential style of Cuban vocal music that crossed international frontiers and gained universal recognition. One of its earliest proponents was José Pepe Sánchez, a teacher and pioneer in defining the different stylistic characteristics of the bolero. Many boleros, like Sanchez's "Tristezas," feature two sections of 16 bars each, separated by an instrumental section played on guitar and known as the pasacalle. This type of bolero can be played in a major or minor key, sometimes alternating between both. In traditional Cuban bolero, the fusion of Spanish and Afro-Cuban elements is complete, as evidenced in the guitar accompaniment and its influence on the melody: the musical-percussive accent of the Cuban cinquillo is imposed on the text in duple meter, or 2/4 time. (Spanish bolero always uses 3/4 time.) The bolero began to evolve in the 1920s when skilled composers and pianists changed the configuration of the cinquillo by putting it onto the accompanying left hand of the piano part to make melodic/harmonic decorative figures. Little by little, composers began to use the texts of well-known poets (as in "Aquellos ojos verdes," with lyrics by Adolfo Utrera and music by Nilo Menéndez), letting the verses imply their own rhythm and depriving the cinquillo of its traditional hegemony. The bolero continues to develop and evolve, always maintaining its identity, even when interpreted by different instruments and even with the addition of percussive instrumentation from the son. These influences confirm that the development of this style of bolero is purely Cuban and not affected by other countries, as some suggest. However, the international success of the Cuban

bolero in duple meter is due in part to the creativity of significant composers, such as the Mexican Agustín Lara, who possessed a distinctive melodic-poetic style. In Puerto Rico, composers such as Rafael Hernández also developed the duple-meter bolero considerably. Over the years, the bolero has been fused with other forms to create hybrids, such as bolero-moruno, bolero-mambo, and bolero-beguine, which are commonly used by Mexican and Cuban composers. The power of the bolero is eternal. Even with the recent invasion of rock-influenced music, one can still hear the sensual rhythm of Cuban bolero as the percussion alters the accents and timing (Rosendo Ruiz Jr., "El bolero cubano," 238–39).

Bolero, Sexteto. Formed in Havana in 1935 by Tata Gutiérrez (vocalist and claves player) with Félix Chapotín (trumpet); José Vega (tres and second voice); Julio Galindo (double bass); Eliseo Zequeira (tres); and José Manuel ("El Chino") Cattiera (bongó). The sextet adapted the son style for different foreign movie soundtracks. It had a radio show on the Loma del Mazo station. The band exists today under the direction of Enrique Pérez and performs at popular festivals.

Bolet, Alberto. Violinist and symphonic conductor. Born in Havana. Brother of the pianist Jorge Bolet. Alberto Bolet took up the violin and cello at the age of seven and later studied music at the Mateu Conservatory in Guanabacoa. He finished his studies on the violin at the age of fifteen at the Falcón Conservatory, under the guidance of Casimiro Zertucha, then moved to Madrid. There, he graduated from the National Conservatory, where Enrique Hernández de Arbos was his teacher. In Spain Bolet worked as a violinist in cafés and theaters, then went to Paris to perfect his knowledge of the violin with Fermín Touche. He performed in Italy, Germany, Austria, and Belgium. In 1925 he traveled to the United

States and worked in the symphony orchestras of Detroit, Sacramento, and Phoenix. In 1939 he returned to Cuba, where he became musical director of CMZ radio. In 1942 he was appointed assistant to Erich Kleiber, the director of the Havana Philharmonic Orchestra. From 1943 to 1951 he directed various orchestras in Latin America and North America, then returned to Havana where he established himself as associate director of the philharmonic orchestra. After 1954 he conducted symphony orchestras in Europe and the United States, where he lived.

Bolet, Jorge. Pianist. Born 15 November 1914, Havana; died 16 October 1990, San Francisco, California. At the age of twelve Bolet went to study at the Curtis Institute in Philadelphia, where he graduated in piano in 1935. At the institute he was under the tutelage of David Saperton, and also worked with Josef Hofmann and Emil von Saner. From 1939 to 1942 Bolet was a professor of piano at the Curtis Institute, and from 1968 to 1977 he was a professor at the School of Music at Indiana University, until he returned to the Curtis Institute, where he remained for many years. One of the last exponents of the bravura, a Romantic tradition of piano playing exemplified by Rachmaninoff and Horowitz, Bolet was associated especially closely with the works of Franz Liszt. After enjoying a limited reputation for much of his career, he gained a larger popular following in the 1970s.

Boletín de Música. Periodical created for the promotion of issues and topics related to Latin American music and edited by Casa de las Américas, a cultural institution based in Havana. Its first issue was published in 1969. It carried news about Cuban music to Latin American countries and also registered the musical achievements of people throughout Latin America. It included articles and lists of works by Cuban composers. The outstanding professor, musicologist, and composer Argeliers León directed the music department at Casa de las Américas until 1991.

Boloña, Alfredo. *Bongó* player and guitarist. Born 1890, Havana; died 1964. Boloña helped introduce the *son* musical style to Havana, where, for over half a century, he was a promoter of musical groups and events. Initially a *bongó* player, he eventually switched instruments to concentrate on the guitar. He organized a number of *son* sextets that gained immense popularity with the dancing public. His own group, Sexteto Boloña, recorded under the Columbia label. He was not only the group's director but also played the *marímbula* and sang. In 1926 Boloña traveled to New York to record. He is the author of many *sones*, including the famous "Guigüína yirabo," which was covered by many different *son* groups of that era.

Boloña, Sexteto. The guitar and *bongó* player Alfredo Boloña founded this *son* group in Havana in 1915. At that time, the musicians were Hortensia Valerón (vocalist), Manuel Menocal (*tres*), Manuel Corona (guitar), Victoriano López (maracas), and Joaqín Velazquéz (*bongó*). In 1926 the band became a sextet and it traveled to New York, where it made several recordings. Subsequently, new musicians joined the band: Abelardo Barroso and Mario Rosales (vocalists), José Interián (trumpet), and Loreto Zequeira (*bongó*). The group split up in 1935.

bombo criollo (Creole bass-drum). A European instrument, adapted and creolized by some Latin American peoples and characteristically used by Cuban military bands. It has a metal or wooden body, about 50 centimeters in diameter, with two drumheads fastened by hoops. It is played either

with a mallet or with the hand. It is used in street congas in Cuba.

Bombú, Ignacio. Guitarist and composer. Born 1914, Guantánamo; died 29 November 1973, Santiago de Cuba. In 1920 Bombú was living in Santiago de Cuba, where he was known as "Cucho el Pollero" because he was a door-to-door chicken salesman. In the 1930s Bombú played the guitar and sang at festivals in Santiago. He is the author of "Amargas penas," "Avileña," and "Adiós a la vida" (which was dedicated to Renato Guitart shortly before his death in the battle of Moncada), and of the popular *son*, "Cuatro pollos, cinco reales," as well as other pieces.

Bonachea, Arturo. Composer and saxophonist. Born 12 April 1897, Remedios; died (?), Havana. First studied with the Spanish musician Ernesto Jarque and later was taught cello and piano by Armando Ledeux, María Luisa Chartrand, and César Pérez Sentenat. Bonachea was also a disciple of Manuel M. Ponce and Pedro Sanjuán. He was a clarinet player in the bands of Cienfuegos and Marina de Guerra and later with the Havana Symphony Orchestra. Bonachea later joined the Havana Municipal Band as a saxophonist and also worked as a professor of music, and composed for piano, voice, orchestra, and chamber music groups.

bongó. An Afro-Cuban instrument consisting of two small drums, joined by a wooden piece. The drums are almost identical, about 20 centimeters across and of similar height; the slightly larger one is a *hembra* (female) and the smaller one is a *macho* (male). Originally the drum heads were tuned by fire; today tuning keys are used. The player holds the drums between his knees and beats the drumheads with his fingers and with the palms of his hands. The *bongó* is of markedly African origin. When it reached Havana from the eastern province of Oriente as an accompanying instrument in *son* groups, it became

immensely popular. In Oriente, it originally consisted of two small drums, resembling those used in *tahona* groups, joined together by a leather strap which the player placed over his knee, with one drum beside him and the other between his legs. Sometimes only one small drum was used. According to Ortiz, "the *bongó* is the most valuable synthesis in the evolution of twin drums in Afro-Cuban music" (Ortiz, *Los instrumentos de la música afrocubana*, 4:447).

Bonich, Juan. Music and theater critic. Born 25 December 1888, Havana; died 6 March 1939. Trained as a journalist and was a columnist and critic for the newspaper El Mundo in Havana. Bonich was a theatrical impresario and toward the end of his life founded a national opera company.

Bonilla, Diego. Violinist. Born 1898, Manzanillo; died (?), Havana. Began his musical studies with the Manzanillo Music Band and later studied the violin at the Manzanillo Musical Institute with the teacher Rodríguez Carballés. Bonilla moved to Havana when he was fourteen to study with Juan Torroella. He won many awards, and in 1921 he won a grant that enabled him to study in Europe. In 1931 he toured the United States and Mexico, returning to Cuba that same year to join the Havana Municipal Conservatory as a professor. He was later appointed director of the conservatory.

bonkó enchemiyá. Abakuá drum that Ortiz defines as standing a meter high, in the shape of a truncated cone, about 23 centimeters in diameter at the drumhead and about one-third smaller at its open base. The body is about 1 centimeter thick. The drum is played slightly tilted, one end resting on the ground, with the body of the drum leaning against a stone or some other low object. A *monibonkó* musician sits astride the drum and beats on the drumhead with his hands, while another musician, the *monitón*, squatting at the foot of the drum, beats the lower part of the wood with two sticks (*itónes*). Sometimes the *bonkó enchemiyá* is held vertically, in which case the musician stands to play it. When the musician is marching, the drum hangs to the player's left from a strap across his right shoulder (Ortiz, *Los instrumentos de la música afrocubana*, 4:35). The *bonkó enchemiyá* is one of the trio of Abakuá drums known as *enkómo*.

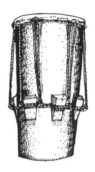

The *enkómo*, along with the *ekón*, two *itónes*, and two *erikundí*, constitute an Abakuá musical ensemble.

Bonne, Enrique. Composer. Born 15 June 1926, San Luis, Oriente. Director of the group Tambores de Oriente. Bonne spent his adolescence in Palma Soriano and then moved to Santiago de Cuba. He was taught music by his mother until he went to secondary school; he later discontinued his academic studies in order to dedicate himself to the study of music. He is author of the *cha-cha-chás* "Italian Boy" and "Cha-cha-chá de la reina," the *danzones* "Confidencial" and "Granito de arena," the *guarachas* "Que me digan feo, se tambalea," "A cualquiera se le muere un tío," and "No quiero piedras en mi camino," and the *sones* "Míralo aquí" and "Guajira simalé." Bonne often used popular refrains in his songs and would frequently use those refrains as titles. In 1960 he performed with his group Tambores de Oriente, which featured fifty percussionists, in theaters, on television, and at carnivals throughout Cuba.

Borbolla, Carlo. Composer. Born 1902, Manzanillo; died (?), Havana. Member of a musical family that made organs for dances. After initially teaching himself, Borbolla went to Paris in 1926 to study piano with Pierre Lucas and composition with Louis Aubert. He also took organ lessons with Constar Fermín. In 1930 he returned to Manzanillo and turned to constructing organs. He wrote chamber music for piano and the piece *Tres bailables manzanilleros* for string orchestra, as well as *sones* for piano, arguably his most important contribution. His compositions were always distinctly Cuban. In collaboration with Carmen Valdés, Borbolla also wrote

educational music that incorporated folkloric elements for teaching students.

Borbolla, Luis. Piano accompanist. Born at the beginning of the twentieth century, Manzanillo; died 1979, Havana. Borbolla studied in Manzanillo with the sisters Matilde and Amalia Badía and later perfected his piano technique with the pianist Alberto Falcón in Havana. He was a distinguished piano accompanist. He worked with some of the best singers in Cuba and abroad, as well as at the Pro-Musical Art Society. He traveled twice to Europe with the soprano Iris Burguet, in 1961 and 1966, performing in the Soviet Union, Germany, Bulgaria, Poland, and Czechoslovakia. He also played in the United States, Spain, France, and Italy, and studied voice technique with the contralto Gabriella Besanzoni and the tenor Tito Schipa.

Borcelá, Amado. Singer and percussionist. Born 14 July 1934, Havana; died 1966. Also known by the pseudonym Guapachá. For some years, Borcelá worked as an upholsterer. He was an innovator within Cuban popular music and sang with a specific and unusual style, close to *guaracha*. He briefly worked in radio, television, theater, and cabaret, and also made an excellent record with Jesús Valdés's combo. He died in the middle of a blossoming career.

Borges, Lino. Singer. Born 1936, Batabanó. Started as a singer in music groups in Batabanó. Borges went on to join the Conjunto Saratoga, with which he remained for twenty years, recording and appearing on radio and television programs as well as performing live. He is a notable interpreter of bolero and works as a soloist in nightclubs.

Borja, Esther. Singer. Born 5 December 1913, Havana. Raised in Santiago de las Vegas, where she began singing in festivals and religious ceremonies. In 1934 Borja qualified as a teacher in the Havana Normal School. In 1935 she was introduced to the public by Ernesto Lecuona at the Principal Comedy Theater, and the following year traveled to Argentina with Lecuona and toured the rest of the continent. On her return to Cuba she took part in operettas and *zarzuelas*. Borja gave a recital of Cuban music at Carnegie Hall in 1943 and toured the United States five times with Sigmund Romberg. She had a beautiful mezzo-soprano voice, clear diction, and a good feel for melody. She took part in radio programs and performed on television and in theaters throughout the country. She made many records, performed in various films, and helped create the television program *Album de Cuba*. She is one of the most notable and long-lived performers in the history of Cuban song.

Botet, Maria Enma. Composer. Born 1903, Matanzas. Botet was the author of choral music as well as pieces for solo piano and for voice and piano, including "Suite cubana" and "Cajita de música que toca una cubana." She was dedicated to teaching music and made great contributions in the realm of musical education.

botija. An earthen jug, like those used long ago to transport oil, with a perforation or small hole on one side through which the player blows. The sound is manipulated by the movement of the player's hands over the mouth of the instrument (Ortiz, *Los instrumentos de la música afrocubana*, 5:340). The *botija* is used in *son* groups and sometimes in *comparsas* as a

rudimentary substitute for the double bass. According to Ortiz, it is of African origin and was formerly called a *bunga*.

Boudet, Pedro. Violinist and composer. Born at the beginning of the nineteenth century in Santiago de Cuba; died 1880. Organist in the Cathedral of Santiago de Cuba who in 1878 inherited the role of choirmaster from Cratillo Guerra. Boudet also played violin and composed various works, including a mass for voice and orchestra.

Boudet, Silvano. Violinist, pianist, composer. Born 27 November 1828, Santiago de Cuba; died 9 March 1863. Cousin of Pedro Boudet. Silvano Boudet was a notable violinist who won awards at the Paris Conservatory. He was conductor of the Cathedral Orchestra in Santiago de Cuba and composed religious music, including *misas*, *lecciones*, and pieces for violin ("El canto del canario," "Recuerdo a mi madre," and "El ave entre las flores") and for piano ("Pensamientos melancólicos" and the *contradanza* "La retozona").

Bousquet, José Domingo. Violinist. Born 13 August 1823, Havana; died 6 April 1875. Studied first with Gavira and then with Rappetti. In 1842 Bousquet went to Paris, where he continued studying violin with André Robberechts, of Belgium. In 1856 he began a long tour of Europe. He played in various cities in the United States, and on his return to Cuba spent time performing and giving violin lessons.

Bovi, Arturo. Tenor. Born (?), Rome, Italy; died (?), Havana. Sang in various operas in Italy and later in Cuba, where he lived with his wife Tina Farelli. They ran a musical academy where they nurtured artists of the bel canto style.

Boza, Antonio. Composer, violinist; also played clarinet, flute, cello, double bass, organ, and various wind instruments. Born mid–nineteenth century in Santiago de Cuba; died end of the nineteenth century. Son of Pedro Noalsco Boza and brother of Lino. Antonio Boza composed religious pieces, waltzes, and dances. Among his *danzas* for *orquesta típica*, the most outstanding is "La francesita" because of its use of the *cinquillo*, a form commonly found in Cuban music that contains elements of Haitian song. Boza was assassinated by the colonial Spanish authorities at the end of the nineteenth century because of his separatist ideas and for attempting to leave Santiago de Cuba.

Boza, Lino. Composer, clarinetist, conductor of orchestras and bands; also played clarinet, violin, viola, cello, double bass, and flute. Born 1840, Camagüey; died (?). From a family of musicians; son of Pedro Nolasco and brother of Antonio. Lino Boza's family moved when he was very young to Santiago de Cuba. He is the author of waltzes, rigadoons, potpourris, marches, religious pieces, and, above all, *danzas*, such as "El chivo negro," "La cachita," "El camisón," and "La Elvira," which became very popular in the mid–nineteenth century. From 1860 he led the Band of the Fire Brigade in Santiago de Cuba. He taught music to young students in Santiago. His dance orchestra was famous throughout the eastern province. In 1879 he went to Haiti, where he spent three years, and then to Panama, where he founded a musical academy that was run by his son after his death.

Boza, Pedro Nolasco. Dance orchestra director. Born end of the eighteenth century in Camagüey; died 1870, Santiago de Cuba. Father of Antonio and Lino Boza. Pedro Nolasco Boza lived from an early age in Santiago de Cuba. His orchestra performed short poems about everyday life in Santiago de Cuba that he had set to music and often accompanied theatrical events.

Brindis de Salas, Claudio. Violinist, double bass player, dance orchestra director. Born 30 October 1800, Havana; died 17 December 1872. Brindis de Salas's orchestra, La Concha de Oro, was the most popular ensemble in the salons of Havana at the beginning of the nineteenth century. He was a student of the teacher Ignacio Calvo. His father, Luis Brindis, was a first sergeant of the Royal Artillery Corps; because of this, Claudio gained favor from wealthy people, who patronized his studies. He composed dances with a distinctly Cuban flavor and nearly always dedicated them to people from the insular aristocracy. He was the author of the operetta *Congojas matrimoniales*. Brindis de Salas was a lieutenant in the Morenos Leales Batallion, and in 1844 his musical career was interrupted by his connection with

the famous Escalera conspiracy. He was expelled from the island by the government of Leopoldo O'Donnell. He returned in 1848 and was imprisoned for nonfulfillment of his sentence; two years later, he was released. In 1864 he began giving concerts throughout Cuba with his two sons. In his old age, he lost his sight, and he spent his last few years alone. He wrote a *melodía* dedicated to General Concha that was printed in 1854. He also wrote poetry. His son Claudio José Domingo Brindis de Salas was a brilliant violinist known around the world. *See also* (La) Concha de Oro, Orquesta.

Brindis de Salas, Claudio José Domingo. Violinist. Born 4 August 1852, Havana; died 1 June 1911, Buenos Aires, Argentina. Claudio José Domingo began his studies with his father, Claudio, and then studied with Redondo and with the Belgian musician Vandertgucht. He finished his music studies in Paris, where he won First Prize at the Paris Conservatory and made a triumphal tour of the principal cities of Europe. He was dubbed "the black Paganini" by the press. In Europe he received many honors and decorations, including the Caballero de la Legión de Honor, the Barón, and the Ciudadano Alemán. He was also made the court chamber musician by Emperor William II of Germany. He married a German noblewoman. The "Barcarola" is one of his best-known works. Claudio José Domingo Brindis de Salas returned to Cuba greatly glorified and began a tour of the Americas. He later lost all his glory and fame and died an ill man.

Brito, Alfredo. Flutist, composer, arranger, orchestra director. Born 6 June 1896, Havana; died 17 December 1954. Studied with Armando Romeu, who helped him perfect the art of flute playing. He later learned to play the clarinet, saxophone, and piano, and studied harmony with the maestro Pedro Sanjuán. At the age of seventeen he played the flute with Antonio María Romeu's orchestra. He traveled to New York with Don Azpiazu's orchestra, playing saxophone. There, he recorded an arrangement of "El manisero" by Moises Simons that enjoyed an enormous success, selling a million copies for the RCA Victor label. On his return to Cuba, Brito founded the Orquesta Siboney; he later traveled with the orchestra to Spain, France, and Portugal. He was a member of Paul Whiteman's jazz orchestra, which he directed for several months. Brito wrote the soundtracks of several films, including *Rumba*, *Yo soy el héroe*, and *Prófugos*. He was also the author of classical works: sonatas for violin and piano, orchestral works, songs, a *fantasía*, and, most notably, the popular *danzones* "Acelera," "La choricera," "El volumen de Carlota," and "La flauta mágica" (with Romeu). In addition, he was musical director of Channel 2 Cuban television.

Brito, Julio. Composer and orchestra director. Born 21 January 1908, Havana; died 30 July 1968. Taught music by Pedro Sanjuán. At the age of sixteen, like his brother Alfredo, Julio Brito joined the orchestra of Don Azpiazu as a saxophonist, but he later turned to drums, also playing guitar and vibraphone. His first compositions, "Tus lágrimas" and "Florecita," were written in 1931, and shortly after, he became very popular, especially for the work "Ilusión china." He later wrote "Trigueñita," "Oye mi guitarra," "Flor de ausencia," "Mira que eres linda," "Serenata guajira," "Si yo pudiera hablarte," and in 1937 "El amor de mi bohío." Brito spent most of his professional life as an orchestra director. He wrote the music for various films, including *Tam Tam* and *Embrujo antillano*. He was a pioneer of live musical radio broadcasts, interpreting his songs on programs that garnered a large listening audience. In 1946 he became president of the Society of Cuban Composers.

broadcasting, Cuban music and. Owing in part to its proximity and close economic ties to the United States, Cuba was among the first countries to develop radio broadcasting, preceded only by the United States itself, England, and France. As late as 1933, Cuba ranked among the most developed nations in this sense, having established sixty-two stations—the highest number in all of Latin America. The first station capable of national broadcasts, PWX, began transmitting in 1922; numerous local, low-power broadcasting stations had been established a year or two earlier. Live broadcasts on PWX featured outstanding soloists of the symphony and philharmonic orchestras, as well as dance orchestras. The most prominent radio station of the 1930s that featured live and recorded music was CMQ. It made the voices of Pablo Quevedo and Eusebio Delfín famous throughout the island and introduced the famous musical talent show *La Corte Suprema del Arte*. Other stations of the period include Radio Cadena Azul, owned by the Trinidad Brothers, and Radio Habana Cuba, both of which eventually joined forces toward the end of the decade and came to be known as Unión Radio.

In the 1940s, CMQ and RHC/Unión continued broadcasts with figures such as Miguelito Valdés and Joseíto Fernández; these stations soon began competing with Radio Cadena Suaritos, Radio Progreso, and Mil Diez. Countless other musicians established their careers on the radio at this time as well, including Celia Cruz and the Sonora Matancera, the *conjunto* of Arsenio Rodríguez, and Antonio Arcaño's *charanga*. This and the following decades represented a period of phenomenal growth for the broadcasting industry. By 1958, the island already boasted more than 145 radio stations, including five national broadcasters and forty-five short-wave and seven FM stations. Cuba was also one of the first Latin American countries to establish its own local television broadcasts, establishing three television channels in the mid-1950s. Weekly television programs such as *Jueves de Partagás*, *El Cabaret Regalías*, *El Show de Mediodía*, and *Bar Melódico de Farrés* served as a powerful medium for the dissemination of many forms of music and dance, both within Cuba and abroad.

Since the Revolution of 1959 and the shift from commercially oriented to state-controlled enterprises, Cuban broadcasting has not been as powerful a medium for popular music. Many of the original owners of radio and television stations left the country in the early 1960s, and by 1961 all had been nationalized. The format of programming shifted for many years away from what the public may have wanted to hear toward material—including music—

used to educate the public about particular issues or create support for the government's political agenda. Still, the period since the mid-1980s has witnessed a resurgence of commercial music on TV programs including *Mi salsa* and radio stations such as Radio Progreso, Radio Taíno, and Radio Ciudad de la Habana.

Broadway, Orquesta. Formed by a group of Cuban musicians conducted by Eddie Zervigón in New York, 1962. The original members were Eddie (flute), Rudy Zervigón (violin), Kibbin Zervigón (*güiro*), René Hernández (piano), Roberto Torres (vocalist), and other Cuban and Puerto Rican musicians. The *son* was the basis of the orchestra's sound, but it also incorporated new arrangements as well as *pachanga* and salsa. It played an important role in promoting Cuban music in the United States and abroad.

Broch de Calvo, Natalia. Pianist. Born 1830, Matanzas; died 19 December 1876. Began her musical studies in Matanzas with Fernández Caballero. Broch de Calvo moved to Havana in order to improve her musical skill under the guidance of Nicolás Ruiz Espadero. She gave recitals in Havana and then traveled to Paris and London, but died during the return journey from London to Cuba.

Brochi, Juan. Band director. Born at the beginning of the nineteenth century in Florence, Italy; died 1900, Havana. Brochi lived most of his life in Cuba, where, in 1856, he organized and led the music band of the Spanish Army's Engineer's Corps. He gave many concerts with the band until the year before his death.

Brooks, Alfredo. Composer and orchestra conductor. Born 13 December 1884, Santiago de Cuba; died (?). Studied with various teachers, among them the pianist Maria Mitchell. Brooks traveled abroad for many years, studying cello, harmony, composition, and conducting. He also studied in the Victor Herbert Academy in the United States. On his return to Cuba he worked as an orchestra conductor. His compositions included the religious pieces "Ave María," for voice and piano; "Angelus," for voice and orchestra; "Tres cuartetos y melodía"; "El guajirito" (*capricho*), for piano; and "Nirvana" and "Santiaguera" (*canciones*).

Brouwer, Leo. Composer, guitarist, percussionist, orchestra director. Born 1 March 1939, Havana. Brouwer was born into a musical family: he is the grandson of Ernestina Lecuona. He was first taught guitar by his father and then went on to study with Isaac Nicola. He is self-taught in harmony, counterpoint, form, and composition. He studied with Caridad Mezquida, Edward Diemente, Vincent Persichetti, and others, and completed his education in 1960 at the Juilliard School of Music and in the music department at Hartford University. In 1961 he became a teacher of harmony and counterpoint at the Amadeo Roldán Conservatory, and in 1963 also began teaching composition there. He was also musical adviser to Cadena Nacional (radio and television). A magnificent guitarist, Brouwer has toured many countries, performing and taking part in festivals in Aldeburgh, Avignon, Edinburgh, Spoleto, Berlin (Fetwochen), Toronto, Arles, and Martinique, as well as at the most important musical centers in both Eastern and Western Europe. He played the guitar part in the opera El *cimarrón* by the German composer Hans Werner Henze. In 1972 he received a DAAD grant from Berlin, and he has also given seminars in Toronto (at Guitar '75), Arles, Martinique, and Mexico. He has recorded many successful records. His style has encompassed serialism, postserialism, and aleatoric performance, and he has directed pioneering works. He is the director of the Experimental Department of the Cuban Institute for Movie-Making, Art, and Industry, where he continues to work as a composer.

Buelta y Flores, Tomás. Orchestra director, composer, professor, cello and viola player. Born 1798, Havana; died 11 October 1851. During the first half of the nineteenth century, Buelta y Flores's orchestra became very popular. He composed *contradanzas, danzas,* and other popular pieces, such as "La bella Irenita," "El sarao de Peñalver," "El patriotismo habanero," "La valentina," the waltz "Cristina," and religious pieces. He was a titled musician with the Royal House of Charity and the first sergeant to benefit from the Morenos Leales Batallion of Havana. He was thought to have been connected with the so-called Black Conspiracy of 1844, an association that later caused him some problems. When he died, he left behind a great fortune, including houses and slaves.

Buena Vista Social Club. The Buena Vista Social Club, which was formed in 1997, soon became a phenomenon and the world's most successful world music project, spawning a film of the same name. In 1998 the album *Buena Vista Social Club* won a Grammy Award for Best Tropical Album. The following musicians participated in the project: Ry Cooder (guitar), Joachin Cooder (dumback), Rubén González (piano), Carlos Gonzalez (*bongó*), Lazaro Villa (congas and *güiro*), Barbarito Torres (laúd), Luis Barzaga (*coros*), Compay Segundo (guitar), Alberto Valdes (maracas), Manuel "El Guajiro" Mirabal (trumpet), Cachaito Hernandez (bass), Juan De Marcos Gonzalez (conductor), Orlando Lopez, Salvador Repilado, Julienne Oviedo, Eliades Ochoa, Ibrahim Ferrer, Manuel ("Puntillita") Licea, Omara Portuondo, and Julio Alberto Fernandez.

Bueno, Enrique. Composer and director. Born 1885, Santiago de Cuba; died 1954. Headed the Music Band of Santiago de Cuba for many years, which won awards in different national competitions. Bueno also directed a dance band. He is the author of *danzones, canciones,* and the "Himno a Santiago de Cuba."

bufos habaneros. The origin of the *bufos habaneros* (Havana comic theater) can be pinpointed to a performance on 31 May 1868 at the Villanueva Theater. But long before then, the theaters of Havana had presented plays that were the precursors of the so-called Havana *bufos,* whose originators were Francisco Covarrubias (1775–1850), José Agustín Millán (c. 1810–c. 1863), and Bartolomé José Crespo (1811–1871). This musical-theatrical form originated in Italy and developed in France. It is characterized by a light and humorous plot line and is deeply rooted in the most authentically popular expressions. In Cuba, the genuine antecedents were the one-act farce and the theatrical *tonadilla* (lighthearted song) of Spanish origin. From 1868 theaters in Havana such as the Cervantes became exclusively devoted to the *bufo* genre, which reflected national feelings by giving voice to the the Cuban people's ardent aspirations for independence. As a consequence, the Spanish authorities closed down the Cervantes for some time and repressed demonstrations that resulted from performances of the *bufos.* On 22 January 1869, during a performance of *Perro huevero aunque le quemen el hocico,* by Juan Francisco Valerio, army volunteers raided the Villanueva Theater and shot at the audience, which was composed mostly of Cubans who reacted to the patriotic references in the play by voicing their anticolonialist feelings. There were numerous casualties.

The composers Francisco Valdés Ramírez and Enrique Guerrero contributed to the musical development of the genre, and their popularity spread beyond Cuba. In 1882 a company of Havana *bufo* comedians performed in Mexico. By 1880 Los Bufos de la Sala had become extremely popular. Almost all plots in *bufo* theater are based on three characters: a Negro, a *gallego* (Spanish man), and a mulatto woman. Through them, the bourgeois life in prerevolutionary Cuba is satirized and the genuine values of the people are reaffirmed. The plays generally contain vulgar expressions, which some contend detract from their effectiveness. They "were divided into tableaux separated from each other by music, with a final tableau consisting of a strident fanfare by the whole company" (González Freire, *Teatro cubano,* 157–58). Throughout the twentieth century several theaters granted space to the *bufo* companies: the Moulin Rouge, where Arquímedes Pous performed outstandingly; the Martí Theater; and, above all, the Alhambra. Among the most outstanding playwrights in the genre were Federico Villoch (1866–1927), Gustavo Robreño (1873–1957), Mario Sorondo, and Carlos Robreño (1903–1972). The most significant composers of music for the *bufo* genre were Jorge Ánckermann (1877–1941), Manuel Mauri (1857–1939), and José Mauri (1855–1937). The most popular plays were *La casita criolla,* by Villoch and Ánckermann, and *El velorio de Pachencho,* by the Robreño and the Mauri brothers. (Both plays have recently been restaged.) The stage of the Alhambra was witness to brilliant acting by Amalia Sorg, Luz Gil, Blanca Becerra, Regino López, and Adolfo Colombo, among others, while comic sopranos such as Alicia Rico and Candita Quintana excelled at the Martí Theater, alongside actors such as Alberto Garrido and Federico Piñeiro. "*Bufo* comedians played a considerable role in the evolution of Cuban popular music. It was thanks to them that all types of urban and *campesino* songs and dances were brought to light, became widely known, and were mixed with other styles. The demands of the stage diversified genres born out of the same roots. Black music acquired a permanent standing. The Alhambra was, for thirty-five years, a genuine conservatory of national rhythms" (Alejo Carpentier, *La música en Cuba*, 196).

Burés, Félix. Violin and piano teacher. Born in the middle of the nineteenth century in Barcelona; died 1919, Cárdenas. Arriving in Cuba to live, Burés spent many years as a teacher at the National Conservatory. In Cárdenas, he founded the Beethoven Academy.

Burguet, Iris. Soprano. Born 23 October 1922, Havana; died (?). Burguet was a specialist in the German lied song style. After studying in Havana, she went to Munich, Germany, to study under Karl Walter Schmidt, and then to Vienna, where she took lessons with Viórica Ursuleac de Krauss. Burguet sang all styles of music, and in 1952 she began performing in the important cities of the world. In Cuba, she gave recitals and performed as a soloist with the National Symphony Orchestra.

Burke, Elena. Singer. Born 28 February 1929, Havana; died 2002. Original name was Romana Burgues. In 1941 Burke gave her first performance for a program of amateur artists on CMQ radio. In 1942 she turned professional, subsequently performing on the radio stations Mil Diez, Cadena Roja, COCO, and Radio Progreso, and at the cabarets Sans Souci and Zombie. In 1945 she performed at a number of Havana theaters: the Encanto, Alkázar, América, Riviera, and Fausto. She then traveled to Mexico and Jamaica with the choreographer known as "Rodney," singing in *Las mulatas de fuego* (which also featured Celia Cruz). Upon returning to Cuba, she sang with the quartets of Facundo Rivero, Orlando de la Rosa, and Las d'Aida, with whom she traveled to the United States, Canada, Venezuela, and Mexico. Her longest

association was with Aida's quartet, which she left in 1958 to perform as a soloist. In her solo performances, she was accompanied by the guitarist Foilán and by such pianists as Frank Domínquez, Meme Solís, and Enriqueta Almanza. Subsequently, she traveled throughout most of Europe and the United States. In 1964 she represented Cuba at the Cannes Festival. Beginning in 1962 she hosted a radio program entitled *A solas contigo*. She also appeared in two Cuban films, *Llanto de luna* and *Nosotros la música*, and performed throughout Cuba, and on radio, television, and in the theater. Burke sang mostly in the *fílin* genre. Even after her death, she remains one of Cuba's most popular singers.

Buxeda, Elías. Teacher and band director, violinist, pianist. Born 1894, Sagua la Grande; died (?). In 1902 Buxeda moved to Camajuaní, where he studied music with his father (who had the same name). In Remedios, he was taught by Fernando Estrems. In 1907 he returned to Sagua la Grande and studied with Antonio Fabre, then joined the Municipal Band of Sagua la Grande as *requinto* player and toured several Latin American countries. He returned to Cuba and lived in Camajuaní, where he founded a musical institute and also directed the Municipal Band of Placetas.

C

Cabaleiro Cervantes, Ernestina. Pianist. Born 4 November 1896, Havana; died 12 August 1976. Her mother was the illegitimate daughter of Ignacio Cervantes Kawanagh and Guadalupe Ibañez Hernandez. Cabaleiro Cervantes taught piano, theory, and harmony. She studied piano with Maria Luisa Chartrand, and then with Alberto Falcon at the Havana Municipal Conservatory. In 1914 she was granted a scholarship to continue studying music in Germany, but she could not make the trip because of the outbreak of World War I. She gave several concerts in Havana, sometimes playing with José Echaniz. For many years, she was a music professor at the Municipal Conservatory and gave private lessons in piano, theory, and harmony. She taught several generations of Cuban musicians, including Ignacio Villa ("Bola de Nieve").

Cabel, René. Singer. Born 9 March 1914, Havana. Full family name was Rene Cabezas. Cabal took singing lessons with Arturo Bovi. In 1930 he made his debut singing ballads and boleros. Beginning in 1934, he was accompanied on his recordings and in his performances by the orchestra of the Hermanos Castro. He sang in concerts sponsored by Ernesto Lecuona. In 1937 Cabel traveled to Mexico, where he recorded for the Peerles label and later signed a contract with RCA Victor. He has toured the United States and almost all of Latin America. Cabel is known as "the tenor of the Antilles" and has lived in Bogotá, Colombia, since 1964.

Cabrera, Rafael. Director, composer, clarinetist. Born 9 November 1872, Bayamo; died 14 September 1967. Cabrera's father, Manuel Muñoz Cedeño, taught him music, and at the age of ten he was playing the clarinet in his father's orchestra. At fifteen, he composed his first musical play. When his father died in 1895, he became the orchestra's director. During the War of Independence, he joined the Liberation Army. Once the war was over, he returned to Bayamo as a member of the Banda Mambisa. Cabrera founded the Bayamo Municipal Band in 1913 and was its director until 1962. He taught music to his own sons. He wrote the *Capricho sinfonico*, as well as songs, dances, *danzones*, waltzes, hymns, and marches.

Cabrera, Ramón. Composer. Born 1925, Bayamo; died 15 December 1993, Madrid. Among his most famous songs are the bolero "Tu voz," the bolero-*cha* "Esperanza," and the songs "Guantánamo," "Santiago de Cuba," "Manzanillo," "Palma Soriano," and "Marianao," which became hits for Benny Moré. His songs "Santiaguera," "Bayamo," and "Banes" were sung by Tito Gomez. From the 1970s until his death, he lived in Spain.

Cabrisas-Farach, Duo. An original vocal duo composed of lead and accompanying voice, with traditional guitar played by Irene Farach (born in Caibarien) and Jesus Cabrisas (born in Matanzas). Formed in Havana during the 1950s, the group was immediately hired to perform on radio, television, and theater and made several records. Its repertoire includes traditional Cuban songs.

Cachao. *See* Lopez, Israel.

cadena (chain). A step in the *contradanza* dance style. "The man, dancing within the women's line, gives his right hand to his dancing partner, asking her to reach for the left hand of the dancer beside her, who has already done the same. With their hands free, the four dancers can continue in a double-S shape for eight measures so that they execute what is known as a double chain. If they continue for only four measures and don't repeat the steps, the figure is called a half chain." (Pichardo, *Diccionario provincial casi razonado de voces cubanas.*)

Caignet, Félix B. Composer. Born 31 March 1892, San Luis, Oriente; died 25 May 1976, Havana. When Caignet was seven years old, his family moved to Santiago de Cuba. As an adolescent, he began work as a writer and a journalist. His songs "Te odio," "Mentira," and other compositions, such as "Frutas del Caney" and "Carabali," were very popular and remain in the repertoire of several singers. He also wrote several successful radio soap operas, including the classic El *derecho de nacer.*

Cairo, Pablo. Composer and guitarist. Born 29 June 1917, Corralillo; died 14 April 1978, Havana. Cairo spent his childhood in Cienfuegos and later moved to Havana. He was a singer with the Hermanos Dihigo Orchestra. In the 1940s, his *guarachas* "El tibiri-tabara," "Pa' fricase los pollos," "Que va, viejo," "Como me da la gana," "Vive como yo," "Y que mi socio," and "La rumba tiene valor" were popular.

Caissé, Alberto. Composer of *guarachas* and singer. Born 1 October 1908, Holguin. Also played guitar and maracas. Among Caissé's most popular songs are "La media naranja," "El siju," "To' el mundo quiere bailar," and "Cancanito." For many years, he sang with his own band in Havana night clubs.

Caíto. *See* Diaz, Carlos Manuel.

cajón. An instrument made from a commercial wooden box used for packing. It is used as a substitute for the drum among very poor people or in impromptu situations, as well as in playing the rumba. The *cajón* is played with both hands. Two types are generally used: boxes like those formerly used to pack cod, and smaller candle boxes.

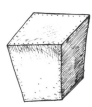

Calderón, Jorge. History graduate, journalist, movie critic, writer. Born 17 April 1939, Havana. Calderón worked as a researcher for the Institute of Ethnology and Folklore, and his works have appeared in many publications. He also worked as a scriptwriter and as an adviser and assistant director for several documentaries produced by ICAIC. He is the author of *Amparo, millo y azucena* (a memoir written in 1970), *Maria Teresa Vera* (1986), and *Nosotros, musica y el cine*, published in Mexico in 1997.

Callava, Calixto. Composer of bolero, *son*, and rumba. Born 14 October 1930, Havana; died 16 December 1990. Callava started playing rumba as a child in the Havana neighborhood of Belen. He sang and performed in the groups Guaguancó Maritimo-Portuario and Yoruba Andabo. He wrote the bolero

"La añoro," the *sones* "La Tumba Brava," "Retozon," and "Tumbayaya," the *mozambique* "Lo bailo solo," and the *guaguancos*, "El callejon de los rumberos," "Guaguanco sabroso," "Mi guaguanco si da la hora," "Taguiri," "El congo," and "Tiembla la tierra." Callava worked in the port of Havana until his death, and his songs reflect that environment.

Calle, Oscar. Pianist, orchestra director, composer. Born 1898, Matanzas; died (?). Began studying music in his native city and then piano with Fernando Carnicer in Havana. In 1928 Calle left for Paris, where he performed as a pianist and orchestra director. He later toured several European cities. He is the author of the rumbas "Ay, mama!," "Invitacion a la rumba," "Lo es rumba," "Changó," and "Quiero una conga," and the *canciones* "Horas lejanas," "Para mi," "Nunca lo quisiera." He also wrote musicals. In 1941, he moved to Havana, where he continued working as a pianist.

Calvo, Ela. Singer. Born 18 February 1932, Havana. A balladeer, Calvo started singing in 1955 in nightclubs and on radio and television. She has given concerts in Cuba, Germany, Spain, Italy, Cyprus, Bulgaria, Poland, Venezuela, Jamaica, Mexico, Peru, Panama, Chile, and Angola.

Calzadilla, Ramón. Baritone. Born January 1934, Havana. Studied with Arturo Bovi and the contralto Maria Pissarevskaya and also in Italy and Romania. Calzadilla has performed in Switzerland, France, Holland, Portugal, the United States, Costa Rica, Brazil, and several Eastern European countries. In 1960 he won First Prize at Italy's Beniamino Gigli International Singing Contest. In 1962 he won international singing contests in Toulouse, France, and in Italy, where his award was presented to him by Tito Schipa. In Cuba, he has starred in many concerts and operas and sung on radio and television. He is Cuba's most renowned opera singer. He currently lives in Colombia, where he continues to sing and give lessons.

Calzado, David. Violinist and orchestra director. Born 29 January 1958, Havana. From a family of musicians that includes his father, Sergio, an excellent singer. David Calzado was a violinist in various orchestras, including Ritmo Oriental, before forming his own dance band, Charanga Habanera, in 1988. He later became the band's director. He remains at the forefront of the group, which has made important musical innovations.

Calzado, Osmundo. Orchestra director and arranger. Born 4 December 1942, Santiago de Cuba. A music graduate from the University of Oriente, Calzado played the clarinet in the Oriente Symphony Orchestra from 1963 to 1967, when he became director of the Orquesta de Música Moderna of Oriente. Since 1985 he has been the director of the Orquesta Cubana de Música Moderna. He has directed several music festivals in Cuba and abroad and has conducted radio and television orchestras in Germany, Poland, Bulgaria, Czechoslovakia, and the United States.

Calzado, Rudy. Singer. Born 27 November 1929, Santiago de Cuba. Started as a vocalist with several bands in his native city and also in Havana. Calzado then moved to New York, where he has performed with leading Afro-Cuban bands, including Machito's Afro-Cubans. He is a master of all genres of Cuban music.

Camacho, Nelson. Pianist. Born 1 May 1948, Santa Clara. Camacho's first piano lessons were at the Falcon Conservatory with Professor Zoila Benitez; he then perfected his skill with Professor Cesar Perez Sentenant. He became Esther Borja's accompanist in 1972. He has performed on radio and television and made several records, and has also written Cuban dances and concert songs.

Camacho, Nicolás. Singer. Born in the middle of the nineteenth century; died at the beginning of the twentieth century. Camacho was one of the first Cuban bolero singers, along with Pepe Sanchez. He was a member of a group of troubadours from Plaza de Marte, and he participated in the War of Independence under the leadership of General Antonio Maceo in 1895, achieving the rank of lieutenant.

Cámara, Juan Antonio. Composer. Born 1917, Havana. Studied composition with Amadeo Roldán and José Ardévol. Cámara was a member of the Grupo de Renovación Musical. He wrote the Sonata for piano (1942), the Suite for flute, clarinet, and bas-

soon (1942), and the Trio for oboe, viola, and piano (1945). He has also written harmony for Cuban and Spanish folksongs for choral singing.

Camara de La Habana, Orquesta. See Havana Chamber Orchestra.

Camayd, Raúl. Baritone. Born 13 August 1937, Holguín; died 28 July 1991. Studied music in his hometown with Esther Mallo and later in Havana with Ricardo Sevilla and Francisco F. Dominicis. Camayd took lessons with the Bulgarian Liliana Yablenska. Camayd is also a law graduate from University of Havana. He founded the Oriente Lyric Theater in 1962, sang as a soloist with the National Symphony Orchestra, and performed with the National Lyric Theater. He toured several countries, singing in twelve languages. His repertoire included operas, operettas, and songs.

Camero, Cándido. Percussionist. Born 22 April 1921, San Antonio de los Baños. Camero's first instruments were tres guitar and double bass, but in 1946 he took up percussion instruments: the bongó and the conga drums. In 1953 he turned to jazz, accompanying Duke Ellington, Dizzy Gillespie, Billy Taylor, and others. He has made records with important jazz bands and the most significant Latin bands in the United States, where he lives.

campesino group. A band that performs Cuban folk music, such as the punto guajiro, the zapateo, and the guajira. Such ensembles originated in the eighteenth century. The modern campesino ensemble includes various guitars, a laúd, a three-stringed tres guitar, a güiro (a percussion instrument made from a dried gourd), claves, and sometimes other accompanying instruments. See also guajira, música.

canción. Musical genre whose roots are in the light Spanish popular song and other Spanish song forms, including tiranas, polos, and boleros, along with the Italian operatic aria, French romanza, Neapolitan song, and the slow waltz. Argeliers León noted that at the beginning of the nineteenth century, canción was characterized by twisting and intricate melodies, the same sorts of ornamental turns found in gruppetti and appoggiatturas, and dark, enigmatic, and elaborate lyrics. Later, the form assumed the nineteenth-century sentiment of independence: *canciones* became idyllic love songs to symbols of Cuban identity, such as a palm tree, a mockingbird, or a girl from Bayamo. Their two-part melodies became more fluent; they were written in phrases and periods and sung in thirds and sixths. Their sound was dominated by the vocal duo and the accompanying guitars. Some *canciones* became quite popular (León, *Música folklórica cubana*, 185–88). Initially, it could be said that these compositions were written by the Creole population of Cuba, who opposed the ruling Spanish oligarchy but, with minor exceptions, perpetuated musical styles associated with Europe. Not only the native bourgeoisie but also the anonymous songwriters from the working classes used the same musical patterns as their counterparts across the Atlantic. Songs like "La Corina" (anonymous), "La Bayamesa" (Cespedes, Fornaris, and Castillo), and even "Es el amor la mitad de mi vida" (J. Martin Varona) from the operetta El *brujo* were written in 3/4 time. The essence of the Cuban bolero, however, gradually began to influence the *canción* by way of small details (anacruses, deceptive cadences, and so forth), also imparting a tropical lassitude and melodic sensuality. Another influence of the Cuban bolero on the form came through its distinctly Cuban lyrics. Beginning in the the third quarter of the nineteenth century and extending through the traditional *trova* movement in Santiago de Cuba led by José "Pepe" Sánchez, Sindo Garay, Alberto Villalón, Manuel Corona, Rosendo Ruiz, and others, the *canción*, which at that point had adopted duple meter, further rid itself of certain European influences and became truly Cuban. A strong Cuban character was apparent in the accompaniment of the popular troubadour's guitars and in the way the genre expressed the feelings and aspirations of the population. Over time, the *canción* has naturally evolved into its current identity, incorporating local percussion instruments and fusing with other genres, such as the *son*.

canción de cuna. Variant of the *canción*. Its themes revolve around putting a baby, usually a black baby, to sleep. The lyrics of the *canción de cuna* often contain somewhat pejorative imitiations of black dialect. Another kind of lullaby, of Spanish origin, is widespread in Latin America, but it is entirely different from the Cuban variety.

Cané, Humberto. Double bass player, guitarist, arranger. Born 22 January 1918, Matanzas. Son of Valentin Cané, founder of the Sonora Matancera band. Humberto Cané started to play the *tres* guitar in his father's band in 1935. He also accompanied Chano Pozo in the Conjunto Azul and later in the Conjunto Camacho. In 1945 he moved to Mexico, where he founded a band, the Humberto Cané Orchestra, with Benny Moré as lead singer. In 1949 he founded the Conjunto Yeyo y Cané, with Yeyo Estrada. He played the double bass in several jazz orchestras and Mexican trios. In 1962 he moved to Los Angeles.

Caney, Conjunto. The trumpet player and vocalist Benito Llanes formed this group in Havana in 1969. Its repertoire includes all the Cuban dance styles. The group has performed on radio and television, at festivals, in cultural centers, and at theaters and has recorded many LPs. It has also played backup for many singers. It performs what is considered "traditional" Cuban music.

Cantos de Altares de Cruz. A Catholic fiesta that brought celebrants together on the evening of 3 May, at an altar in a house or a religious place, to celebrate Santa Cruz. The fiesta involved dancing, singing, drinking, and eating, and was widely celebrated across the island, especially in the eastern provinces. During the celebrations, songs with a particular form and content that were exceptionally Spanish in style were performed around the cross. Only a few people still know these songs today.

Cañizares, Dulcila. Music writer and composer. Born 1 March 1936, Santiago de las Vegas. Studied music and graduated from Havana's Normal Kindergarten School. Primarily a pianist, Cañizares has also written poetry and worked as a journalist. She is the author of *Gonzalo Roig* (1978), a biography of the great Cuban musician; *Julio Cueva* (1991); *La trova tradicional cubana* (1992); and *Musica religiosa en Cuba* (1993). She has written for most Cuban periodicals and currently works for Editorial Letras Cubanas.

(Las) Capellas. A vocal duo formed by the sisters Daysi and Marta Baró that made its debut in 1958. The duo's repertoire includes Cuban songs, particularly love songs, although it also plays Afro-Cuban music. Las Capellas mostly sings a cappella but sometimes is accompanied by piano. The duo has performed on radio and television and in nightclubs.

capricho. A variant of the *canción* patterned after the *capriccio* of Western classical music. It is usually written in a lively tempo and is characterized by comical or capricious lyrics.

Carabalí Izuamá. A social and musical union founded centuries ago by the Carabalí Afro-Cubans in Santiago de Cuba. Records prove the association already existed by the end of the nineteenth century, when it was headed by the seven Nápoles brothers. Its headquarters are still in the Santiago neighborhood of Los Hoyos. The carabalí was established as a council, and during the War of Independence it assisted the liberation cause known as the Mambí. During the first years of the Republic, it was incorporated as a society, and in its early years its members came out for carnival to perform their songs and dances. The instruments played by the Carabalí Izuamá group are the *bombo criollo*, a small drum called a *fondo*, a *hierro* (iron), and a *maruga* or *chachá*. At present, the society exists as a folkloric group.

Carbó Menéndez, José. Composer. Born 13 May 1921, Santiago de Cuba. Carbó Menéndez's songs have become very popular through versions performed by well-known singers. He has composed the boleros "Hablemos de los dos," "Ya me cansé de ti," "Embrujo antillano," and "En tu ausencia"; the *sones* "El baile del sillón," "La televisión," "El pasito tun tun," and "A burujón puñao"; the *danzón* "Avenida 486"; the *cha-cha-chá* "Pínchame con tenedor"; and the *guarachas* "Se murió Panchita," "Cao cao maní picao," "Quimbo quimbumbia," and "Palmeras." For many years, Carbó Menéndez was a member of the board of directors of the Society of Cuban Composers, and he also worked for the Peer and Cia. publishing house. He has written about music for different newspapers and magazines. He currently lives in the United States.

Carbonell, Luis. Declamator and pianist. Born 26 July 1932, Santiago de Cuba. Began reading poetry on CMKC radio in his native city and also worked as a piano accompanist. Carbonell traveled to the United States, where he performed at New York's Hispanic

Theater and at Carnegie Hall. In 1948 he returned to Cuba and performed in theater and on radio and television. He has given readings of Afro-Caribbean poetry in several Latin American countries and in Spain. In 1955 he recorded three LPs with the Cubaney record company. In recent years, he has made many recordings for EGREM.

Carcassés, Bobby. Composer and singer of Cuban jazz music. Born 29 August 1938, Camajuaní. A multi-instrumentalist with an original singing style, Carcassés's performances also include dance and mime. His musical style fuses several Cuban musical genres (rumba, *son*, *guaracha*) with jazz. He worked for the Havana Musical Theater for many years and, at present, he performs as a soloist. His hit compositions include "Blue-guaguancó."

Cárdenas, Félix. Guitarist and singer. Born 6 November 1912, Matanzas. For thirty-two years, Cárdenas directed the Lira Matancera band and, later, the Estudiantina Matancera. His compositions include the *sones* "Puntillita," "Lo que sea," "Yo pico un pan," "Juan sin traba," and "Ya Mantilla se botó"; the bolero "Oye una canción para ti"; the *guarachas* "Chanchuyo" and "El cuento del sapo"; and the conga "Oye el bombo."

Cárdenas, Hermenegildo. Composer of popular songs. Born 1910, Havana; died 1975. His song compositions include "Marinerito, marinerito" (*son*), "El naranjero del amor" (*pregón*, with Obdulio Morales), and the *afro* hit "Un brujo en Gaunabacoa."

caringa. An Afro-Caribbean dance and song that became very popular in the early nineteenth century. The lyrics, of Afro-Cuban origin, are repeated over and over: "Toma, toma y toma, *caringa* / A los viejos palo y jeringa" (Take it, take it, take it away, *caringa* / All the hard times and annoyances). Nowadays this song is included in the repertoire of folkloric groups.

Carioca. *See* Noroña, Gilberto.

Carlés, Maggie. Singer. Born 1947, Havana. Made her debut in 1967 as a pop and rock singer. For many years, Carlés was half of a duo with Luis Nodal. She has performed on radio and television and in nightclubs and has toured widely. She spent one season in a Paris nightclub. She currently lives in Miami.

Carlos Emilio. *See* Morales, Carlos Emilio.

carnaval, comparsas de. The processions held on 5 January that are vital to the celebration of the Day of the Kings, commemorating the Adoration of the Kings. The *comparsas de carnaval* date back to colonial times. Different Afro-Cuban societies would group themselves into "nations"—Congos, Lucumís, Mandingas, Carabalís, and Ararás—and parade through the streets of the capital until they reached the Palace of Government, where they greeted authorities and received a Christmas gift. Initially, each group wore its own characteristic indigenous costumes and ornaments. Slowly, however, the groups began incorporating costumes and objects given to them by their masters as presents or bought cheaply at small shops. By the second half of the nineteenth century, the traditional indigenous dress of the Afro-Cuban societies—the blue-striped shirts, red percale pants, and feather hats of the Congos and Lucumís; the blue silk turbans of the Mandingas; and the straw-frayed borders, ornamented shirts, tubular hats, and cowbells of the *íremes* in the Abakuá groups—had been replaced by cutaway coats, bowler hats, and other dress copied from their masters' outfits. The music and dances performed also became a fusion of styles. The Cuban conga, for example, adopted elements from Cuba's white European ancestors and became amalgamated, or "hybridized," although without losing its African roots. In 1937 the costumed carnival groups began performing in the Havana carnival on a permanent basis, parading along the Prado Promenade with their distinctive choreographies, dances, and songs. The groups included El Alacrán, from the neighborhood of El Cerro; the Marqueses, from

Atarés; Las Boyeras, from Los Sitios; Los Dandys, from Belén; La Sultana, from Colón; Las Jardineras, from Jesus María; Los Componedores de Batea, from Cayo Hueso; El Príncipe del Raj, from Marte; Las Mexicanas, from Dragones; Los Moros Azules, from Guanabacoa; El Barracón, from Pueblo Nuevo; and Los Guaracheros, from Regla. Carnivals in Santiago de Cuba and other eastern towns have their own characteristics. Performed in July, these celebrations spread throughout the entire city, and the population is more actively involved. The music and dances are also different. In the east the main musical instruments are *bocú* drums, the *galleta*, and the *corneta china*, and costumed participants include groups from the El Tívoli, Los Hoyos, and La Placita neighborhoods, as well as the old *cabildos* (unions) of Cocoy, Carabalí Izuamá, and Carabalí Olugo, all of whom parade along the Trocha. Carnival songs and dances have always been a very rich source for popular music.

Carnicer, Fernando. Professor and composer. Born 1865, Madrid, Spain; died 1936, Havana. Before coming to Cuba Carnicer was already a professional musician and had won awards. In Havana, he taught music at several music schools before founding his own. In 1917 he taught harmony and counterpoint at the Havana Municipal Conservatory. He wrote three symphonies, two operas, studies for the piano, and some religious music.

Carpe, Raúl. *Tres* player. Born 5 October 1905, Guadalupe; died (?). At the age of five, Carpe moved with his family to Guantánamo, where he became one of the most active players of the *tres* guitar. He played the kind of *son* music known as *changüí*, which originated in the region.

Carpentier, Alejo. Writer and musicologist. Born 26 November 1904, Havana; died 24 April 1980. After dropping out of the University of Havana's architecture school, Carpentier studied literature, music, and art criticism. For many years, he was a critic in Havana, Paris, and Venezuela. He was a member of the Grupo Minorista, from which he promoted the new aesthetic trend advocated by the *Revista de Avance*. In 1928 he moved to France, where he contributed the texts for operas, ballets, cantatas, and operettas, in collaboration with the composers

Edgar Varese, Darius Milhaud, Marius François Gaillard, and the Cubans Amadeo Roldán and Alejandro Garcia Caturla. In 1937 he attended the Second Congress of Intellectuals in Defense of Culture in Spain. In 1939 Carpentier returned to Havana, where he researched musical works. He discovered scores by the composer Esteban Salas that had been lost in the archives of the Santiago de Cuba cathedral. From 1945 to 1959 Carpentier lived in Caracas. He returned to Cuba after the triumph of the Revolution. He is the author of *Ecue-Yamba-O* (1993); *La musica en Cuba* (1946); *El reino de este mundo* (1953); *El acoso* (1956); *Guerra del tiempo* (1958); *El siglo de las luces* (1962); *Tientos y diferencias* (a collection of essays, 1964); *Derecho de asilo* (1972); *El recurso delmetodo* (1974); and *Concierto barroco* (1974). He has also published the two-volume *Crónicas* and *Ese musico que llevo dentro*, a three-volume compilation of his work published in the magazine *Carteles y Social* and in other publications from 1921 to 1974. He also wrote *La consagracion de la primavera* and *El arpa y la sombra* in 1979. His last book, *Razon de ser*, was published in 1980. He won the Miguel de Cervantes Award in 1978 and the Medicis Award in 1979.

Carreras, Oscar. Violinist. Born 25 December 1944, Matanzas. Attended the National School of Art. Carreras played the violin in the Matanzas Symphony Orchestra and later studied at Moscow's Tchaikovsky Conservatory. He is currently a soloist with the National Symphony Orchestra and has given concerts around Cuba. He is also a professor at the Higher Institute of Art.

Carriazo, Lorenzo. Professor and composer. Born 30 June 1840, Havana; died 10 July 1899. A pupil of Nicolas Ruiz Espadero, Carriazo wrote several dances for piano, including "La siempre viva" and "Cosas." He taught many musicians in Havana.

Carrillo, Isolina. Composer and pianist. Born 9 December 1907, Havana; died 21 February 1996. Had many hit songs in the 1940s. Carrillo was under contract to the radio station RHC Cadena Azul and also directed the vocal group Siboney. She worked as a piano accompanist and choral director. Some of her most famous songs are "Canción sin amor," "Sombra que besa," and "Increible," but her most lasting and popular composition is "Dos gardenias." She also wrote many indexes for the Cuban Institute of Radio and Television.

Carrillo, María Teresa. Soprano. Born (?), Havana. Represented Cuba at the 1950 Salzburg Festival and also performed on radio and television and gave concerts. Carrillo took lessons with Elizabeth Schumann in New York. She was a member of the American Opera Society. In Havana, she starred in many operas.

Casamitjana, Juan. Flutist, composer, professor, musical director. Born 1805, Spain; died 1882, Paris. Moved to Santiago de Cuba in 1832, where he founded a music school, directed bands and orchestras, and composed music. In 1836 he transcribed the folkloric *cocoyé* songs from the Oriente province. Casamitjana borrowed from the folklore of Santiago de Cuba for his compositions. He wrote several *canciones*. He taught music to Laureano Fuentes Matons and Rafael Salcedo. In 1866 he moved to Paris, where he staged an opera.

Casanova, Héctor. Singer. Born 19 November 1942, Havana. Since the 1960s, Casanova has lived in New York. One of the most outstanding singers of salsa music, he has performed with Johnny Pacheco's orchestra and as a soloist. He has recorded many albums.

Casanova, Nancy. Pianist. Born 17 July 1941, Havana. Studied music at the Havana Municipal Conservatory and graduated in 1964. Casanova later attended the Warsaw Higher Music School, working for five years with professor Trombini Kazuro. In Havana, she performed under the direction of Natalia Hornowska. She has given concerts in Czechoslovakia, Bulgaria, Poland, Yugoslavia, and the Soviet Union. In Cuba, she has given piano recitals and performed with the National Symphony Orchestra. She is a professor at the National School of Art.

Casas, Adolfo. Tenor. Born 2 December 1947, Pinar del Rio. Studied music at the Pinar del Rio Conservatory and graduated from Bulgaria's State Conservatory, where he took singing lessons with Sima Ivanova. In 1962 Casas joined the Pinar del Rio Lyric Theater. In 1976 he starred in Puccini's *La Boheme* at the Plovdiv Opera Theater in Bulgaria, where he won two awards. He has performed in many countries. In Cuba, he has played the lead role in operas and operettas, and in such vocal and symphonic works as Bach's *Magnificat*, Mozart's Requiem, and Beethoven's Ninth Symphony. He is a soloist with the Cuban Opera and a professor at the Higher Institute of Art.

Casas Romero, Luis. Composer and band leader. Born 24 May 1882, Camagüey; died 30 October 1950, Havana. Studied music at the Escuelas Pías from the age of nine. At the age of twelve, he played flute with the orchestra of the Santa Cecilia Popular Society. In 1895, when the War of Independence resumed, Casas Romero joined the Liberation Army (Mambí), and after the war was over, he returned to Camagüey, where he founded a children's band and played in a dance band. For economic reasons, he also worked as a typesetter. In 1904 Casas Romero moved to Havana, after signing a contract to be director of the orchestras at the Martí Theater. He played the flute in most of Havana's most significant orchestras at the beginning of the twentieth century, and also directed the Payret Theater orchestra. His *criolla* song "Carmela" (1909) marked the beginning of that genre in Cuban music. He per-

formed in Mexico, Santo Domingo, Canada, and the United States. After returning to Cuba, he became a professor, specializing in flute, harmony, and composition. In 1913 he was appointed deputy director of the army's staff band and became its director in 1933. Casas Romero's most popular *criollas* are "El mambí," "Soy cubano," "Mi casita," and "Camagüeyana." He also composed marches, operettas, overtures, dances, and musicals, and wrote several articles for Cuban magazines. He was decorated for his creative work. *See also* criolla.

Cascabel, Agustín. Composer. Born (?); died (?). Author of the most popular mid–nineteenth-century *contradanzas*, such as "La chalupa," "La bruja," "Súplicas," "No hablemos mas del asunto," "La Antoñita," and "Tu madre tiene la culpa," as well as of waltzes like "El chivo cojo." Cascabel also wrote marches and *canciónes*.

Cascarita. *See* Guerra, Orlando.

Casino, Conjunto. Formed in Havana in 1937. The group became a *conjunto* in 1940. It traveled to Mexico to perform on the radio and in nightclubs. In 1945 the band traveled to Puerto Rico and the following year to Venezuela. In 1947 it gave concerts all around Cuba. Conjunto Casino became very popular and made many records. At the peak of its fame, in 1950, its musicians were: Roberto Espí (bandleader and vocalist); Roberto Faz (vocalist); Agustín Ribot (guitar and backing vocalist); Alberto Armenteros, José Gudín, and Miguel Román (trumpets); Roberto Alvarez (piano); Cristobal Dobal (double bass); Orlando Guzmán (*bongó*); and Carlos Patato Valdés (conga). Later, new musicians joined the band, including Orlando Vallejo, Rolito Rodrigues, and Fernando Alvarez (vocalists) and Ñico Cevedo

and Rolando Baró (piano). The group has performed in many countries and at home, and it still plays on radio and television and at festivals.

Casino de la Playa, Orquesta. *Jazzband* founded in 1937 in Havana by Miguelito Valdés, Anselmo Sacasas, Walfredo de los Reyes, Liduvino Pereira, Guillermo Portela, Alfredo Saenz, José M. Peña, Ernesto Vega, Antonio González, and Luis Rubio. Its name was taken from the venue where the group first worked. One of the best Cuban *jazzbands*, it recorded numerous records and made five brief performances for American television. The band appeared in several Cuban films and continued performing up until the 1950s.

Castellanos, Tania. Composer. Born 27 June 1920, Regla; died 8 December 1988, Havana. Her name originally was Zoila, but she took a pseudonym for political reasons. A metallurgical worker, in 1939 she became a member of the Socialist People's Party and a union leader. She took music lessons and was associated with the *fílin* movement. Castellano represented Cuba at various international events. After the triumph of the Revolution, she was appointed to several positions in the cultural and political sectors and also at the Cuban Institute of Radio and Television. She composed the songs "En nosotros," "Recordaré tu boca," "Prefiero soñar," "Me encontrarás," "Vuélvete a mí," "Inmensa melodía," "Canción a mi Habana," "Evocación," "Cuba, corazón de nuestra América," "Me niego," "Por los Andes del orbe," "Canción a los niños," "Por Angela," "Soldado de mi patria," and "Desde Yara hasta la Sierra," among others.

Castillo, Elías. Guitarist and *tres* player. Born 20 July 1924, Ceiba Mocha; died 1974, Havana. In Matanzas, Castillo played in several trios until he moved to Havana with the Trío Matancero. A self-taught musician, he was one of the most original *tres* and guitar stylists. For many years, he accompanied the guitarist and singer Carlos Querol. Together with Ñico Rojas, he performed in concerts and on radio and television shows. He also played in Los Bocucos band.

Castro, Orquesta Hermanos. *Jazzband* founded in 1929 in Havana by saxophonist Manuel Castro with his brothers Antonio, Andrés, and Juan. The band started out playing on Radio Salas. In 1932 it traveled to New York. On returning to Cuba it played in hotels, on the radio, and at other venues. The band went to Venezuela, where it appeared at the Tropical Club and on Radio Cultura. It appeared in the film *Havana Cocktail*, produced by Warner Brothers. It traveled to Puerto Rico, subsequently recorded various records, and remained active until 1960, when members of the band formed the resident orchestra for Radio Progreso.

Castro Romeu, Zenaida. Orchestra and chorus director. Born 4 December 1952, Havana. Studied piano and orchestra and choral direction at the Amadeo Roldán Conservatory and at the Higher Institute of Art. Castro Romeu has directed the Cuban National Symphony Orchestra and chamber music groups in Cuba, Nicaragua, Spain, Sweden, and Germany. In 1989 she directed Michel Legrand's "Conciertoratorio," with Legrand as a soloist. She is a professor at the Higher Institute of Art and directs the Camerata Romeu.

Castroverde, Hortensia de. Soprano. Born (?), Havana. Made her professional debut in 1937 accompanied by the Havana Symphony Orchestra. Castroverde was a soloist with the Havana Municipal Band under its director Gonzalo Roig. She sang operas as well as *canción*, and she performed on radio and television. She currently lives in the United States.

Caunedo, Jesús. Saxophonist, clarinetist, flutist. Born 24 August 1934, Havana. Began playing in jazz bands in 1953. Together with other Cuban musicians, Caunedo founded the Cuban Jazz Club. In 1960 he settled in New York, where he played with Machito, Tito Puente, and others. In 1976 he moved to San Juan, Puerto Rico, and continued his career as a renowned musician. He recorded the solo albums *Fire and Sugar* in 1973 and *Puerto Rican Jazz* in 1986.

Cavailhón, Emilio. Composer, guitarist, singer. Born 14 March 1939, Guantánamo. A self-taught musician, Cavailhón played with the group Los Llamas and the Pepin Vaillant band. He is the author of the *guarachas* "La chica complicada," "Guerra a la ambición," "Guardafronteras," "La chica del granizado," "El camisón," "La quiero término medio," and "Suena el piano Ruben." He currently studies at the Professional Training School and performs as a soloist throughout Cuba.

cedazo. A figure of the *contradanza*. The *cedazo* is a waltz, though it is in 2/4 time, reduced to the eight measures that are repeated in the second part (with which the dances are always finished), or else to thirty-two measures, regardless of the previous figures (Pichardo, *Diccionario provincial casi razonado de voces cubanas*).

cencerro. A Cuban imitation of the Ñáñigo *ekón*, which is often played in popular-music orchestras. It is simply a cowbell from which the clapper has been removed. It is struck on its outside with a piece of metal or hard wood and produces two different sounds, according to the point at which it is struck: a high-pitched sound if struck on its narrower part, near the handle, and a low-pitched sound if struck on its wide rim or the perimeter of its opening (Ortiz, *Los instrumentos de la música afrocubana*, 2:270).

Centro de Investigación y Desarrollo de la Musica Cubana. *See* Cuban Music Research and Development Center.

Cervantes, Ignacio. Pianist and composer. Born 31 July 1847, Havana; died 29 April 1905. Took his first piano lessons with Nicolas Ruiz Espadero. In 1865 Cervantes entered the Paris Conservatory, where he was taught by Antoine Francois Marmontel and Charles Alkan. In 1866 he won a piano award playing Hertz's Fifth Concert. In 1868 he won another piano and harmony award. Cervantes was a candidate to receive the Rome Award, but he was forbidden to compete for it because he was a foreigner. He was admired by such composers as Rossini, Liszt, and Paderewski. In 1870, after a short stay in Madrid, he returned to Cuba. Cervantes was the first Cuban composer to breathe European air after Raffelin. His repertoire as a pianist included Beethoven, Chopin, Mendelssohn, Liszt, and Bach. He performed as orchestra director for an opera company in the Payret Theater, and he also gave piano lessons. In 1875, the Captain General, a great fan, urgently summoned Cervantes to him. "Ignacio Cervantes," the Captain General advised, "we now know for sure that the money you collect with your concerts is being handed to the rebels. Get out of here before I am forced to have you arrested!" The Captain General then asked Cervantes where he would go. Cervantes informed him, "To the United States. . . . It is Cuba's closest country, so I will be able to continue doing there what I was doing here." Surprised by this, the Captain General let him go (Carpentier, *La música en Cuba*, 121–22). In the United States and Mexico, Cervantes gave concerts to raise funds for the War of Independence and then returned to Cuba at the end of the Ten Years' War. When the war resumed in 1895, he again left the country. In 1900, when the war against Spain was completely over, he returned to the island and began working as orchestra director in the Tacón Theater. In 1902 he represented Cuban music at the Charleston Exhibition. It would be his last trip abroad. Cervantes addressed the issue of the national accent in music as a problem that could be solved only by the peculiar sensibility of the musician. He worked with the philosophy that his nationality was inborn, not a result of what he had been taught. Cervantes was one of the first musicians in the Americas to consider nationalism to be a consequence of a people's distinct character; he was thus a great forebear to later composers (Carpentier, *La música en Cuba*, 124).

Cervantes, María. Pianist and singer. Born 30 November 1885, Havana; died 8 February 1981. A singer of genuinely Cuban folk music. The daughter of Ignacio Cervantes, María Cervantes took music lessons with him. She also studied with professors Gonzalo Nuñez and Enriqueta García. In 1930 she became a very popular singer, pianist, and composer, and made records in the United States. She sang in a very clear and passionate style. She wrote "Lejos de ti," "Ignacio," "Los lunares," "Tomasa," and "Gratitud." On 22 April 1964 she performed in a concert at the Fine Arts Palace. Cervantes was active as a musician until her death.

Cervantes, Orquesta. Band playing in the French *charanga* style popular in Havana during the early part of the twentieth century. It was directed by the flutist Leopoldo Cervantes. Other members were Antonio María Romeo (piano), Ramón Cervantes (violin), Avelino Ceballos (double bass), Remigio Valdés (timbales), and José de la Merced (*güiro*). The group was one of the first *charanga* bands in Cuba.

Céspedes, Pancho. Composer and singer. Born 28 February 1956, Havana. Began as an amateur singer on the television program *Todo el mundo canta* and later became a soloist. Céspedes has sung mostly light romantic songs. He is the author of "Vida loca," "Si tú te vas," "Señora," and "Pensar en ti." He is now known internationally and has for many years lived in Mexico City.

Cevedo, Ñico. Composer and pianist. Born (?), Havana; died 23 December 1988, Miami. Played the piano in the Kubavana and Casino bands before going to the United States in 1954. Cevedo wrote the boleros "Ya lo puedes decir," "Amor burlado,"

"Por que me besaste," "Alma muerta," "No lo puedo evitar," and "No me hables de amor."

chachá. Name given to the Cuban cylindrical metal rattle used in the *tumbas francesas* of the eastern provinces. It is usually profusely adorned with ribbons of many colors and is shaken while held high in the air. Its cylindrical body has flat covers on both its ends and a handle inserted in its central part. There is no doubt that the *chachá* comes from Haiti (Ortiz, *Los instrumentos de la música afrocubana*, 2: 315–317). *Chachá* is also one of the names given to the Carabalí *comparsa* rattles, more commonly known as *maracas de canasta* or *erikundí*.

cha-cha-chá. Song and dance style derived from a specific type of *danzón* known as "danzones de nuevo ritmo" and influenced by the *son*. These *danzón* variants were developed by the López brothers, Orestes and Israel, when they were members of the band Arcaño y Sus Maravillas. Enrique Jorrín created the actual *cha-cha-chá* at the end of the 1940s. Jorrín says of his invention: "I composed some *danzones* in which the musicians would sing short choruses and, as that pleased the audience, I continued to develop it. In the *danzón* 'Constancia,' I included some well-known *montunos*, and the way the audience participated in the chorus made me write more *danzones* in that same style. I also asked everyone in the orchestra to sing in unison, so that the lyrics could be heard more clearly and strongly. . . . That concealed the quality of the musicians' voices—for they were not professional singers. In 1948, I changed the style of a Mexican song by Guty Cárdenas, 'Nunca,' by leaving the first part as it was and providing the second part with a different rhythm underneath the melody. This caused such a great sensation that I decided to compose music based on the last part—the third trio section, or *montuno*—independently of the *danzón*. Then I came up with 'La engañadora' in 1951. It had an introduction, an A part repeated, then a B part and a return to A, and it ended with a coda in the way of a rumba. When I started composing, I watched the steps of the dancers during the *danzón*-mambo and noted the difficulty that most syncopated rhythms created. The dancers' steps were not following the 'out of time' structure—that is to say, they were moving to the second and fourth beat of the bar (2/4). Syncopated rhythms and melodies made it extremely difficult for the dancers to place their steps in accordance with the music. So I started composing melodies that marked the time more clearly, trying to include as few syncopations as possible. . . . This led to moving the emphasis that is produced on the fourth eighth-note in the mambo to the first beat in *cha-cha-chá*. With melodies nearly danceable by themselves and the balance between melodies on strong beats and weak beats, the *cha-cha* was born." *See also* Jorrín, Enrique.

chambelona. A popular song performed to a conga rhythm. The song has been well known since the Liberals introduced it during the 1916 election campaign, which culminated in the seizure of power by their opponent Mario García Menocal and the failed "revolution" of February 1917. By mixing the structure of an old Spanish song with rhythmic elements of Congolese origin, Rigoberto Leyva composed this work, which has been sung on Cuba's streets for decades. Over the years the lyrics have changed in order to make them more relevant to new political campaigns, but the melody has remained constant.

changüí. Variant of the Cuban *son* that originated in the region of Guantánamo. One of the most ancient forms of *son*. Today there is a group that performs it in its homeland, under the sponsorship of the Ministry of Culture. *See also* son.

Chapottín, Félix. Trumpet player. Born 31 March 1909, Havana; died 20 December 1983. Director of the band carrying his name. Chapottín studied music with Professor Venancio González. When he was eleven years old he joined the Children's Band of Guanajay, playing *cajón*, tuba, onoben, and trumpet. For seven years he was director and trumpet player in the Chambelona de Guanajay Band. In 1927 he returned to Havana and played with the Sexteto Colón for a short time before joining the Sexteto Habanero. He also played with several other sextets, including Munamar, Pinin, Agabama, Universo, Boloña, Bolero, Carabina de Ases, América, and Jóvenes del Cayo. In the 1940s, Chapottín joined the Arsenio Rodríguez Band, which in 1950 took Chapottín's name and was directed by him after the founder moved to the United States. Chapottín is the most renowned trumpet player of the *son* style. His solos are famous for their unique style and high-pitched sound. He has composed many popular *sones* and *guarachas*, including "Mentiras criollas."

charanga. A type of musical group also known as *charanga francesa*. This type of ensemble made its appearance in the early years of the twentieth century as a variation of the typical dance or wind orchestra. *Charangas* mostly played *danzónes*, but when the *cha-cha-chá* appeared in 1951, the new dance style was an ideal vehicle for the *charanga*-style musical groups. The original instrumentation consisted of flute, violin, piano, double bass, *paila* ("Creole tympani"), and gourd scraper (*güiro*). These instruments were later augmented with a conga drum, two more violins, and three singers.

Charanga Cubana. A *charanga* created in 1960 by the National Council for Culture to perform *danza*, *danzón*, and other genres. The band featured Aurelio Herrera (flute); Guillermo González (piano); Miguel Valdéz, Miguel Borbón, Cristóbal Paulin, and

Octavio Muñoz (violins); José Cordero (violoncello); Miguel Angel Colombo (double bass); Rafael Blanco (timbales); Iván Hernández (conga); and Francisco Vergara (*güiro*).

Chase, Gilbert. Musicologist. Born 1906, Havana. Died 1992. Lived in the United States. Chase began his studies with Max Dritter and Max Wald and continued at Columbia University and the University of North Carolina. He worked as a music critic for many U.S. and European publications, was associate editor of the *International Encyclopaedia of Music and Musicians*, was the Latin American expert in the Music Division of the Library of Congress, and was Professor of History of American Music at Columbia University. Chase was also director of the music school attached to the University of Oklahoma and a member of the American Musicology Society. In 1955 he was elected First Vice President of the Inter-American Council of Music. He is the author of *Music in Spain, Guide to Latin American Music,* and *History of Music in the United States,* among other works.

Chavez, Ramon. Tenor. Born 29 June 1938, Florida. Chavez graduated from the voice program at the Perumbesco Conservatory in Romania and became a member of the Cuban National Opera. He has sung as a soloist in many different operas and has performed solo concerts of music by composers from the seventeenth, eighteenth, and nineteenth centuries. He has toured Europe and Mexico.

Chaviano, Flores. Guitarist and composer. Born 10 December 1946, Caibarién. Studied with Isaac Nicola at the National School of Art. Chaviano has worked intensively, giving concerts and galas, both in Cuba and abroad, and has toured Czechoslovakia and the German Democratic Republic. In 1974 he was granted the Guitar Award by the Writers and Artists Union of Cuba. Among his works are *Requiem a un sonero* (dedicated to Miguel Matamoros), *Homenaje a Víctor Jara, Variaciones sobre un tema yorubá,* and Poem for flute and guitar. He has also written music for children. Chaviano recorded an album of works for the guitar by different Cuban authors. He studied composing under the guidance of Sergio Fernandez Barroso at the Higher Institute of Art. He has presided over the Hermanos Saiz Brigade of Music and

has worked as a guitar teacher at the Amadeo Roldán Conservatory in Havana. He lives in Spain.

Chediak, Esperanza. Soprano. Born (?), Havana; died 6 December 1981, Tampa, Florida. In 1944 Chediak made her debut at the National Theater in the *zarzuela La Plaza de la Catedral,* with libretto by Francisco Meluza Otero and music by Ernesto Lecuona. She subsequently performed the Cuban lyrical repertoire, especially Lecuona's works. In Cuba, she sang in theaters and on television. In the early 1960s she left for the United States, where she continued to sing.

chekeré. A type of gourd of African origin, also known as an *agbé* or *aggué. Chekerés* are large gourds, 50 or more centimeters long, that are dried, made hollow, and almost completely covered, except on the two ends, by a cord mesh netting to which numerous colored beads are attached. These beads strike the outside of the gourd when the instrument is shaken. The gourd is empty inside, with no stones or percussing objects, which makes it different from the maraca and the *chachá;* its empty, resonating cavity produces a loud sound when the beads hit it from the outside (Ortiz, *Los instrumentos de la música afrocubana,* 2:124). It is shaken and gently hit with both hands in a variety of ways to produce different sorts of sounds. Its function has broadened in recent years; it is no longer used only in religious ceremonies and is now popular with dance-music and concert-music groups.

Chirino, Willy. Singer, pianist, bass player, percussionist, drummer, composer. Born 5 April 1947, Consolación del Sur, Pinar del Río. His full given name is Wilfredo. In 1961 Chirino left for Miami with his family. He directed his first musical group at the La Salle School and made his first album in 1973. He subsequently performed in theaters, at festivals, and on radio and television, and has recorded almost twenty albums. His individual style—which he calls "the Miami sound"—is a mixture of Cuban and American music. He is the director of a musical group whose members are mostly Cuban. His hit songs include "Soy," "Gracias a la música," "Demasiado," "Yo soy un tipo típico," and "Doña Soledad."

Tomás Casademunt

Choral Society of Santiago (Orfeon Santiago). Created by the conductor Electo Silva in Santiago de Cuba in 1960, this choral ensemble performs traditional and modern Cuban pieces and polyphonic works from previous centuries. The performances are always a cappella, with arrangements made by Silva. The group has received awards in contests and festivals. *See also* Silva, Electo.

Chorens, María Luisa. Popular singer. Born (?), Havana. Singer of Cuban and Latin American songs. In 1952 and 1953 Chorens received the ACRI (Association of Cuban Critics) Award for Best Popular Singer of Cuba, and in 1955 she was elected Queen of Radio and TV. In 1961 she left for the United States.

Chori. *See* Shueg, Silvano.

Ciérvide, María. Soprano. Born (?), Havana. Ciérvide's first performances were with the Trío Luis Rivera, and she formed another trio with Zoraida Marrero and Georgina Du'Bouchet. With Du'Bouchet, she formed the famous Duo Primavera, which performed for many years. In 1964 Ciérvide was selected Best Singer by the Union of Show Critics of Florida. She now lives in the United States.

cinquillo. A musical figure that creates a constant underlying rhythm in many pieces. In this construct, one grouping of five syncopated notes alternates with another of four notes that is not syncopated. The two groups together form a rhythmic cell characeristic of much Cuban music. The syncopated group represents the "strong" side of the rhythm and is followed by the "weak," nonsyncopated side. Along with the *tresillo* (essentially the "triplet side" of the *son clave* pattern; *see* son) the *cinquillo* is one of the most widespread rhythms in the circum-Caribbean area. It is found in many Cuban genres and also in Puerto Rican *bomba*, Haitian *merèngue*, and in the music of nearby countries on the mainland, as well as in North American ragtime. Within Cuba, the *cinquillo* appears prominently in light classical music written for the piano during the nineteenth century and based on popular dance repertoire, such as the *danzas* and *contradanzas* of Ignacio Cervantes and Manuel Saumell. In their compositions, the *cinquillo* is found in primary melodic lines and also in supporting bass figures. The *danzón*, a direct descendant of the *danza* and *contradanza*, is probably the musical form most closely associated with the *cinquillo* that is still performed today. *Danzón clave* (*see* clave rhythm) consists of a *cinquillo* or similar pattern followed by four quarter-notes. The entire phrase is usually performed on the timbales using a series of open and closed tones on the head to create timbral variety.

Cirártegui, Juan Bautista. Organist. Born 1792, Spain; died (?), Havana. Came to Cuba with his family when he was ten and studied music in Havana. In 1821 Cirártegui became the organist at the Havana Cathedral, replacing Cayetano Pagueras. He played the church organ for more than forty years, wrote several musical pieces, and also studied painting, sculpture, and mathematics.

Cisneros, Orquesta de Gabriel. Formed in the early part of the twentieth century by the trombonist Gabriel Cisneros and other musicians who came from Mariano Mendez's band. Other musicians were: Safora (double bass), Domingo Corbacho (cornet), Ricardo Ramos (ophiclenic), Agustin Ezarduy (first violin), Juan Torroella (second violin), José Travieso (first clarinet), Margarito (second clarinet), Demetrio Pacheco (timbales), and Marquetti (*güiro*).

Clara y Mario, Duo. Formed by Clara Morales and Mario Rodríguez in 1953, who started playing at school balls and cultural events in Regla and Havana, and also performed in nightclubs and on the radio. The duo was particularly popular after 1961. Its repertoire included Cuban traditional and love songs.

Clark, María Luisa. Soprano. Born (?), Holguín. Clark studied singing in Holguín. She is a member of the Holguín Lyric Theater, has starred in Cuban operas and operettas, and performed on radio and television. She is one of Cuba's most renowned sopranos.

clave rhythm. The concept of clave in Cuban music refers to the use of a constantly repeating rhythmic figure, usually two measures in length, that serves as the structural basis for the rest of the composition's rhythms and melodies. It derives ultimately from West African notions of timeline patterns. In the majority of Cuban folkloric and popular music, but not all, repeated isorhythmic figures of this sort are found. The claves (wooden sticks) perform the rhythmic figures most often, but the rhythm can also be played on wood blocks, timbales, metal bells, and other objects. Clave rhythms typically contrast a syncopated figure in one measure against a relatively straight rhythm in the following measure. This alternation demands that the syncopated side of the pattern be synchronized to an extent with the strong beats in the melodies and additional rhythms of the composition. If such synchronization does not occur, the musicians will provoke a rhythmic error known as "crossed clave" or "being out of clave." Distinct clave rhythms exist for the *son*, the rumba, the *danzón*, Yoruban-derived religious music, and other genres.

claves. A Cuban instrument that has its origin in the Havana musical milieu. It evolved from wooden pegs that were used in the construction of boats. According to Oneyda Alvarenga, the claves are a musi-

cal instrument that consists of two round sticks, about a *jeme* (six inches; about the length of a hand) long, made of hard, sonorous wood, that are struck against each other to keep rhythm (Alvarenga, *Música popular Brasileña*, 255).

clave song. Folkloric genre that was created by inhabitants of the Afro-Cuban neighborhoods surrounding the port of Havana and that later spread into the city of Havana and to Matanzas, Cárdenas, and Sancti Spiritus at the beginning of the twentieth century. Two of the best-known clave groups, known as *coros de clave*, were La Unión and El Arpa de Oro, whose peak of activity occurred during Christmas festivities. Clave choirs consisted of mixed choral groups singing in the style of Spanish choral ensembles. A male soloist would set the key of the song with a nonlexical melody (a "diana") and would improvise variations on the verses sung by the choir. A "censor" would offer advice as to the best use of language in each composition. Songs were created from a mixture of African and Spanish elements. The Spanish influence was present in the songs' melodies, expressions, and in the frequent use of *campesina* music rhythms. Since clave songs originated in poor neighborhoods where blacks were a majority, however, Afro-Cuban rhythms also had a strong presence. Although no drums were used, a percussionist would softly beat on an old stringless guitar known as a viola or bass, and on claves, for percussion. Other variants of clave emerged later—for example, the Ñáñiga clave used the Abakuá dialect; and theater clave was created and developed by Cuban musician Jorge Anckermann. Singers of the traditional *trova* also adapted the genre to their style. Finally, the clave for the theater stage served as a point of departure for the creation of a new genre of popular music: the *criolla*. The first of these, "Carmela," was written by Luis Casa Romero in 1909.

Clave y Guaguancó. Rumba group formed in the 1960s under the direction of Mario Alán, together with Agustín Piña, Andrés Gutiérrez Malanga, and Miguel Ángel Mesa. Dedicated to the interpretation of *coros de clave*, rumba, toques, and songs of the Yoruba, Congo, Arará, and Abakuá. At the beginning, the group used *cajones*, or boxes, as percussive instruments but later incorporated drums and other

Mo Fini

percussion instruments. The group was directed by the researcher, vocalist, and percussionist Amado Dedeu and has toured America and Europe.

Clenton, Arturo. Composer and violinist. Born 1 April 1916, La Boca, Panama. Has lived in Cuba since he was four. A tailor, Clenton studied music with Professor Pablito Rodríguez and later entered the Felix Ernesto Alpizar Conservatory, where Casimiro Zertucha taught him to play the violin. He also studied at the Society of Cuban Composers and the Professional Training School. He has played with different bands. Father of the singer of the same name, Clenton wrote the bolero "Dos perlas"; the *danzones* "El escrupuloso," "Rescatando el corazon," and "Melodía de la juventud; and the symphonies *Prestidigitacion* and *Fragmentos del futuro*.

Clerch, Joaquín. Guitarist. Born (?), Havana. Leopoldina Nuñez, Martha Cuervo, and Efrain Amador were his professors. A graduate from the Higher Institute of Art, Clerch has given concerts in Cuba and abroad. He made a record with the Cuban record company EGREM. He has won many awards, including the 1987 UNEAC (Union of Cuban Writers and Artists) Award, the Havana International Guitar Festival Award, and the 1987 Toronto International Composition Festival First Prize. He currently lives in Sweden.

Coalla, Hortensia. Soprano. Born 1907, Havana. Studied singing and piano at Havana's Municipal Conservatory. In 1926 Coalla made her debut with Ernesto Lecuona's company. As a young woman, she dubbed silent motion pictures. She also performed in theaters and on the radio. She toured many countries with Lecuona, singing some of his songs. In 1949 she discontinued her musical career for a time. She later moved to the United States, where she

has performed once again in concerts dedicated to Ernesto Lecuona's music. Lecuona called her "Cuba's most beautiful voice."

Coca, Lino Fernandez. Composer, pianist, professor. Born 1830, Havana; died (?), United States. Composer of *contradanzas* such as "Ave Maria," "La Unica," "Tres lunares," "La reina del bando azul," "Pienso en ti," "El lamento," and "El vaya y venga," which were hits in the mid–nineteenth century and during the Ten Years' War of 1868–78. In 1869 he moved to Mexico. Coca's works were published by Desvernine and Edelmann and reprinted after the triumph of the Revolution by the José Martí National Library.

Coccó, José Antonio. Born (?); died (?). Director of the Havana Principal Theater for many years. He also choreographed several ballets and wrote the two-act opera *Fátima y Zelima: Las dos prisioneras*, which was staged for the first time on 12 October 1825. This opera and those by the Italian Cristiani, who lived in Cuba for several years, are representative of the musical genre at that time.

cocoyé. Songs and dances from the eastern provinces that were based on the Dahomeyan music coming from Haiti. When French colonizers and Haitian slaves emigrated to eastern Cuba at the end of the eighteenth century, they brought their songs and dances with them, and these were soon being performed in the Santiago de Cuba carnivals. In 1849 the Spanish musician Julián Reinó made an arrangement of the song "El Cocoyé," which had been transcribed by the Catalonian musician José Casamitjana, and saw it performed in the Plaza de Armas in Santiago. *See also* Casamitjana, José.

Codina, Joaquín. Singer and guitarist. Born 2 July 1907, Manzanillo; died 4 May 1975, Havana. In 1932 Codina moved to Havana, where he became a popular attraction in nightclubs and on the radio, performing a repertory of traditional Cuban songs. He also worked as a bookkeeper and hosted a program on Radio International.

Coimbra, Marino. Clarinetist, professor, band leader. Born (?); died 10 February 1913, Cienfuegos. Coimbra's orchestra earned great prestige and played at balls in Cienfuegos and other parts of Cuba.

Coliseo Theater (later, the Principal). The first theater built in Cuba, located in Havana, and modeled on European theaters. It was conceived by General Captain Marqués de la Torre, and the construction was directed by the engineer Antonio Fernández Trevejo. It was completed in 1775 or 1776 (researchers cannot agree on the precise date). In 1794 it was closed for reconstruction. It reopened in 1803, completely renewed and renamed the Principal Theater. The first Italian opera companies to visit Cuba, starting in 1834, performed there. After the opening of the grand Tacón Theater in 1838, its status decreased. It was seriously damaged by a hurricane in 1844 and demolished in 1846. The Luz Hotel was later built on the same site.

Collado, Carmen. Choir teacher. Born 6 May 1942, Havana. Collado has been a professor with the Amadeo Roldán Conservatory, the National School of Art, and the Higher Institute of Art, and is also a choral director.

Collazo, Bobby. Composer and pianist. Born 22 November 1919, Havana; died 9 November 1989, New York. Studied music and later formed a vocal quartet. Collazo's first success, in 1949, was with "Rumba matumba." After a long stay in Mexico, he went to Santo Domingo in 1947, then returned to Havana, but moved to New York in 1952. He composed many hit songs, including "Vivir de los recuerdos," "Tenía que ser asi," "Tan lejos y sin embargo te quiero," "Que te has creido," "La ultima noche que pasé contigo," "Lejanía, Luna de Varadero," "Esto es felicidad," and "Nostalgia habanera." He also wrote the rumba "Serenata mulata." He is the author of a book about Havana's show business, *La última noche que pase contigo: 40 años de la farándula cubana.*

Collazo, Fernando. Singer and composer. Born 1909, San Antonio de los Baños; died 16 October 1939, Havana. Worked as a cigar maker. Collazo began singing Cuban traditional song before joining a number of *son* bands in Havana. In 1930, he founded the Septeto Cuba. He starred in the first talking picture shot in Cuba, *Maracas y bongó,* and

also sang with different bands. He wrote boleros and *sones* and toured several countries.

Collazo, Julio (Julito). Percussionist, singer, musicologist. Born 1925, Havana. At the age of fifteen Collazo played the *batá* drums in a band. A pupil of Pablo Roche, he played with rumba bands and costumed groups in the Havana carnival. In the 1950s, he moved to New York, where he promoted Cuban folk music. He has worked with the Katherine Dunham Company and in the orchestras of Mongo Santamarka, Tito Puente, Eddie Palmieri, Xavier Cugat, and others. He is the director of the New York Cuban Folkloric Group.

Colson, Guillermo. Musician and painter. Born 1 May 1775, Paris; died 3 February 1850. Lived in Cuba for many years and opened a piano academy in Havana. Among his pupils were Nicolas Ruiz Espadero, Pablo Desvernine, and Fernando Aritzi. From 1836 to 1843 Colson directed the San Alejandro Painting School. Articles from that time proclaim Colson a skillful pianist. He also painted Cuban landscapes. In 1844 he returned to France.

columbia. *See* rumba.

combo. A type of group that emerged in Cuba in the 1950s under the influence of Puerto Rican bands that imitated America's "combos"—ensembles made up of different instrumental sections, each containing one instrument. In Cuba, they were a response to the needs of small nightclubs that could not afford large orchestras. Combos interpreted all styles of music, and generally consisted of trumpet, saxophone, piano, double bass, drums, Cuban percussion, and electric guitars, but the lineup could be flexible. Combos proliferated at the end of the 1960s, moving from nightclubs into all fields of popular music in the country.

Comellas, José. Pianist and composer. Born 21 February 1842, Matanzas; died 9 February 1888, Havana. Studied in Leipzig, Germany. Comellas was a music professor in Baltimore for many years. His works were very popular, particularly the *Sonata brillante* for piano. He was also a well-known performer.

Companioni, Miguel. Composer. Born 29 July 1881, Sancti Spiritus; died 21 February 1965, Havana. Father was a captain in the Liberation Army. Companioni lost his sight at the age of eleven. When young, he worked as a baker, a telegraph operator, and a pharmaceutical salesman. Then, in 1902 he assembled a group to perform the popular music of the time. He learned to play the guitar well and gave guitar lessons. In 1911 he traveled to New York for a medical examination and was told he would never see again. He also studied piano, flute, violin, and double bass. He played piano in theaters and cinemas. He ran his own dance band, which played in the province. He directed Easter choral concerts, which included his own compositions. Among his most famous works are "La lira rota," "Alelí," "Amelia," "La fe," "Por qué latió mi corazón," and, in particular, "Mujer perjura." He was awarded a medal for his fifty years as a composer by the Society of Cuban Composers.

(La) Concha de Oro, Orquesta. This band was formed by the violinist Claudio Brindis de Salas in Havana at the beginning of the nineteenth century and was in great demand in the ballrooms of the island's aristocracy. The ensemble played the European music of the time—*contradanzas*, minuets, *rigodones, cuadrillas, lanceros*—typical of a wind orchestra. The band would occasionally have as many as one hundred members.

conga. Style of song and dance, performed originally in carnival processions and originating from African slave celebrations. Conga incorporates various types of drums (*see* conga drum, below). The style was appropriated by politicians during the early years of the Republic in an attempt to appeal to the masses before elections. The dance actually became more of a march, characterized by its distinctive conga rhythm. Dancers would lift a leg in time with the music, marking the beat with strong motion of the body (Grenet, *Música popular cubana*). It later came to be a freer dance form: "It has two time elements; in the first, the accented notes of the rhythm coincide with the strong and weak beats, while in the second, the strong beat is the third beat of the rhythm structure, but the weak beat converts into a semi-quaver in relation to the fourth (last) note of

the bar. The melodic phrases are short, each being usually of 2 or 4 bars, and the number of bars of the whole piece varies between 28 and 36. Sometimes the conga adopts the ternary form (A-B-A), sometimes the binary, and sometimes it consists of only one theme, repeated however as many times as necessary for the text" (Durán, *Recordings of Latin American Song and Dances*.) This music and dance form has become totally assimilated into Cuba's musical heritage and has been used in many film soundtracks. It was popularized in the 1940s in the United States by Cuban singer-percussionist Desi Arnaz and by the Spanish bandleader Xavier Cugat.

conga drum. A drum of African origin, almost always made of staves and iron hoops, about a meter long, barrel-shaped, and open at the bottom with only one ox-leather drumhead affixed to the body by nails (Ortiz, *Los instrumentos de la música afrocubana*, 3:392). In ancient times, it was tuned by fire; today, it is tuned by adjusting metal lug keys. It can be played with the player seated, standing, or marching. The musical genre that commonly features this drum is also known as *conga*.

conga group. The group that provides the music for carnival processions, it originated from festivities celebrated by African slaves in Cuba. Drums and percussion instruments of varying sizes are used, including the conga drum, *tumbador*, *quinto* and *bombo*, cowbells (*cencerros*), and modified frying pans (*sartenes*), as well as wind instruments such as the trumpet and *corneta china*.

conjunto. Type of musical group that developed around 1940 as a result of the expansion of the traditional *son* septet. Its repertoire was mostly *son* but also included boleros and *guarachas*. The instrumental lineup usually consisted of piano, double bass, *bongó*, congas, *tres* guitar, four trumpets, and three singers who sometimes also played maracas and claves. The *tres* was usually the lead instrument.

Conjunto Folklórico Nacional. *See* National Folkloric Ensemble.

Conservatorio. A national magazine published from 1943 to 1951, it was produced by the Havana Municipal Conservatory. Its first editor was Ithiel León. According to José Ardévol, that era was "restless, waiting for live music, and [the magazine was] a vehicle for new things." Orlando Martinez edited the magazine for a time in the 1950s. The magazine played an important role in promoting the best Cuban music during the 1940s and 1950s.

Conservatorio de Alejandro García Caturla. *See* (Alejandro) García Caturla Conservatory.

Conservatorio Municipal de La Habana. *See* Havana Municipal Conservatory.

Conservatorio Nacional. *See* National Conservatory.

Conservatorio Provincial de Oriente. *See* Provincial Conservatory of Oriente.

Conte, Luis. Percussionist. Born 16 November 1954, Santiago de Cuba. Left Cuba in 1971 for Spain and later lived in Los Angeles, where he studied music. Conte later embarked on a successful career as a drummer, playing with musicians like Pat Matheny, Al Dimeola, Tania María, Dave Valentín, Celia Cruz, Maná, Luis Miguel, Simone, Daniela Romo, Julio

Iglesias, María Behania, Madonna, Stevie Wonder, and Diana Ross. He has played Latin jazz, Afro-Cuban music, salsa, and pop. He teaches percussion in the Dick Grove School, Los Angeles.

contradanza. Dance genre included among the so-called line or square dances, or *piezas de cuadra*, whose origins lie in the European contradance born in Normandy and brought to Cuba by the French at the end of the eighteenth century, though it was already familiar to a small sector of the population who had been introduced to it from Spain. At the beginning of the nineteenth century, there was a notable development in Cuba of the "Creole contradance," whose dance forms were known as *paseo*, *cadena*, *sostenido*, and *cedazo*. "The first two were calm, the last two lively and *picante*. There were *contradanzas* in 6/8 time, but many were that way because of the time signature and not rhythmically; rather they were characterized by 3/4 time" (León, *Música folklórica cubana*, 128–31). They consisted of two parts, each 16 bars in length. African musical elements are always present in this dance form. With the passage of time, the dance evolved from a communal one to one performed by couples. There also developed differences between the *contradanza* of Havana and that of the Oriente. The Havana version was seen to be more elegant, and that of the Oriente to be more "of the people." The oldest known *contradanza*, the "San Pascual Bailón," was published in 1803. The *danzón* is descended from the *contradanza*. From 1842 onwards, the sung form of the *contradanza* gave way to the *habanera*.

Contreras, Orlando Palma. Born 22 May 1926, Soriano; died 8 February 1994, Medellín, Colombia. Contreras began as a vocalist in various groups in Havana, such as Kalamazoo and that of Arty Valdés, then joined the dance band of Neno González. He was later a member of the Conjunto Musicuba. From 1961 onward he became a successful soloist. In 1964 he left Cuba and continued his career as a bolero singer in several countries, particularly the United States and Colombia.

Contreras, Silvio. Pianist, composer, dance orchestra director. Born 3 November 1911, Havana; died 14 January 1972. Led the *charanga* Hermanos Contreras in the 1930s. Contreras was also a pianist with other popular groups. He is the author of *danzones*, including "Masacre," "Ya está el café," and "Rey de reyes."

Coral de La Habana. *See* Havana Choir.

Corbacho, Orquesta de. Formed by the cornet player Domingo Corbacho in Havana in the 1920s and considered a wind orchestra, or *orquesta típica*.

Corman, Tomás. Composer and orchestra director. Born 1895, Spain; died 9 November 1957, Havana. Studied the *bandurria* (a type of Spanish lute) under Lazarriaga. When Corman was thirteen, his father, a guitarist, took him to Mexico, where they played as a duo. On returning to Havana, they performed in the Albian Theater. As a pianist, Corman organized his own *charanga* band, which stayed together for about thirty years. He was also musical director of the Alhambra Theater and author of the *danzones* "Maldita timidez," "Rachel, Íreme," "Gelleticas de María," "Me voy para Alemania," "La Mayendía," "Quien tiró la bombá?," "El pagaré," and "El dulcero."

corneta china. An instrument of Asian origin, absorbed into Cuban music. It was introduced by the many Chinese indentured workers who arrived in Cuba during colonial times. Its Cuban origin is in Havana's Chinatown, where the Asian *comparsas* known as Los Chinos Buenos played it in the city's carnivals. It is said that around 1910 it was taken to the *comparsas* of Santiago de Cuba by the sol-

diers of the "permanent army," and since then, it has remained a principal element in the congas of Santiago. Its five high-pitched, shrill, and strident notes easily penetrate the dense texture of the carnival drums.

coro de claves. *See* clave song.

Corona, Manuel. Composer and guitarist. Born 17 June 1880, Calbarién; died 9 January 1950, Havana. One of the "greats" of the Cuban *trova* movement. Corona moved to Havana with his family in 1895 and was a tobacco worker as a child. He later dedicated himself to music, and—with his guitar—led a bohemian, artistic existence. His *canción* "Mercedes" was very popular in 1908, and later works became part of Cuba's national heritage. They include "Longina," "Santa Celia," "Doble inconsciencia," "Las flores del Edén," "La Alfonsa," "Una mirada," "Adriana," and "Aurora"; as well as the *guarachas* "El servicio obligatorio," "Acelera Ñico, acelera," and "La choricera," inspired by everyday Cuban reality at the time. Corona also wrote works in response to those of other authors: for example, "Animada" is an answer to "Timidez" by Emilio Ballagas; "Gela amada" is an answer to "Gela Hermosa" by Rosendo Ruiz Sr.; and "La habanera" is an answer to "La Bayamesa" by Sindo Garay. Corona died a poor man.

Coro Polifónico Nacional. *See* National Polyphonic Choir.

Corrales, Alberto. Flutist. Born (?), Guanabacoa. Graduated in 1981 from the Higher Institute of Art. Since 1974 Corrales has given performances of chamber, symphonic, and popular music throughout Cuba. He has been a soloist in the Havana orchestra and elsewhere. He was a flutist in the National Concert Band. Corrales has toured various countries and recorded albums, two featuring traditional *danzones*. He has received many awards at international events.

Corrales, Julián. Violinist. Born 17 August 1954, Guanabacoa. Studied at the conservatories of Guillermo Tomás and Amadeo Roldán, at the National School of Art, and at the Korsakov Conservatory in Leningrad. In 1975 Corrales joined the Opera and Ballet Orchestra and later the National Symphony Orchestra. He has worked with the symphony orchestras of Peru, Santo Domingo, and Russia. He taught violin at the Higher Institute of Art and in conservatories in Peru and Santo Domingo. He is currently first violin in the National Symphony Orchestra of Cuba.

Cortés, José Luis. Flutist, composer, arranger, director. Born 5 October 1951, Santa Clara. Studied flute at the National School of Art. Cortés was a member of Los Van Van and then Irakere until, in 1988, he left to form NG (Nueva Generacion) La Banda. He has performed with this group on radio, television, in theaters and nightclubs, and at dances all over Cuba, and has toured the United States, Europe, and Asia. While continuing to play flute, he recently began to sing with the band as well. He is the author of "Rucu Rucu de Santa Clara," "Échale limon," "La bruja," "Cha Cortes," "No te compliques," "Pónle el biberón," "La expresiva," and "Santa palabra."

Cosmopolita, Orquesta. *Jazzband* created in 1938 in Havana by Vicente Viana. Humberto Suárez was the bandleader. It was widely acknowledged as the best accompanying orchestra to work in theaters and on the radio during the 1940s and 1950s. For twenty years it was resident at the American Theater. At the height of its greatest fame, its members included Carlos Faxas (piano); José A. Montalvan (double bass); Joaquín Benítez, Orosmán Zayas, and Orestes Gelabert (saxophones); Florencio Hernández, Félix Prieto, and Eddy Martínez (trumpets); José M. Valdéz Orovio (trombone); Jesús González (conga); and O. Viana (drums). The group kept playing until the beginning of the 1960s.

Costa, Oriol. Professor, director, composer. Born 1836, San Feliú de Guixols, Spain; died 1892, Sagua la Grande. When young, Costa moved to Sagua la Grande in Cuba, where he passed a musically active life. He founded a musical academy there that produced various notable musicians, such as the famous flutist Ramón Solís. He was the director of various bands and head of the local church choir. He organized choirs and groups and wrote religious and non-religious works.

Coto. *See* Antomarchi, Juan Antonio.

Coto, Pedro. Pianist and composer. Born 12 December 1938, Caibarién. Studied with José M. Montalván, Hilda López, and Enrique Bellver. Coto became known in Havana as the pianist in various dance orchestras, especially the Orquesta del ICRT. He was also an arranger. He received musical guidance from Adolfo Guzmán. He is the author of the *canciones* "Vive y sé feliz" and "Canción para un regreso."

Crespo, América. Soprano. Born 22 October 1922, Aremisa; died 21 May 1995, Miami. Lived in Havana from an early age. Crespo began playing for the program *La Corte Suprema del Arte* on CMQ radio in 1940 and in 1943 joined the RHC Cadena Azul. She has performed on many occasions with Ernesto Lecuona. She developed a repertoire of Cuban and international lyrical songs. Crespo toured and gave concerts all over Latin America. In the United States she performed at Carnegie Hall and at other world-famous venues and on television. She has lived in the United States since the 1960s.

criolla. The term *criolla* is said to derive from the phrase *canción criolla*, or Creole song. This Cuban genre developed in the late nineteenth century and is similar in style to many other forms of the lyrical, romantic vocal repertoire of the period, including the *canción* itself, the *guajira*, and the bolero. *Criollas* are most closely associated with the composer Luis Casas Romero, who is said to have been the first to make them widely popular. He apparently took inspiration from turn-of-the-century *coros de clave* as performed in working-class black neighborhoods and in carnival celebrations. Indeed, there appears to be little to distinguish compositions such as Jorge Ánckermann's "Mares y arenas," a clave, from *criolla* compositions of the same period (Grenet, *Popular Cuban Music*, 27). *Criollas* consist of a brief introduction and two sections generally of sixteen measures (Grenet, *Popular Cuban Music*, xli). Often the two larger sections contrast a minor key in the first part with a major key in the second. *Criollas* are written in a relatively slow tempo in 6/8 time and may have been influenced by Colombian genres such as the *bambuco* (Sánchez de Fuentes, *El folk-lor en la música cubana*, 60) and/or musical forms of Spanish origin in triple meter. The guitar style that accompanied them initially is said to have been influenced by *música campesina*. Many *criollas* were first heard in the *bufos* (comic popular theater). One of the first composers to adopt the *criolla* was Gaspar Villate y Montes (1851–1891). Perhaps the most famous *criolla* composition is "Carmela" (1909) by Casas Romero.

Crucet, Felix. Guitarist and composer. Born 12 January 1822, Spain; died (?). Worked as a lawyer while he was an active musician. In the middle of the nineteenth century, Crucet excelled as a concert guitarist in Paris. He also played the violoncello and wrote pieces for the guitar. He lived in Matanzas.

Cruz, Celia. Singer. Born 21 October 1925, Havana; died 16 July 2003, Fort Lee, New Jersey. Began on Radio García Serra and later on Radio Mil Diez. Cruz produced a program of Afro-Cuban music on Radio Cadena Suaritos. She studied music at the Havana Municipal Conservatory. In 1950 she recorded with La Sonora Matancera and continued to be associated with the group for many years. From 1947 on she appeared in cabaret shows in Havana, such as those at the Sans Souci, the Tropicana, and the Monmartre. She performed on radio, TV, and in theater. She has recorded over one hundred albums and has appeared in several films. In 1960 she moved to the United States, where she has sung with the greatest figures in Latin music. She has toured virtually the entire

world. Cruz is one of the greatest singers to have emerged from Latin America.

Cruz, Felix. Cornet player. Born in the middle of the nineteenth century, Puerto Rico; died (?), Havana. Cruz directed an *orquesta típica* that carried his name from the end of the nineteenth century to the beginning of the twentieth century. From 1888 to 1898 he was at the height of his career as a cornet player and director of his band.

Csonka, Paul. Born 1905, Vienna, Austria; died (?). Although Austrian, Csonka composed all his known works in Cuba; those he wrote in Austria were lost during the war. He is the author of Five religious cantos (1941), for voice, organ, and piano; "Nocturno español" (1939), for clarinet and chamber orchestra; Sonata for soprano and piano (1940), with a poem by Mariano Brull; *Danza de Salomé* (1943), for two clarinets and chamber orchestra; the *Mirándolina* suite (1944); *Suite francesca* (1948), for a quartet of recorders; *Melisandra* (1945), a cantata for five soloists, female choir, and orchestra, based on a poem by Pablo Neruda; *Cantar de los canatares* (1948), for mezzo soprano, mixed choir, and two pianos; Concertino for oboe, bassoon, and orchestra (1951); *Cuarteto de cuerdas* (1944); Variations without a theme (1952), for violoncello and piano; among other works.

cuarteto. Type of musical group with two distinct forms: (1) the *cuarteto de sones*, which developed at the beginning of the twentieth century and usually consists of a guitar, *tres*, *botija*, and claves (the guitarist and claves player sing); and (2) the vocal quartet, which developed around 1950 under the influence of American doo-wop groups and consists of four voices of different pitch, harmonizing in all styles of music.

Cuarteto de La Habana. See Havana Quartet.

Cuba, Sexteto. Band created by the singer Fernando Collazo in Havana, 1930. The other members were Enrique Garcia (lead vocalist and claves), Oscar Pelegrin (*tres*), José Interián (trumpet), Afredo Rivero (double bass), Heredio Loinaz (maracas), and Marino González (*bongó*). In 1933 a piano was introduced into the sextet, played by Armando Valdéz

Torres. The group was famed for the uniform elegance of its stage costumes.

Cuba Musical. Founded by the composer José Marín Varona in Havana at the beginning of the twentieth century, this magazine recorded the key events in the development of Cuban music at the beginning of the Republic. It showed how music struggled to survive in a hostile and frustrating environment, and it also registered the remarkable work being done by Cuban artists, whose talent and dedication contributed to overcoming that environment.

Cuban Choral Society (Orfeon Cuba). Created and conducted by Juan Viccini in Santiago de Cuba. During the 1950s, it played an important role in the promotion and teaching of music in Santiago de Cuba.

Cuban Music Research and Development Center (Centro de Investigación y Desarrollo de la Musica Cubana, CIDMUC). Founded on 18 July 1978, under Decree no. 25 passed by the Council of Ministers, this department is attached to the Ministry of Culture. Its purpose is to promote and encourage the study and development of Cuban music and also to carry out musical research and provide information using scientific methods. It advises the Ministry of Culture on the historical and social aspects of music and it sponsors conferences, seminars, symposiums, and publications on music. The director is the musicologist Olavo Alen.

Cuba Theater. *See* Reina Theater.

cuchara. A peculiar element within Cuban musical folklore. The *cuchara* is the common teaspoon, which, in Cuba, has become a musical instrument in rumba groups. A member of the rumba ensemble takes a *cuchara* in each hand and marks rhythm by tapping the spoons on the wooden body of a drum, a *cajón*, any piece of wooden furniture, or, most commonly, a small wooden board.

Cucho el Pollero. *See* Bombú, Ignacio.

Cuervo, Caridad. Singer. Born 1 April 1946, Havana; died December 1998. In 1952 Cuervo began her career as a singer of *guaracha* and *afro* songs, and continued in presentations at nightclubs and on radio. She recorded albums and toured Mexico, Venezuela, Colombia, Panama, and Ecuador. Her work is characteristic of Afro-Cuban folkloric music.

Mo Fini

Cueto, Rafael. Guitarist and singer. Born 14 March 1900, Santiago de Cuba; died 7 August 1991, Havana. Member of the famous Trío Matamoros. Cueto joined various troubadour groups from Santiago until he formed the Trío Matamoros with Siro Rodríguez and Miguel Matamoros. Before that he had worked at many different jobs. He was a self-taught guitarist. He created the *tumbao*—the rhythmic model that consists of a combination of bass and percussion instruments and that results in the outstanding and quintessential Cuban musical flavor. Cueto's many compositions included "Algo me dejaste," "Pico y pala," and "Los carnavales de Oriente." *See also* tumbao.

Cueva, Julio. Trumpet player, composer, orchestra director. Born 12 April 1897, Trinidad; died 25 December 1975, Havana. Cueva was already playing the cornet with a local children's band by the age of ten and later began to compose *danzones*. In 1916 he became the clarinetist of the Santa Clara Municipal Band. He joined the orchestra of the Arquimedes Pous theater company and toured all of Cuba. In 1923 he founded the Trinidad Municipal Band, which he directed for several years. In 1929 he moved to Havana and played with the Hermanos Palau Orchestra and with Moises Simons and Don Aspiazu. The latter took him to the United States and Europe. After quitting Aspiazu's band, Cueva remained in Europe as a trumpeter and bandleader for ten years. In 1924 he signed a contract with the Paris cabaret La Cueva, which was named after him. The Spanish Civil War found him in Madrid, where he sided with the Republican government and directed the Fourth Division Band on the battlefield. When the Republicans were defeated, Cueva left for France, only to be intercepted and imprisoned in a concentration camp for seventy-eight days. In 1940 he returned to Cuba and founded his own band, which became very popular. His hit songs include "El golpe de bibijagua," "El Marañón," "Rascando rascando," and "Tingo talango."

Cuevas, Ezequiel. Guitarist. Born (?); died (?). Studied music in Havana and was later a student with Domingo Prat in Spain. Upon returning to Cuba Cuevas gave recitals in various venues. He made notable recordings, including "Capricho arabe" by Tarrega and "Malagueña," an Adalusian folk piece.

Cugat, Xavier. Violinist, bandleader, cartoonist. Born 1 January 1900, Gerona, Spain; died 27 October 1990, Barcelona, Spain. Cugat came to Cuba with his family when he was four. He studied violin with professor Joaquin Molina and played with the Havana Symphony Orchestra. In the late 1920s he went to the United States, where he helped introduce tropical music. He starred in many motion pictures as leader of his own orchestra. He directed many renowned American singers, as well as the Cubans Miguelito Valdes and Desi Arnaz. He also worked as a cartoonist for newspapers and magazines.

Cumba, José Dolores. Composer of religious and dance music. Born (?); died (?). Cumba was an outstanding musician in Havana in the nineteenth century. He sang in churches and directed orchestras and bands. He played several musical instruments — in particular, the cornet.

Cumba, Juan. Double bass and ophecleide player. Born (?); died (?). Cumba was a famous nineteenth-century musician who played in orchestras accompanying operas and operettas. In 1881 he had to flee Cuba because of his patriotic activities against the Spanish. For many years he directed the Veracruz Federal Band in Mexico.

Cuní, Miguelito. Singer. Born 8 May 1920, Pinar del Rio; died 3 March 1984, Havana. Began singing with Rolando Luis's Yamile Band in his native town. In 1938 Cuní joined the Ernesto Muñoz Band, and he also sung with Arcaño y Sus Maravillas. In 1940 he joined Arsenio Rodríguez's band and later sang with Benny Moré's Banda Gigante (in 1956), with Bebo Valdes's band (in 1959), and with Felix Chapottin's band during the 1950s and 1960s. Cuní toured Venezuela, Panama, the United States, and Curaçao, made several records, and starred in the motion picture *Nosotros la musica*, as well as many other Cuban films. He wrote "Todos bailan la guajira" and the *son* "Guachinango," as well as the bolero "Las ansias mías." He remains one of Cuba's greatest *son* singers.

Curbelo, José. Pianist and director. Born (?), Havana. Graduated from Havana Municipal Conservatory. At sixteen Curbelo began playing with the Gilberto Valdes band. In 1938 he founded Orquesta Riverside. A year later, he emigrated to New York, where he studied with Hal Overton and also played with Xavier Cugat. In 1941 he formed his own jazz band, which featured renowned musicians such as the Puerto Rican singer Tito Rodríguez and the percussionist Tito Puente. Curbelo switched from performance to management and helped promote tropical music in the United States.

D

D'Aida, Cuarteto. Founded in 1952 by pianist Aida Diestro, this vocal ensemble has performed Cuban music for forty years. Its original members were Elena Burke, Moraima Secada, Omara Portuondo, and Haydée Portuondo. When the original performers turned soloists, they were replaced by new voices, including those of Leonora Rega, Lilita Peñalver, Xiomara Valdés, and Teresa García. The quartet traveled to Mexico, South America, the United States, and many European countries; performed on radio, on television, and in theaters and cabarets; and recorded albums.

Dana, Alice. Soprano. Born 16 September 1903, Havana. On graduating in singing from Tina Farelli and Arturo Bovi's Academy, Dana made her radio debut in 1922. She had an outstanding career in Cuban theater and music halls. She was a soloist in the Havana Choir. After 1935, she concentrated for the most part on teaching singing. In 1938, she sang the vocal part in Beethoven's Ninth Symphony, conducted by Amadeo Roldán and Mario Muñoz, and repeated that performance in 1946, under the conductor Leopold Stokowski.

dance in Cuban music. During the nineteenth century many European dance companies visited Cuba, bringing music and dance from the European repertoires. Pedro Simon notes that the debut of Fanny Elssler, one of the great ballerinas of the nineteenth century, at the Tacón Theater in Havana on 23 January 1841 marked an important event in the history of dance in Cuba, as did the premiere of the ballet Giselle, also performed at the Tacón by the Los Ravel

company on 14 February 1849, eight years after it was first choreographed in France (Simon, "La música cubana en la danza"). Also in the nineteenth century, the emerging Cuban dance music was played in folk and popular music contexts, using choreographies created through a symbiosis of Hispanic and African elements. The danzas of Manuel Saumell and Ignacio Cervantes are examples of such assimilation. Andres Pautret's choreographed performance of La Matancera, with music by the black composer Ulpiano Estrada, at Havana's Principal Theater in 1824 was another milestone in the evolution of a distinctly Cuban style of dance (ibid.).

Significant events during the first half of the twentieth century included a visit to Havana by Anna Pavlova and her company in 1915; the foundation in 1931 of the Ballet School of the Pro-Musical Art Society, where Alberto, Fernando, and Alicia Alonso began their outstanding careers; and the performance of the first Cuban musical piece for ballet, Dioné, composed in 1940 by Eduardo Sánchez de Fuentes, choreographed by Milenoff, and accompanied by the Havana Symphony Orchestra conducted by Gonzalo Roig. The main roles of the ballet were danced by Fernando and Alicia Alonso. It premiered in the Auditorium Theater (later renamed the Amadeo Roldán Theater). Two years later, Joaquín Nin composed the music for Alicia Alonso's first choreographed piece, La Condesita. The year 1943 saw the premiere of Forma, with music by José Ardévol and choreography by Alberto Alonso, based on a text by José Lezama Lima. Alicia and Fernando Alonso, together with Alexandra Denisova, danced the lead roles to music played by the Havana Choir ensemble, conducted by María Muñoz de Quevedo. That same year, Harold Gramatges composed the score to the ballet Icaro by Sergio Lifar, and the following year Gramatges worked on a prelude for El mensaje, choreographed by Alberto Alonso. In 1947 Antes del alba was staged, with music composed by Hilario Gonzalez and choreography by Alberto Alonso. In 1948 Alicia Alonso founded her own company under the name Ballet de Cuba (now the Cuban National Ballet). Two years later, Alberto Alonso created his own dance company, in which he performed different pieces based on Edgardo Martín's Cuatro fugas and Paul Csonka's Fantasia cubana. In 1951 Alicia Alonso presented Fiesta Negra, composed by Amadeo Roldán. This piece was taken by Alicia Alonso and Igor Youskevitch to the

Metropolitan Opera House in New York under the title *Pas de deux tropical*. That same year, Alicia Alonso enjoyed great success when she danced the title role in *Lydia*, composed by Francisco A. Nugué. Other composers of the era also worked for the ballet: Ramiro Guerra choreographed *Habana in 1890* to music by Ernesto Lecuona; the score of *Toque* was written by Argeliers León; and *Songoro cosongo*, a symphonic piece by Felix Guerrero, and *Son para turistas*, by Juan Blanco (both based on poems by Nicolás Guillén), were also performed as ballet. In 1957 *La rebambaramba*, which Amadeo Roldán had composed in 1928, premiered. The libretto was written by Alejo Carpentier and the piece was choreographed by Alberto Alonso, with Sonia Calero dancing the leading role.

With the triumph of the Revolution, the dance movement was strengthened. In 1959 the Ballet de Cuba was reorganized and new companies were created, including the Modern Dance Ensemble and the National Folkloric Ensemble. In 1962 Alicia Alonso, together with Banegas and Parés, performed Carlos Fariñas's *Despertar*, which has a strong political content. Ramiro Guerra choreographed the dances *Mulato* and *El Milagro de Anaquilléto* to music by Amadeo Roldán. The music for the latter is considered an important Cuban composition created specifically for dance. Other composers, including Leo Brouwer, Enrique González Mantici, Olga de Blank, Roberto Valera, Juan Blanco, Carlos Malcolm, Argeliers León, Jorge Berroa, and Sergio Fernández Barroso, have also written music specifically for ballet and modern dance; other pieces, by Cuban composers José White, Amadeo Roldán, Gilberto Valdés, and Gisela Hernández, have been adapted for use with dance. On its tours throughout the world, the National Folkloric Ensemble has performed to Afro-Cuban music from the Yorubas, Congos, Ararás, and Abakuás. The Modern Dance Ensemble, today known as National Dance, regularly includes in its repertoire pieces that are drawn from the African cultural tradition, mixed with Afro-Hispanic-Cuban elements and accompanied by percussive instruments. Many Cuban dance pieces written and performed since the Revolution have received awards at international festivals.

danza. Along with the *contradanza*, the *danza* represents one of the most popular styles of dance repertoire in early and mid-nineteenth century Cuba. It was danced by couples who did not touch but instead faced each other in lines or squares, as was the fashion at the time. The tempo of the pieces was relatively brisk and could either be in triple or duple meter, or might alternate between the two. Traditional *danzas* typically began with a repeated eight-measure introduction called a *paseo*. This appears originally to have been a moment in which couples would rest briefly or walk on or off the floor. The bulk of the composition consisted of two contrasting repeated sections following the introduction, often sixteen measures in length, called the *primera* and *segunda* (Sánchez de Fuentes, El folk-lor en la música cubana, 17–25). *Danzas* remained popular through the 1870s, after which they increasingly lost popularity to the *danzón*. The most well-known *danzas* today are the stylized pieces for piano written by such composers as Ignacio Cervantes and Manuel Saumell that have become a standard part of Cuban classical repertoire.

danzón. A dance genre derived from the Cuban Creole tradition. The name is a derivation of *danza*. The *danzón* is a collective dance organized in couples who dance under arches of flowers. It was particularly popular in the second half of the nineteenth century. The first *danzón*, "Las alturas de Simpson," was written by Miguel Faílde and premiered on 1 January 1879 at the Liceo de Matanzas. It is written in 2/4 time and is slower, has more cadence, and is more varied than the *contradanza* or *danza*. The *danzón* "begins with an introductory eight measures, repeated to make a total of sixteen before the entrance of the clarinet. Although there are no interruptions from one section to the other, and the rhythm is maintained at the same tempo (a slight acceleration toward the end is hardly noticeable), we can say that the first part is faster than the second, since it is written for the agility of the clarinet. When a *charanga* performs a *danzón*, the flute is substituted for the clarinet, which allows for the display of virtuosity in passages written with fast notes, where the flutist can show his or her skill on the traditional five-key, high-pitched wooden instrument. The introduction is then repeated to create a bridge to the entrance of the brass (or violin, in the case of the *charanga* format), which, due to the longer duration of their notes, has a slower pace. It has thirty-two beats, returning to the repeated introduction. The final section is almost always the fastest movement" (Grenet, *Popular Cuban Music*, xxxli).

The origins of the *danzón*, Odilio Urfé explains, came about when José Urfé imposed a new rhythmic element on the *son oriental* with the structure of his famous *danzón*, "El bombín de Barreto" (1910), which established the present format of the Cuban *danzón*. Urfé altered the *danzón's* traditional choreography, allowing more freedom with the introduction of new steps (Urfé, *El danzón*).

danzonete. Song and dance genre, derived from the *danzón* and mixed with the *son*, that also possesses a prominent vocal part. It was created by Aniceto Díaz in 1929, in Matanzas, with the song "Rompiendo la rutina." Odilio Urfé explains that Díaz maintained the introduction and violin part from the *charanga*-style *danzón*, but also added a vocal section culminating in a short coda (Urfé, *El danzón*). The solo singer plays an important role in this genre: he or she is the center of attention. The song's *montuno* almost becomes a *guaracha*.

Davidson, Eduardo. Composer. Born 30 October 1929, Baracoa; died 10 June 1994, New York. His name was originally Claudio Cuza. Davidson moved to Havana during the 1950s and started working as a scriptwriter for radio shows. In 1959 he popularized the rhythmic song "La pachanga," which was an immediate success. He followed it with other pieces in the same style: "Lola Catula," "Agua de mar," and "La niña traviesa." He later wrote "Pancho calma," "Sobando el son," "Sabor de Cuba," "El último bembé," "Al cantío de un gallo," and the boleros "La renuncia," "Novia de año nuevo," and "Yo volveré." He moved to the United States in 1960.

décima. A ten-line poetic form derived from Renaissance Spain that is believed to have first become popular in Cuba during the eighteenth century. Each line of the text typically contains eight syllables and follows a strict rhyme scheme (an *espinela*) in the form A-B-B-A-A-C-C-D-D-C. *Décima* poetry serves as the basis for a great deal of the *música guajira* performed by immigrants from Spain and the Canary Islands. The lyrics can be precomposed or improvised by the singers at the moment of performance. *Música guajira* songs employing *décimas* often use stock melodic phrases common to many other pieces; the primary focus is on the poetry and the skill with which singers are able to invent rhyming couplets and *décimas* based on particular themes.

Delfin, Carmelina. Composer and pianist. Born (?), Havana. From the 1920s Delfin worked with Ernesto Lecuona and traveled abroad with his company. She is the author of lyric-romantic songs such as "Al recordar tu nombre." She gave piano concerts in which she played her own music and that of other Cuban composers. She has lived in New York since the 1940s.

Delfin, Eusebio. Composer, guitarist, baritone singer. Born 1 April 1893, Palmira; died 28 April 1965, Havana. When he was a child, Delfin moved to Cienfuegos, where he studied and graduated as an accountant in the Hermanos Marista school. He studied guitar with Professor Barrios and Vincente Gelabert and sang with Sánchez Torralbas, who was from Valencia, Spain. In 1916 Delfin sang for the first time in public in the Terry Theater in Cienfuegos. Beginning in 1921, he recorded many albums of Cuban songs, solo and with other singers such as Rita Montaner, Esteban Sansirena, and Luisa María Morales. Delfin donated 200,000 pesos (about $8000) from his record sales proceeds to charity in Cienfuegos. According to Gonzalez Rubiera, Delfin was not an outstanding guitarist, but he did come up with the influential notion of changing the style used to accompany boleros. In the 1920s, boleros were usually accompanied by sweeping strings; Delfin, however, changed the accompaniment to a semi-arpeggio style. The new rhythm became extremely popular among the *trova* singers and the public alike. Another characteristic of his style was repeating the rhythm by a time and a half, then leaving in silence the weak part of the second beat. Delfin always used that structure prior to making a change in harmony (Gonzalez Rubiera, "Armonia aplicada a la guitarra"). The music accompanying Delfin's bolero "¿Y tú que has hecho?" illustrates that principle. Delfin also put poetry to music, since he considered that the duty of musicians. He composed "La guinda" from Pedro Mata's poem; "Con las alas rotas," with text by Mariano Albaladejo; and "Migajas de amor" from a poem by Lázaro Galarraga, among others. However, he also wrote his own lyrics, as well as the music, for two exceptional pieces: "¿Y tú qué has hecho?" and "Qué boca la tuya." In 1922 he gave some music concerts in Cuba together with Eduardo Sánchez de Fuentes. In 1924, when Tito Schipa came to Cuba, Delfin accompanied him on the guitar for the songs "Cabecita rubia" and "La guinda."

Delgado, Isaac. Singer. Born 11 September 1962, Havana. Studied at the Amadeo Roldán Conservatory and in the Ignacio Cervantes School of Professional Achievement. Delgado also received classes in vocal technique from Professor Mariana de Gonich. He started his singing career with the group Proyecto, directed by Gonzalo Rubalcaba, later joining Pacho Alonso's orchestra, the Galaxia band, and NG La Banda. In 1991 Delgado founded his own dance band and has recorded eleven CDs. He has performed in theaters, dance halls, and on radio and television all around Cuba; he has also toured Spain, Colombia, Panama, Mexico, Peru, Italy, France, Austria, Holland, Czechoslovakia, Venezuela, Germany, Switzerland, Denmark, Puerto Rico, the Dominican Republic, the United States, and Canada. He is one of the most notable singers of boleros, *son*, *guaracha*, and the new generation of salsa. He has also composed many songs.

Delgado, Manuel. Composer. Born end of the eighteenth century in Santiago de Cuba; died 1852. Was called "Maestro Delgado." By the year 1847 he was at the peak of his fame among dancers, mainly due to his pieces "El palete," "La estrujadora," and "La sopimpa." He continued to write music at an advanced age.

Delgado, Manuel. Guitarist and composer. Born 1876, Santiago de Cuba; died 7 November 1925.

Studied music briefly but could not finish his training for economic reasons, and so went to work as a cigar roller. Delgado was known by the nickname Manuelico. He lived for some years in Bayamo and in El Cristo, but it was mainly in Santiago de Cuba that he became involved with the troubadour (*trova*) movement. He became a well-known guitar accompanist and wrote *canciones* including "La gacela," "Aquel beso robado," "Aida," "La música expresada," "La morita," "Artista enamorado," and "Adorada," as well as *sones* and *guarachas*.

Delgado, Pepé. Composer and pianist. Born 17 May 1920, Las Tunas; died 18 December 1990, Miami. When he was eighteen years old, Delgado moved to Havana and became the pianist for the Niagara band. Later, he joined Los Jóvenes del Cayo, and the Orquestas Casino and Colonial. He is remembered for his popular boleros "Dueña de mi corazón," "Quédate conmigo," "Cosas del alma," "Díme la verdad," "Cuando tú me quieras," "Tus ojos," "No pienses así," and "Culpable." He also wrote the *cha-cha-chá* "Me voy a la luna." Delgado was also an eminent arranger. At the beginning of the 1960s he moved to Mexico City, then to Puerto Rico, and then to the United States.

dengue. Cuban musical genre created by Dámaso Pérez Prado at the beginning of the 1960s. It follows the mambo style, with roots in the *guaracha-son* and elements of the conga. The characteristic rhythm is provided by a piece of iron beaten with a pair of drum sticks, the same note repeated throughout the song.

Desvernine, Pablo. Pianist. Born 31 July 1823, Havana; died 1910. Took his first piano lessons from Maestro Juan Federico Edelmann and went to Paris to continue his studies under the guidance of Kalkbrenner and Thalberg. Desvernine also studied the harp and the violin. He gave concerts in several European and American cities. He worked as a piano teacher in New York, where his disciples included Howard MacDowell. In 1856, back in Havana, he founded the magazine *Revista Musical, Artística y Literaria*. He is the author of many pieces for the piano. In 1869 he settled in Cuba and dedicated himself to teaching music. His compositions include *Serenata*, with lyrics by Mendive.

Diago, Virgilio. Violinist. Born 1897, Tampa; died 1948, Mexico City. Started studying violin at fifteen with Juan Torroella at the National Conservatory, where he finished his training. Diago was awarded First Prize in Violin when he graduated in 1919. Following the founding of the Havana Symphony Orchestra, he played first violin. He also played the viola in dance bands and is considered to be one of Cuba's most outstanding violinists.

Díaz, Angel. Singer, guitarist, composer. Born 23 December 1921, Havana. Son of the *trova* singer Tirso Díaz. Angel Díaz studied legal management and diplomatic law at the University of Havana and music at the Popular Music Seminary under the guidance of Vicente González Rubiera ("Guyún"). He was a member of the *filin* movement since its inception, when the founding members of the group met at his house. His compositions include "Rosa Mustia."

Díaz, Aniceto. Composer. Born 17 April 1887, Matanzas; died 10 July 1964. Creator of the Cuban *danzonete*, which involved the use of elements from the *son* style. Díaz played the flute, piano, and ophicleide. He was a member of Miguel Faílde's orchestra, the Orquesta Faílde, at the end of the nineteenth century and, years later, led his own orchestra. In 1929 he premiered his first *danzonete* ("Rompiendo la rutina") at the Matanzas Casino Español. At the time, he played flute. He also composed *danzones*, such as "El trigémino," "El cocodrilo," "Zona franca," "Dulce imagen," and "Engreída." In 1944 he moved to Havana, where he ran his orchestra for another four years.

Díaz, Carlos. Singer. Born (?), Havana. Carlos Díaz was the soloist in the Hermanos Castro orchestra during the 1950s, recording unforgettable boleros. Later, he performed with the Orquesta Casino de la Playa, then began a solo career. He moved to Miami in the 1960s.

Díaz, Carlos Manuel ("Caíto"). Singer and maracas player. Born 8 November 1905, Matanzas; died 28 September 1990, New York. In 1924 Caíto was a founding member of La Sonora Matancera, with whom he sang lead vocals and played maracas. He made solo recordings and composed the songs "No te boté," "Hoy sé que vuelves," "Merengue arrimao," and "Así es Borinquen." His famous falsetto voice established a chorus style for Spanish Caribbean music.

Díaz, Miguel Angá. Percussionist. Born 15 June 1961, San Juan y Martínez. Began his studies at the Provincial School of Art in Pinar del Rio; then studied in Havana in the School for Art Instructors. Díaz was a percussionist in the Afro-Cuban Jazz ensembles Opus 13 and Irakere and has been a guest in other groups in Cuba and abroad. He has played congas in Latin jazz concerts with Chick Corea, Billy Cobham, Michel Camilo, Nana Vasconcelos, and Arturo Sandoval.

Díaz, Raúl. Conga player. Born 1915, Havana. Raul Díaz was a connoisseur of the Congo and of Abakuá folklore. He was a consultant to the musicologist Fernando Ortiz. He was initiated into the secrets of the sacred drum and its language by Pablo Roche. His father participated actively in the War of Independence against the Spanish crown.

Díaz, Ricardo. Composer. Born 9 June 1926, Havana. Studied at the Havana Municipal Conservatory and was percussionist in many bands. Ricardo Díaz is the author of the boleros "Cuando comienza el amor," "Díme en qué momento," "Pocas veces se dice la verdad," and "Muchas veces"; as well as of the bolero-mambo "En el juego del amor"; the rhythmic bolero "Tú no sabes de amor"; the *guarachas* "Domitila," "A bailar pachanga," "Malembe," and "Quítate el chaquetón"; and the rumbas "Fiesta brava," "A la pelota con Carlota," and "Ese atrevimiento," in addition to many other popular songs.

Díaz, Tirso. Composer and guitarist. Born 24 September 1895, Güira de Melena; died 16 July 1967, Havana. One of the founders of the Nano Quartet (1912), in which he played the guitar for some years. For decades, Tirso Díaz accompanied different singers and composed songs, including "Ana," "Eloisa," "Como la vida," "Solo oigo al corazón," and "Entre las palmeras."

Díaz, Trío Servando. Founded in 1937 in Havana by the singer and guitarist Servando Díaz, with Otilio Portal and Octavio Mendoza. The trio performed on radio and television and at theaters. They were known as "the smiling troubadors" and made many records of boleros and *guarachas*. They also toured throughout the Americas. Years later, Mario Recio, José A. Pinares, and Angel Alday entered the trio, in turn. In 1960 Servando settled in Puerto Rico and continued performing there. He died there on 2 April 1985.

Díaz, Ulpiano. Percussionist. Born 1920, Pinar del Río; died 1990, Havana. Ulpiano Díaz started playing music as a child. He was a timbales player in many *charanga* orchestras in Havana, including the orchestras of Félix González and Tata Alfonso and in Arcaño y Sus Maravillas, Fajardo y Sus Estrellas, and Estrellas Cubanas. He is considered an innovator in Cuban percussion. He traveled widely abroad.

Díaz Albertini, Rafael. Violinist. Born 13 August 1857, Havana; died 11 November 1928, Marseilles. Started studying violin with José Vandertguch and Anselmo López. In 1870 Diaz Albertini went to Paris to work for Alard. In 1875 he was awarded First Prize in Violin at the Paris Conservatory. He gave concerts all around the world and toured Europe with Wolf and Camille Saint-Saëns. In 1894 he visited the main Cuban cities with Ignacio Cervantes. The following year he returned to France, where he served as a member of the jury at the Paris Conservatory.

Díaz Ayala, Cristóbal. Historian and musicologist. Born 20 June 1930, Havana. Doctor in Law and Social Sciences and Doctor in Public Law at the University of Havana. In 1960 Díaz Ayala moved to Puerto Rico. From 1979 to 1995 he produced and hosted the radio show *Cubanacán*, which featured Cuban music. In 1981 he published *Del Areito a la nueva trova: Historia de la música cubana*, and in 1988, *Si te quieres por el pico divertir: Historia del pregón latinoamericano*. The first volume of his *Discografía de la música cubana (1898–1925)* was published in 1994. He has written articles about Cuban music in publications all over the world and has lectured at many institutions. His collection of Cuban music, which he donated to Florida International University, is among the most extensive in the world.

Díaz Calvet, Rey. Composer and instrumentalist. Born 16 November 1919, Havana. Also a conductor.

As a pianist, Díaz Calvet has played in many popular dance music bands. He is the author of "Me gustas" and other *canciones*.

Díaz Cartaya, Agustín. Composer. Born 25 September 1933, Marianao. One of the attackers of the Moncada Garrison in Santiago de Cuba in 1953. Díaz Cartaya is the author of "Himno del 26 de julio," "Marcha de América Latina," and other pieces that draw on folk songs.

Díaz Comas, Vicente. Composer. Born (?), Spain. Settled in Havana in the mid–nineteenth century; also a Doctor in Civil Law. Díaz Comas is the author of the *contradanzas* "La tropical," "Ajiaquito con casabe," "La azucena," "La siempreviva," "El secreto," "Almibar puro," "La pin-pin," "La cariñosa," "Dolores dame café," and "Los ojos de Filita." He has also composed marches, anthems, polkas, waltzes, and *zapateos*, as well as the opera *La esmeralda*. He died in a shipwreck on the way to Spain; he had been traveling to give Queen Isabel II a "royal album" containing a collection of his musical pieces dedicated to her.

Díaz de Herrera, Chalía. Soprano. Born 17 November 1863, Havana; died 16 November 1948. Studied singing with Angelo Massanet in Havana, and with Emilio Agramonte in New York. Díaz de Herrera started her professional career in 1894 in the United States. In 1895 she debuted at La Scala in Milan. She participated in concerts to raise funds for the Cuban War of Independence. She performed opera seasons in Cuba, Mexico, Venezuela, Spain, Italy, and the United States. She settled in Cuba in 1946.

(Las) Diego. Composing and singing duet formed by the sisters María Luisa and Teresa Diego. From a young age they played on the radio and television in Havana. In 1980 they moved to the United States, where they have continued playing in nightclubs, theaters, and on radio and television. They have recorded many LPs and are the authors of the songs "La loca," "Fuego," "Yo sin él," and "Perdóname." They have toured throughout Latin America.

Diestro, Aida. Pianist, arranger, director of the Cuarteto D'Aida. Born 1928, Havana; died 28 October 1973. From early childhood, Diestro revealed a gift for music. She played the piano and was dedicated to popular music. In 1952 she formed an eponymous vocal quartet, which performed the best Cuban music and traveled around the world. She was a founder-member of the *filin* movement.

Diez, Barbarito. Singer. Born 4 December 1909, Bolondrón; died 6 May 1995, Havana. When he was four, Diez moved to the town of Manatí, the location of a sugar factory, in the province of Oriente. There, he began his artistic career as a music enthusiast. In 1930 he moved to Havana, and the following year joined a trio formed by Graciano Gómez and Isaac Oviedo. In 1935 he started singing with Antonio Maria Romeu's dance band, which later became the Barbarito Diez Orchestra. He performed in Puerto Rico, the Dominican Republic, and the United States. Diez recorded eleven LPs of his extensive repertoire of Cuban *danzones*.

Diez, Humberto. Baritone. Born 1930, La Maya, Oriente. Took singing lessons at the Hubert de Blanck Conservatory, Havana. Diez has performed leading roles in operas staged in Cuba, was a soloist at the Lyric Theater, and performed in concerts all around Cuba. He currently lives outside Cuba.

Diez Nieto, Alfredo. Director, professor, composer. Born 25 October 1918, Havana. Studied with Jaime Prats, Pedro Sanjuán, and Amadeo Roldán. Diez Nieto later went to New York, where he completed his training with Steuermann, Wagner, and Mahler. He has taught in several Cuban schools. In 1965 he organized and conducted the Popular Symphony Concert Orchestra, formed by musicians from dance companies. He has composed symphonic music (including *Primera sinfonía*), chamber music, a wind quintet, and vocal music. He is a professor of harmony at the Higher Institute of Art.

Diorama Theater. This building, used by the famous French painter Juan Francisco Vernay as a diorama — a scenic representation in which a translucent painting is seen from a distance through an opening — was turned into a theater and opened in 1829. It was mainly used for staging drama, but some opera and ballet were also presented. It was located at the junction of Indústria and San José Streets, where the Campoamor Theater is currently located. The theater was demolished in 1846.

Dobal, Cristobal. Double bass player and composer. Born (?), Havana; died 1992, Miami. Dobal played in different bands, but is particularly remembered for his work with the Conjunto Casino. He wrote some very successful boleros, including "Inteligentemente" and "Comprensión." At the time of his death, he lived in the United States.

Domínguez, Frank. Composer and pianist. Born 9 October 1927, Matanzas. Began writing songs in the 1950s while still a university student. His first presentation was on a television show for amateur artists. Domínguez is the author of such well-known songs as "Refúgiate en mi," "Tú me acostumbraste," "Pedacito de cielo," "Luna sobre Matanzas," "Me recordarás," "Mi corazón lloró," "Cómo te atreves," "Si tu quisieras," "Imágenes," "El hombre que me gusta a mí," and "La dulce razón." He has been the piano accompanist for several Havana nightclubs and has directed a combo. He lives in Mexico.

Dominicis, Francisco (Fernández). Tenor. Born 28 November 1883, Havana; died 3 February 1968. Disciple of Pablo Meroles and Weremunda de Vieta.

After starting his career in Cuba, Dominicis moved to Italy to broaden his knowledge and polish his technique. He sang at La Scala in Milan. He subsequently performed in many European cities before returning to Cuba, where he gave singing lessons until his death.

Dreke, Mario ("Chavalonga"). Author, singer, dancer, musician. Born 25 April 1925, Havana. Since the 1940s Chavalonga has been considered one of the most outstanding performers of African rhythms and rumba. Among his most popular *guaguancós* are "Palo quimbombó," "Los barrios unidos," "Muñequita," and "Oye lo que te voy a decir." He was a founder of the National Folkloric Ensemble and is currently the director of a company carrying his name.

Duarte, Ernesto. Pianist, composer, arranger, director. Born 7 November 1922, Jovellanos; died 1988, Madrid. After working with other bands, Duarte created his own dance orchestra, which was considered to be one of the most important bands in 1950s Cuba. He played jazz, accompanying many well-known singers, and his arrangements set a landmark in popular music. He is author of the boleros "Anda dilo ya," "Codicia," "Cómo fue," "Ven aquí a la realidad," and "No digas." His most famous *danzón* was "Cicuta tibia." Among his *sones* are "Miguel," "Nicolasa," "Dónde estabas tú," and "El baile del pingüino." He is also the author of the *cha-cha-chá*, "No te vuelvas loco."

Duchesne Cuzán, Manuel. Orchestra conductor. Born 10 November 1932, Havana. Completed his higher education at the Havana Municipal Conservatory. His professors there were Harold Gramatges, José Ardévol, and Edgardo Martín. Duchesne Cuzán began studying conducting with Enrique González Mántici and finished his training with Igor Markevich. He has conducted orchestras in Chile, Argentina, Venezuela, the Soviet Union, Peru, Brazil, Mexico, Ecuador, Poland, Czechoslovakia, Hungary, China, Korea, Romania, Germany, and Bulgaria. In Cuba, he has led many orchestras, including the orchestra of the National Lyric Theater. He was the head of the music department at the Cuban Institute for Movie-Making, Art, and Industry and a professor at the Alejandro García Caturla Conservatory. He is general director of the National Symphony Orchestra and head of the symphonic music division at the Ministry of Culture. He is also head of conducting at the Higher Institute of Art. His career has been characterized by the wide range of music he has conducted with different orchestras. He has introduced modern pieces from abroad into the Cuban repertoire and has contributed to the promotion of new Cuban music outside of Cuba.

Duchesne Morillas, Manuel. Flutist, orchestra conductor, bandleader. Born 14 June 1902; died 25 October 1990. In 1939 Duchesne Morillas began playing the flute in the Havana Municipal Band and later became its deputy director. In 1970, after Gilberto Roig's death, he was appointed director of the National Concert Band.

Dulzaides, Felipe. Pianist. Born 1917, Havana; died 23 January 1991. Dulzaides was co-founder of the Cuarteto Llópiz-Dulzaides. In the 1960s he created his own band. His songs were strongly influenced by American music. His most famous song was "Es muy fácil." Dulzaides made several recordings with his own group and with several outstanding female Cuban singers.

Dupuy, Berta. Singer. Born (?), Guantánamo. Started singing on a radio program for children in her hometown and later became a member of the Choral Institute in Guantánamo. Dupuy took singing lessons with the professor Clara Creagh. In Havana, she became successful through José Antonio Alonso's show on CMQ television. She was also taught by Isolina Carrillo. In 1958 the members of the ACRI (Association of Cuban Critics) chose her as Cuba's best singer. She performed at the many cabarets in Havana until settling in the United States.

E

Echaniz, José. Professor and pianist. Born 1860, Azcoitía, Guipuzcoa, Spain; died 5 December 1926, Guanabacoa. Echaniz came to Cuba in 1877 and settled in Guanabacoa. He is the father of the well-known pianist of the same name. He was an organist and professor at the Escuelas Pías, the director of the department of recitation at the Guanabacoa Lyceum, a professor at the National Conservatory, and director of the Orfeón Vazco in Havana. In 1916 he founded the Arizti Academy in Guanabacoa. On many occasions, he has played piano duets with Ignacio Cervantes.

Echaniz, José, Jr. Pianist. Born 4 June 1905, Guanabacoa; died 1973, New York. When he was seven, Echaniz studied music with his father, then continued his training with the Spanish teacher Ignacio Tellería. He improved his mastery of the piano at the Falcón Conservatory, and at age fourteen gave a series of concerts around the island. In 1920 he traveled to perform in New York and then toured various American cities. He subsequently traveled to many countries, sometimes returning to Cuba, but mostly working from the United States. He appeared on the same program with Lucrecia Bori and Tito Schipa. He was director of the Milliken Conservatory of Music in Decatur, Illinois.

Edelmann, Juan Federico. Pianist, professor, editor. Born 17 February 1795, Strasbourg, France; died 20 December 1848, Havana. Son of the Alsatian musician with the same name. Juan Federico Edelmann studied at the Paris Conservatory and in 1832 settled in Havana and dedicated himself to teaching. Among his disciples were Manuel Saumell, Desverine, Fernando Arizti, and Arizti's children Eugenia, Ernesto, Federico, and Carlos. He was director of the Santa Cecilia Philharmonic Society. In 1836, he founded his own publishing house, where he printed and promoted the works of Cuban musicians.

Egües, Rembert. Composer and vibraphonist. Born 4 February 1949, Havana. Son of the flutist Richard

Egües. Rembert Egües studied at the Amadeo Roldán Conservatory. He was a member of the staff band of the Revolutionary Armed Forces. He played in Felipe Dulzaides's band. He is the author of the *sones* "En gris," "Como cada mañana," "Amar, vivir," and of the symphonic pieces *Recuentos* and *Ser joven*. In 1976 he received an award in a contest organized by the Cuban army. He was vice-president of the music section of the Writers and Artists Union of Cuba. He lives in Paris.

Egües, Richard. Flutist, composer, arranger. Born 26 January 1926, Cruces. His original family name was Eduardo. Egües studied with his father and belonged to the Santa Clara Municipal Band. Later, he moved from one dance band to another, until in 1953 he joined the Orquesta Aragón. His distinctive flute style has contributed to the unique sound that characterizes this orchestra. He is a multi-instrumentalist and author of the popular songs "El bodeguero," "El cuini," "Sabrosona," "Bombón cha," "Cero penas," "El trago," "El cerquillo," and others. He has also played in classical music concerts.

Tomás Casademunt

ekón. A percussion instrument made of iron, similar to a clapperless cowbell, with a handle about 10 or 15 centimeters long. The body of the bell is concave, bell-shaped or nearly conical, generally made up of two small, roughly triangular plates about 30 centimeters long, that meet in an arch at their center, are welded or riveted on their two longer sides, and are open at the ends. It is held by the handle and beaten with a wooden stick, and it produces a metallic sound somewhat less sonorous than that of a small bell (Ortiz, *Los instrumentos de la música afrocubana*, 1:239). The *ekón* originated with Abakuá music, although it is now also used in popular music, mainly by conga groups. There is also a double-*ekón*, called *jimagua* (twin).

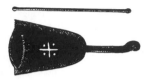

ekué. A friction drum used in the secret ceremonies of the Abakuá society, considered to represent the voice of the divine through its powerful evocation of a leopard's roar. It is played only by a small number of qualified musicians within the Ñáñigo groups. The sound is produced by the friction created when the hand rubs a rod which is held against the drumhead; the drum acts as a sounding-board and produces a harsh sound (León, *Música folklórica cubana*, in Ortiz, *Los instrumentos de la música afrocubana*, 5:205).

Eli, Victoria. Musicologist. Born 25 June 1945, Havana. Studied at the International Conservatory in former East Germany, at the Alejandro García Caturla Conservatory, and at the Higher Institute of Art, where she majored in musicology. Eli is a researcher at the Cuban Music Research and Development Center and teaches at the Higher Institute of Art. She has a Ph.D. in Musicology from Humboldt University in Berlin, Germany. She has written several papers on Cuban music and has participated in national and international conferences on the subject.

Embale, Carlos. Son and *guaguancó* singer. Born 3 August 1923, Havana; died 12 March 1998. Embale's career started at the Corte Suprema del Arte show at the end of the 1930s, when he sang in the Septeto Boloña and the Septeto Bolero, and with Neno

González's dance band, Fantasía. From 1946 to 1954 he sang with the Conjunto Matamoros. In 1976 he joined Ignacio Piñeiro's Septeto Nacional. He recorded many *sones* and an LP of *guaguancós* with Muñequitos de Matanzas and the Coro Folklórico. He was director of the *guaguancó* band carrying his name.

enkómo. Trio of Abakuá drums that includes the *opiapá* (the largest lead drum that produces the deepest tone), the *kuchí-yeremá* (the medium-sized drum that produces a middle tone), and the *binkomé* (the smallest drum that produces a sharp tone) (Ortiz, *Los instrumentos de la música afrocubana*, 4:24–25).

Enrizo, Rafael ("Nené"). Guitarist. Born 24 October 1897, Havana. Enrizo played popular music, mainly *trova* songs. By the age of eight, he was already playing with his brother and sister Enrique and Candita. He eventually began formally studying music with Antonio Rodríguez. At fifteen, he gave concerts with the *trova* singers in Havana, where he worked as a barber. For many years, he played in a duet with his brother and composed songs.

Ensueño, Orquesta. Jazzband formed in Havana under Guillermina Foyo, and with García Cano and the Pérez Alderete sisters. Afterwards, other musicians joined. For many years, the lead vocalist was Carmen Calza. The group's repertoire included Cuban, Latin American, and American songs, as well as waltzes, and it toured Mexico, Panama, Venezuela, Colombia, and the United States, and disbanded in the 1950s. Orquesta Ensueño is acknowledged as the first all-women jazzband in the history of Cuban music.

erikundí. One of the percussive instruments in the Abakuá musical ensemble. More generally known as a maraca, the instrument is typically played in sets of two. Erikundí are made from gourds, tin, or wicker. Those made from wicker are used for ritual purposes in Abakuá ceremonies. The receptacle for each maraca is cylindrical, tapering to a conical shape at the end, where a rope or wicker handle is attached. The sound of the erikundí is produced when the player shakes one of the two maracas, causing the small seeds or pellets inside the sealed resonating cavity to collide with one another. The two erikundí produce different sounds—one low and rumbling, the other high and sharp. (Ortiz, Los instrumentos de la música afrocubana, 2:103–111.) See also chachá.

Escalante, Karelia. Pianist. Born 12 April 1939, Havana. Studied at the Amadeo Roldán Conservatory and later in Paris and Moscow. Escalante has given many concerts with the National Symphony Orchestra. At present, she is a professor at the National School of Art and at the Higher Institute of Art.

Escalante, Luis. Trumpeter. Born 25 August 1915, Guantánamo; died 7 May 1970, Havana. Played in different jazz bands and in the Orquesta Cubana de Música Moderna. Escalante was a soloist with the National Symphony Orchestra. He made several recordings of solo trumpet and is considered to be one of the most outstanding trumpet players in Cuba.

Escalona, Miguel. Composer and instrumentalist. Born 26 October 1949, Camagüey. Started his career in 1968 as part of the nueva trova movement. Escalona plays accordion and guitar. The lyrics of his songs are, for the most part, poems written by Cubans, though some he has picked up from abroad. Escalona is an actor in the Guiñol Theater in Camagüey and has also written music for children. He is the author of "Esa mujer," "La casa y la sorpresa" (text by the Cuban poet Pablo Milanes), "Eclipse de amor," "Pablo," "Yo tengo un amigo muerto" (text by José Martí), and "Canción a Ignacio Agramonte," among others. At present he is studying at the School of Musical Achievement in Camagüey.

Escarpenter, Sara. Soprano. Born (?), Havana. In the 1950s, Escarpenter began singing the Cuban lyrical repertoire, performing zarzuelas (operettas) and operas. She has performed on radio and television and in the theater. In the 1960s she settled in the United States, where she teaches singing.

Escorcia, Franciso. Composer. Born 4 December 1917, Havana. Played in different Cuban trios. In 1943 Escorcia's song "Quedará el recuerdo," performed by Salvador García Gallardo, won the Kolynos Contesta at Radio CMQ. Later, he composed the boleros "Rezo en la noche," "Cómo puedes pensar," "Vestido nuevo," "Doce veces," "El caso mío," "Será mi última carta," and "En culaquier momento."

Escudero, Daniel. Tenor. Born 30 December 1929, Havana. Studied singing at the Levy and Hubert de Blanck conservatories, and in other institutions in Russia and Bulgaria. Escudero was a tenor in the staff band of the army. He also sang on the radio, television, and in theaters. He performed in opera seasons at the Auditorium theater. In 1964 he joined the Cuban National Opera as a solo tenor and sang in Don Pasquale, Rigoletto, La Traviata, Madame Butterfly, The Barber of Seville, The Merry Widow, and The Marriage of Fígaro. He has played an active role in the promotion and organization of musical events.

Escuela Nacional de Música. See National School of Music.

Escuela de Superación Profesional. See School of Professional Achievement.

Espí, Roberto. Singer. Born 26 May 1913, Cienfuegos; died 14 May 1999, Havana. After performing with many dance orchestras, Espí joined the Conjunto Casino in 1941 and sang with the group for many years. His repertoire comprises boleros and canciones, and he made several recordings. Espí was a member of the famous Conjunto Casino's trilogy of singers, along with Roberto Faz, Agustín Ribot, and later Orlando Vallejo.

Espinosa, Juan. Pianist. Born 5 October 1939, Guanajay. Studied music in his hometown and later entered the International Conservatory in Havana, under the direction of María Jones de Castro. Espinosa also worked with Jorge Bolet and Lawrence

Davis. In the 1950s, he started as a piano accompanist to well-known Cuban and visiting singers. Since 1964 he has been the repertory pianist of the National Lyric Theater. He has accompanied many Cuban singers on tours and festivals and has recorded two LPs with the outstanding baritone Ramón Calzadilla. He was awarded the Friendship Medal of the Republic of Vietnam. Recently, he received an award in a contest held in Tokyo, Japan.

Esteban Theater. *See* Sauto Theater.

Estefan, Gloria. Singer. Born 1 September 1957, Marianao. Her maiden name is Fajardo. When she was eighteen, Gloria began singing with the Miami Latin Boys, whose director and percussionist was her future husband Emilio Estefan. In 1976 the band changed its name to the Miami Sound Machine. Its players were Emilio Estefan (accordion), Marcos Avila (bass), Enrique (Kike) García (drums), and Gloria (vocals). Beginning in 1984, the group became very successful, with a string of hits that included "Dr. Beat" and "Conga." It subsequently became one of the most famous international pop bands, playing the mixture of Cuban rhythms (conga, rumba) and rock known as "the Miami sound." Later, Raul Padilla (bass) and Joe Galdo (keyboards) joined the band, together with other instrumentalists, and Emilio moved over to play Cuban percussion. Gloria Estefan turned solo, backed by the Miami Sound Machine, in the late 1980s. She is considered one of the most important pop singers worldwide and has recorded many successful, award-winning albums and CDs, including the Cuban-music-influenced *Mi tierra*.

Estivil, Osvaldo. Pianist and conductor. Born (?), Havana; died 3 May 1992, Miami. In the 1940s, Estivil started his career as a piano accompanist, arranger, and conductor. Cosmopolita was one of the many bands he played with. He lived for many years in the United States.

Estrada, Ulpiano. Conductor, violinist, composer. Born 1777, Havana; died 1847. Estrada was a teacher of violin. He directed the orchestra at the Principal Theater from 1817 to 1820 and was head of the Extramuros Theater orchestra as well. In addition, he was director of a famous band that played at the dances frequented by the urban aristocracy of his day. He composed classical *contradanzas* and more elaborate musical pieces. He was the musical director of many operas that were staged in Havana in the first half of the nineteenth century. According to Alejo Carpentier, Estrada was so fond of the minuet de corte that he kept on playing it, after it had fallen out of fashion (Carpentier, *La música en Cuba*). In 1824 his *La matancera* (waltz), with choreography by Andrés Pautret, was premiered at Havana's Principal Theater.

Estrada, Yeyo. Singer. Born (?), Havana. Estrada was born in the Jesus María neighborhood of Havana and sang with different bands in the city until 1945, when he moved to Mexico City. There, he sang boleros, *guarachas*, *sones*, and *mambo* with many orchestras, including that of Pérez Prado. He subsequently formed the Yeyo and Cané Orchestra, with Roberto Cané, and together they made several recordings. Recently, he has been working as a music editor and promoter in Mexico.

Estrellas Cubanas, Orquesta. Created by Félix Reina (violinist and bandleader) in Havana, 1959. Some members came from the José Fajardo Orchestra. The founding members were Julián Guerrero (flute); Dámaso Morales (double bass); Raul Valdéz (piano); Ulpiano Díaz (timbales); Filiberto Peña (conga); Gustavo Tamayo (*güiro*); Sergio Calzado, Luis Calzado, and Ruddy Calzado (vocalists); and Elio Valdéz, José Ferrer, and Félix Reina (violins). Later, new musicians joined the band, including Armando Hechevaría (flute), and José Vargas, Berto González, and José A. Moya (violins).

Estrems, Fernando. Professor. Born 17 December 1872, Valencia, Spain; died 1940, Santa Clara. Started studying music in Valencia and continued his training at the Madrid Conservatory, where he graduated in piano, harmony, and theory. After a short stay in Puerto Rico and Cuba, Estrems returned to Valencia, but in 1903 he settled in Cuba, where he opened music academies in Puerto Padre, Manzanillo, Remedios, Caibarién, and Santa Clara. His schools have a very high standard of training for instrumentalists.

Estudiantina Oriental. Also referred to as the Estudiantina Invasora. Formed in Santiago de Cuba toward the end of the nineteenth century, the ensemble played various rhythms, including bolero, *son*, and *guaracha*. The lineup consisted of *tres*, xylophone, timbales, maracas, claves, and guitars, with two vocalists. In several cities, groups of youths, almost always white, created similar bands but with different instruments. Today, the Estudiantina Oriental is conducted by trumpeter Inaudis Paisán.

Exaudi, Coro. Choral ensemble founded in Havana in 1987 and directed by María Felicia Pérez. Its first concert was in March 1988 at the National Museum. It has been widely acclaimed both in Cuba and abroad.

Experimentación Sonora del ICAIC, Grupo de. Founded in 1970 and sponsored by the Cuban Institute for Movie-Making, Art, and Industry (ICAIC), with Leo Brouwer as the bandleader. The group developed an experimental trend within Cuban and Latin American music, creatively transforming the basic influence of folklore. Its members were Sara González (vocals); Pablo Milanés, Noel Nicola, and Silvio Rodríguez (vocals and guitar); Leonardo Acosta (saxophone); Eduardo Ramos (bass); Emiliano Salvador (piano); and Sergio Vitier and Pablo Menéndez (guitar).

F

Fabré, Antonio. Composer, flutist, pianist, teacher. Born 8 November 1875, Sagua la Grande; died 23 January 1953. Made a significant contribution to the development of music in his hometown. Fabré trained a large number of pupils who would eventually be acclaimed both in Cuba and overseas. He wrote "Barceuse," "Dora," "Patria," and other pieces for piano, orchestra, and band. He also wrote *zarzuelas*.

Fabré, Cándido. Singer and songwriter. Born 20 September 1957, San Luis, Oriente. Sang with the Hermanos Salazar group and the Samurai combo. Fabré joined the Original de Manzanillo band in 1983 and sang with them for ten years, recording seven LPs. An intuitive, spontaneous musician, he has sung *guarachas*, boleros, and, mostly, *son* pieces. He has toured Mexico, Colombia, Venezuela, Nicaragua, Guadeloupe, Canada, Belgium, England, Germany, France, and Spain. Fabré formed his own band in 1993, with whom he has recorded three CDs. He is the writer of the *son* pieces "Coge el camarón," "Acabo de llegar," "La guagua," "Soy cubano, soy de Oriente," "¿Quién ha visto por ahí mi sombrero de yarey?," "Guayabita del Pinar," "A la hora que me llamen voy," and "El cinturón del taxi," among others.

Mo Fini

Faílde, Miguel. Composer, cornetist, conductor. Born 23 December 1852, Caobas, Municipality of Guacamaro, Matanzas; died 26 December 1921. Creator of the *danzón*. Faílde was a member of a family of musicians. As a child, he moved with his family to the city of Matanzas, where he lived thereafter. His father, the trombonist Cándido Faílde, initiated him into the study of music. At age twelve, he played the cornet with the firemen's band of Matanzas. He later took harmony and composition lessons with the French professor Federico Pecher, and later still, he took up viola and double bass, performing in classical music concerts. He subsequently taught music. Faílde participated in underground conspiratorial activities against Spanish colonial rule. In 1871 he formed his own *orquesta típica*, the Orquesta Faílde, which became well known both in Matanzas and throughout the country. In 1879 he performed his composition "Las alturas de Simpson," the first *danzón*, which he later followed with "Antón Pirulero," "Los tirabuzones," "La malagueña," "A La Habana me voy," "El mondonguito," "El Malakoff," "Cuba libre," "Yaka-hula," "El amolador," "Los chinos," and "La diosa japonesa." Faílde also wrote dances, waltzes, *pasodobles*, and marches. In 1920 he performed for the last time at the head of his band, in Palos.

Faílde, Orquesta. Founded in Matanzas in 1871 by Miguel Faílde (cornet), creator of the Cuban *danzón*, along with Pascual Carrera (ophiclenic), Pancho Morales (first violin), Juan Canteros (second violin), Anselmo Casalin (first clarinet), Eduardo Faílde (second clarinet), Cándido Faílde (trombone), Eulogio Garrido (double bass), Andrés Segovia (timbales), and Isidro Acosta (*güiro*). The instrumentation subsequently changed with the incorporation of new members into the ensemble: Julián Jiménez (trombone), Aniceto Diaz (ophiclenic), Eduardo Betancourt (violin), and Benito Oliva (timbales). In 1903 the Orquesta Faílde made its first and only trip to Havana where it was successfully received at the carnival. It collapsed in 1921 on the death of Miguel Faílde.

Fajardo, José Antonio. Flutist, composer, bandleader. Born 18 October 1919, Guane. Studied flute in his hometown; settled in Havana in 1933. Fajardo played successively with the bands led by René Alvarez, Armando Valdespí, Paulina Alvarez, Antonio María Romeu, Neno González, and Antonio Arcaño. In 1949 he formed his own band, Fajardo y Sus Estrellas, which played at dances throughout Cuba as well as on the radio and on television. He wrote "Los tamalitos de Olga," "Ritmo de pollo," "De bala," "Fajardo te pone a gozar," and other numbers.

Fajardo has lived in the United States since 1961, where he continues to lead his band and where he has recorded thirty-three LPs.

Falcón, Alberto. Pianist and teacher. Born 21 May 1873, Matanzas; died 1961, Havana. Studied at the Hubert de Blanck Conservatory. Later, while living in France, Falcón won the competition for the piano professorial chair at the Bordeaux Conservatory. In France he also studied composition under the direction of Jules Massenet. Falcón toured several European cities as a pianist and gave piano concerts in Cuba. Back in his homeland, he also engaged in teaching and became director of the conservatory in Havana that bore his name. There, he encouraged the development of chamber music and created a chamber music orchestra. Along with other outstanding figures, he was a member of the Honor Committee at the Paris International Conservatory. He was also a member of the National Academy of Arts and Humanities. He wrote chamber music pieces for piano and one comic opera.

Fallótico, José. Composer, pianist, entertainer at musical shows. Born at the end of the eighteenth century, Havana; died (?). A writer of *tiranas*, Fallótico also wrote *zarzuelas* and pieces for piano. He was extremely well known in the capital's music business world. His work as concert player, composer, and arranger was unequalled by any other musician of his time. He organized dances and various musical events at private houses in Havana. One of his pieces for piano, *Los entredós de los demonios* (1791), was widely acclaimed.

Fals, Santiago. Choir conductor and composer. Born 14 June 1943, Santiago de Cuba. Was also a trumpet player with popular music bands. Fals studied music at the Esteban Salas Conservatory, in his hometown, and at the National School of Art. He has been conductor of the Coro Madrigalista of Santiago de Cuba and a teacher at the Esteban Salas Conservatory. He was the conductor of the Oriente Symphony Orchestra from 1966 to 1976 and has composed choral pieces.

Fantoli, Maria. Soprano. Born Rome, Italy; died (?), Havana. Settled in Havana in the 1920s. Fantoli performed in operas and sang in Cuban lyric music concerts. She was a member of Ernesto Lecuona's troup and also taught music.

Farah María. *See* García, Farah María.

Farelli, Tina. Soprano. Born 16 April 1879, Rome; died 26 June 1966, Havana. Sang operas first in Italy, then in Cuba, and settled in Havana at the beginning of the twentieth century with her husband Arturo Bovi. Together, they founded the Farelli-Bovi Academy, where several generations of Cuban musicians were trained.

Fariñas, Carlos. Composer. Born 28 November 1934, Cienfuegos. His first contact with music occurred within the framework of his family. Fariñas later settled in Havana, where he studied under the direction of José Ardévol, Harold Gramatges, and Enrique González Mántici. In 1956 he studied with Aaron Copland at the Berkshire Music Center in the United States. From 1961 to 1963 he studied at the Tchaikovsky Conservatory in Moscow. Back in Cuba, Fariñas worked as a teacher and music adviser and was director of the García Caturla Conservatory. His compositions include *Muros, rejas y vitrales* (for orchestra); *Atanos* and *Tres sones sencillos* (for piano); *Oda a Camilo* and *Despertar* (ballets); *Tientos* (a prize-winning piece at the Paris Biennial Contest for Young Composers in 1970); *Diálogos, Relieves,* and *Hecho historia* (ballets); *De Rerum Natura* (for chamber music orchestra); Sonata for violin and cello; and several string quartets. Fariñas introduced many avant-garde elements in his compositions, using dodecaphonic, serial, and aleatory techniques as well as electro-acoustic environments. He also composed music for motion pictures. Fariñas was director of the music department at the José Martí National Library and was the 1987 winner of the Annual Recognition Award given by the Writers and Artists Union of Cuba.

Farrés, Osvaldo. Composer. Born 13 January 1902, Quemado de Güines; died 22 December 1985, New Jersey. Started out in 1932 as an illustrator for *Carteles* magazine. Farrés hosted the radio show *Bar melódico de Osvaldo Farrés,* which later became a TV show. He also worked as a publicity agent. He wrote the *canciones* and boleros "Toda una vida," "No me vayas a engañar," "Acaríciame," "No, no y no," "Qué va,"

"Ni sé qué voy a hacer," "Qué será, será," "Chinito, chinita," "Piensa bien lo que me dices," "Acércate más," "Quizás, quizás," "Estás equivocada," "Para que sufras," "Tres palabras," and "Madrecita"; the *cha-cha-chá* "El teléfono"; and the *guarachas* "Mis cinco hijos" and "Un caramelo para Margot." His compositions have been performed by leading singers and arranged as instrumental pieces for symphony orchestras. He settled in the United States in 1962.

Faz, Roberto. Singer. Born 18 September 1914, Regla; died 26 April 1966, Havana. At age thirteen, Faz sang with the Bellamar Children's Sextet, formed by his father, in Regla. He later joined the Sexteto Cubano and, successively, the bands Hermanos Lebatard and Habana. After some time with Alberto Ruiz's Conjunto Kubavana, Faz joined the Conjunto Casino in 1943, with whom he sang for thirteen years and recorded a number of records that covered a wide range of genres, including bolero, *son,* and *guaracha.* In 1956 he formed his own band, which successfully toured Cuba and other Latin American countries.

Faxas, Carlos. Bandleader and pianist. Born 30 October 1921, Manzanillo. Has lived in Havana since he was eleven. Faxas studied with Pérez Sentenat, Enrique Aparicio, and Félix Guerrero. He worked as a pianist with popular music bands, including the Cosmopolita *jazzband.* During the 1950s, he led an eponymous quartet. He was jailed during Batista's dictatorship for underground revolutionary activities and subsequently conducted the small band that secretly recorded the "26th of July March." Exiled to the United States, he returned to Cuba after the Revolution. He was secretary-general of the Union of Cuban Musicians. In recent years, he led a music group and has worked on the Isle of Youth.

Fe, Alfredo de la. Violinist. Born 6 January 1954, Havana. Son of the singer bearing the same name. Fe studied violin at the Havana Municipal Conservatory and was a member of several school bands. In 1965 he settled in New York, where he studied at the Juilliard School of Music. At the age of twelve, he performed with the band led by Cuban flutist José Fajardo and, subsequently, with Roberto Torres's Latin Dimensions. He was a member of Tito Puente's Latin Jazz Ensemble from 1979 and the salsa band Tipica 73 in the 1980s. He was an active member of the Grupo Folklórico y Experimental Nuevayorkino. He has been based in Colombia for the past fifteen years.

Feijóo, Samuel. Folklorist, poet, writer. Born 1914, San Juan de las Yeras; died 14 July 1992, Santa Clara. Outstanding researcher of Cuban folkloric and popular music, especially that of his home province. Feijóo has published poetry, short stories, essays, and novels. He is also a sketch artist and painter. His work to achieve the diffusion of Cuban popular art has been praiseworthy. His articles on musicological appreciation and diffusion can be found in the magazines *Islas* and *Signos*, both of which he edited.

Feliú, Santiago. Songwriter and singer. Born 1962, Havana. Feliú's songs began to be broadcast in the early 1980s. His music is representative of the line within the *nueva trova* movement that has been strongly influenced by rock music. Among his most outstanding songs are "Para Bárbara" and "Vida." He has sung with his group in Cuba, Latin America, and Europe.

Feliú, Vicente. Songwriter and singer. Born 11 November 1947, Havana. Member of the *nueva trova* movement. Since the movement first emerged around 1967, Feliú has been an active member, contributing songs and performing. His compositions include "El seguidor," "Monumento al obrero desconocido," and "Créeme." He has also adapted to music poems by García Lorca and Heraud.

Fellové, Francisco. Writer and interpreter of Cuban popular music pieces. Born 7 October 1923, Havana; died (?). Among his best-known numbers are the *guarachas* "Mango mangüé," "Para que tú lo bailes," and "Sea como sea." In the 1950s, Fellové recorded several records that were widely broadcast on the radio. He has applied his original style to pieces from the *guaracha* repertoire. He has lived in Mexico for many years.

Fellové, Julián. Saxophone player. Born 1922, Guanabacoa. Fellové played with various groups, among them the Hermanos Martínez *jazzband*, before heading for Spain with Jaime Camino's *jazzband*, and then to Paris with the Benny Bennett Orchestra. He later toured Europe and in 1958 formed his own band, which played at the Brussels Exhibition. Returning to Cuba in 1966, he joined the resident players at the Kawama and Oasis nightclubs in Varadero Beach. He has played saxophone with the Orquesta Cubana de Música Moderna since 1967.

Fergo, Tony. Composer. Born 13 January 1923, Havana. His full name is Antonio Fernández Gómez. Worked as a publicist first in Cuba and later in Panama. Fergo wrote the boleros "Alma vanidosa," "En la palma de la mano," "Conformidad," "Sonámbula luna," "Cita a la una," "Algún día," and "Mala memoria," as well as the mambo-boleros "La televisión" (cowritten with Carbó Menéndez) and "Luna lunera."

Fernández, Alba Marina. Mezzo-soprano. Born 9 October 1920, Havana. First studied at a conservatory in Havana, then spent nine years in New York, where she studied singing at the Juilliard School of Music and sang on NBC. Fernández toured Mexico, Venezuela, Puerto Rico, and Colombia. In Cuba, she has appeared in many operas and *zarzuelas*, as well as on radio and television. She has performed with

Maurice Chevalier, Libertad Lamarque, Nat King Cole, María Félix, Eddie Fisher, Hugo del Carril, and other outstanding singers.

Fernández, Antonio ("Ñico Saquito"). Composer, singer, guitarist. Born 17 January 1902, Santiago de Cuba; died 4 August 1982, Havana. Worked as a foundry man for many years. At age fifteen, Fernández began to study guitar with Félix Premión, and some time later started singing as a troubadour. He formed a quartet in the 1930s, but dissolved it to join the Cuarteto Castillo, with which he played for the next ten years. In the 1940s he played with Guillermo Mozo's Grupo Típico Oriental at the Montmartre nightclub in Havana. After spending some time in his hometown, Fernández returned to Havana at the head of a quintet, Los Guaracheros de Oriente. In Havana, the group played on the radio station RHC Cadena Azul and on Radio Cadena Suaritos. His songs often offered critical commentary on the country's political situation. The group left for Venezuela in 1950 and returned to Cuba in 1960, having been hunted by the Venezuelan secret police for its revolutionary activities. Among Fernández's most outstanding songs are the *guajira* "Al vaivén de mi carreta," and the *son-guaracha* pieces "Compay gallo," "María Cristina," "Jaleo," "No dejes camino por vereda," "La negra Leonor," and "¿Qué te parece, mi compay?"

Fernández, Coralia. Singer and actress. Born 23 August 1927, Regla; died 1 August 1988, Havana. Singer of country music. Coralia Fernández was the wife of and artistic partner to Ramón Veloz. She sang on radio and on television and performed dramatized novels and short stories for radio and television.

Fernández, Frank. Pianist. Born 16 March 1944, Mayarí. Started studying piano at age four with his mother, and later under the direction of Esteban Forés in his hometown. After settling in Havana, Fernández played in nightclubs and cabarets. He entered the Amadeo Roldán Conservatory, where he studied harmony, music history, and piano with Margot Rojas. He is the winner of the piano contest held by the Writers and Artists Union of Cuba. Fernández later left for the Soviet Union on a scholarship to study with Merchanov. He has performed as

a soloist and with the National Symphony Orchestra, in Cuba and in several cities abroad. He has also written choral music and has recorded albums of both Cuban and international classical music.

Fernández, Gonzalo. Flutist. Born 1930, Sagua la Grande; died 1998, Houston. Started out playing with the Hermanos Quintero band in his hometown and later joined Mario Fernández's band in Havana. In 1958 Fernández left for Mexico, where he joined the Orquesta América. He spent eighteen years in Paris and then settled in New York, where he played with Latin dance (salsa) bands and on several excellent records.

Fernández, Joseíto. Singer. Born 5 September 1908, Havana; died 11 October 1979. Sang with trios, sextets, and *orquestas típicas*. In the 1930s, when *danzonete* was at its height, Fernández first sang with the Raimundo Pía y Rivero band, and then set up his own *danzón* group. Around that time, he wrote his now world-famous *son-guajira* "Guantanamera," which was recorded by the American singer Pete Seeger. "Guantanamera" was created one night when it occurred to Fernández to end his show playing a *son-guajira* instead of the customary rumba. As he sang, he improvised stanzas in the style of the typical

Cuban country ballads (*décimas*), praising the virtues and beauty of the women who live in the town where that night's dance was being held. Of all the *guajiras* created that way, only "Guantanamera" remained in the band's repertoire—"for sentimental reasons," as Fernández himself has stated. These days, it is common practice to include stanzas from José Martí's "Versos sencillos" within the piece. For many years, Fernández sang on the radio, using his *guajira* "Guantanamera" as the backing to stories about current events in Cuba. Another of the many boleros and *guarachas* he wrote is "Elige tú, que canto yo."

Fernández, Teresita. Singer, guitar player, songwriter. Born 20 December 1930, Santa Clara. Fernández grew up in a family of art and music lovers and learned to play the guitar with Benito Vargas, a troubadour from her home province. In general, she should be considered as a self-taught artist, with only minimal musical education. In later years, she came into contact with some old troubadours, among them the Martí sisters. Her first performances took place in her hometown, where she sang her own songs, accompanied by her guitar, at family gatherings. One night, the pianist Bola de Nieve presented her to the public at the Monseigneur Restaurant in Havana, and she subsequently sang at the Coctel nightclub and performed on a number of radio and television shows, as well as in small Havana theaters. Her songs are a mixture of poetry and melody where the majority of themes are about nature and everyday life. She has set to music José Martí's "Ismaelillo" and Gabriela Mistral's "Rondas" and has written songs for children ("Tía jutía," "Canta pajarito"), as well as songs filled with intimate lyricism ("La gaviota," "Pinares de Mayarí").

Fernández, Wilfredo. Singer. Born 18 March 1924, Mayarí. Started singing professionally on radio shows in Havana in 1946. Fernández later toured several Latin American countries, singing *sones* and boleros. In Cuba, he has performed on the radio, on television, at theaters, and in nightclubs. He settled in the United States in 1968.

Fernández Barroso, Sergio. Composer. Born 4 March 1946, Havana. Studied piano under César Pérez Sentenat in Cuba, and with Vaclav Dobias and Karl Janacek at the Higher Music Academy in Prague. Fernández Barroso has taught counterpoint and fugue, as well as morphology, at the National School of Art since 1968, and at the Amadeo Roldán Conservatory, in Havana, from 1968 to 1970. He is director and producer of the radio show *Música contemporánea* on CMBF Radio Musical Nacional, where he is also musical adviser. He was director of the music department at the José Martí National Library and at the University of Havana between 1970 and 1973. He has written symphonic, chamber, and vocal music, as well as pieces for electro-acoustic environments. He won the Chamber Music Award at the 26th of July Contests in 1973 and 1974. Fernández Barroso's music has been performed in Peru, Spain, France, Bulgaria, Czechoslovakia, Poland, and elsewhere. Among his most outstanding pieces are Quartet for strings (Chamber Music Award, 1973); Concerto for oboe and orchestra (1967); Concerto for piano, percussion, and audience (1968); *S. XIX-69*, *La casa de Bernarda Alba* (ballet), for grand wind orchestra, percussion, nine mixed voices, and electronic music (1969); *Noema I* (electronic music); Concerto for electric guitar and vocal orchestra; *Plásmasis* (ballet, 1971); Concerto for one or several bow instruments and four sound sources; *Yantra*, for the musician's imagination (1972); *Noema II*, for solo singer, cello, guitar, piano, and audiotape, with text by José Martí (1973); *Yantra II*, for double wind septet (Chamber Music Award, 1974); *Yantra III* (for guitar and audiotape); *Chile*, testimony for unaccompanied choir (First Vocal Music Honorary Mention at the MINFAR 26th of July Contest, 1974); and *Noema III*, for singer and piano, with text by José Martí (1975).

Fernández-Brito, Ninowska. Pianist. Born 25 December 1944, Havana. Started studying piano at the Havana Municipal Conservatory; graduated from the Tchaikovsky Conservatory in Moscow in 1972. Fernández-Brito has given concerts with the National Symphony Orchestra and toured Latin America and Europe. He teaches piano at the Higher Institute of Art.

Fernández Coca, Lino. *See* Coca, Lino.

Fernández G., Pablito. Singer. Born 11 January 1962, Havana. Began singing in rock and pop groups and was a member of Dan Den, playing *son*, salsa, and rumba. He later sang with Opus 13 before forming his own group, Pablito F. G. y Su Élite. He has been responsible for creating an individual style of salsa and Cuban *timba*. He has toured widely and recorded several CDs.

Fernández Iznaola, Ricardo. Guitar player. Born 1949, Havana. Studied in Spain with professor Saínz de la Maza, and in Caracas, with Alirio Díaz. Fernández Iznaola has toured many countries as a concert player. He has recorded ten LPs of classical and contemporary guitar pieces and won many awards. He currently teaches at the Center for Music Studies in Denver, Colorado.

Fernández Porta, Mario. Pianist and songwriter. Born 16 February 1917, Guanabacoa; died 13 December 1996, Miami. Performed as an accompanist to singers on radio shows in Havana. In 1938 Fernández Porta toured Mexico as a dancer with an art troupe. Later, he began to sing to his own accompaniment on piano, and also performed on piano in concerts organized by Ernesto Lecuona. His compositions include "Oyeme," "Realidad," "Fuiste tú," "Qué me importa," "Mentiras tuyas," "Ya no me acuerdo," "No vuelvo contigo," "Ya no vuelvo a querer," "Todavía," "No te alejes," "Vivo sin ti," "Qué lástima me da," and "Para mi Cuba mi son." Fernández Porta won various awards for his work as a songwriter both in Cuba and overseas and played at the most important nightclubs and restaurants both in Cuba and in the United States. He left for Puerto Rico in 1960. He later moved to Santo Domingo and then back to the United States.

Ferrer, Ester. Pianist. Born 6 February 1916, Havana. Started studying with Fidela Lanz at age seven; continued with Margarita Carrillo at the Havana Municipal Conservatory. Ferrer has performed with the Havana Philharmonic Orchestra and the National Symphony Orchestra and has given many solo concerts. She teaches at the Amadeo Roldán Conservatory (formerly the Havana Municipal Conservatory). An outstanding accompanist, she currently works with the violinist Evelio Tieles.

Ferrer, Ibrahim. Singer. Born 20 February 1927, Santiago de Cuba. Sang in his hometown with the groups Jóvenes del Son, Sorpresa, Wilson, Maravillas de Beltrán, Los Modernistas, and Orquesta Chepín. Ferrer later joined Los Bocucos, whose leader was the singer Pacho Alonso. With the Buena Vista Social Club and the Afro-Cuban All Stars band, he has recently gained worldwide recognition as a singer of *son* music in the style of the easternmost provinces. He has been accompanied on tours of Europe by his own backup band.

Ferrer, Pedro Luis. Songwriter, singer, guitar player. Born 17 September 1952, Yaguajay. Studied in the music section of the National School of Art. Ferrer has sung in concerts on radio and television and has written the incidental music for plays. His songs include "Mariposa," "Boca que partes la boca," "Al son del pitazo," "Operación sitio," "Canto negro," and "Ronda de la puerta del enemigo" (with text by Félix Pita Rodríguez), and among his *son* compositions are "Son de la muerte esdrújula" and "Mario Agüé."

festivals. During the Republican Era, there were a few festivals held to encourage the development of music in Cuba, but it was only after the Revolution that festivals gained momentum. The first Cuban Music Festival, held in 1961, featured the National Symphony Orchestra, chamber music ensembles, choirs, and outstanding soloists, and presented an assortment of highly elaborate Cuban pieces. In 1962 the first Latin American Music Festival, held at the Amadeo Roldán theater, had a similar musical content, but broadened to encompass pieces written by composers from all over Latin America. The program included music by Heitor Villa-Lobos, Alberto Ginastera, Blas Galindo, Camargo Guarnieri, Silvestre Revueltas, and other representatives of Latin American music, including some contemporary Cuban composers. In 1962 the Santiago de Cuba National Choral Music Festival was launched, and ever since, choirs from every province have presented their repertoire of Cuban pieces and universal classics. In the same year, musicologist Odilio Urfé organized the first Popular Music Festival, where for several days, audiences could enjoy samples of the best popular and folkloric music and traditional dancing. The National Band Festival is held every year in various cities around the island; bands from all over the country participate, keeping alive a musical expression of the utmost historical importance. At open-air concerts (*retretas*) in parks and public spaces, the bands have made an invaluable contribution to the spread of artistic values and knowledge. The Creative Music Festival is held in the city of Matanzas every year to encourage the writing of Cuban songs. A prestigious jury awards prizes to the best songs, which are subsequently broadcast on the radio and on television. The Benny Moré Memorial Festival is organized every year in Santa Isabel de las Lajas, the singer's hometown, as a tribute to the outstanding representative of popular Cuban art. The Trova Festival in Santiago de Cuba (and, occasionally, in other cities such as Havana and Sancti Spiritus) invites the participation of singers performing material from the *trova* tradition, both past and present, accompanied by their own guitars. On several occasions, Varadero Beach has been the site of the International Song Festival, where well-known singers from several countries have performed for a largely Cuban audience. Contemporary music festivals have also been held in Havana, under the auspices of the music section of the Association of Cuban Writers and Artists, for the purpose of facilitating auditions, analyses, and discussions of works created in various countries. Also, national amateur festivals are regularly held.

Figarola, José. Writer and singer of *trova* songs. Born 20 June 1893, Santiago de Cuba; died (?). Figarola started his life as a musician, and was singing in theaters at the age of sixteen in a duo with Blanca Becerra. His most important mentor was Sindo Garay, but he also studied with Pepe Sánchez and Emiliano Blez. In 1908 he joined the famous Quinteto de Trovadores Santiagueros, whose other members were Luis Felipe Ports, Bernabé Ferrer, Emiliano Blez, and Pepe Sánchez. He led the Trío Oriental, featuring the singers Ferrer and Blez. His song compositions were "La poesía," "Muñequita de carne," and "Un beso en el alma."

Figueredo, Pedro. Lawyer, literature and music enthusiast, pianist. Born 29 July 1819, Bayamo; died 17 August 1870. In 1868 Figueredo enlisted in the Liberation Army, where he was given the rank of general. In that same year, he wrote the lyrics and music for "La Bayamesa," which was sung for the first time on 20 October 1868, and which later became Cuba's national anthem. He was imprisoned by the Spanish in 1870 and sentenced to death by firing squad in Santiago de Cuba.

Figueroa, Antonio. Violinist, teacher, composer. Born 11 June 1852, Santiago de Cuba; died 14 September 1892. Brother of the violinist Ramón Figueroa. Antonio Figueroa studied under the direction of Alard and White at the Paris Conservatory. Back in Cuba, he played violin at the music chapel in the Santiago de Cuba Cathedral. He later taught music at the San Basilio el Magno Seminary. He wrote transcriptions for quartet and small orchestra and several dances.

Figueroa, Manuel. Songwriter and band leader. Born at the beginning of the nineteenth century, Santiago de Cuba; died at the end of the nineteenth century. By the mid-1800s, his band was very well known in Santiago de Cuba and its nearby towns. Figueroa wrote the song "Soñando."

Figueroa, Ramón. Composer and violinist. Born 1862, Santiago de Cuba; died 4 March 1928. From 1882 Figueroa excelled as a violin player. In 1895 he settled in the Dominican Republic, where he organized and took part in fundraising concerts for Cuba's anticolonial cause. He was a member of the Cuban Revolutionary Party. He returned to Santiago de Cuba at the end of the war and engaged in teaching music, like his father, Manuel Figueroa. He founded the Academy of Fine Arts in his hometown. An outstanding violinist, he also wrote elaborate dance tunes. To some musicologists, he was the most important reformer of the Cuban *danza*. His compositions include "Capricho cubano," as well as waltzes, hymns, and marches. He died while listening to his children and friends playing Haydn's *Seven Words*.

Filarmónica de La Habana, Orquesta. *See* Havana Philharmonic Orchestra.

Filarmónico Mensual. The first music magazine published in Cuba, it debuted in 1812. It seems to have lasted for only a short period: just two issues have been found. There are few references to this magazine.

fílin music. Inspired by American music (its name derives from the English word "feeling" and conveys its emotional aspects), *fílin* music is a genre within the Cuban *canción* style that arose in the 1940s as a response to the need to reappraise the *canción* repertoire. It has significant roots in the traditional *trova* movement: its songs are performed to the accompaniment of a guitar, and *fílin* singers, like performers of *trova*, were traditionally from very poor backgrounds and had little knowledge of formal musical theory and technique. In the decade preceding the emergence of *fílin*, Cuba's music had gained worldwide recognition. Developments in broadcasting capabilities had disseminated Cuban music among a wider audience. Its melodies had gradually lost their quietude and achieved new modulations, and the links between tonal and extratonal harmony triads had become tighter and broader. *Danzón-charanga* bands broadened their technical scope; syncopated rhythms gained popularity among such bands as Arcaño y Sus Maravillas; the old *son* septet lost favor to a new kind of ensemble, the *conjunto*; and new arrangements trumped performance in importance. Eventually songs that were noticably antecedents to the *fílin* style became popular, including those written by Adolfo Guzmán, Bola de Nieve, René Touzet, Margarita Lecuona, Facundo Rivero, Francisco Cuesta, Enrique Pessino, Orlando de la Rosa, and others. The early members of the *fílin* movement—Luis Yáñez, César Portillo de la Luz, José Antonio Méndez, Niño Rivera, Ñico Rojas, Elena Burke, Froilán, Rosendo Ruiz Jr., Aida Diestro, and Frank Emilio—held meetings at the home of Tirso Díaz, located on Hammel Alley, near the intesection of Infanta and San Lázaro streets in Centro Habana. The *fílin* movement was collaborative, the product of the joint efforts of many artists. Arrangers in the *fílin* movement, among them Bebo Valdés, Niño Rivera, Pedro Jústiz, Tania Castellanos, and Peruchín, played a large part in shaping the movement's characteristics. There is a strong element of Debussy's impressionism, which had reached Cuba by way of American music. Thematically, *fílin* songs were private and poetic, and the fact that they were told rather than sung gave singers absolute freedom while performing them.

Fleites, Virginia. Composer. Born 1916, Havana. Studied composition with Amadeo Roldán and José Ardévol. Fleites was a member of the Grupo de Renovación Musical. She wrote *Invenciones* (1941), *Dos sonatas* (1942), *Fugas* (1943), Small suite for piano (1943), and Sonata for cello and piano (1944). She resides in the United States.

(La) Flor de Cuba, Orquesta. Formed in the mid–nineteenth century in Havana by Juan de Dios Alfonso, composer and clarinetist. It performed the dance music of the day—*contradanzas*, minuets, *rigodones*, *lanceros*, and *cuadrillas*. The instrumentation was that of an *orquesta típica*, or wind orchestra, with cornet, trombone, ophiclenic, two clarinets, two violins, double bass, timbales, and *güiro*. This is the orchestra that was performing when Spanish soldiers launched a savage attack on the audience at the Villanueva Theater in Havana in 1869.

Flores, Antonio. Singer, guitar player, composer. Born (?); died (?). Very popular in Havana at the beginning of the nineteenth century. Flores performed *tiranas* to the accompaniment of his own guitar and displayed great improvisational skill; his *tiranas* seemed to emerge spontaneously during his performances. Due to his command of the genre, he was known as "El Tirano."

Floro and Miguel, Duo. Duo formed by Floro Zorrilla and Miguel Zaballa that performed from 1912 to 1926. Both singers played the guitar, with Floro as first voice and Miguel as second. They sang at theaters and movie houses in Havana and toured various Latin American countries. They recorded over one hundred records.

flute, aboriginal. A wind instrument used by the Indo-Cubans, as well as by many other Amerindian peoples. It was a small pipe made from cane or, preferably, from the bones of birds or other animals. It

had several holes and a rudimentary mouthpiece. One of these flutes was recently found in eastern Cuba, the only one to have been found in the Antilles.

Flynn, Frank Emilio. Pianist. Born 13 April 1921, Havana; died 2001(?), Havana. Flynn lost his sight at age thirteen but nevertheless still finished high school. He began to play piano as a child, with no knowledge of musical theory and guided only by his marvelous ear. As a young man, he played the piano with a typical Cuban music band, having studied music with the aid of the Braille system, under the direction of Dr. Julio Azanza. He later performed in nightclubs, hotels, and cabarets, as well as on radio and television. Flynn continued his studies with professor César Pérez Sentenat. For years he led the Orquesta Cubana de Música Moderna, whose members include double bassist Pepito Hernández, drummer Guillermo Barreto, conga player Tata Güines, and *güiro* player Gustavo Tamayo. Flynn recorded a large number of albums, most notably those featuring piano dances written by Manuel Saumell, Ignacio Cervantes, and Ernesto Lecuona. He has toured all over Cuba and performed at New York's Carnegie Hall in the late 1990s with his group Los Amigos.

fondo. The second of two *bongó* drums, also called *segundo*. The first *bongó* drum is called *primo*, or *quinto*, and has a higher pitch than the *fondo*. *See also* bongó.

Formell, Juan. Composer, double bass player, arranger, bandleader. Born 2 August 1942, Havana.

The son of a musician, Formell became familiar with music as a child. In 1959 he joined groups led by the pianists Peruchín and Guillermo Rubalcaba, as well as the house band at the Caribe cabaret. In 1968 he joined the Orquesta Revé, whose traditional *charanga* style he revolutionized with the introduction of his own pieces and arrangements in which the typically Cuban patterns were enriched with up-to-date musical elements. In 1969 he formed his own band, the Orquesta Van Van, which has become one of the most outstanding groups of recent decades. His successful compositions include "Ya lo sé," "Lo material," "Yo soy tu luz," "De mis recuer-

dos," "Qué será de mí," "La flaca," "Yuya Martínez," "Así," "Marilú," "La Habana joven," "Que se sepa," "Chirrín-chirrán," "Aquí se enciende la candela," "Ponte para las cosas," "El buey cansa'o," "Sandunguera," "Qué pista," "No juegues conmigo," and "Soy todo" (with lyrics by Eloy Machado). With his group, he has toured many Latin American, European, and African countries, and has recorded many albums and CDs. His band performs on radio and television and at theaters and nightclubs. His songs are regarded as classics of popular Caribbean music.

Fornés, Rosita. Singer. Born 11 February 1923, New York. Fornés was born in New York by chance, when her Spanish parents who lived in Cuba traveled there for a short stay. They returned soon after. Her full name is Rosalía Palet Bonavia, but the public has always known her as Rosita Fornés. As a lyric soprano, she has made numerous presentations at theaters, singing *zarzuelas* and operettas; she is also an outstanding and versatile singer of popular songs. She has performed in fifteen films and toured Mexico, Venezuela, Honduras, the United States, and other countries, and spent several successful years in Spain. She made her first public appearance, as a teenager, in *La corte suprema del arte*, a TV show for amateur singers, and made her professional debut under the guidance of Ernesto Lecuona, whose company she joined at age seventeen. She has made many records and has performed constantly in recent years.

Fortín, Tomás. Orchestra conductor. Born 29 April 1949, Santiago de las Vegas. Studied violin and viola. Fortín played the viola with the National Symphony Orchestra. In 1982 he graduated as a conductor from Moscow's Tchaikovsky Conservatory. He has conducted the Matanzas Symphony Orchestra and orchestras accompanying opera productions. Fortín toured several countries as the leader of various orchestras and has conducted the Brindis de Salas Chamber Music Orchestra and the National Philharmonic Orchestra.

fotuto. An Indo-Cuban instrument, also called *guamo*, constructed from a large, tubular sea shell. The end of its spiral is broken so that the musician can blow through it, to produce very loud,

hoarse sounds. Early European and Asian cultures used this sonorous device, and it was found throughout the Americas. The indigenous inhabitants of Cuba used it in their *areítos*. José Rivero de la Calle notes that work has been done to show the extreme variety of sounds *guamos* can produce. At the Montané Museum at the University of Havana, for instance, a *guamo* was made from a hollowed-out boulder that produced a third-octave C, a third-octave A, a second-octave A, and a second-octave E flat. (Rivero de la Calle, *Las culturas aborígenes en Cuba*, 155–59).

Frades, Amelita. Singer. Born 1928, Havana; died 9 August 1984. Made her first public performances on the radio stations Lavín, Mil Diez, and Radio Cadena Suaritos. Frades appeared with the bands of Obdulio Morales and Rodrigo Prats, singing mostly boleros. She toured Mexico and Venezuela in 1956, and returned to Mexico in 1984. In Havana, she performed at the El Rincón del Bolero nightclub in the Capri Hotel and also on radio, television, and in theaters.

Fraga, Modesto. Flutist, teacher, music band conductor. Born 24 February 1861, Cárdenas; died 1932, Havana. Was first flute with the Havana Municipal Band on its foundation in 1899. From 1902 onward Fraga was the band's deputy director, and in 1923 he replaced Guillermo Tomás as director, a position he held for four years. While teaching flute at the Havana Municipal Conservatory, he was responsible for training several brilliant Cuban flutists. He performed in orchestras, playing repertoires of classical music, opera, and *zarzuela*, and his compositions for them included *danzones* and mazurkas.

Fragoso, Argelia. Singer. Born 14 May 1958, Havana. Studied singing at the Amadeo Roldán Conservatory and the Manuel Saumell Academy, then took choral conducting at the National School of Art, where she graduated in 1975. As a child, Fragoso gave some television performances. She was awarded the Dresden Festival Prize in the German Democratic Republic and the Grand Prize at the Sochi Festival in the Soviet Union. In 1976 she sang at the Sopot Festival and received the press award. She has performed in Berlin, Prague, Moscow, and Sofia. Fragoso sang the theme song of the Eleventh World Festival of Youth and Students, held in Havana in 1978. She studies choir conducting at the Franz Liszt Higher School of Music, in Weimar.

Fragoso, Guillermo. Composer and guitarist. Born 2 April 1953, Havana. Studied at the Amadeo Roldán Conservatory and at the Higher Institute of Art. Fragoso has performed as guitar accompanist and has written *Variaciones sobre Lube-Lube* (a Congo chant, 1976); *Octógono*, for brass instruments (1978); and Concerto for guitar and orchestra (1980), as well as popular songs. She teaches at the National School of Art.

Franco, Rosario. Pianist. Born 28 June 1930, Havana. Made her first public presentation as a child, in 1941, with the Havana Symphony Orchestra conducted by Gonzalo Roig. Franco studied with professors Sara Estrada and José Luis Vidaurreta and later with Claudio Arrau. She continued to a higher grade at schools in France, the United States, and Germany. She has given solo concerts, accompanied by various orchestras, on tours of Europe and Latin America.

Frank Emilio. *See* Flynn, Frank Emilio.

Frías, Lino. Pianist and composer. Born (?), Havana; died 21 May 1983, New York. Studied at the Havana Municipal Conservatory. Frías played with Carabina de Ases and the group led by Arsenio Rodríguez. In 1944 he joined the band La Sonora Matancera, with whom he spent thirty-two years. In the United States, he participated in recordings with Tito Puente, Sonora Alegre, Conjunto Son de la Loma, and Roberto Torres's ensemble. His style constituted a turning point in the development of Afro-Caribbean music. He wrote "Yemayá," "Mata siguaraya," "Oyela, gózala," "Pan de piquito," "Oye este mambo," "Guíllate," "Suena mi bajo," "Bésame puchunguita," "Con maña sí," and the boleros "Vuelve muñequita," "Encanto de mujer," "Convencida," and "Has vuelto a mí."

Frontela Fraga, Regino. Pianist and bandleader. Born 7 September 1908, Catalina de Güines; died 18 February 1991, Havana. Studied under the direction of Melania Acosta at the Santa Cecilia Academy and at the Havana Municipal Conservatory. Frontela

Fraga played the piano with Valerio Moreira's band. In 1940 he formed Moreira's *charanga* band, Melodías del 40, which he led until 1976. He wrote the *charanga-son* pieces "Tunas-Bayamo," "Esta melodía," and "El niño prodigio."

Fuente, Benito de la. Composer and singer. Born 29 May 1948, Holguín. Sang with the Holguín choir. From 1976 onward, Fuente sang with the Havana group Mayohuacán. His compositions include "El corazón de La Habana," "Oxígeno," "Dama antigua," "Supermundo," and "Como cuando viene un ciclón." He currently sings and plays guitar with Benito y Compañía, which he also leads.

Fuentes, Justo. Composer. Born 11 November 1921, Havana; died, 4 April 1949. Studied odontology at the University of Havana and was deputy president of the Federation of University Students (FEU). Fuentes was murdered on leaving the radio station COCO, where he was director of the show *The Voice of FEU*. He was a founding member of the *filin* movement and wrote "Burla" and "Cenizas y olvido," among other songs.

Fuentes, Pedro María. Composer. Born 1858, Santiago de Cuba; died (?). Studied in his hometown under the direction of his father and Juan de la Moya. Fuentes later settled in Havana and traveled to the United States, where his music was widely acclaimed. He wrote numerous piano dances, which were often played and praised, among them "Misterio de un botón," "La reglita," "La dulce María," "La Nena," "Un recuerdo," "Ay, Julia," "Gratitud," "Sabrosita," "Melancolía," "La trigueña," and "Las dos cubanas."

Fuentes Matons, Laureano. Composer, violinist, orchestra conductor, multi-instrumentalist. Born 3 July 1825, Santiago de Cuba; died 30 September 1898. Studied with Juan París, Hierrezuelo, and Juan Casamitjana. An outstanding violinist since a teenager, at the age of fifteen Fuentes Matons won the position of first violin at the music chapel of the Santiago de Cuba Cathedral. He studied Latin and philosophy at the San Basilio Seminary in Santiago de Cuba. Throughout his life, he wrote a large number of works, most of which have been preserved to this day. His music, with its classicist basis, exhibits a clearly Romantic style of expression. He wrote both secular and sacred music, excelling mostly in the latter. Among his liturgical pieces are masses, hymns, responses, psalms, lessons, antiphonies, invitatories, graduals, sequences, Benedictus, and others; his *Stabat Mater* is highly regarded. He also wrote the symphonic poem *América*, several orchestral overtures, chamber music (six sonatas; two trios for violin, flute, and piano; and various trios for string instruments), numerous pieces for piano and violin (melodies, waltzes, songs, ballads, *romanzas* and boleros), *danzas* and *danzones*, mazurkas and marches, the zarzuelas *Me lo ha dicho la partera*, *El viejo enamorado*, *Desgracia de un tenor*, and *Dos máscaras*, the opera *Seila*, and the typical *canciones* "La candelita" and "Currucucú." In 1893 he published a historical essay, "Las artes en Santiago de Cuba."

Fuentes Pérez, Laureano. Pianist and composer. Born 14 September 1854, Santiago de Cuba; died 27 December 1927, Havana. Son of Laureano Fuentes Matons. Laureano Fuentes Pérez was an outstanding pianist. He wrote *Rapsodia cubana*, "Elegía," "Marcha triunfal," and "Idilio," the fantasies "Oriente" and "Brulé," the capriccios "La mocita" and "Galimatías," the waltz "Alina," and several dances.

Fumero, José Claro. Composer, trombonist, instrumentalist. Born 12 August 1906, Matanzas; died 1977, Havana. Studied with Oscar Verweire, conductor of the Matanzas Music Band, who taught him to play the tuba. Fumero performed in Narciso Velazco's *orquesta típica*, and later with Aniceto Díaz's band and the orchestra of Rafael Somavilla Sr. He wrote the boleros "Mi amor, mi fe y mi ilusión" and "Aquella mujer," the conga "¿Y a mí qué?," works for the band entitled "Un juguete," "Pass silencio," and "Los carabalíes," and several *danzones*.

G

Gadles Mikowsky, Solomon. Pianist and teacher. Born 1936, Havana. Studied with César Pérez Sentenat, Argeliers León, and Luis Pastoret. In 1956, Gadles Mikowsky settled in the United States, where he continued his studies at New York's Juilliard School of Music. He is the author of *Ignacio Cervantes y la danza en Cuba*, published by Editorial Letras Cubanas in 1988.

Galán, Natalio. Composer, musicologist, teacher. Born 1917, Camagüey; died 30 December 1985, New Orleans. Studied in his hometown with Luis Aguirre, and in 1936 settled in Havana, where he studied composition at the Municipal Conservatory. Galán composed chamber music, and later wrote some Variations for small orchestra (serial pieces) and the opera *Los días llenos* (with script by Antón Arrufat). He taught at the Havana Municipal Conservatory. He moved to the United States in 1947, and after a few short stays in Cuba, settled permanently there, first in New York and then in New Orleans. He is the author of the book *Cuba y sus sones* (1983), an important contribution to the study of Cuban music.

Gallart, José. Pianist and composer. Born 19 December 1890, Guantánamo; died 16 August 1946. Studied with Rafael Salcedo in Santiago de Cuba. In 1899 Gallart accompanied Claudio José Domingo Brindis de Salas on piano in Guantánamo. In 1900 he traveled to the United States, where he graduated as a civil engineer five years later. Back in Cuba in 1907, he studied harmony and composition on a "distance education" basis under professor Alfred Wooder. Some time later, he obtained diplomas in counterpoint and fugue in Philadelphia, and qualified as a piano teacher and obtained a doctorate in music in England. His compositions include "Dulce recuerdo," "Desilusión," "Germania," "El ruiseñor," "Gardenia," "Mable," and "Azucena."

galleta. Type of drum similar to the *bombo* (bass drum) but squatter, it is used in the carnival congas in the eastern region of the country. A similar instrument is used by Mozambican musical groups.

Gálvez, Zoila. Soprano. Born 19 May 1899, Guanajay; died 26 November 1985, Havana. Her father, José Gálvez, was a colonel in the Cuban Liberation Army. Zoila Gálvez started studying piano at the Hubert de Blanck Conservatory in Havana and trained as a singer under the Italian teachers Tina Farelli and Arturo Bovi, completing her studies in Milan under the guidance of Professor Giacomo Marino. She made her debut as a soprano in Milan and stayed in Italy for four years, singing at concerts and in opera performances. Her first presentation in Rome was in 1924, as leading singer in Verdi's *Rigoletto*. She made her debut in Havana with the Havana Symphony Orchestra, conducted by Maestro Gonzalo Roig. Gálvez performed in 1925 at the Pleyel theater in Paris and then successfully toured Spain, Mexico, and other countries. She was a leading soprano singer in the Miller and Lyles Company in New York during 1927 and 1928. In 1929, she toured the United States. She was very active in Cuba, where she gave numerous opera, lyric song, and lied concerts. Several Cuban pieces were written especially for her voice. She sang on many Cuban radio shows, and occasionally on television. In 1951 she gave a memorable concert at New York's Town Hall, and two years later an even more impressive presentation at Carnegie Hall. From 1927, she taught singing at the Havana Municipal Conservatory. She has received countless tributes and distinctions both in Cuba and overseas.

Garay, Sindo. Songwriter, singer, guitar player. Born 12 April 1867, Santiago de Cuba; died 17 July 1968, Havana. The most outstanding writer of *trova* songs in Cuba. Garay composed his first song, "Quiéreme trigueña," at the age of ten. As a teenager, he worked as a circus clown and acrobat. He learned to read and write by copying the signs outside stores in Santiago de Cuba. He worked for a short period at a leatherworker's shop. During the War for Independence against Spain, he served as liaison between the rebels. He gave all his children Indian names in honor of Cuba's aboriginal inhabitants. Garay was a leading figure in Santiago de Cuba's *trova* movement, along with Pepe Sánchez and others. At the end of the nineteenth century, he traveled to Santo Domingo, Puerto Rico, and several South American countries, and in 1906, settled in Havana, where he sang to his own guitar accompaniment. A self-taught musician, he possessed extraordinary musical intuition. According to Vincente Gonzales Rubiera, Garay used chromaticism in his music with simplicity and accuracy, achieving surprising results. He was dissatisfied with the inherent the simple diatonic nature of tonality and expanded it by alternating some of its sounds. In the major tonality, he would alter the sixth descendingly to produce the sixth minor and thus attained a minor subdominant within the dominant that he used profusely. Garay was predisposed to the sound the dominant ninth minor chord. He used creative sonorities to produce the harmony for the second voice, a form that was new to the *trova* movement (Gonzalez Rubiera, "Armonia aplicada a la guitarra"). Along with Alberto Villalón, Rosendo Ruiz, and Manuel Corona, Garay is one of the greatest representatives of traditional *trova*. In 1928 he traveled to Paris with Rita Montaner and other Cuban musicians and spent three months there performing Cuban songs. Once back in Cuba, he sang with his children Guarina and Guarinex on various radio stations (Cuban Telephone, Radio Salas, Mil Diez, CMZ, and Cadena Azul) and made countless recordings. Among his most outstanding songs are "La tarde," "Perla marina," "Rendido," "Labios de grana," "Clave a Maceo," "Retorna," "La baracoesa," "Adiós a La Habana," "Mujer bayamesa," "La alondra," "El huracán y la palma," "Fermania," "Rayos de oro," "Tardes grises," "Ojos de sirena," and "Guarina."

García, Chamaco. Singer. Born 14 May 1938, Santiago de las Vegas. His full name is José Antonio. García started singing as a child in groups such as Los Hermanos Castro. In 1958 he began performing solo in theaters and cabarets. In 1960 he left Cuba for a tour of Mexico and remained in the city of Mérida for ten years. He then settled in the United States. He has recorded various Cuban song albums and has sung at the New York Metropolitan Opera House. He works as an actor on radio and television.

García, Farah María. Singer. Born 17 December 1944, Havana. Studied at the School for Art Instructors. García was a member of Meme Solís's quartet. She started singing solo in 1969, and performed on radio and television and at theaters. She has given many concerts of traditional and modern Cuban song, and was awarded a prize at the Sopot Song Festival in Bulgaria in 1977.

García, Freddy. Singer. Born 1933, Céspedes; died 1961, San Juan, Puerto Rico. At age twelve García moved to Havana to work in domestic service. She was discovered by the musical director of the nightclub at the Casino del Capri while singing informally in a bar that was popular with artists, and she made her debut appearance in the Casino some time later, thus beginning a sensationally successful career. Her large physique—she is estimated to have weighed three hundred pounds—was easily overlooked when her low voice resonated with its unique sensitivity. She recorded one splendid LP of unforgettable songs. She died young during a stay in Puerto Rico.

García, Lázaro. Songwriter and singer. Born 1948, Cienfuegos. Began his career as a member of the *nueva trova* movement in the 1970s. García was the director of the 5 de September group from Cienfuegos. His compositions include "Al sur de mi mochila," "Carta de provincia," "Si de tanto soñarte," and "Tejiendo un rostro en la canción."

García, Luis. Singer. Born 1936, Havana. Started his singing career during the 1950s as a member of the *filin* movement. García left for Spain in 1968 and sang in Madrid, then settled in the United States, where he has continued to sing and accompany himself on piano. He has recorded twenty-three LPs. He wrote the songs "Mi manera de ser," "Así canta el corazón," and "Oferta."

García, Miguel. Choir conductor and composer. Born 8 September 1981, Havana; died 1981. Studied at the Havana Municipal Conservatory, then moved to Santiago de Cuba, where he completed his most outstanding music work. García was the founding member, along with Hernández Balaguer, of the music faculty at the University of Oriente. He conducted the Coro Madrigalista choir, and was also teacher and director at the Esteban Salas Conservatory. He wrote choral and orchestral pieces, incidental music for theater plays, and choral transcripts. He was also musical director at the National Council for Culture.

García Caturla, Alejandro. Composer, violinist, conductor. Born 7 March 1906, Remedios; died 12 November 1940. Started studying music in his hometown, first with Fernando Estrems and then with María Montalván, both of whom provided him with a solid background. On settling in Havana to study law at the university, García Caturla also took up harmony, counterpoint, and fugue classes under the direction of Pablo Sanjuán. In June 1928 he left for Paris, where he studied with Nadia Boulanger. The idea of the trip to France resulted from his acquaintance with twentieth-century innovative musical trends and from his own aesthetic views. About García Caturla, Boulanger stated, "Seldom have I had a pupil as gifted as him. . . . He is a force of nature: you'd better leave it alone so it can manifest itself." Back in Cuba in October 1928, while working as a lawyer, he continued to develop as a composer and wrote countless pieces that place him among the great composers in Latin America. His hometown City Hall awarded him the title Eminent and Distinguished Son on 6 October 1928, and named the art room at the José María Espinosa Museum after him. In September 1929 he traveled to Europe once more, this time with composer Eduardo Sánchez de Fuentes, to participate in the Ibero-American Symphonic Festivals at the Barcelona International Exhibition, where his "Tres danzas cubanas" for symphony orchestra was performed. On that occasion, he made contact with some of the most important Spanish musicians of the time: Ernesto Halffter, Bartolomé Pérez Casas, and Adolfo Salazar. Then he headed for Paris again, where he premiered his "Poemas" for singer and piano. On 30 November of that year, he returned to Havana. He was not able to attend the premiere of *Bembé*, the first version, written in Paris at the request of conductor Marius François Gaillard. In 1932 he founded the

Caibarién Concert Society, whose orchestra he conducted and where he fulfilled many functions, including transcribing scores for the instruments at his disposal in pieces by composers as diverse as Vivaldi, Mozart, Debussy, Ravel, Gershwin, Cowell, and Falla. In 1938 the culture division of the Ministry of Education awarded him First Prize at the 1937 National Music Contest for his *Obertura cubana*. He also received an honorary mention for his Suite for orchestra at the same contest. García Caturla's symphonic pieces have been performed in Cuba, Moscow, Philadelphia, Los Angeles, Mexico, Caracas, Barcelona, Seville, and Paris. Among those who have conducted them are Pedro Sanjuán, Amadeo Roldán, Marius François Gaillard, Nicolas Slominsky, Ernesto Halffter, Bartolomé Pérez Casas, Carlos Chávez, Silvestre Revueltas, Erick Kleiber, Leopold Stokovsky, Gonzalo Roig, Enrique González Mántici, José Ardévol, Manuel Duchesne Cuzán, and Roberto Sánchez Ferrer. He played the violin and the viola with the Havana Symphony Orchestra under the conduction of Gonzalo Roig, and with the Philharmonic Orchestra, conducted by Pedro Sanjuán. He started out as a pianist playing *danzón* and American music in a *jazzband* of which he was later director, and played a few concerts, the level of which is indicated by the pieces performed: Beethoven's Sonata quasi una fantasia, Albeniz's *Triana*, Halffter's *The Gypsy's Dance*, Debussy's *Two Arabesques*. He also played Debussy's *Preludes* at a lecture delivered by Alejo Carpentier on the French composer. Although not an "impeccable" pianist, in the sense that the term is usually applied to concert players, many of his performances, including those of Liszt's Rhapsody no. 6 and the dances written by Cervantes and Lecuona, were memorable. He also played saxophone, clarinet, and percussion instruments. A baritone singer, he participated in concerts organized by Jorge Ánkermann and Ernesto Lecuona, where he sang with such quality singers as Rita Montaner, Mariano Meléndez, and Maria Fantoli. From an early age he practiced journalism as both a social columnist and a theater critic, and he also wrote articles about teaching music and on new music of the day. He was a keen sportsman, playing tennis and rowing. His art is a synthesis of national and universal values and of traditional and modern concepts, harmoniously combined. So, *son* and

minuet, bolero and pavane, *comparsa* and *giga*, *guajira* and waltz, *bembé* and symphonic poem, rumba and sonata all go hand-in-hand in his compositions, expressed in a language that combines the traditional nature of Cuba's cadential forms, the modality of its folk chants, and the peculiar character of melody wrought in the Cuban style with the chromatic aggressiveness of the European avant-garde of that time, polyharmony, and polyrhythm. His lasting universality is deeply rooted in Cuban culture. García Caturla did not consider his career as a lawyer to be a mere living; his concern for justice led him to participate in significant social movements, such as the reform of the Electoral Code and the writing of an influential essay on juvenile delinquency. His permanent fight against social and artistic conventions led to his death: he was murdered at age thirty-four by a defendant who was due to be sentenced mere hours later. He left behind eleven children and the legacy of an exemplary life, a valuable contribution to Cuban culture, and a large collection of letters that have been published under the title *Alejandro García Caturla: Correspondencia*.

(Alejandro) García Caturla Conservatory. Located in the Marianao municipality of Havana, which is supported by the Cuban Ministry of Culture. The building was renovated in 1960. Its faculty has played an outstanding role in the training of young instrumentalists. Its first director was Nilo Rodríguez.

García Lorca Theater. *See* Tacón Theater.

García Montes, María Teresa. Promoter of musical culture. Born 23 June 1880, Havana; died 10 October 1930, New York. Studied piano with Mazzucelli, Pablo Desvernine, and Hubert de Blanck. Garcia Montes was president of the Pro-Musical Art Society from its foundation on 2 December 1918. In 1928 her campaign for the construction of the Auditorium Theater (later to become Amadeo Roldán Theater) was of decisive importance.

García Orellana, Rosario. Soprano. Born (?), Havana; died (?). Started out singing on radio in Havana. García Orellana was a member of Ernesto Lecuona's company. She recorded numerous records for RCA Victor, mostly lyric songs by Cuban composers.

García Perdomo, Ricardo. Songwriter. Born 20 April 1917, Cienfuegos; died 12 September 1966, Miami. Wrote boleros that became very popular and were widely broadcast in Cuba and overseas, including "Total" and "Qué te cuesta."

García Porrúa, Jorge. Composer. Born 9 June 1938, Havana. Studied at the Castillo Conservatory, the Amadeo Roldán Conservatory, and the National School of Art. A music teacher at several schools, he has also been musical adviser at several theaters. He won the National Chamber Music Award at the UNEAC contest in 1970. He has written music for theater and for film. Among his compositions are Three preludes and Themes with variations and fugue (for piano), Requiem and Vietnam (for symphony orchestra), Diálogo con la charanga, String quartet, Sonata (chamber music), and other songs and choral pieces.

García Wilson, Herminio. Tres player. Born 25 April 1904, Guantánamo. Self-taught tres guitarist. A member of several son groups from Guantánamo. From the 1930s, he led his own group. In 1929 García Wilson wrote the basic rhythmic dance coda for "Guantanamera" and also composed the son pieces "En casa de Epifanita," "Lola se quiere casar," and "Los celos de Cachita."

Gavira, Joaquín. Violinist, composer, teacher. Born 1780, Havana; died 1880. As a child, Gavira was soprano singer at the Havana Cathedral. A member of the Militia Corps, he lived in extreme poverty. In 1802 he started playing cello in the Cathedral Chapel, then moved to second violin. In 1811 he founded the first Cuban chamber music group—a classical music trio whose other members were Mazzuchelli and Manuel Avilés. He contributed to the development of musical art in the capital. In 1852 he was appointed choirmaster. He composed religious music and also taught violin for many years. One of his pupils was the eminent José Domingo Bousquet.

Gaytán, Eddy. Accordionist, vibraphone player, composer, arranger, bandleader. Born 30 June 1929, Santa Fe, Argentina. In 1950 Gaytán settled in Cuba, where he has played an active role in the development of Cuban music. He leads the combo bearing his name, with whom he has performed in nightclubs, on the radio and television, and on numerous recordings. Gaytán has a large number of arrangements to his credit, all the time renewing his mode of expression. He is the composer of the popular pieces "El sabor de la Rampa" (joropo) and "Quizás la luna" (cha-cha-chá).

Gelabert, Vicente. Guitarist. Born (?), Barcelona, Spain; died (?), Quemado de Güines. Studied under the direction of Francisco Tárrega. Gelabert settled first in Havana, and then in towns in the province of Santa Clara, mainly Caibarién and Quemado de Güines. He gave concerts and played at numerous artists' gatherings. He was known for his technical skills, as well as his bohemian life.

Gil, Blanca Rosa. Singer. Born 26 August 1937, Perico. As a child, Gil moved with her family (sisters Rita and Mercedes are also singers) to Havana, where she studied music. She traveled to Venezuela, where she sang on television shows. Back in Havana in 1957, she sang at cabarets, on radio and television, and recorded several LPs of boleros that became very popular. She toured Mexico, Colombia, and the Dominican Republic. In 1962 she traveled to Mexico, where she stayed for some time until she moved to Puerto Rico. In recent years, she has performed sacred music.

Ginés, Teodora. A legendary figure in Cuba's musical history. Believed to have been born in Santiago de los Caballeros in the Dominican Republic, and to have played mandolin in a group with her sister Micaela Ginés and several Spanish musicians. This group is said to have played at popular festivals. Some time later when Ginés was living in Havana with Micaela and the Sevillian bass violinist Pascual de Ochoa, as well as the Malagan Pedro Almanza, and the Portuguese Jacome Viceira, she performed their "primitive" compositions at dances and other gatherings. The famous "Son de la Ma' Teodora," which some believe to be the ancestral son piece, has been attributed to her, but Alberto Muguercia has denied the truth of this statement, basing his opinion on the apocryphal nature of the tale of the attribution and on the lack of documentary evidence to support Laureano Fuentes's statements about these supposedly "primitive" musicians (see Muguercia, "Teodora Ginés: ¿Mito o realidad histórica?"). Odilio Urfé explains that there are no documents attesting to the real origin of the legendary "Son de la Ma' Teodora." Though there are reliable testaments to the relationship between the *son* and the Ginés sisters from historians, musicologists, and other specialists, there is an obvious contradiction between the versions of the composition analyzed by Laureano Fuentes in his book *Las artes en Santiago de Cuba* and that analyzed by Bachiller and Morales in *Cuba primitiva*. Urfé attests that it is impossible to accept "Son de la Ma' Teodora" as an example of Cuban music of the sixteenth, seventeenth, or eighteenth centuries, because the composition was first transcribed in the mid–nineteenth century, a time when what is considered today to be typical Cuban music was first beginning to emerge. There is no reliable way to verify whether the "Cuban-ness" of "Son de la Ma' Teodora" is a result of the musical development achieved prior to the nineteenth century—a period of "cultural darkness" in Cuba—or of the flourishing of the "Cubanisms" that characterize the beginning of the nineteenth century and resulted in the appearance of the contredanse, Cuban theater, and folkloric chants. (Urfé, *Islas Magazine*.)

Giro, Radamés. Guitar player and musicologist. Born 30 July 1940, Santiago de Cuba. Started studying music in his hometown and continued at the School for Art Instructors in Havana. Giro accompanied singers on his guitar and played with various groups. He became an outstanding editor of music books. He is the author of *Leo Brouwer y la guitarra en Cuba* (1986) and *Heitor Villa-lobos: Una sensibilidad americana* (1990). He has also made several compilations of articles on Cuban music.

Gloria Matancera, Conjunto. Created by the singer Juan Manuel Diaz in Matanzas in 1929. Initially a septet, on moving to Havana in 1931, it was expanded into a *conjunto*. It is still active, playing popular dance music. Its most outstanding members have been the singers Roberto Sánchez and Cheo Junco.

Gómez, Graciano. Writer and singer of *trova* songs. Born 28 February 1895, Havana; died 22 May 1980. At age fourteen, studied flute with Professor Máximo del Castillo. Later, he studied guitar with the Mexican, Ramón Donadio. In 1912 Gómez formed a quartet with Floro Zorrilla, Miguel Zavalla, and Juan Cruz. In the 1920s he sang and played guitar at the Vista Alegre Café, a place popular with Havana's musicians. In 1929 he founded the group Matancero, which toured the Caribbean and recorded for the RCA Victor record company. He led the resident group at the Plaza Hotel from 1930 to 1934 and performed in New York in 1938. In the 1940s Gómez sang at the Montmartre Cabaret with the Cuarteto Selecto, whose other members were Barbarito Diez, Isaac Oviedo, and Rolando Scott. He transposed poems to music, especially those by Sánchez Galarraga. He toured Cuba under the sponsorship of the National Council for Culture, giving popular music concerts with his Quinteto Típico. He composed "Cita en tinieblas" and "Yo sé de una mujer" (*canciones*); "En falso" (bolero); "Flores" (*criolla*); "Habanera ven" (*guajira*); and "Crocante maní" (*pregón*: street vendor's cry).

Gómez, Pedro. Songwriter and singer. Born 27 January 1932, Gibara. Studied music with his father, Olavo Gómez, in whose band he began performing as a singer. Pedro Gómez settled in Guantánamo in 1951, then moved to Holguín, where he sang with the Banda Hermanos Avilés. In 1972 he moved to Santiago de Cuba, where he continued performing. He wrote the *son* pieces "Calle Enramada," "Mi viejo barrio," "Mi tierra montuna," and "Son del Guacanayabo."

Gómez, Rafael ("Teofilito"). Composer. Born 20 April 1889, Sancti Spiritus; died 1971. Known in the music business world as "Teofilito," after his father, the violinist Teófilo Gómez. Besides guitar, he also plays flute, clarinet, double bass, accordion, and bell. In 1919 he became a member of the Philharmanic Association Los Lirios, aimed at diffusing and developing music in Sancti Spiritus. As a young man, he conducted and composed pieces for the choir to perform during Christmas celebrations in Jesús María, a neighborhood of Sancti Spiritus. He played clarinet in the Sancti Spiritus Music Band in his hometown and wrote *trova* songs, including his best-known, "Pensamiento." He also wrote "Temo al olvido," "Si volvieras a mí," "Ayer pensando en ti," and "No sé por qué," plus the *danzón* "Nenita I," with instrumentation by Antonio María Romeu. He performed at *trova* concerts, leading the Trío Pensamiento, whose other members were Miguelito Companioni and Augusto Ponte.

Gómez, Tito. Singer. Born 1920, Havana. Sang all genres of popular Cuban music. Tito started performing in 1939 with the Sevilla Baltimore Band, and for decades was lead singer with the Riverside Orchestra, a *jazzband* that became enormously popular through performances on radio, television, and at theaters and nightclub cabarets. He later sang with the Orquesta Jorrín before going solo. He has recorded many LPs. Gómez adds a personal, Cuban flavor to the *canciones*, *sones*, and *guarachas* in his repertoire.

Gómez, Zoila. Musicologist and teacher. Born 6 October 1948, Havana. Studied at the Amadeo Roldán Conservatory; plays organ and piano. Gómez also studied at the Center for Popular Music in Havana. She carried out postgraduate studies in musicology and the history of Cuban music at the Higher Institute of Art. She won the biography award at the Pablo Hernández Balaguer Contest, sponsored by the National Council for Culture in 1974, for her paper on Amadeo Roldán. She works at the Editorial Arte y Literatura as head of the art section.

Gómez Cairo, Jesús. Musicologist. Born 26 October 1949, Jagüey Grande. Studied at the National School of Art, and later at the Leningrad Institute of Music and Theater in the USSR. Back in Cuba, Gómez Cairo taught at the Higher Institute of Art. He has published essays and articles on Cuban music, and has delivered lectures and talks both in Cuba and overseas.

Gómez Labraña, Jorge. Pianist. Born 10 November 1942, Barcelona, Spain. At age nine, moved to Cuba with his family. In 1952 Gómez Labraña started studying music with Professor Caridad Mezquida at the Peyrellade Conservatory. In 1959 he headed for Paris to study piano. In 1962 he traveled to Hungary to continue his piano studies. Since his return to Cuba, he has played numerous concerts all over the island. He teaches at the National School of Art and is secretary of the music section of the Writers and Artists Union of Cuba. He attended the Bartok Seminar, in Budapest. He is one of Cuba's most highly qualified pianists.

Gómez Pírez, Rubén. Pianist and teacher. Born 10 May 1918, Matanzas. Studied music with Esther del Castillo; later played piano with several popular music bands. Gómez Pírez pursued advanced music studies with maestro Justo Ojanguren. He performed as a piano accompanist in Havana. From 1962 onward, he was pianist with the Matanzas Symphony Orchestra, which he later conducted for some time. He was also director of the Matanzas Vocational School of Music. Today, he plays piano with the Matanzas Lyric Group. He has written *canciones*, waltzes, short preludes, and symphonic pieces.

Gonitch, Mariana de. Singing teacher. Born 5 February 1900, Saint Petersburg; died 14 January 1993, Havana. Has sung opera all over the world, with figures as outstanding as Chaliapin and Tito Schippa. Gonitch settled in Cuba in 1943, and made an important contribution to Cuba's culture by training many of today's best Cuban singers.

González, Alfredo. MC at musical events and *trova* singer. Born 1895, Havana; died 1979. Started singing at parties and other gatherings in 1915, alongside Manuel Corona, Rafael Enrizo, and others. González later opened the famous Peña de Sirique at his El Cerro home, which was frequented by enthusiasts of traditional music for over half a century. In 1935 he sang with the Cuarteto Vueltabajero. For years, he organized regular gatherings of musicians at Havana's Central Park, which were attended nightly by Sindo Garay, Hilarión Cabrisas, Nené Rizo, and Manuel Corona, among other musicians. In 1962 the Peña reopened in his mechanic's workshop, where popular music lovers met every Sunday amidst his working tools.

González, Benito ("Roncona"). Rumba dancer, musician, singer. Born end of the nineteenth century, Jovellanos; died 1950, Havana. As a young man, González engaged in activities organized by rumba groups. Nicknamed "Roncona," he was a very funny and extremely popular figure. He later settled in Havana and with the encouragement of Amado Trinidad joined the folk music shows on radio RHC

Cadena Azul, playing percussion and singing rumbas. He wrote the Afro-Cuban piece "Lamento de un congo real."

González, Berto. Troubadour. Born 1 November 1916, Santa Clara. Learned to play the guitar and started his musical career as a *trova* singer on Havana radio, under the name "El trovador tropical" (the tropical troubadour). González sang traditional Cuban songs. He has lived in Miami since 1972.

González, Celina. Singer. Born 16 March 1929, Jovellanos. As a child, moved to Santiago de Cuba with her family. At the age of sixteen, González took up singing Cuban *punto* (popular country music) in a duo with Reutilio Domínguez (b. 1927, Guantánamo) on the radio station Cadena Oriental de Radio. The pairing become very popular. In 1948 Celina and Reutilio landed a contract with Radio Cadena Suaritos, in Havana, and later with Cadena Azul and other radio stations. They also performed in a number of films, including *Rincón criollo* and *Bella, la salvaje* and toured several Latin American countries. In 1964 the duo stopped performing and Celina appeared as a solo singer of country music. Reutilio died in 1971 in Guantánamo. Celina sings on the radio and on television. She regularly tours abroad, singing duets with her son, the singer Lázaro Reutilio. The Celina y Reutilio duo wrote *son montuno* compositions such as "Que viva Changó" and "Yo soy el punto cubano," which are still popular today.

González, Celio. Singer. Born 29 January 1924, Camajuaní. Spent some time in Camagüey, then settled in Havana. González sang with the groups Jóvenes del Cayo, Luis Santí, and Sonora Matancera, before going solo. In 1959 he traveled to Mexico

City on a contract with the Odeon record company and settled there. He has frequently performed on radio and television and at theaters and nightclubs, and has recorded several LPs. An outstanding bolero singer, he has also sung almost all genres of Cuban popular music.

González, Enrique ("La Pulga"). Songwriter and singer of popular music. Born 1890, Santiago de Cuba; died 1 January 1957. Was a member of vocal groups with Ñico Saquito and others. González wrote *canciones*, boleros, *guajiras*, and *guarachas*. His music is cheerful, funny, and very Cuban. Among his best-known songs are "Injusta duda" and "Lupina."

González, Félix. Leader of dance orchestra, composer, ophicleide player. Born 1887, Madruga; died 1967, Havana. At age sixteen, González started studying music in his hometown with Professor Ramos. In 1894 he played typical Cuban music in the bands of various towns around Havana while continuing to work as a shoe repairer. In 1896 he moved to the capital to resume his ophicleide studies under the direction of Tomás Olivera, and joined Enrique Peña's band when it was founded in the early years of the Republic. In 1915 González set up his own group. He was founding president of the Musical Casino Society. With his band consisting of eleven musicians, he recorded for RCA Victor and Columbia Records and played at dances all over the island. His wind ensemble has been active longer than any other in the country—for fifty-two years. He composed numerous *danzones*.

González, Fernando. Singer. Born 20 March 1927, Santiago de las Vegas. Started out as singer with the group Conjunto X and later sang with La Sonora band. Between 1948 and 1950 González performed in Spain with Avilés's band Gong, then back in Cuba, he joined Ernesto Duarte's group. He was later a member of Rumbavana and Casino. He has recorded various boleros and also sung solo.

González, Hilario. Composer, pianist, teacher, researcher. Born 24 January 1920, Havana; died c. 2000. Studied piano with Jasha Fischermann, and harmony first with José Ardévol and then in Venezuela with Vicente Emilio Sojo and Anthony de Blois Carreño. With the latter, he also studied counterpoint and fugue. González also took a short conducting course with Serguin Celibidache and studied choir conducting with Angel Sauce. He conducted the Coral de Venezuela and formed a youth orchestra that helped disseminate Esteban Salas's music in that country. While living in Caracas, between 1947 and 1960, he taught piano at the Music Preparatory School and was head of production at the National Popular Theater, where he wrote the music for *Hernani*, *Esperando al zurdo*, *El juez de los divorcios*, and other plays. In 1960 he returned to Cuba, where he taught piano at the Amadeo Roldán Conservatory and the Center for Popular Music. He was a founding member of the Grupo de Renovación Musical, which he left after various disagreements. He has written articles on music and art for several Cuban publications, particularly the UNEAC magazine, *Gaceta del Caribe*. He worked as a music researcher at the National Museum of Music. His compositions include: Three preludes in conga (1933); Two danzas (1938); Sonata in A minor (1942); Suite of Cuban canciones, for singer and orchestra (1943); Concerto in D (premiered with the Havana Chamber Music Orchestra, conducted by José Ardévol, with the composer on piano); *Sinfonía*, concerto for piano and orchestra (1946); *Antes del alba* (ballet; premiered by the Pro-Musical Art Society with choreography by Alberto Alonso, stage decoration by Carlos Enríquez and with Alicia Alonso in the leading role; 1947); "Las puertas abiertas" (with lyrics by Augusto Rodríguez Barroso, 1964); *Los zapaticos de rosa* (mini-opera performed a capella and based on a poem by José Martí); and also more than seventy lieder, among them those based on poems by José Martí (some premiered by the National Symphony Orchestra, conducted by Roberto Sánchez Ferrer with soprano singer Iris Burguet), and by Nicolás Guillén, Roberto Fernández Retamar, Fayad Jamís, Antonio Machado, Emilio Ballagas, Baudelaire, Cintio Vitier, Leopoldo Lugones, and Dante Alighieri.

González, Jorge Antonio. Journalist and researcher into Cuba's lyric theater. Born 24 August 1912, Havana. González has published the book *Operas cubanas y sus autores* and the first volume of *Historia del teatro habanero*. He has written for several magazines and wrote the *Pequeña enciclopedia del ballet en Cuba* and *La composición operística en Cuba*. He worked for fifteen years at the information center for the National Council for Culture.

González, Joseíto. Pianist, arranger, bandleader. Born 1 November 1940, Matanzas; died 3 April 1997, Havana. At age four, moved to Marianao with his family. González studied piano at the Marianao Municipal Conservatory. In 1954 he formed the group Ritmo y Melodía. He later played the piano with Mario Fernández's band and led the resident orchestras at the cabarets in the Riviera and Capri hotels. In 1968 he became leader of the group Rumbavana. In 1988 he took over the lead of Orquesta Riverside. He was an outstanding arranger of popular Cuban music.

González, Juan de Marcos. Musical director, arranger, *tres* guitarist. Born 1954, Havana. At the beginning of the 1980s González founded the septet Sierra Maestra, which brought about a rebirth of traditional *son*. In 1996 he formed the Afro-Cuban All Stars, which brought together a group of legendary Cuban musicians, many in retirement. In 1997 he received a Grammy award for his work on the *Buena Vista Social Club* record.

González, Manolín. Singer and composer. Born 1956, Guantánamo. Studied medicine and for this reason is known as the "salsa doctor." He plays guitar and in his early career as a singer performed mostly *nueva trova*. He is the son of the *guajira* singer Fefita Hernández. He performs with an excellent group. His song compositions include "Una aventura loca," "Arriba de la bola," "A pagar allá," and others in Cuba's new salsa-timba style.

González, Maruja. Soprano. Born 1904, Mérida, Mexico. When she was one year old, her father died and her mother returned to Cuba and registered her as a Cuban citizen. González was an outstanding member of Ernesto Lecuona's Company, with which she premiered numerous Cuban zarzuelas and toured many Latin American and European countries. She sang in many Spanish zarzuelas and was very successful in theaters in Spain with zarzuelas and operettas. Her last official performance was in 1965, in San Juan, Puerto Rico. She now resides in the United States.

González, Mundito. Singer. Born 1948, Bayamo. His given name is Edmundo, but he is known as "Mundito" in the music business. González started his singing career in his hometown in 1963. After living in Santiago de Cuba for some time, he settled in Havana, where he sang at shows and cabarets, on the radio, television, and at theaters. He has toured Mexico, Costa Rica, Venezuela, and Colombia.

González, Neno. Pianist and songwriter. Born 20 August 1903, Havana; died 8 June 1986. Son of pianist Luis González, who taught him music. In 1924 Neno González formed his own charanga band, which he led for over four decades. In 1932 the band was noted for its excellence with danzonete, fronted by the singer Paulina Alvarez. The band also performed danzones, boleros, and cha-cha-chás. González wrote the dances "Improntu" and "Contratiempos," the danzones "Circunstancial" and "Mi danzón," and the canciones, "Al fin llegaste" and "Calladas razones."

González, Nicolás (El Güinero). Clarinet player. Born (?), Güines; died 1892. Already by 1837 El Güinero was an outstanding clarinetist. He was a teacher and director of the firemen's band in Güines, his hometown, and founder and director of a popular dance band. He was decorated in 1881 by King Alfonso XII for his artistic merits.

González, Orquesta de Félix. An orquesta típica, or wind orchestra, formed by the ophiclenic player and composer Félix González in Havana, 1915. In its heyday, it also included Alfredo Garcia (cornet), Dolores Betancourt (trombone), José Belén Puig (clarinet), José Urfé (clarinet), Miguel Angel Mendieta (violin), Benito Moya (violin), Guillermo Maherve (double bass), Demetrio Pacheco (timbales), and Ulpiano Diaz (güiro). This orchestra recorded several LPs.

The ensemble performed for fifty-two years, longer than any other band of the same type, and only folded after the death of its director, Félix González, in 1967.

González, Orquesta de Neno. French charanga group created by the pianist Luis Gonzalez, known as "Neno," in Havana, 1926. Its earliest lineup included Belizario Lopez (flute), Alfredo Urzais (violin), Fernando Urzais (double bass), Federico Gonzalez (drums), Primitivo Guerra (timbales), Eladio Diaz (güiro), and Neno González (piano). Later, José Antonio Diaz replaced Belizario Lopez on flute. During the 1930s, the band became popular for playing danzonete and because Paulina Alvarez was its vocalist. The following musicians were also members: José Raymant (flute), Carlos del Castillo (violin), Pedro López (double bass), Angel López (timbales), Juan Febles (güiro), and Neno González. The orchestra is still active, now directed by Neno's son Carlos González, and it plays mainly cha-cha-chás and features new musicians.

González, Orquesta de Nicolás. Orquesta típica, or wind orchestra, formed in the 1850s in Güines by the clarinetist Nicolás González, who is known as "El Güinero." They played at dances in Güines and in Havana Province. When González died in 1892, the clarinetist José Travieso became the director, but the group split up a few years later.

González, Rubén. Pianist. Born 26 May 1919, Santa Clara; died 8 December 2003. At the age of six, he moved to Encrucijada with his family. González studied in Cienfuegos with Amparo Rizo, and back in Santa Clara, graduated as a schoolteacher. He completed four years of medicine at the University of Havana, then moved into music, starting as a pianist with groups from his province. In 1940 he settled in Havana, where he played with Paulina Alvarez's and Paulín's charanga bands, and also with the band led by Arsenio Rodríguez, as well as with Kubavana, Senén Suárez's combo, and the jazzbands Siboney and Orquesta Riverside. In the 1950s he worked with Orquesta América, Jorrín, and the CMQ. He performed in Venezuela between 1957 and 1961. He has toured Latin American countries and recorded an LP of piano instrumentals. He was recently enormously successful all over the world with his recording of the

Buena Vista Social Club and the *Afro-Cuban All Stars* albums, and with his solo albums *Introducing . . . Rubén González* (1997) and *Chanchullo* (2000). He appeared in the Wim Wenders film *The Buena Vista Social Club*.

Mo Fini

González, Sara. Singer of *nueva trova*. Born 1951, Havana. In 1966 González started studying viola at the Amadeo Roldán Conservatory; she could already play the guitar. She joined the *nueva trova* movement in 1971, and then the Grupo de Experimentación Sonora, sponsored by the Cuban Institute for Movie-Making, Art, and Industry. She has written many songs, the most outstanding of which is "La victoria" (about the American invasion on Playa Girón—the Bay of Pigs). She has composed music for poems by José Martí. She has performed in Italy, Mexico, and other countries.

González, Vinicio. Trumpet player, flutist, composer. Born 2 February, 1922, Santiago de las Vegas; died 4 January 1994, Havana. Studied music with Edmundo Escalante. González played with the bands Azul Tropical, the Astros de René Alvarez, Niágara, Diablo Rojo, Nueva América, Kubavana, and Jóvenes del Cayo. He later led the band Emoción. He wrote the *son* pieces "En el mes de mayo," "Oye, vanidosa," and "El chivo," and the *cha-cha-chá* "Los quince."

González, Virgilio. Songwriter. Born 27 November 1907, San Luis; died 14 October 1985, Havana. *Tres* guitar player and double bassist with several septets, including El Rojo. González was a composer of many popular songs, including the bolero-*son* pieces "Clara," "Le dije a una rosa," and "No me persigas"; the *pregones* "El caramelero" and "El manguero"; the *son* "Rompe saragüey"; and the *guaracha* "La ola marina."

González Abreu, Leonardo. Violinist and composer. Born 19 June 1706, Laguna de Tenerife, Canary Islands; died at the end of the eighteenth century, Santiago de Cuba. González Abreu settled in Santiago de Cuba as a very young man and went on to marry a local harpist, Bernarda Rodríguez Rojas. Their family would be entirely devoted to music for several generations. He wrote *seguidillas*, boleros, and Christmas carols, and played a prominent role in the organization of popular music events in Santiago de Cuba.

González Allué, Jorge. Pianist, composer, orchestra conductor. Born 10 February 1910, Camagüey. As a child, González Allué studied piano under the direction of a female cousin and later with professor María Larín. At the age of fifteen, he graduated from the National Conservatory where he had studied piano, harmony, and musical theory. He has taught music. In 1935 he founded a *jazzband*. He has studied Cuban and Latin American musical folklore, and has presented shows of folk music, given piano concerts, and toured several Latin American cities at the head of his band. He has adapted two music poems by Nicolás Guillén and written songs and scores for orchestra. He works as a pianist in Camagüey.

González Mántici, Enrique. Orchestra conductor, violinist, composer. Born 4 November 1912, Sagua la Grande; died 29 December 1974, Havana. Started studying music with his mother; then studied violin with José Valls. González Mántici later studied composition under the direction of Rafael Castro and Emilio Grenet, and conducting under Erich Kleiber. He took courses in violin and conducting at the Tchaikovsky Conservatory with the maestros Anosov, Gauk, and Guinsburg. He played the first violin in the Havana Symphony Orchestra and the Havana Quartet and conducted the orchestra of the radio station Radio Mil Diez. He was the founding director of the Radio CMQ orchestra. He was also the musical director of the Pro-Musical Art Society and director of the orchestra that accompanied the National Cuban Ballet. He founded the National Institute of Music. In 1951 he conducted the Symphony Orchestras of Leipzig and Berlin and the orchestra of USSR Radio. Three years later, he toured South America with the Cuban Ballet and conducted the leading orchestras in Santiago de Chile, Buenos Aires, and Uruguay. In 1961 he was appointed conductor of the newly created National Symphony Orchestra. In 1962, he was honorary guest at the Tchaikovsky International Contest in Moscow. In 1964 he was a member of the violin jury at the Enescu Contest, in Bucarest. In 1963 he toured the Soviet Union and China as a conductor and performed at the head of the Leningrad Symphonic-Philharmonic Orchestra, of the Symphony Orchestra on Moscow Radio, and of orchestras from Armenia, Georgia, Baku, and the Peking Central Symphony Orchestra. He also performed in Poland, the German Democratic Republic, Romania, Hungary, and Bulgaria, and accompanied soloists such as David Oistrav, Leonich Koga, Mtislav Rostropovich, Evelio and Cecilio Tieles. He taught orchestral practice at the National School of Art. Among his most outstanding pieces are First concerto for violin and orchestra (1953); Pregón and danza for orchestra (1954); Second concerto for violin and orchestra (1957); Three pieces for piano; Cimarrón (for Alberto Alonso's dance company); Guerrillero (a march, 1960); Tríptico vocal, for soprano and piano (with his lyrics); Concert symphony for cello and orchestra; Tríptico, for string orchestra; Trio for clarinet, oboe, and bassoon; El circo and Mestiza (ballet based on "Cecilia Valdés," 1966); and Obertura Cuba.

González Rojas, Luis. Pianist. Born 1 December 1931, Rancho Boyeros. Studied piano at Carmen González's Academy, then at the Hubert de Blanck Conservatory, and finally at the Juilliard School of Music in New York. Back in Cuba in 1959, González Rojas taught at the Alejandro García Caturla Conservatory, in Marianao. He performed with the National Symphony Orchestra in several European countries. As of 1967 he has continued his musical career in the United States and has since given concerts in various cities around the world. He teaches piano at the University of Missouri.

González Rubiera, Vicente ("Guyún"). Guitarist and harmony teacher. Born 27 October 1908, Santiago de Cuba; died, 1987, Havana. Started studying guitar in his hometown under the direction of Pepe Banderas and Sindo Garay. During the 1930s, in Havana, Guyún became the most outstanding performer of vocal and instrumental Cuban and Latin American music. His sons were accomplished guitar accompanists, and he trained many pupils who would eventually form a Cuban school of popular guitar. He wrote a valuable book, La guitarra: Su técnica y armonía, in which he describes a new technique that recommends the use of the little finger of the right hand and the thumb of the left hand to achieve fuller harmonies. In transcribing works for guitar, he has devised a novel system. He also wrote the Diccionario de acordes and Un nuevo panorama de la modulación y su técnica, in which he does away with the prevailing criteria about so-called distant tonalities; neither book has been published. He was highly praised by Andrés Segovia during his visit in Cuba. He was a teacher at the Popular Music Center and with the Society of Cuban Composers, and technical adviser at the School for Art Teachers. He taught aesthetics and the psychology of harmony.

Gonzalo, Miguel de. Singer. Born (?), Santiago de Cuba; died 13 November 1975, Havana. Performed for some time as an amateur singer in his hometown before joining the Orfeón Cuba choir. Around 1940 Gonzalo settled in Havana, where he joined Armando Valdespí's band. He sang on the radio stations Mil Diez, RHC Cadena Azul, and CMQ, and eventually on practically all of the country's radio and television stations, as well as in theaters. He is considered to be one of the forefathers of the fílin movement, which began in the 1940s.

Gramatges, Harold. Composer, pianist, teacher. Born 26 September 1918, Santiago de Cuba. Started studying piano under the direction of Dulce María Serret at the Provincial Conservatory of Oriente; then under Flora Mora at the Havana Municipal Conservatory, where he also studied harmony, composition, aesthetics, and music history with Amadeo Roldán and José Ardévol. In 1942 Gramatges traveled to the United States to study at the Berkshire Music Center, under the direction of Aaron Copland and Serge Koussevisky. In 1945 he founded and directed the orchestra at the Havana Municipal Conservatory, where he also taught harmony, composition, aesthetics, and music history from 1944 to 1958. In 1958 his Symphony in E won him the Reichold Prize for the Caribbean and Central America, awarded by the Detroit Orchestra. He was a member of the Grupo de Renovación Musical and president of the Nuestro Tiempo cultural society from its foundation in 1951 until 1960. He attended a congress of the Inter-American Music Association in Mexico and the Stockholm Peace Congress in 1958. After the Revolution, he was appointed adviser to the music department of the General Section for Culture and participated in the reform of music teaching systems and in the creation of the National Symphony Orchestra. In 1959 he was a member of the music jury at the World Festival of Youth and Students held in Vienna. Between 1961 and 1964 he was Cuban ambassador to France. From 1965 to 1970 he headed the music department at Casa de las Américas. In 1970 he was appointed adviser to the national music section of the National Council for Culture. He has written works for mixed choir and solo singers based on texts by Juan Ramón Jiménez, Góngora, Rafael Alberti, and Justo Rodríguez Santos (1940–1942), and also *Icaro*, for percussion and piano (a ballet commissioned by Alicia Alonso); Sonata for piano (1943); Duo for flute and piano; Trio for clarinet, cello, and piano (1944); Prelude for the ballet *Mensaje al futuro* (1944); Symphony in E (1945); Capriccio for flute, clarinet, viola, and cello (1945); Concertino for piano and wind instruments (1945); Serenade for string orchestra (1947); "Dos danzas cubanas" (*son montuno*, 1948); Sinfonietta for orchestra (1955); *Tríptico*, for singer and piano (with words by José Martí, 1957); Quintet for wind instruments (1957); Divertimento for brass quartet (1957); Tocata for large concertina (1961); *In Memoriam* (a tribute to Frank País, 1961); *La muerte del guerrillero*, for reciting actor and orchestra (1968); Motive I for piano (1969); Motive II for flute, horn, celesta piano, vibraphone, xylophone, and percussion (1970); Cantata for Abel (1973); Concerto for guitar and orchestra (1974); and *Diseños* (1976). In 1997 he was awarded the Tomás Luis de Victoria Prize in Spain.

Granda, Bienvenido. Singer. Born 30 August 1915, Havana; died 9 July 1983, Mexico City. Started singing Cuban popular music as a child, and performed on the Havana radio stations CMQ, RHC Cadena Azul, Radio Cadena Suaritos, and Radio Progreso. Granda sang with the Septeto Nacional and the Hermanos Martínez jazzband, then joined La Sonora Matancera, with whom he worked for many years until he went solo. He performed in Colombia and Central American countries before settling in Mexico City. Though he performed in various Cuban and Caribbean styles, his speciality was bolero, to which he brought a characteristic originality, style, and timbre.

Grandy, Miguel de. Lyric theater director and tenor. Born 29 September 1909, Havana; died 18 January 1988, Miami. Made his debut presentation as a lyric singer in 1927 at the Havana Regina theater with Ernesto Lecuona's *Alma de raza*. Grandy later performed in several zarzuelas written by Lecuona: *María la O*, *Rosa la china*, *La de Jesús María*, *La Plaza de la Catedral*, and *Lola Cruz*, as well as *Cecilia Valdés* by Gonzalo Roig and Amalia Batista Prats. He premiered several operettas in Cuba and gave an outstanding performance in *La viuda alegre*. He toured Latin American countries and Spain as both a tenor and an actor. He was the first Latin American lyric singer to record with RCA records. He has directed countless Cuban plays. In 1973 he settled in the United States. His last performance as a singer was in 1976, in the zarzuela *Luisa Fernanda* in New York, and his last work as a director was in Miami, in 1987.

Grenet, Eliseo. Composer, pianist, orchestra conductor. Born 12 June 1893, Havana; died 4 December 1950. At the age of five, he began studying piano; at nine, he premiered his own musical revue *La geografía física* at a school party; and at thirteen, he played piano at La Caricatura, a silent movie theater. At sixteen, Grenet conducted the orchestra at the Havana Politeama. In 1926 he toured the country as head of the orchestra that played for the Arquímedes Pous Company. Later, he traveled to several Latin American countries with a group of musicians. In 1932, a few months after returning to Cuba, he was forced to leave the country because he was being persecuted by henchmen in the service of tyrannical President Gerardo Machado. He returned to Havana after the downfall of the Machado regime, a year later. In 1936 he left for New York, where he contributed to the dissemination of Cuban music there, and introduced the Cuban conga. From New York, he traveled to France, Spain, and other European countries, and returned to Cuba some time later. He wrote scores for the films *Escándalo de estrellas*, *Conga bar*, *Estampas coloniales*, and *Milonga de arrabal*, and for many theater plays, including *Niña Rita*, *La canción del mendigo*, *Bohemia*, *Como las golondrinas*, *La virgen morena*, and *El submarino cubano*. He also adapted the poems of Nicolás Guillén to music in the work *Motivos del son*. In 1948 he won First Prize at the Cuban Song Contest for "El sitierito." Among his most outstanding musical compositions are the *danzón* pieces "La mora," "Si me pides el pesca'o," "Si muero en la carretera," and "Papá Montero"; the *canciones* "Las perlas de tu boca," "Tabaco verde," and "Lamento esclavo"; the *pregones* "Rica pulpa" and "El tamalero"; the *congo-tangos* "Espa-bílate" and "Mamá Inés"; the *son* pieces "Facundo," "Lamento cubano," and "Negro Bembón"; and, perhaps most prominently, the *sucu-sucus*, which were his re-creation of folk songs from the Isle of Youth, "Felipe Blanco" and "Domingo Pantoja."

Grenet, Emilio. Composer. Born 1908, Havana; died 1941. Brother to Eliseo and Ernesto Grenet. Emilio wrote "Sabia ausencia" (*canción*), "La torrecilla" (*pregón*), and "Curujey," "Vito Manué," "Yambambó," and "Quirino con su tres" (*son* pieces). In the latter, he added music to the poems by Nicolás Guillén. In 1939 he published the book *Música popular cubana*. In 1930 he lost his left arm and leg as a result of an attack by a shark as he swam at the Havana shore. He traveled to Spain and France. He also composed the choral piece *Maracas y bongó*.

Grillo, Frank. *See* Machito.

Gris, Orquesta. French *charanga* band created by the composer and pianist Armando Valdés Torres in Havana, 1930. Miguel Valdés (violin), Antonio Arcano (flute), Severo Safora (double bass), Rafael Blanco (timbales), Oscar Pelegrín (*güiro*), and Fernando Collazo (vocalist) were also part of the band. Later, new musicians joined the orchestra: Cecilio Vergara (*güiro*), Aurelio Herrera (flute), Mario Jiménez (vocalist), Nilo Espinosa (violin),

Luisito Valdés (vocalist), Iván Hernández (conga), Rodolfo O'Farrill (cello), and Gerardo Pedroso (vocalist). The group split up in the 1950s.

guaguancó group. One of three subtypes (*yambú*, *guaguancó*, *columbia*) of the rumba music groups. Guaguancós appeared in the early nineteenth century. The group is organized simply, comprising musicians that play a *cajón*, a small candle box, spoons, and claves—or, slightly more elaborately, conga drums of various sizes and pitches, a *tumba* and *quinto*, spoons, and claves. An essential feature of this style of ensemble is one or two improvising singers.

guaguancó music. *See* rumba.

guajira, música. Genre of Cuban song similar to the *criolla*. Its lyrics deal with country situations in an idyllic, bucolic manner. The songs use rhyming stanzas, almost always following the pattern of Cuban *décima* poetry. It is characterized by a combination of 3/4 and 6/8 rhythm patterns. Its first section is written in a minor key, its second in a major key, and it always ends above the dominant of the tone in which it is written (Sánchez de Fuentes, *El folklor en la música cubana*, 56). Aside from its original meaning, the term *guajira* also has been used since the middle of the twentieth century to refer to dance compositions in slow 4/4 time that fuse elements of the *son* and the *guajira*.

guamo. *See* fotuto.

Guanche, Gerardo D. Band musician. Born 24 September 1889; died 13 August 1961. Music teacher and clarinet player. He was a member of the Guanabacoa Municipal Academy and the Guanabacoa Music Band.

Guapachá. *See* Borcelá, Amado.

guapachá music. A variant of *guaracha* that reached its peak during the 1960s. *See also* Borcelá, Amado.

guaracha. A genuine Cuban style of song and dance whose origins are found in the confluence of African and Spanish musical elements. Originally an element of typically Cuban nineteenth-century comic theater (*bufo*), it later moved into the dance halls. Throughout the nineteenth century, the *guaracha*'s structure, comprising couplet and refrain, led to a new format characterized by a solo singing section, followed by a response from a chorus. It eventually lost its alternation and was merged with the forms of binary songs (Leon, *Música folklórica cubana*, 88). Rhythmically, *guaracha* exhibits a series of rhythm combinations: 6/8 with 2/4. Its lyrics are, in general, picaresque, burlesque, and satirical, mirroring the atmosphere of the time and dealing with popular affairs or humorous events.

Guaracheros de Oriente. Quartet founded by Ñico Saquito, first voice and maraca player, along with Florencio Santana ("Picolo") on second voice and guitar; Gerardo Macías ("El Chino"), third voice and guitar; and timbales player Félix Escobar, known as "El gallego." From 1940 onward, they started appearing on radio shows and at theaters and nightclubs in Havana, performing *guarachas* and *son* pieces in the style of the eastern provinces. They have toured almost all of Latin America. Ñico Saquito left the group in 1955, and the rest of the group continued as a trio. They settled in the United States in 1959, and in 1962 moved to Puerto Rico.

guataca. A metal blade of a hoe, used as a percussion instrument in the Afro-Cuban rituals of Arará and Congo groups, among others. The blade is held between the thumb and the forefinger by the hole left by the hoe handle and is struck with a metal stick. *See also* hierro.

Güel, Luisa Maria. Popular singer and songwriter. Born 1940, Havana. Made her debut on radio and television and at theaters in the Cuban capital dur-

ing the 1960s. In 1968 Güel left for Spain, where she continued her artistic career. She was winner of the First Prize at the Malaga Song Festival, where she sang Manuel Alejandro's "No me vuelvo a enamorar." She toured various Latin American countries and the United States. She was awarded First Prize at the Edith Piaf contest in France and has recorded numerous LPs.

Guerra, Digna. Choir conductor. Born 6 August, 1945, Havana. Studied at the Havana Municipal Conservatory. Guerra conducted the choir at the Cuban Institute of Radio and Television. She later studied at the Berlin Higher School of Music in the German Democratic Republic. At present she conducts the National Choir, where she has played a decisive role in the spread of knowledge of both Cuban and international choral music. She teaches at the Higher Institute of Art and is head of the music department at Cuban Television.

Guerra, Georgia. Soprano and singing teacher. Born 23 April 1940, Havana. Studied since the age of eight with her mother, Carmen Valdés, and later with José Ardévol. Guerra sang in choral groups and studied vocal technique with the Colombian bass singer Luis Forero. In 1959 the Cuban Revolutionary Government granted her a scholarship to New York, where she studied at the Juilliard Academy and at the Julius Hart School. Back in Cuba in 1960, she started performing as a soloist, singing a varied repertoire that ranged from classical vocal music and opera to Latin American and Cuban pieces. She has taught at the National Theater and has trained many popular music singers. She perfected her technique under the direction of Mariana de Gonitch. She is specifically devoted to chamber music and now performs as a soloist.

Guerra, Gratilio. Composer. Born 2 July 1834, Santiago de Cuba; died 5 March 1896. Studied music in his hometown and later moved to Havana, where he lived for several years. Guerra played the piano and organ and was choirmaster at the Santiago de Cuba Cathedral. Most of his work is sacred music—masses, litanies, psalms, anthems, antiphonies, and lessons for requiem masses. His Danzas for piano are among the scarce secular music that has been preserved. It is often said that his style carries an Italian influence, but Viennese classicism is also present in his pieces. Guerra taught piano and was a conductor. He returned to his native city of Santiago de Cuba after his stay in Havana.

Guerra, Jesús. Songwriter. Born 20 February 1920, Cienfuegos; died 31 January 1995, Alicante, Spain. Guerra wrote *guarachas* that were very popular in the 1940s. They include "A mí qué," "Bigote de gato," "Dónde vas María," and also the *cha-cha-chás* "Tú verás," "Margot," "Baila Violeta"; and the *son* pieces "Un meneíto namá" and "Semilla de marañón." He settled in France in the 1950s and moved to Spain in 1985.

Guerra, Luis ("Tata"). Composer and percussionist. Born 9 June 1934, Guanabacoa. Guerra was a percussionist in a number of dance bands: Almendra, Cuban Swing, Sonora del Caribe, Los Melódicos, Aldemaro Romero, Chucho Sanoja, Porfi Jiménez, and Simon Diaz. In 1956 he moved to Colombia and since 1960 has lived in Venezuela. His compositions include "Son Matamoros," "Aché para todos," "Siete potencias," "De ti depende," "Son de la escopeta," "El gato y el ratón," "Mas feo que yo," and "Zapato viejo." He is percussionist in the trio Hermanos Rodríguez.

Guerra, Marcelino ("Rapindey"). Songwriter and guitarist. Born 1914, Cienfuegos; died 1996, Alicante, Spain. Around 1930, Guerra joined Ignacio Piñeiro's Septeto Nacional, and later was guitarist and second voice with various sextets, including Borgorellá's Sans Souci. His boleros and *son* compositions were very popular and were widely acclaimed and performed during the 1930s. He used lyrics

Tomás Casademunt

by Julio Blanco Leonard in his pieces. Outstanding among his compositions are the boleros "Se fue," "A mi manera," "Convergencia" (with lyrics by Bienvenido Gutiérrez), and "Quién será"; as well as the *son* pieces "Canto para ti," "Buscando la melodía," "Me voy pa'l pueblo," "Un lamento en las tinieblas," and "Pare cochero." He settled in New York many years ago, and has since moved to Spain.

Guerra, Orlando ("Cascarita"). Cuban popular music singer. Born 14 September 1920, Camagüey; died 1975, Mexico City. Made his debut as a singer in his hometown. In the 1940s, Guerra sang with Hermanos Palau and with Julio Cueva's bands in Havana and achieved huge popularity, particularly for his rendering of *guarachas*. He possessed a peculiar and graceful style and great skill at improvisation. His extravagant clothes and his catch-phrases hit the headlines more than once. After appearing for years in Cuban cabarets and on radio and TV, he left for Mexico City, where he continued his artistic career. He recorded countless hits and acted in several films.

Guerra, Rey. Guitarist. Born 1950, Santa Clara. Graduate of the Higher Institute of Art. Guerra started his career as a concert player in 1977 giving concerts throughout Cuba. He has performed as a soloist with the Havana and Matanzas Symphony Orchestras. He has successfully toured the United States, Poland, Cyprus, the Soviet Union, Sweden, Germany, Spain, Hungary, Holland, Greece, Italy, Czechoslovakia, Turkey, Yugoslavia, and Nicaragua. He has won various awards. He teaches at the Higher Institute of Art.

Guerrero, Enrique. Composer, songwriter, pianist, teacher. Born at the beginning of the nineteenth century, Havana; died 1887. Although he wrote several songs and *contradanzas* such as "La Kalunga" and "La que a ti te gusta," Guerrero achieved his greatest success with *guarachas*, of which he leaves behind wonderful examples. His lyrical themes were based on Havana's Afro-Cuban traditions. His popularity reached its height around the second half of the nineteenth century. He directed traditional Cuban comic theater companies, for which he wrote several pieces that were harshly criticized because of the bold expressions he used in them. In 1869 he wrote a clave song, "La Belén," for two singers, choir, and orchestra. Among his most outstanding *guarachas* are "La pluma de tu sombrero," "La prieta santa," and "Mi bandera cubana."

Guerrero, Félix. Composer and orchestra conductor. Born 13 January 1917, Havana. Started his musical studies with his father. Guerrero studied piano, harmony, and composition with César Pérez Sentenat, Pedro Sanjuán, and Amadeo Roldán, and also studied at the Juilliard School in New York. In 1952 he went to Paris, where he took lessons with Eugene Bigot and Nadia Boulanger. He conducts orchestras on radio and television and in theaters. He has taught at the García Caturla Conservatory. He also conducts orchestras accompanying ballet and opera performances. He has composed for piano and orchestra, and also scores for use in plays and with motion pictures. He has written Concerto for clarinet and orchestra; *Tríptico campesino*, for singer and orchestra; *Cuadros sonoros*, for horn and orchestra; *Suite cubanam*; and *Homenaje al Sóngoro cosongo*.

Guevara, Ofelio. Songwriter. Born 7 April 1941, Santiago de Cuba; died, 7 October 1973, Havana. Brother of Walfrido Guevara, with whom he cowrote many compositions. Ofelio wrote the lyrics to songs such as "No quiero matarte," "La canción del borracho," and "No puedo perdonarte." He wrote the *canción* "Aleida," as well as other *canciones* and boleros.

Guevara, Walfrido. Songwriter. Born 9 December 1916, Santiago de Cuba. During the 1930s, made his debut as a writer and singer of *trova* songs and *guarachas*. Walfrido Guevara formed a duo with Raúl Barbarú in Santiago de Cuba; then both settled in Havana in 1940, appearing subsequently on radio Mil Diez. He later sang successively with José Antonio Valentino and Santiago Fulleda, before forming a duo with Juvenal Quesada in 1947. He wrote the *canciones* and boleros "Un juramento de amor," "Derrotado corazón," "Canción del borracho," and "No quiero matarte"; the *son montuno* "Qué cinturita"; the *cha-cha-chá* "Bésala y cásate"; and many popular *guarachas*, such as "Qué buena es la nochebuena" and "Dengue con dengue." He now works as a guitar accompanist for the traditional *trova* trio Los

Idaídos, whose other members are Ida Laguardia and Antonio Rodríguez.

Guillot, Olga. Singer. Born 9 October 1925, Santiago de Cuba. At the age of five, Guillot moved to Havana with her family. She made her debut presentation at the age of nine, singing tangos. Soon after, she formed the Hermanas Guillot duo with her sister Ana Luisa, and they won a prize on the television contest *La corte suprema del arte*. She sang with Isolina Carrrillo's vocal group Siboney, with which she recorded her first hit, "Stormy Weather," in the mid-1940s. Olga Guillot sang solo on the radio stations Mil Diez, RHC Cadena Azul, and CMQ. She toured most Latin American and many European, Asian, and African countries. In 1964 she gave a gala concert at Carnegie Hall in New York and sang at the Paramount Theater on Broadway. She was also offered concerts at the Olympia Theater in Paris. She has won numerous awards and accolades, among them thirty gold records. She has recorded more than seventy LPs of unforgettable boleros. She took roles in movies and television soap operas. After residing for many years in Mexico City, she then moved to New York, and currently lives in Miami.

güiro. An instrument widely used in Cuban popular music that probably originated with the Bantu people, although Cuban aborigines may also have used it. It has also been called *calabazo* or *guayo*. It is a percussive idiophone made from the cylindrical fruit of the *güiro* (gourd), between 30 and 50 centimeters long, and about 10 centimeters in diameter, with a curved peduncle. It is held with the left hand, and the fingers (or sometimes just the thumb) are introduced through a hole on the back of the instrument. On its outer front surface are a number of equidistant parallel grooves, transverse to the axis

of the *güiro* and 1 or 2 millimeters deep. When a hard, thin stick is rapidly rubbed against these grooves, the stick jumps from one ridge to the other, successively striking them and producing a raspy sound that is used for accompaniment and to stress rhythm (Ortiz, *Los instrumentos de la música afrocubana*, 2:168). The *güiro* is sometimes also struck on its even surface, as if it were a clave.

Gutiérrez, Agustín. Bongo player. Born 28 August 1900, Havana. Was a member of Septeto Habanero, with whom he toured the United States in 1925. Gutiérrez later played with Ignacio Piñeiro's Septeto Nacional, with Septeto Agabama, and with the Conjunto Matamoros. He performed on the radio stations RHC Cadena Azul and Mil Diez. He also played with the Havana Symphony Orchestra under the conduction of Kleiber and held percussion contests with other leading drummers from Cuba and North America. He played with the group Conjunto de Claves y Guaguancó. He has been a member of the National Folkloric Company since 1963.

Gutiérrez, Bienvenido Julián. Composer. Born 22 March 1890, Havana; died 10 December 1966. An intuitive and spontaneous musician with no technical knowledge, Gutiérrez could not play any instrument and he required the aid of transcribers to put his ideas on paper, but he started composing for the Havana choir Los Roncos and later wrote music for *son* sextets. His *son* and *guaguancó* pieces, as well as his *guarachas* and boleros, were widely broadcast in Cuba. He wrote extensively, and his most remarkable creations are "Sensemayá," "El huerfanito," "Tú te acordarás," "El habitante," "Hagan juego," "El diablo tuntún," and "Convergencia."

Gutiérrez, Horacio. Pianist. Born 1950, Havana. At the age of eleven, Gutiérrez appeared as a soloist with the Havana Symphony Orchestra. In 1962 he moved to Los Angeles with his family. He graduated from the Juilliard School of Music. He has performed with the most prestigious orchestras in the world and recorded classical piano masterpieces. He has given concerts in the most important theaters of the United States, Canada, Latin America, Europe, and Asia. He is one of the most brilliant pianists working today.

Gutiérrez, Julio. Pianist, composer, orchestra conductor. Born 12 January 1918, Manzanillo; died 15 December 1990, New York. Gutiérrez was a competent pianist by the age of seven, and at fourteen, formed an orchestra in his hometown. In 1940 he moved to Havana and joined the Casino de la Playa band as pianist. In 1948 he formed his own *jazzband*, with whom he played at cabarets and on radio and television shows and toured the Dominican Republic, Brazil, Venezuela, Colombia, Chile, Uruguay, Argentina, and Spain. Back in Cuba, he was appointed musical director of Channel 4 television. In 1960 he traveled to Mexico and later settled in New York, where he remained an active arranger, conductor, musical director, pianist, and composer. He spent several periods performing in Puerto Rico's hotels and nightclubs. He composed *canciones* and boleros, including "Llanto de Luna," "Inolvidable," "Qué es lo que pasa," "Se acabó," "Desconfianza," "Un poquito de amor," "Arriba," and "Mírame más." He launched his own record company, J & G, in New York.

Gutiérrez, Welfo. Singer. Born 23 September 1942, Santiago de Las Vegas. Started his career as a child singing in a quartet. In the early 1970s, while living in the United States, Gutiérrez joined the Sonora Matancera band as a singer. He remained in the United States for many years, then moved to Mexico City, where he formed his own group, which performed on radio, television, and at nightclubs. He has recorded eleven LPs of boleros, *son* pieces, *guarachas*, rumbas, and salsa numbers.

Guyún. *See* González Rubiera, Vicente.

Guzmán, Adolfo. Composer, pianist, music transcriber, conductor. Born 13 May 1920, Havana; died 30 July 1976. Started his piano studies at the age of eight, and four years later began to study instrumentation. In 1937 Guzmán was piano accompanist for the Argentinian group Los Romanticos Gauchos. In 1938 he played on the radio station CMW Cadena Roja. In 1939 he made his first tour of Cuba. He conducted the resident band at the Zombie Club cabaret and was musical director at Radio Mil Diez. He accompanied the Argentinian singer Alberto Gómez on piano on RHC Cadena Azul, and on Gómez's tour of Santo Domingo in 1944. In 1948 he toured the Dominican Republic again. He conducted the Habana Casino band and played with the orchestra at the Campoamor Theater. He supported and took part in the strike of the kitchen staff at the Zombie Club. He inaugurated the Warner Theater (today the Yara movie house). Between 1951 and 1959, Guzmán worked in television on Channel 4 and was conductor of the Orquesta Riverside. In 1960 he was appointed founding president of the Cuban Institute for Music Copyright, created by Cuban Revolutionary Government Law No. 860. Together with Isolina Carrillo, he organized the giant choir of the Cuban Workers' Association. He was a guest delegate at the meeting of the World Confederation of Composers in Madrid. He was a member of the jury and musical director at the Festival of Cuban Music held in Varadero in 1975. As president of the Cuban Institute for Music Copyright, he visited Czechoslovakia, the German Democratic Republic, and Paris. He conducted the orchestra at the Havana Musical Theater. He was a member of the Cuban delegation to Expo 67 in Montreal, Canada. In 1970 he conducted the orchestra of the Cuban Institute of Radio and Television and also the orchestra of the Varadero International Song Festival. In 1971 he traveled to Santo Domingo as musical adviser to the Cuban delegation at the Twelfth Pan-American Games. In 1975 he wrote the music for the Cuban TV series *Ulises, Los Tres Mosqueteros,* and *Los Insurgentes.* In 1976 he participated in the contest La Edad de Oro and in another contest organized by the FAR. He was decorated with the Twentieth Anniversary Award and the Medal of the Twenty-fifth Anniversary of the Creation of the National Council for Culture. The Cuban Workers' Association awarded their National Work Hero honorary distinction to him posthumously. Among his outstanding compositions are Concerto for piano and orchestra and the *canciones* "No puedo ser feliz," "Cuando tú me quieras," "Lloviendo," "Al fin amor," "Profecía," "Te espero en la eternidad," and "Es tan fácil mentir."

H

habanera. Dance and music genre with origins in the *danza.* It reached its peak as a style of dance music in the second half of the nineteenth century. Its structural elements have appeared in pieces by European composers such as Albeniz, Ravel, Bizet, Debussy, Faure, and Saint-Saëns, and it was also influential in the genesis of some Latin American genres, particularly the Argentine tango. It would later disappear as a dance but remained as a vocal genre, of which "Tú," by Sánchez de Fuentes, is an example. "The *habanera* is characterized by a melodiousness expressive of the Cuban ambience, which combined with its rhythmical cadence, gives it lyricism and elegance. It is written in 2/4 time. The introduction precedes two constituent parts of between eight to sixteen bars each. The metric structure is binary and regular, even when a rhythmical variant is adopted in the first part" (Grenet, "Música cubana," 65).

Habanero, Sexteto. Formed in Havana in 1920. Its original name was the Cuarteto Oriental and later it expanded to become the Sexteto Habanero. The founding musicians were Felipe Nery (maracas and vocalist), Gerardo Martínez (vocalist and claves), Carlos Godínez (tres), Gerardo Martínez (vocalist and claves), Guillermo Castillo (guitar), Antonio Bacallao (*botija*), and Oscar Sotolongo (*bongó*). Later, Cheo Jiménez (vocalist), Abelardo Barroso (vocalist), Agustín Gutiérrez (*bongó*), José M. ("El Chino") Incharte (*bongó*), and Miguel García (vocalist) joined the band. The group became a sextet when the trum-

peter Enrique Hernández arrived in 1927. He was subsequently replaced by Félix Chapotín. Sexteto Habanero performed in several movies, including *La puerta del infierno*, recorded many LPs, and traveled abroad. In 1926 it was awarded First Prize at the Cuban Song Competition for its version of "Tres lindas cubanas," composed by Guillermo Castillo. The contest was held in Frontón Nuevo. Sexteto Habanero is still active and still gives concerts.

Hansel and Raúl. Duet made up of Hansel Martínez and Raúl Alfonso, singers and musicians. Both were born in Havana, but when they were three and four years of age, respectively, they moved to Miami with their parents. Hansel and Raúl were originally stars in the group Charanga 76. In 1980 they formed their own group and traveled in several countries. They recorded a number of LPs. Hansel recently became a soloist with the Eighth Street Orchestra. They play salsa music with an original timbre.

Havana Chamber Orchestra (Orquesta Cámara de La Habana). José Ardévol created the orchestra in 1934 and it played a remarkable role in the promotion of international chamber music, in particular works by contemporary Cuban authors. It split up in 1952 due to the effects of the Batista dictatorship.

Havana Choir (Coral de La Habana). Founded in 1931 by Maria Muñoz de Quevado, the Havana Choir was the first choral organization established in Cuba. It brought together singers and conductors in performances of works otherwise unknown in Cuba at that time.

Havana Municipal Band (Banda Municipal de La Habana). Founded in 1899 and conducted by

Guillermo Tomás. Since its founding, it promoted public auditions in the capital. It was also instrumental in the training of musicians. After Guillermo Tomás, it was conducted by Gonzalo Roig, and on his death, by Manuel Duchesne Morillas. It is currently known as the National Concert Band.

Havana Municipal Conservatory (Conservatorio Municipal de La Habana). On 2 October 1903 the O'Farrill School of Music, under the direction of Guillermo Tomás, was opened. In 1910 it was decided the school would be renamed the Havana Municipal School of Music, and it was opened as such on 1 April 1911. In 1935 it was renamed the Havana Municipal Conservatory of Music. Beginning in 1936 it was directed by Amadeo Roldán, and in the 1940s by Diego Bonilla. It published the *Conservatorio* magazine and sponsored an orchestra and a choral group. It is considered the most important institution for training Cuban musicians and is currently known as the Amadeo Roldán Conservatory.

Havana Philharmonic Orchestra (Orquesta Filarmónica de La Habana). Created in 1924 by Pedro San Juan. The formation of the orchestra played a significant and decisive role in the promotion of non-Cuban symphonic music in Cuba. In 1932 Amadeo Roldán became the conductor, amid well-documented official indifference and an economic crisis. The early instability of the orchestra was overcome by its dedicated musicians and the efforts of its conductor, but due to his precarious health, Roldán was replaced by Massimo Freccia in 1939, and in 1944 Freccia was replaced by Ereich Kleiber, who continued to promote and refine the orchestra. Outstanding guest conductors included Juan José Castro, Alberto Bolet, and Igor Malkevitch. The orchestra disbanded at the end of 1958.

Havana Quartet (Cuarteto de La Habana). Created in 1906; played chamber music in concert rooms and theaters in Havana. It was formed by Juan Torroella (first violin), Arturo Quiñones (second violin), Antonio Mompó (cello), and Constance Suárez (viola). In 1927 Amadeo Roldán formed a second Havana Quartet. In 1961 the quartet, renamed the National Quartet, was once again re-created with Szymisa Bahur, Gonzalo Valledor, Lazaro Sternic, and Ernesto Xancó. The quartet played for three years, conducted by the violinist Maruja Sanchez.

Havana Symphony Orchestra (Orquesta Sinfónica de La Habana). The idea of a symphonic institution was first mentioned in a conversation between Ernesto Lecuona and Gonzalo Roig, and the Havana Symphony Orchestra was launched in Havana on 2 September 1922. The conductor was Septimio Sardiñas. After he resigned, he was replaced by Edwin Tolón. The symphony gave its first concert on 29 October 1922, at the National Theater. The program pieces included *Oberón*, by Weber; *Escenas Pintorescas*, by Massenet; Concerto no. 2 in G minor, op. 22, for piano and orchestra by Saint-Saëns, with Ernesto Lecuona as soloist; *Visión*, by Rhienberg; the aria from the Suite in G by Bach; and the *Tannhauser Overture*, by Wagner. The orchestra played for twenty years, thanks to the efforts and hard work of its conductor and the professors who, with no economic resources, premiered in Cuba many pieces from an international and national repertoire. Pablo Casals, Juan Manén, Adela Verne, Julián Carillo, Ernesto Halffter, José Echánez, and many others have been guest conductors. The orchestra folded in the 1940s.

Hechavarría, Juan de Dios. Born mid–nineteenth century, Santiago de Cuba; died c. 1950, Havana. Creator of one of the precursors of the Cuban bolero. His songs have a festive tone. He was very close to Pepe Sánchez.

Henríquez, María Antonieta. Professor and researcher of Cuban music. Born 9 November 1927, Havana. Studied music with Margot Díaz Dorticós and Paul Csonska, and at the Havana Municipal Conservatory. Henríquez also studied philosophy and letters at the University of Havana. She belonged to the board of the Nuestro Tiempo cultural society, which confronted the tyrannical Batista regime. She undertook the teaching of music in 1948, and as a critic, published a number of articles in *Última Hora*, *Nuestro Tiempo*, and *Hoy*. At the advent of the Revolution, she was appointed national assistant director for music of the National Council for Culture, and was in charge of teaching music from 1960 to 1964. In 1962 she represented Cuba at the Congress on Music and Its Audience, convened by UNESCO,

in Rome. In the same year, she attended the Warsaw Fall Festival. In 1974 she participated in the CIMCIN Seminar, "Museums of Music," in Stockholm. In 1973 she was appointed adviser for music at the Institute of Infancy. She has published songbooks for daycare centers and drawn up guidelines for the musical education of preschool children. In 1977 she was appointed coordinator of the Ministry

of Culture's music commission. Between 1971 and 1983 she was the director of the National Museum of Music. She has published several works based on her research on Cuban music.

Henríquez, Reinaldo. Singer. Born 21 August 1915, Santiago de Cuba; died 8 June 1987, Havana. First performed on the radio and in the theater in his hometown. Henríquez came to Havana in 1939 and sang for the radio stations CMQ and RHC Cadena Azul, supported by Amado Trinidad. In the early 1940s, accompanied by the pianist Orlando de la Rosa, he performed songs from Cuba, Mexico, and elsewhere. He was one of the pioneers of the *fílin* movement. In 1942, due to the economic conditions in Cuba, he traveled to the United States and sang for many years on a CBS radio coast-to-coast program. Some of his records of Latin American songs became very popular. In 1955 he returned to Cuba, working as a sound technician while continuing to perform. He worked at the ICRT until the time of his death.

Hermanos Bravo. This group has been playing boleros, *son*, and conga since the 1950s but is best known for its congas. Hermanos Bravo is the most established conga group today in Cuba and is di-

Mo Fini

rected by Esteban Bravo. A recent record release is *Conga tu carnaval.*

Hernández, Edilio. Tenor. Born 20 December 1936, Havana. Studied singing at the Ignacio Cervantes Conservatory and at the Higher Institute of Art. In 1970 Hernández joined the chorus of the Cuban National Opera. In 1974 he went on tour in Europe as a lead singer in the Cuban zarzuela *Cecilia Valdés*. He has sung lead in various operas and also performed pieces in the Cuban lyrical repertoire.

Hernández, Gisela. Professor, composer, chorus conductor. Born 15 September 1912, Cárdenas; died 23 August 1971, Havana. Studied piano, harmony, counterpoint, orchestration, history of music, and aesthetics with María Muñoz and José Ardévol, and later with Gustav Strabe in the United States. Hernández was a member of the Grupo de Renovación Musical. She became a conductor of the Havana Chorus in 1947, and a year later joined the Hubert de Blanck Conservatory as a professor. She published educational works and was an adviser to the National Council for Culture. She composed orchestral works, chamber music, and piano pieces; incidental music for theater; and, most significantly, ten choral and twenty vocal works—some from texts by Cuban poets—and music for children. Among her compositions are Choral suite, Zapateo, Prelude, and *Canciones infantiles cubanas.*

Hernández, Israel. Bass singer. Began his professional career in the chorus of the National Lyric Theater. Hernández later performed as a soloist in various operas. He has given recitals in Cuban theaters and has toured a number of countries.

Hernández, Ivette. Pianist. Born 1933, Havana. At seven years of age, Hernández gave a piano recital at the University of Havana. She studied at the Havana Municipal Conservatory and later in New York under Claudio Arrau and Sidney Foster. She was a finalist in the piano contest organized by Young People's Concerts. She traveled to France in 1950 to study at the Paris Conservatory, where she won First Piano Prize. She was awarded the Harriet Cohen Medal in London (a medal awarded to each year's three most outstanding pianists). She also won First Prize at the Gottschalk International Contest in New Orleans. Hernández made concert tours of America and Europe and made several recordings. She returned to Cuba and gave recitals throughout the country and concerts with the National Symphony Orchestra. She established herself in Spain in the mid-1960s. She has made an outstanding career as a pianist.

Hernández, María Luisa. Singer. Born (?), El Cobre, Santiago de Cuba; died (?). Began her singing career in her home region. Hernández moved to Havana in 1946 and sang *guajiras, sones*, boleros, and *guarachas* for radio broadcasts. She also performed on several television programs and made numerous commercial recordings, becoming known as "La India de Oriente." She established herself in the United States in 1960 and is now based in Miami. She has performed in nightclubs and theaters and has recorded many LPs, including several for labels run by the Miami-based Cuban singer Roberto Torres.

Hernández, Oscar. Composer. Born 15 August 1891, Havana; died 3 March 1967. Took music lessons from the maestro Félix Guerrero Sr. Hernández entered the world of troubadour singing and formed a trio with Manuel Corona and Juan Carbonell, in which he sang and played the guitar. The group separated in 1919, and he then joined other troubadours, with whom he remained for several years. He later devoted himself to composing. His *canciones* and boleros, which are still sung, include "Rosa Roja," "Ella y yo" (known as "El sendero"), "Mi ruta," and "Para adorarte." He won the First Prize in the Cuban Song Competition in 1955 with Justicia de Amor.

Hernández, Pedro. Composer, violinist, professor. Born 26 November 1912, Havana. Studied violin with professors Antonio Caballero and Joaquín Molina, along with other musical subjects at the Havana Municipal Conservatory. Hernández has been a member of several ensembles, including Romeu, Ideal, Frank Emilio's band, Arcaño y Sus Maravillas, Ernesto Muñoz's band, Fajardo y Sus Estrellas, Jorrín, CMQ, and Barbarito Diez. He has been a professor of singing, music theory, and violin. He is the author of the danzones "Una cosita pá gozá," "Mi gran pasión," "Cabaña en las nubes," and "Juventud de Atarés", as well as the Concierto de Varsovia and other pieces inspired by symphonic works.

Hernández, René. Pianist, arranger, composer, conductor of popular orchestras. Born 21 January, Cienfuegos; died 5 September 1977, San Juan, Puerto Rico. After working in Havana as a pianist with the Casino de la Playa and the Julio Cueva orchestras, Hernández traveled to the United States where he formed various ensembles and orchestras. He was an arranger for many outstanding dance bands and popular music singers, including Tito Rodríguez and, most notably, Machito's Afro-Cubans during their golden era from 1946 to 1966. In the 1970s he created arrangements for the pianist Eddie Palmieri. He was a pioneer of big-band mambo and Afro-Cuban jazz in the United States.

Hernández, Rodolfo. Composer, professor, organist. Born 30 September 1856, Santiago de Cuba; died 21 March 1937. Studied flute, piano, and violin under Laureano Fuentes Matons. With Juan Cardona, he studied harmony, composition, and organ. At sixteen years of age, Hernández became an organist and choirmaster at the Asilo San José and later at the Santiago de Cuba Cathedral. During the struggle for independence, he cooperated with the emigrants, offering concerts to raise funds for the war against Spanish colonialism. After the war, he returned to Santiago de Cuba, where he continued to give concerts and conducted the Haydn Society Orchestra. His compositions include the zarzuelas El asalto and Geografía física; the religious piece "Misa en do mayor"; Danzas and Twelve studies for piano; several pieces for orchestra, such as Intermezzo, Gavota, and Caprichosa; as well as other short pieces for piano. He also published texts on theory and harmony.

Hernández, Yolanda. Soprano. Born 27 May 1945, Havana. Her early studies were at the Municipal Conservatory (today, the Amadeo Roldán Conservatory) and she pursued higher studies in Poland. Hernández joined the National Lyric Theater in the late 1960s. She has sung leads in operas and has given recitals in Cuba and abroad. She has performed on television and recorded one LP. She played the leading role in the opera Halka.

Hernández Balaguer, Pablo. Cellist, musicologist, professor. Born 13 July 1928, Havana; died 31 January 1966. Studied cello with Ernesto Xancó and later continued his music studies in Barcelona. He studied musical theory in Prague, Budapest, and Moscow. Hernández Balguer was a professor of music at the University of Oriente and the director of the province's Archives of Music. He did extensive research on the history of Cuban music. He was a professor at the Esteban Salas Conservatory and composer of several pieces. He published several works on Cuban music, including Breve historia de la música cubana, Catálogo de música de los archivos de la Catedral de Santiago y del Museo Bacardí, and Obras de Esteban Salas. He also carried out research at the archives of the Santiago de Cuba Cathedral, which resulted in his work, Los villancicos, cantadas y pastorelas de Esteban Salas.

Hernández Zubarán, José. Professor and composer. Born 1860, Trinidad; died 1918, Cienfuegos. Although born in Trinidad, Hernández Zubarán made his musical career in Cienfuegos, where he moved when very young and raised a large family. He made some admirable efforts in composing zarzuelas (including Eureka, 1897), but his best works were typical airs, waltzes, and danzones.

Herrera, Aurelio. Flutist. Born 15 October 1901, Havana. Studied under Enrique Fuentes ("El Rubio") and later at the Havana Municipal Conservatory under Modesto Fraga. Herrera was a flutist with Orquesta Gris and also with the Charanga a la Francesa of the National Council for Culture.

Herrera, Elena. Orchestra conductor. Born 15 August 1948, Cabaiguán. Studied conducting at the Higher Institute of Art and was a professor of music history. From 1980 on, Herrera conducted the Matanzas Symphony Orchestra and other orchestras in Cuba and abroad. She was also a piano accompanist. In 1985 she became the conductor of the Theater and Dance Center Orchestra.

Herrera, Florentino. Composer and flutist. Born 6 February 1895, Havana; died 3 December 1929, Switzerland. Studied music in his hometown. Herrera was granted a scholarship to pursue further studies in New York, and he later traveled to Paris, where he studied composition with Vincent d'Indy at the Schola Cantorum. He was a remarkable flutist; his performances earned him success both in the United States and in Europe. His compositions were impressionistic but drawn from his Cuban roots, as in his *Capricho cubano* for orchestra, *Danzas cubanas* for piano, his chamber music, his *Cantos sin palabras* for piano, and his choral pieces. His premature death deprived music of a promising figure.

Herrera, Huberal. Pianist. Born 28 May 1829, Mayarí. Studied with Hortensia Rojas and Arcadio Menocal in his hometown. Herrera completed his studies of harmony, counterpoint, and music teaching in Havana. He has given recitals in halls and theaters and on radio and television, and has toured Europe and Asia. He has played as a soloist with the National Symphony Orchestra. He currently performs as a soloist.

Herrera, Lázaro. Trumpet player. Born 17 December 1903, Guara. Joined Ignacio Piñeiro's Septeto Nacional as a trumpet player in 1927. Herrera transcribed Piñeiro's *sones* and rumbas for trumpet. He created a trumpet mode within the genre.

Herrera Drake, Manuel. Guitarist. Born 1 January 1926, Máximo Gómez sugar mill, Camagüey. Studied under Vicente González Rubiera. Herrera Drake has pursued a career as a guitarist while simultaneously working as an X-ray technician and pursuing studies in medicine. He has performed in concert numerous times, playing *danzones* on the guitar.

Hevia, Liuba María. Composer and singer. Born 14 December 1964, Havana. Studied singing with Angel Menéndez and guitar with Vicente González Rubiera. Later studied at the Rafael Somavilla Center and at the Ignacio Cervantes Professional School. Hevia has followed the *nueva trova* line, but with a

repertoire within the *guajiro* style. She has toured several countries and recorded a number of CDs.

Hierrezuelo, Caridad. *Guaracha* and *son montuno* singer. Born 10 August 1924, Santiago de Cuba. Hierrezuelo came from a family of troubadours and *soneros*. She is the sister of Lorenzo and Reinaldo (Los Compadres). She began her career in the CMKC radio in the 1950s. She was vocalist with the group Maravillas de Beltrán. She spent many years as a soloist performing on radio, television, and at theaters and festivals. She has toured outside Cuba and made various records.

Hierrezuelo, Lorenzo. Composer, guitarist, singer. Born 5 September 1907, El Caney, Oriente; died 16 November 1993, Havana. Hierrezuelo was heir to a family troubadour tradition (his parents were singers at the end of the nineteenth century) and was descended from a line of Indo-Cubans (his grandmother was a Siboney). When he was thirteen years old he went to Santiago de Cuba with his guitar to sing in cafés and at family parties. He formed a trio with two troubadour friends, Julio and Edelmiro, and traveled with them to Havana in 1930. When his two friends returned to Oriente, he stayed in Havana and joined the Trío Lírico Cubano, and later the Hatuey Quartet and Justa García's ensemble, always as a second voice and guitarist. After 1937 he sang with María Teresa Vera as one of Cuba's most popular duets until 1962, when María Teresa retired due to ill health. He composed *sones* and *guarachas*. He formed the Los Compadres duo with Francisco Repilado (Compay Segundo) and later continued to perform with his own brother, Reinaldo. He represented Cuba in several countries abroad. He composed the *sones* "Venga guano, caballeros," "Caña quemá," "No quiero llanto," "Sarandonga," and "Baja y tapa la olla."

Hierrezuelo, Reinaldo. Guitarist and *tres* player, singer. Born 30 December 1926, Santiago de Cuba. Born into a family of musicians, among whom Caridad Hierrezuelo (singer) and Lorenzo Hierrezuelo (composer, guitarist, and singer) were also outstanding. During the 1940s, Reinaldo Herrezuelo was part of the Cuarteto Patria. He came to live in Havana in 1950 and joined various groups; then in 1935, with Lorenzo, he formed the Duo Los Compadres. He later performed as a soloist. In 1960 he sang with the César Concepción Orchestra in New York. He has recorded several LPs. He is currently a member of the Vieja Trova Santiaguera.

hierro. A certain class of metal percussion instruments of African origin, struck with metal and sometimes wooden sticks. Although theoretically this category could include any percussion instrument made from metal (including spoons, pots and pans, bells, and metal rattles), the term *hierro* most often refers to such instruments as the *guataca* (hoe blade) and the *sanmartín*. These instruments maintain a steady rhythmic pattern within the dense percussive texture of Afro-Cuban music.

Horruitiner, Margarita. Professor of piano. Born 15 July 1910, Santiago de Cuba. Studied piano with several teachers, and took singing lessons from Maestro Fernández Dominicis. Horruitiner has given recitals in many halls in Cuba. She became a teacher, working at the García Caturla Conservatory, in Marianao, and at the Professional School.

I

Ibáñez, José ("Chicho"). Composer and singer, *tres* player. Born 22 November 1875, Corral Falso (today, Pedro Betancourt); died 18 May 1987, Havana. Had an original way of playing and singing *sones* and songs, which was the result of his unusual voice and a rare technique of playing the *tres*. During his lifetime, Ibáñez took the *son* from the streets and plazas and into nightclubs. All through the 1920s he was forced to sell his *sones* to musical groups and composers for economic reasons. Among his works are the *sones* "Tóma mamá que te manda tía," "Evaristo," "No te metas Caridad," "Ojalá," "Luis Toledano, patinador"; the bolero-*sones* "Yo era dichoso," "Al fin mujer," "Besarte quisiera," "Cuando era niño," "Mi existencia se redime," and "No me perturbes"; and the *guaguancós* "Qué más me pides" and "La saya de Oyá." He also sang Afro-Cuban Abakuá music and gave recitals throughout the country.

Ideal, Orquesta. French *charanga* formed in Havana in 1938 by the flutist Joseíto Valdés along with Pedro Hernández (violin), Miguel Angel Colombo (double bass), Humberto Bello (piano), Angel López (timbales), and José Dávila (*güiro*). They performed at dances and on the radio and recorded LPs. The orchestra disbanded in the 1950s.

Iglesias, Raúl. Pianist. Born 18 May 1933, Havana. Studied at the Municipal Conservatory (today the Amadeo Roldán Conservatory). Iglesias studied at the Budapest Conservatory, beginning in 1962, and graduated in 1968. He has performed as a soloist with the symphony orchestras of Camagüey, Las Villas, and Matanzas; and also with the National Symphony Orchestra. He has performed as a piano accompanist. He is currently a pianist-repertoirist at the School of Opera at the Higher Institute of Art.

Inciarte, Joaquín. Guitarist, violinist, pianist, professor. Born (?); died 1884, Santiago de Cuba. Arrived in Santiago in 1836 and established himself as a teacher. His pupils included José and Emilio Bacardí. He was an outstanding performer.

Inciarte, Rafael. Composer, conductor, saxophonist, clarinetist. Born 24 January 1909, Santiago de Cuba. Descended from a line of musicians, Inciarte began to study music with his father at nine years of age. He took clarinet lessons from Narciso Carmona and received guidance from Maestro Antonio Moedhano. As a child, he played the *güiro* in a popular dance band. At twelve years of age he was already a clarinetist with the Municipal Band of Manzanillo, which his father conducted. Later, in Santiago de Cuba, he played tenor sax with the Municipal Band. He was part of symphony ensembles and of dance orchestras. In 1927 he moved to Guantánamo where he joined the Municipal Band and also organized several music ensembles, initiating many young people into the art of sound. In 1955 he reorganized and conducted the Municipal Band. He was the author of historical works on autochthonous music, particularly that of eastern Cuba, and of popular pieces in collaboration with Luis Morlote, who almost always contributed the lyrics. Among their collaborations are "La jicotea," "Apriétame más," "Todo lo tengo ya," and "Ojos lindos." He was also the director and a professor at the Guantánamo School of Music.

Inciarte, Ruiz Rafael. Professor, double bass player, violinist, cellist, trombonist, cornetist, ophicleidist. Born 25 June 1846, Santiago de Cuba; died 15 November 1940, Guantánamo. For many years, Inciarte worked mostly as a conductor. He took his first music lessons from his father and later was self-taught. He organized and conducted the general staff band of the army of Oriente during the War of Independence, under the command of José Maceo. When the war ended, he held the rank of captain. In 1940 he organized and conducted the Santiago de Cuba Municipal Band. In 1910 he founded the Music Academy and the Children's Band. In 1915 he created the Vista Alegre Band in the capital city of Oriente province, and in 1917, founded the Manzanillo Municipal Band. In 1927 he organized the Municipal Band of Guantánamo, where he was then living. He created small ensembles to play classical music and also conducted a dance orchestra. He taught music to all of his children and also had many disciples. He composed some dance music.

Instituto Nacional de Investigaciones Folklóricas. *See* National Institute for Folkloric Research.

Instituto Nacional de la Música. *See* National Institute of Music.

Irakere, Grupo. Formed in Havana in 1973. Some of the most significant Cuban musicians have played with this band. Since its formation, it has been considered one of the most important Cuban bands. Its original members were Paquito D'Rivera, Germán Velazco, and Carlos Averoff (saxophones); Arturo Sandoval and Jorge Varona (trumpets); Carlos Emilio (electric guitar); Carlos del Puerto (electric bass); Enrique Pla (drums); Jorge Alfonso and Carlos Barbón (percussion); Oscar Valdés (vocalist and percussion); and Jesús "Chucho" Valdés (piano, organ, and bandleader). Its musical roots lie in the basic elements of Afro-Cuban folklore, in traditional dance music blended with other styles from popular American and European music, and in incorporating the new possibilities of electronic music and current musical trends.

Irijoa Theater (later, the Martí). Built in 1883, it was opened by its namesake, Ramón Irijoa, in 1884. Its repertoire consisted mainly of Cuban popular music, but some operas were also staged. The theater was renamed the Martí during the so-called pseudo-republic period of 1902–1959 and buildings were erected in the original front gardens. The present government returned it to its former architectural glory, and today it is the only colonial theater remaining in Havana.

Isidrón, Chanito. Singer of *punto*. Born 26 September 1903, Calabazar de Sagua; died 22 February 1987, Havana. From early childhood, Isidrón worked in the fields, but in 1931 he gave it up and took up his guitar, moving from town to town in the province of Las Villas, playing the traditional *punto guajiro*. Together with other singers of *punto*, he would revive this particularly Cuban folk expression, which had been almost forgotten. He took part in hundreds of *controversias* (sung encounters). He has published prose and verse containing themes of *campesino* (country peasant) life. He came to be known throughout the country by his performances on radio stations in Las

Villas, as well as on RHC Cadena Azul, Mil Diez, Cadena Habana, and Radio Rebelde. He made extensive use of humor in his improvisations.

itón. Two small sticks used to strike Abakuá drums. "Itón" means "wooden stick" in the Efik language of the Calabar region of Nigeria, the origin of Abakuá traditions. A musician hits the smaller part of the bonkó enchemiyá with itónes, producing two tones, high and low (Ortiz, Los instrumentos de la música afrocubana, 1:263–64).

Ivonet, Ramón. Troubadour. Born 1877, Santiago de Cuba; died 27 November 1896, Tumbas de Estorino. At a very early age, Ivonet joined the troubadour performances at the Plaza de Marte, together with Nicolás Camacho, Fermín Castillo, and Alejandro Vian. At the outbreak of the War of Independence in 1895, he joined the Mambí Army (against the Spanish) and was part of General Antonio Maceo's General Staff. In the battlefield, accompanied by his guitar, he sang his own compositions and those by other troubadours, which General Maceo greatly admired. He wrote patriotic songs, such as "Levanta, Cuba, la frente." He died in combat.

iyesá drums. An instrumental ensemble made up of four drums (to which two agogó and a güiro are added): a caja, a segundo, a tercero, and a bajo. The drums are used in the rites and feasts, chants and dances of the Iyesás, a group related to the Yorubá culture of Nigeria. Like the batá drums, iyesá drums are sacred, and possess secret powers (añá). Cylindrical in shape, the drums are made from cedar trunks scooped out by hand. Each end is covered with a drumhead made of goat skin tightened on a hoop of flexible wood called a tibisi. A tension system is operated by zig-zagging bows of cáñamo isleño, which pass inside other bows, arranged in odd numbers and anchored at the hoops to which the goatskin is fixed. A third order of transversal bows tightens the straps in the shape of an N, bringing them together in pairs. Iyesá drums are beaten on one of the drumheads, with sticks about 30 centimeters long and 1 centimeter in diameter, made from the branches of the guava tree or of a wood called hueso, or even from chair cross-pieces. Iyesa drummers will periodically change the position of the instrument

and percuss on the other drumheads. The bajo is the only iyesá drum that is beaten with the bare hand (Martínez Furé, "Los iyesás").

Iznaga, Alberto. Violinist, clarinetist, saxophonist, arranger, conductor. Born 25 July 1906, Havana; died 1995, New York. Studied violin at the Carnicer Conservatory, under the Romanian professor Demetrie Vladescu. Iznaga played with the Havana Philharmonic Orchestra and with the orchestra of the National Theater. He traveled to New York in 1929, where he joined Vicente Sigler's orchestra as a clarinetist and saxophonist. In 1933 he joined the Cooleridge-Taylor quartet, and in 1937 Augusto Coen's band. He later founded the Siboney orchestra, where Frank Grillo ("Machito") began his singing career. He studied at the Juilliard School of Music. His orchestra dissolved in 1952, and he then joined Gilberto Valdés's Charanga as a violinist. He made excellent arrangements for Latin vocalists and for music groups in New York. He retired as an active musician in 1974.

Iznaga, Inocente ("El Jilguero"). Singer (of decimas). Born 28 October 1930, Cienfuegos. "El Jilguero" (the goldfinch) began as a singer of puntos guajiros and montuno genres in the region where he was born. He established himself in 1950s Havana, where he became enormously popular. He performs on radio and on television, and has represented Cuban music on tours abroad.

Izquierdo, Pedro. Composer and percussionist. Born 7 January 1933, Havana; died c. 2000. Known by the name "Pello el Afrokán." Through the tradition of his family, he was initiated into Afro-Cuban folk music at an early age. Izquierdo was a percussionist with several music groups. In 1963 he created a new rhythm, the Mozambique, a mix of various elements of African origin. It gained immediate popularity and became a landmark in Cuban dance music. His compositions include "María Caracoles," "Camina como cómico," and "Ileana quiere chocolate." He conducts his own music group, which has toured various countries.

J

Jarque Gómez, Ernesto. Band and orchestra conductor. Born 21 June 1881, Alcoy, Valencia; died 12 January 1923, Iquique, Chile. Was part of the Military Band in Cazadores, Madrid, where he also conducted orchestras working in lyric theater. Jarque Gómez established himself in Caibarién, Cuba, at the beginning of the twentieth century, and undertook teaching music. He traveled to Peru in 1915 and later to Chile, where he died. In 1954 his remains were brought to Cuba and buried in Caibarién on 6 December 1954.

Jauma, Humberto. Composer. Born 17 December 1908, Santiago de las Vegas; died 22 June 1971. At fifteen years of age, Jauma played the *tres* with the Sexteto Sonora Santiaguera; he was later a guitarist with the Sexteto Mi Tienda and a double bass player with the Azul Tropical ensemble. In 1930 traveled to Mexico, playing with popular orchestras, including those of Alvaro Ruiz, Rafael Hernández, Gonzalo Curiel, and Agustín Lara. There, he began a career as a composer, encouraged by Lara and by the singer Eva Garza. That marked the beginning of a list of popular pieces: the songs "En mi memoria," "Ni novia ni luna," "Qué más da," "Sólo por rencor," "No importa corazón," "Hay algo en ti," "Feliz Navidad," "Si no vuelves," "Noche y día," and "Mi ocaso"; the mambo "Estás como mango"; the *cha-cha-chá* "No te quedes mirando"; and the *guaracha* "Rumberito soy yo."

jazzband cubana. Type of ensemble that originated under the influence of North American music in Cuba, in the 1930s. The *jazzband* served as a vehicle for almost all Cuban and universal genres. It featured the following instruments: piano, double bass, drums, four or five saxophones (two altos, two tenors, one baritone), three or four trumpets, trombone, Cuban percussion (*tumbadora, bongó, paila criolla*), maracas, *güiro*, and singer. The *jazzband* era reached its peak in the 1940s. Popular Cuban styles acquired a new form of expression with the introduction of new sonorities.

Jiménez, Bobby. Singer. Born 21 September 1938, Havana. Besides Cuban songs, Jiménez also sings pieces from the French, Italian, North American, and Brazilian repertoires. He began his career in 1957, singing at the Flamingo Hotel, and later performed on radio, television, and in theaters and nightclubs. He has studied music at the Havana Municipal Conservatory. He lives in the United States.

Jiménez, Generoso. Trombonist and orchestrator. Born 17 July 1917. Began his career as a musician in dance bands and orchestras in his province and later established himself in Havana in several jazzband-type orchestras. In the 1950s, Jiménez joined Benny Moré's Banda Gigante for which he made the arrangements. He recorded an LP, *Trombón majadero*, featuring his trombone solos accompanied by an ensemble. He currently plays with the orchestra of the ICRT. He is the composer of such pieces as "Maíz pa' los pollos."

Jiménez, José ("Cheo"). Singer. Born 1910, Havana; died 1929. Began his career in 1926 singing boleros and *sones* with the Sexteto Facenda and later joined the Hermanos Enrizo ensemble. Jiménez joined the Sexteto Habanero in 1927 and made several recordings with them. He joined Ignacio Piñeiro's Septeto Nacional in 1929 and traveled with the group to perform at the Fair of Seville, but his voice was never heard there; he contracted severe pneumonia and died en route from New York to Seville.

Jiménez, José Julián. Pianist and violinist. Born 9 January 1823, Trinidad; died 1880, Havana. Member of a family with a great musical tradition; his father was an orchestra conductor, and his sons, Nicasio and José Manuel, were outstanding musicians. As an adolescent, José Julián Jiménez traveled to Leipzig, Germany, where he studied piano, violin, and harmony. He was a violinist with the Gewandhause Orchestra in that city. As a soloist and also with his sons, he gave concerts in Cuba and in Europe and the Americas. Although he devoted himself primarily to classical music, he also made contributions in the realm of popular music: he founded a dance band in Havana in 1849, and composed many *danzas* and *guarachas*, which have been popular since the mid–nineteenth century.

Jiménez, José Manuel ("Lico"). Pianist and composer. Born 7 December 1851, Trinidad; died 15 January 1917, Hamburg. Made his early studies of music with his father, José Julián Jiménez, a violinist and composer. When young, "Lico" Jiménez traveled to Europe and studied piano with Carl Reinecke and Ignaz Moscheles, at the conservatory in Leipzig. He later traveled to Paris, where he studied under Marmontel. He met Wagner and Liszt, who praised him as a pianist. He gave successful recitals throughout Europe. In 1879 he returned to Cuba where he gave concerts. He established himself in Cienfuegos as a piano teacher. In 1890 he traveled to Germany and based in Hamburg, where he was appointed a professor at the conservatory. He was the first Cuban composer to cultivate the lied. He composed Symphonic study—*Elegía, Solitude, Murmullo del céfiro, Rapsodia cubana*, and *Valse Caprice*—and also songs and pieces for piano.

Jiménez Crespo, Agustín. Composer, professor, conductor. Born 27 August 1892, Remedios; died 9 October 1976. Was the director of the Music Academy and conductor of the Municipal Band of Remedios. Jiménez Crespo established himself in Santa Clara, where he continued his work, and founded the Symphony Orchestra of Las Villas toward the end of the 1920s. He was also conductor of the Municipal Band of Santa Clara. He composed several band pieces. He taught many noteworthy musicians.

Jimeno, Tomás. Percussionist and musicologist. Born 28 December 1944, Pedro Betancourt. Studied with Rafael Somavilla and Dagoberto Hernández Piloto; took percussion lessons from Domingo Aragú; played with the army's music band. Jimeno began his musical career playing in groups in the Matanzas province. He was later a percussionist with the band led by flutist José Fajardo and with other nightclub orchestras. He has been a professor of percussion at the García Caturla and the Cervantes conservatories in Cuba, where he also conducted research into Afro-Cuban folk music. He has taught in Europe. He currently works at the Odilio Urfé Center of Musical Documentation.

Jorrín, Enrique. Composer, violinist, conductor. Born 25 December 1926, Candelaria; died 12 December 1987, Havana. Studied music at the Havana Municipal Conservatory. Jorrín was a violinist, first with the orchestra of the National Institute of Music under the conductor González Mantici. He joined the *danzón* orchestra Hermanos Contreras in 1941, and there, he cultivated popular music. He later played with Arcaño y Sus Maravillas. In the early 1950s and already with the Orquesta América, he created the new dance music called *cha-cha-chá*. He lived and worked in Mexico from 1954 to 1958. In 1964 he toured Africa and Europe with his orchestra. He wrote orchestrations and music for musical comedies staged in Havana's theaters. In the last years of his life, he conducted the Orquesta Jorrín. His early pieces *danzones*, include "Hilda," "Liceo del Pilar," and "Central Constancia." In his transition period, he composed "Unión Cienfueguera," "Doña Olga," and "Silver Star"; and in his *cha-cha-chá* period, after 1951, his most popular compositions are "La engañadora," "El alardoso," "El túnel," "Nada para ti," "Osiris," and "Me muero."

Jorrín, Orquesta. *Charanga* band created by the composer and violinist Enrique Jorrín. It was founded as a vehicle for the *cha-cha-chá* but has played almost all of Cuba's dance rhythms. The band performed in Mexico from 1955 to 1959, on radio and television, and in theaters and nightclubs. Back in Cuba, they continued performing. In its heyday, the orchestra included Miguel O'Farrill (flute), Enrique Jorrín and Elio Valdés (violin), Rubén González (piano), Fabián García (double bass), Leonides Rodrguez (violoncello), Octavio Calderón and Juan Larrinaga (trumpets), Ricardo León (timbales), Rolando Rodríguez (conga), Pedro Contreras (*güiro*), and Jesús Jorrín and Alberto Bermádez (vocalists). Tito Gómez was the singer during the 1970s and 1980s.

Jovenes Clasicos del Son. Winners of the EGREM Prize in 1997, this talented septet was formed in 1996 and directed by the respected bass player Ernest Reyes, known as "Palma." They mix *son* with salsa and other Latin rhythms, along with blues, funk, and soul. The members have worked with such artists as Candido Fabré, Vocal Sampling, Sonora La Calle, Wynton Marsalis, and Compay Segundo. Their first album, *Fruta Bomba*, distributed worldwide, was a success.

Mo Fini

Jovenes del Cayo, Conjunto. Group formed in the Cayo Hueso neighborhood of Havana. Domingo Vargas was its first bandleader. Miguelito Valdés was the vocalist during the 1930s. In the 1940s it became a *conjunto*, led by vocalist Alfonsín Quintana. At the peak of its popularity its musicians were Alfonso Salinas, Vinicio González, and Vitelio Cruz (trumpets); Pepe Delgado (piano); Franca (double bass); Israel Pérez (conga); Fernando García (*bongó*); and Celio González, Domingo Vargas, and Alfonsín Quintana (vocalists). Conjunto Jovenes del Cayo played Cuban dance music, hosted radio and television shows, recorded several LPs, and performed at dances all over Cuba. The band traveled around Latin America and to the United States, and it also accompanied many Cuban and foreign singers. It split up in 1963.

Joya, Alberto. Pianist. Born 1952, Santa María del Rosario. Studied at the National School of Art under Cecilio Tieles and Vitali Ditsenko. Studied harpsichord with Petr Sefl. Joya has given recitals and concerts in Cuba and in various other countries. He plays works by composers from different areas and of different styles and has also recorded Cuban music.

Junco, Juan Jorge. Clarinetist. Born 9 November 1913, Cienfuegos. Began studying harmony, theory, and clarinet at eight years of age, with his uncle Abelardo Junco. In 1924 Juan Jorge Junco joined the Banda de Exploradores of Cienfuegos, in which he was a soloist a year later. He also played with dance music orchestras. In 1929 he was a soloist in the Cienfuegos Municipal Band. He studied under Maestro Pedro Graces. Established in Havana in 1933, he played solo clarinet in various orchestras, including the Havana Philharmonic. He has been a soloist in the National Symphony Orchestra since 1960. In 1971 he founded the group Nuestro Tiempo, conducted by Maestro Duchesne Cuzán, but he continued working as a professor. He was awarded the National Order for a musical career lasting over thirty years. He is one of Cuba's most outstanding clarinetists.

Junco, Pedro. Composer and pianist. Born 22 February 1920, Pinar del Río; died April 1943, Havana. Began a musical career in his province at an early age. Junco composed thirty-six songs, among them "Soy como soy," "Ya te lo dije," and the very popular "Nosotros."

Junco, Teresita. Pianist. Born 7 October 1946, Havana. Studied at the Havana Municipal Conservatory and pursued further studies at the Tchaikovsky Conservatory in Moscow. Junco has given recitals and concerts with symphony orchestras in Cuba. She has performed in Hungary and in Venezuela and is currently a professor at the Amadeo Roldán Conservatory and at the Higher Institute of Art.

Justiniani, Marta. Singer. Born 2 December 1931, Havana. Began singing as a child and made a career singing popular songs. Justiniani cultivated the *fílin* style, as well as romantic songs. She has performed on the radio and in theaters, and has made many recordings.

Jústiz, Pedro ("Peruchín"). Pianist and orchestrator. Born 31 January 1913, Banes; died 24 December 1977, Havana. Began studying piano at the age of ten, with his mother. In 1928 his family established itself in Antilla, where he studied with his grandfather, Emilio Rodríguez, who was conductor of the Municipal Band. Jústiz studied piano with Juan Pérez, although he was mainly self-taught. He played with the Orquesta Chepín-Chovén in San-

tiago de Cuba in 1933. He moved to Havana and played piano with the *jazzband* Casino de la Playa, Swing Boys, Conjunto Matamoros, Mariano Mercerón, and Armando Romeu. He joined the Orquesta Riverside in the 1950s. Peruchín also played with Julio Gutiérrez and with Benny Moré's Band, for which he made orchestrations. He made several recordings of his piano solos. He composed the bolero "Qué equivocación," and the mambo "Mamey colorao."

K

Kairuz, Kemal. Pianist. Born 1922, Lebanon. Kairuz's family traveled to Cuba when he was two years old, and they established themselves in Antilla, in Oriente province. There, he played piano with the Orquesta Brisas de Nipe, and later moved to Havana, where he played in nightclubs. In the 1950s, he joined the Los Llopis Quartet. Has regularly performed as a piano accompanist with the best singers in the country, and also on radio and television and in theaters.

Karachi, Grupo. Formed in Santiago de Cuba, 1961. It has been playing Cuban music, mainly *son*, salsa, and *merengue* for thirty-five years. Hugo Bueno, Pablo Moya, and Fico Mariol have all been bandleaders. The group performed on radio and television, and at festivals mostly in the West of Cuba. It has recorded many LPs and has traveled abroad.

Karlo, Sergio de. Singer, actor, composer. Born 1910, Havana; died (?). At seven years of age Sergio played the violin; at nine, he composed a bolero, and at fourteen, he sang in the chorus of a musical by Ernesto Lecuona. He traveled with a theater company to Buenos Aires in 1927. On his return, he formed a *jazzband* in Havana, in which he sang North American hits. He acted in a film in Mexico, and was a dancer and movie actor in New York. Karlo composed the bolero "Flores negras" and the rumbas "Parampampán" and "La última rumba." He sang in several nightclubs in New York. In 1940 he substituted for Desi Arnaz in the Broadway musical *Too Many Girls*, and later appeared in a Hollywood film about the life of Rudolf Valentino. He established himself in Mexico in 1950 and became known for his songs.

kinfuiti. "Kinfuiti" is the name of a drum of Congo origin and the rhythm it plays, as well as a particular dance performed to its music. The drumhead is affixed to a wooden barrel-shaped body, between 60 and 80 centimeters high and about 40 centimeters in diameter. The end of a rope or leather strap passes through a hole pierced in the center of the drum-head and extends through to near the open end or mouth of the sounding-body. The *kinfuiti* has been used throughout the island, wherever there have been large groups of Congos and their descendants (Ortiz, *Los instrumentos de la música afrocubana*, 5:150–52).

kuchí-yeremá. The second of the three drums (*enkomo*) of the Abakuá; the other two are *obiapá* and *binkomé*. About 25 centimeters long, the *kuchí-yeremá* is held under the musician's left arm and is beaten on the leather drumhead with the right hand (Ortiz, *Los instrumentos de la música afrocubana*, 4:24).

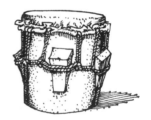

L

old struggles of the Cuban people—black and white —against oppression.

Lago, Trío Hermanas. Founded in 1932, in Havana, by the sisters Cristina, Esperanza, and Graciela Lago. The trio performed on the radio and in theaters. When Esperanza married in 1947, her sister Lucía took her place. Soon after, the group toured Latin America and the United States. In 1950 Esperanza returned to the trio, which then became a quartet until her death in 1954. The sisters performed on radio and television and in theaters and nightclubs. They traveled to New York in 1959, and to Venezuela the following year. From 1961 onward, they toured the country extensively. Since the beginning of their career, their work in introducing Cuban and Latin American songs to wider audiences has been recognized with medals and awards. When Cristina died, Ofelia, another sister, joined the trio. With Lucía Lago as the leading voice, the trio continued to perform in cultural centers and in traditional music events. In 1996 Graciela died. Lucía currently gives sporadic performances.

La Matt, José. Bass and baritone singer. Born (?), Havana. Studied at the Havana Municipal Conservatory. At fourteen years of age, La Matt joined the chorus of the Havana Philharmonic Orchestra, and later became a soloist. He sang in Havana in the most important operas together with renowned bel canto figures. He established himself in the United States in the 1960s, where he has continued to perform in zarzuelas and operas. His voice, which occupied the bass range, in time changed to a baritone, enabling him to sing in both ranges. He has performed in several cities in the United States and Europe.

lamento. A variant of the traditional son that was intended to express the grief and pain of the humble sectors of the Afro-Cuban population but that gave no more than a false, stereotypical image. It devised a melodic and rhythmical structure that scarcely resembled traditional Cuban song and contained no elements of protest, but was characterized by resigned laments that in no way reflected the century-

Landa, Evelio. Composer of popular music. Born 14 April 1922, Havana. Was a chorus singer in several ensembles, among them the René Alvarez orchestra and the Pello el Afrokán ensemble. Landa composed "Me duele el corazón," "Dos lágrimas," and "Carita de cielo" (boleros); "Las mulatas del cha-cha-chá," "Baila mi son," "Dolor y pena" (plenas); "Tamborilero" (afro); "Barín bareta" (guaracha); and "Nace en Cuba el Mozambique" and "Se formó el tiqui-tiqui" (with Pedro Izquierdo).

Landa, Fabio. Cellist, guitarist, pianist, conductor. Born 23 March 1924, Quemados de Güines. Studied with Ernesto Xancó and with Adolph Odnoposoff. Landa played the cello with the National Symphony Orchestra and other musical ensembles. He has composed music for the cinema. Among his works are Fugato theme, for strings; Quinteto, for wind instruments; Toccata, for piano; and Pequeña suite cubana and Canto negro (for cello and piano). Landa was also an arranger and orchestrator of great, refined taste.

Lapique, Zoila. Musicographer and historical researcher. Born 27 June 1930, Havana. A graduate from the University of Havana in library science and history. Lapique has carried out research on Cuban art, particularly in the field of music. Her work on the habanera is outstanding. She currently works at the José Martí National Library. Her book Música colonial cubana (1979) was published by Editorial Letras Cubanas.

Lario, Aldo. Tenor. Born 5 October 1926, Santa Clara. Since 1945 has sung lyrical songs and operatic arias. Lario performed in zarzuelas and operas, and his voice has been heard on radio and television. He was part of the National Lyric Theater ensemble and subsequently performed as a soloist.

Laserie, Rolando. Singer. Born 27 August 1923, Santa Clara; died 1999, Miami. Began his career as a percussionist with ensembles in his hometown; moved to Havana and played drums with several orchestras, including Benny Moré's Banda Gigante. Laserie later played and sang with Olga (Chorens)

and Tony (Alvarez's) group, which performed on Radio Progreso. His recordings of songs in the mid-1950s, with innovative arrangements and appropriate accompaniment by Ernesto Duarte's orchestra, brought him sudden popularity. His voice had a peculiar and distinctive timbre, and he possessed a particular way of conveying feeling in the bolero, the *guaracha*, and other Caribbean genres that set him apart from performers in the same genre. He recorded numerous LPs, and in the 1960s established himself abroad and continued his musical career.

Lastra, Patricio. Composer and singer of *punto guajiro*. Born in La Salud; died (?). Beginning in the 1930s Lastra became an outstanding singer of *décimas* and took part in *campesino* song festivals throughout Cuba. He also sang in radio programs devoted to the *guajiro* genre. He was renowned for his skill at versification, and his tunes were very popular.

laúd. An ancient stringed instrument of Arabic origin. It was played extensively in Spain, from which it was brought to Cuba in the early colonial period. The laúd is widely used in Cuban *guajiro* music, in solos, and, more frequently, as an accompanying instrument. *Campesino* music ensembles prominently feature laúd players.

Lay, Rafael. Violinist, composer, arranger. Born 17 August 1927, Cienfuegos; died 1987. Began his studies of music at age nine with Professor Sara Torres. Lay joined the Orquesta Aragón in 1940 and became its conductor in 1948. He made arrangements for *charanga*-style orchestras and conducted the Popular Concert Orchestra, composed of musicians from several dance bands. His compositions include "Cero codazos," "Envidia," and "Charleston-chá."

Lázaro, Antonio. Tenor. Born 10 June 1938, Guanabacoa. Studied singing at the Hubert de Blanck and the Farelli-Bovi conservatories. Lázaro made his debut as a soloist in 1961 in Verdi's *Rigoletto* at the Auditorium Theater (today the Amadeo Roldán Theater), in Havana. He has given concerts that feature Cuban, Latin American, and European pieces and has toured in Venezuela, Colombia, Puerto Rico, and Mexico. He is a professor at the National School of Art.

Lázaro, Gustavo. Bass singer. Born 1937, Havana; died 29 January 1996, Madrid. Studied with Francisco F. Dominicis. Later Lázaro went on a scholarship to Sofia, Bulgaria, where he perfected his vocal technique and his lyrical repertoire. Lázaro performed in the National Opera of Bulgaria and gave recitals in that country. He performed in various operas in Cuba's National Lyric Theater and gave recitals throughout the Island.

Lazo de la Vega, Manuel. Priest, choirmaster, composer. Born (?); died 1803, Havana. In 1779 he became the choirmaster of the Cathedral of Havana, where he also carried out significant organizational work. He composed Christmas carols.

Lebatard, Orquesta Hermanos. A *jazzband*-style ensemble founded in Havana in 1926 by trumpet player Gonzalo Lebatard. His sons Germán (sax), Luis (sax), Gonzalo (trumpet), and Julio (trumpet) later joined the orchestra, which was eventually conducted by Germán Lebatard. The group played Cuban genres and North American jazz on radio and at many dances throughout the country. The musicians' excellence contributed to the group's singular timbre and style, and its singers were also outstanding. The orchestra continued to play until the 1950s.

Lecuona, Ernestina. Pianist and composer. Born 16 January 1882, Matanzas; died 3 September 1951, Havana. Sister of the renowned Cuban musician Ernesto Lecuona. Ernestina Lecuona studied piano at Havana's Academy of the Centro Asturiano; she pursued higher studies under Madame Calderón, a professor at the Paris Conservatory. As a pianist, she gave innumerable concerts in Cuba and throughout America. As a composer, she left a legacy of songs, including "Anhelo besarte," "Ya que te vas," "¿Me odias?" "Jardín azul," "Ahora que eres mía," "Cierra los ojos," and "Junto al río."

Lecuona, Ernesto. Composer and pianist. Born 6 August 1895, Guanabacoa; died 29 November 1963, Canary Islands. Began his studies of piano with his sister Ernestina, and later studied under Peyrellade, Saavedra, Nin, and Hubert de Blanck. At five years of age, he gave a concert at the Círculo Hispano. At twelve, he composed his first pieces. A year before, he had started working as a pianist for silent movies at the Fedora in Havana. When he graduated from the National Conservatory, he was awarded, by unanimous decision of the board, the First Prize and the Gold Medal of his class (1913). He is the Cuban composer of greatest renown the world over and was a pianist of exceptional quality whose contributions to the Cuban piano tradition are known in particular for their use of distinctive rhythms. He performed internationally and organized orchestras with which he toured several countries in Europe and the United States. He composed nearly six hundred pieces, among them the theater pieces "El sombrero de yarey," "Rosa la china," "Lola Cruz," "María la O," "El cafetal," "El batey," "La tierra de Venus," and "Niña Rita"; and the *canciones* "Siboney," "Damisela encantadora," "Siempre

en mi corazón," "Recordar," "Arrullo de palma," "Tus ojos azules," "Se fue," and "Mariposa." He wrote seventy *danzas* for piano, including "Ahí viene el chino," "Danza negra," "La comparsa," "La malagueña," and "Danza lucumí." He recorded numerous LPs of genuinely Cuban music.

Lecuona, Margarita. Composer. Born 1910, Havana; died 1981, New York. Composed the *canción* "Eclipse"; the bolero "Por eso no debes"; and "Tabú," "Babalú," and other Afro-Cuban pieces.

Ledesma, Roberto. Singer. Born 24 June 1924, Havana. Began his musical career with the Trío Martín, where he sang lead vocals, together with the brothers Ernesto and Eugenio Orta. With the trio he toured several countries in South America. The group dissolved in 1960 and Ledesma became a soloist. Since then he has made an outstanding career as a singer of boleros. He has recorded twenty-five LPs and has been awarded six Gold Records. He currently lives in the United States.

Legarreta, Félix ("Pupi"). Violinist, flutist, arranger, composer, conductor. Born 1930, Havana. Lagarreta began his career as an orchestrator in Cuban orchestras. In 1960 he established himself in the United States, where he has made a brilliant career with both concert performances and recordings. Among his most important LPs are: *Salsa nova* (1962), *Pupi y su charanga* (1975), *Toda la verdad* (1976), *Pupi pa' bailar* (1980), *Pupi–Pachecho, Los dos mosqueteros* (1977), *Habana Jam* (1979), and *Tres flautas* (with Johnny Pachecho and José Fajardo, 1980). He has played in almost all the great salsa orchestras in New York.

Léman, Susy. Lyric singer. Born 11 August 1955, Havana. Her family established itself in New Jersey when she was ten years of age. There Léman began to sing with a Latin group, Fantasy, while at the same time working in an office. In 1976 she made a record of her own compositions, as well as those of other Cuban writers. She has recorded several CDs. Since 1977 she has lived in Miami, where she gives recitals and performs in nightclubs.

León, Argeliers. Musicologist, professor, composer. Born 7 May 1918, Havana; died 1991. Studied education at the University of Havana, where he graduated in 1943. In 1945, León graduated from the Havana Municipal Conservatory, where he studied with Professors Mompó, Luaces, and César Pérez Sentenat. He took his initial lessons in composition from José Ardévol and completed his studies with Nadia Boulanger in Paris. He was granted a scholarship in 1951 to study folklore and music education at the University of Chile. He toured several countries in the Americas, Europe, and Africa, giving courses and lectures, among them: "A Panorama of Cuban Musical Folklore," at the University of Santiago de Chile; "The Negro in Cuban Musical Folklore," at the Ministry of Education, Lima, Peru (1951); "Ethnological Factors of the Cuban People," at the School of Anthropology, Mexico; and lectures at Humboldt University in Berlin in 1967. He took part in several international events: as a delegate at the Eighth International Congress on Anthropological and Ethnological Sciences, Moscow, 1964; and as an attendant of a meeting for the study of music in Latin America, convened by UNESCO and held in Caracas. León has also published in the following foreign journals: *Scientific World*, London; *Algérie Actualité*, Algiers; *América Indígena*, Mexico; and *Abhandlungen und berichte des staatliche Museums für volkerkunde Dresden*, Dresden. Between 1961 and 1970 he was the director of the Institute of Ethnology and Folklore at the Academy of Sciences of Cuba. He also headed the folklore department at the National Theater of Cuba and the music department of the José Martí National Library. He was a professor at the Havana Municipal Conservatory, a professor of African art and Negro cultures in Cuba at the University of Havana, a professor of musicology at the Higher Institute of Art, and head of the music department at Casa de las Américas. His work as a composer is based mainly on folk music but also contains highly

elaborate technical elements. Among his works, the following are outstanding: Symphony no. 2; *Suite cubana*; *Sonata de la Virgen del Cobre*; Quintet for guitar and maderas; *Concertino*; *Cánticos de homenaje*; and *Creador del hombre nuevo* (cantata). The last won him the Chamber Music First Prize in the 26th of July Contest convened by the FAR in 1969. He also composed chamber music and choral and piano pieces, as well as songs. As a musicologist, he published *Un marco de referencia para el estudio del folklore musical en el Caribe*; *Influencias africanas en la música de Cuba* (1959); *Música folklorica cubana* (1964); and *Del canto y el tiempo* (1974), among others.

León, Bienvenido. Baritone. Born 21 March 1888, Havana; died 12 October 1981. León's voice, which acted as the second in harmonic combinations, is considered one of the most mellow voices in Cuban popular music. When he was very young, he established himself in Tampa, Florida, working in cigar factories. There he began his singing career in 1909. He returned to Cuba in 1911 and joined the Cuarteto Nano, with Tirso Díaz (guitar), Domingo Capellejas (falsetto voice), and Romás Nano León (leading voice and conductor). He traveled to New York in 1924 with Juan de la Cruz and Alberto Villalón. Three years later he returned to New York with the Septeto Nacional, with whom he also traveled to Spain. In 1938 he formed his own music ensemble, which performed in nightclubs. In the 1940s, with Alfredo de la Fe, he sang for the Mil Diez radio station.

León, Gina. Lyric singer. Born 19 April 1937, Havana. Studied music with Maestro Candito Ruiz. León sang in several nightclubs in Havana. She has made several very popular recordings of *canciones* and *boleros*. She currently performs on radio and television and in the theater. She has toured widely in Latin America and Europe.

León, Tania. Composer and conductor. Born 1940, Havana. Studied at the Havana Municipal Conservatory. León composed some pieces that were premiered in Cuba. She established herself in New York in 1967, where she was one of the founders of the Harlem Dance Theater, whose music section she heads. She has conducted a number of symphony orchestras in the United States and has composed avant-garde works, including *Momentum* and *Haiku*.

Leyva, Manuel de Jesús. Orchestra conductor, arranger, composer, trumpet player. Born 13 April 1944, Holguín. Studied with Professors Exuperancio Cuayo and Porfirio Sánchez. After having played in several orchestras, Leyva joined the Orquesta Hermanos Avilés in Holguín, with whom he played for seventeen years. He studied orchestration with Juanito Márquez. He was the conductor of the Municipal Band of Holguín. He composed several pieces.

Leyva, Pío. Singer of *son montuno*. Born 5 May 1915, Morón. Began his career playing *bongós* with the Siboney Orchestra in Morón. He later began to sing with trios and popular-music groups. Leyva moved to Camagüey, where he sang with the Orquesta Hermanos Licea and with Juanito Blez's ensemble. In the 1950s, he established himself in Havana, as a soloist. He has made numerous recordings with various ensembles. He is one of the most significant singers of *son montuno*. He has composed "Francisco Guayabal" and other *sones*. In the 1990s he became a vocalist with the Buena Vista Social Club and recorded and toured widely with the Afro-Cuban All Stars.

Li, Jesús. Tenor. Born 27 April 1952, Madruga. Began his singing career in amateur festivals. Li joined the National Opera Theater of Cuba as a soloist in 1971. He has sung leads in operas and *zarzuelas*. He won seventh place in the International Singing Contest in Sofia, Bulgaria, in 1979. He has given lyrical recitals throughout Cuba.

Licea, Manuel ("Puntillita"). Singer. Born 4 January 1927, Yareyal, Holguín; died 2000. First joined music ensembles in his hometown and later moved to Camagüey, where he sang with González Allué's orchestra. In Havana, Licea joined Julio Cueva's orchestra in 1945. With the popularity gained by his interpretation of the "Son de la puntillita," he became known as "Puntillita." When Julio Cueva's orchestra was dissolved in the 1950s, he continued his career as a soloist, singing popular music on the radio, television, and in nightclubs and song festivals. He has made various recordings and has performed abroad. In the 1990s he sang with the Buena Vista Social Club and the Afro-Cuban All Stars, with whom he recorded and traveled widely.

Lima, Ninón. Soprano. Born 28 August 1938, Havana. Studied singing in Havana, and later in Sofia, Bulgaria, where she graduated in 1973. Lima has given numerous recitals in Cuba and has sung in operas. She performs on the radio and television and has given concerts in several European countries. She belongs to the company of the National Opera of Cuba and is a professor at the Higher Institute of Art.

Lima, Radeúnda. Lyric singer. Born 28 August 1923, Vueltas, Las Villas. At eight years of age, sang *tonadas guajiras* accompanied by his brother Raúl Lima, a lute player. Later began to sing *sones montunos* and *guarachas*. Radeúnda Lima performed with the Arredondo and the Castany companies, with the Montalvo and the Santos and Artigas circus, and in radio broadcasts in several cities. She won a prize in the Corte Suprema del Arte. She performed often on the RHC Cadena Azul radio station and was elected Queen of Radio several times. She performed in the United States in 1946. She has made recordings and performed in theaters.

Lima, Raúl. *Laúd* player. Born 1920, Vueltas, Las Villas. Brother of the singer Radeúnda Lima, whose career he has always been linked to as her accompanist. Raúl Lima is one of the most outstanding *laúd* players in Cuba. He currently plays with *campesino* music groups.

Linares, Annia. Lyric singer. Born 5 December 1950, Maracaibo, Venezuela. The daughter of Cuban parents, Linares moved to Cuba in 1963. She began her career as an actress on the radio and television and in the theater. Later, in 1970, she undertook a career as a vocalist. The following year she performed in Peru, where she recorded her first LP with songs by Cuban composers. She later took part in the Sopot Festival, in Poland. She has performed in several countries in the Americas and in Europe. In Cuba, she has performed as a songstress on the radio and television and in theaters and nightclubs. She has recorded several LPs of *canciones* and boleros. She has been living in Miami for several years.

Linares, Antonio. Trombonist. Born 17 January 1927, Guanabacoa. Began his studies of music in his hometown and continued in Havana. Linares has performed as a trombonist in several Cuban popular ensembles, including Benny Moré's band, playing both classical music and popular and dance music. He plays lead trombone with the National Symphony Orchestra. He has taught some outstanding trombonists while a professor at the National School of Art in recent years.

Linares, María Teresa. Professor and researcher of Cuban music. Born 14 August 1920, Havana. Studied at the Municipal Conservatory. Between 1938 and 1947 was part of the Havana Chorus. Linares has been a professor in several music centers, including the Amadeo Roldán Conservatory. She has taught courses at the University of Havana's summer program. Her works have been published in many journals. She is the author of "Ensayo sobre la influencia española en la música cubana," El sucu-sucu de la Isla de Pinos, La música popula, and La música y el pueblo. She worked at the Institute of Ethnology and Folklore at the Academy of Sciences for years, as a member of its advisory committee. She later worked at the Musical Recordings and Publishing House. Until 2000 she was director of the Museum of Music. She is currently affiliated with the Fernando Ortiz Foundation in Havana.

Lombida, Genaro. Pianist and composer. Born (?), Ciego de Avila; died 1983, Miami. Was a piano accompanist and journalist in Havana in the 1940s and 1950s. Lombida played piano accompaniment for the radio program La Corte Suprema del Arte, on CMQ Radio. He composed the bolero "Confidencias de Amor" and other songs.

Lombida, Nestor. Pianist, guitarist, arranger. Born 5 March 1950, Havana. In 1965 Lombida began his studies at the National School of Art, where he was later a professor. He was a pianist with Los Magnéticos ensemble and with the Elio Revé Orchestra. He worked as a pianist and guitarist accompanying several vocalists. He was a music adviser on television programs and musicals. His work as a popular-music journalist has been outstanding.

López, Anselmo. Violinist, publisher, professor. Born 1841, Madrid; died 1920, Havana. Established himself in Cuba in 1858. Through his publishing work, López made an important contribution to the preservation and dissemination of nineteenth-century Cuban music. He was a conductor and heavily involved in musical activity in Havana. He was also a professor of violin.

López, Blas. Singer and choirmaster. Born (?), Bayamo. López was a sacristan in the parish church of Bayamo. Composed the music for the motet that closes "Espejo de paciencia," a narrative poem written in 1608 by Silvestre de Balboa to celebrate the rescue of Bishop Altamirano, who was held captive by the French pirate Gilberto Girón. It is the first known composition by a Creole musician in Cuba.

López, César. Professor and pianist. Born 7 February 1938, Havana. Studied at the Amadeo Roldán Conservatory. López has made a remarkable career as a piano accompanist and performing in chamber music ensembles. He has given recitals and concerts. He has performed in various European countries. He was a professor at the Higher Institute of Art.

López, César. Saxophonist. Born 17 May 1968, Havana. Studied at the National School of Art. López was a member of Bobby Carcasses's band and Chucho Valdés's legendary band Irakere. He is currently the director of his own band, Havana Ensemble.

López, Coralia. Pianist and composer. Born 6 May 1911, Havana. Sister of Israel and Orestes López. Coralia López studied with her father, Pedro López, during her early childhood. She is the author of the danzones "Llegó Manolo," "El bajo que come chivo," "Los jóvenes del agua fría," and of the very popular "Isora."

López, Emelina. Soprano. Born 19 November 1948, Regla. Began her studies singing at the García Caturla Conservatory, in Marianao, in 1968. Later studied at the Professional School under Margarita Horruitiner. López won First Prize for Singing in the contest held by the Writers and Artists Union of Cuba, in 1973. She has given recitals throughout the Island.

López, Israel ("Cachao"). Composer, double bass player, conductor. Born 1918, Havana. Born into a large family of musicians, López joined the Havana

Symphony Orchestra at thirteen years of age. In 1937 he joined Fernando Collazo's orchestra Maravilla del Siglo, and later, as a double bass player, the ensemble Arcaño y Sus Maravillas, for which he composed, with his brother Orestes López, numerous *danzones* set to a "new rhythm," which were precursors of the mambo. He was a double bass player in several orchestras in Havana's theaters and in jazz ensembles. He played with Orquesta Fajardo y Sus Estrellas between 1957 and 1960. He has performed in various countries with important popular music groups. He recorded numerous LPs in New York with groups he conducted and also with other famous salsa groups. His recordings of Cuban *descargas* are highly revered. Among the *danzones* he composed are the classics "Se va el matancero," "Adelante," and "Jóvenes del ritmo." He has composed innumerable arrangements.

López, Jesús. Pianist. Born 30 July 1904, Matanzas; died 6 July 1971, Havana. Studied piano in his hometown and later came to Havana, where he played with several orchestras, among them Collazo's Maravilla del Siglo. López joined Arcaño y Sus Maravillas in 1937, and later played with Fajardo y Sus Estrellas. He is one of the most remarkable Cuban pianists to date, and his style has influenced many instrumentalists.

López, Orestes. Composer, double bass player, cellist. Born 29 August 1908, Havana; died 26 January 1991. Studied music with his father, and later studied piano with Fernando Carnicer. Was also a flutist. In the 1920s López joined the Charanga de Miguel Vázquez ("El Moro") as a double bass player. In the 1930s he founded a *danzón* ensemble with Abelardo Barroso. Later, he founded his own orchestra, Unión. In 1938 he was playing with Arcaño y Sus Maravillas as a cellist, and contributed to the popularity of the "new rhythm," a genuine revolution in Cuban popular music, which was influential in almost all later forms. In that year, he composed his *danzón* "Mambo," which was the genesis of the musical style of the same name, cultivated by his brother Israel López and others. Later the mambo was taken up by Dámaso Pérez Prado, who reelaborated, widened, and developed it and then incorporated it into the *jazzband* format and made it universal. Orestes López was a double bass player in the Havana Philharmonic Orchestra and in the National Symphony Orchestra. He was also the composer of the *danzones* "El que más goza," "Camina Juan Pesca'o," "El truco," "Tan suave," "El coloso," "Atarés y su castillo," and "Rarezas de Melitón."

López, Orlando ("Cachaíto"). Double bass player and professor. Born 2 February 1933, Havana. Studied with his father, the composer and double bass player Orestes López. At thirteen years of age, Orlando López was already playing with René Hernández's Charanga Armonía, and four years later, with Arcaño y Sus Maravillas. He subsequently played with the orchestra of the Bambú nightclub and, in 1954, with the Orquesta Riverside *jazzband*. He simultaneously played in jazz concerts. He has played in the National Symphony Orchestra since 1960. He took lessons from the Czech double bass player Karel Kopriva. He played with the Orquesta Cubana de Música Moderna in 1966. He has performed in almost all socialist countries, and in Panama and the United States. He is a professor of the double bass.

López, Orquesta de Belisario. French *charanga* band created in Havana, 1928, by the flutist Belisario López along with Juan Quevedo and Humberto Trigo (violins), Raúl Valdespí (piano), Guillermo Maherve (double bass), Aurelio Valdés (*güiro*), Gerardo Cabrera (timbales), and Rogelio Martínez (vocalist). Later, Gerardo González (piano), Mario Vaulens (double bass), Facundo Rivero (piano), and Alberto Aroche and Joseíto Núñez (vocalists) were also members. The group was first heard on Radio Progreso Cubano, and there are a few recordings of its music. It disbanded in 1960 when the leader left the country.

López, Oscar. Singer. Born 6 May 1918, Havana. López began his singing career on radio stations in Havana in 1935; he was a vocalist with the orchestras Obdulio Morales, Arcaño y Sus Maravillas, Cosmopolita, and Havana Casino. He sang in concerts with Ernesto Lecuona and, with the Lecuona Company, toured several countries in Latin America. He sang in the films *María la O, Amores de un torero, Yo soy el hombre,* and *Mujer de Tánger*. He has also acted in numerous musicals in Cuba. He lived and worked in Mexico between 1941 and 1946, alternating with working seasons in Cuba and the United States. On returning to Havana, he continued to perform on radio and television and in the theater. He toured in Spain, France, and Switzerland. He established himself in Paris in 1956, where he has cultivated Cuban music with his orchestra. He has made tours of almost all the European and African countries.

López, Rafael. Composer and double bass player. Born 24 October 1907, Bahía Honda; died (?), Paris, France. Played the double bass with several popular-music ensembles. López established himself abroad many years ago and contributed to the dissemination of Cuban music. He is the author of "La sitiera" and other Cuban songs.

López, Severino. Guitarist and professor of guitar. Born 1900, Camagüey; died 1978, Havana. Studied with the Spanish professor Miguel Llobet. After being a concert performer, López began teaching. His pupils included Guyún, José Rey de la Torre, and others. He was a combatant in the Rebel Army in the Sierra Maestra. He also worked as a veterinary surgeon. He transcribed for the guitar.

López Gavilán, Guido. Orchestra conductor. Born 3 January 1944, Matanzas. Studied at the Havana Municipal Conservatory and at the Tchaikovsky Conservatory, in Moscow, where he graduated in conducting in 1973. Has conducted concerts in the Soviet Union, Poland, Hungary, Romania, and Colombia. In Cuba, López Gavilán has been the conductor of the National Symphony Orchestra and of the symphony orchestras of Matanzas, Las Villas, Camagüey, and Oriente. He was president of the music section of the Hermanos Saíz Brigade, public relations secretary of Writers and Artists Union of Cuba, and also the vice president of UNEAC's As-

sociation of Musicians. Among his works are "Variantes," "Tramas," and "Camerata en guaguancó."

López Marín, Jorge. Orchestra conductor and composer. Born 8 May 1949, Havana. Studied at the García Caturla and the Amadeo Roldán conservatories. Between 1969 and 1978, López Marín studied conducting and composing in the Soviet Union with Boris Jaikin and Aram Kachaturian. He has conducted the National Symphony Orchestra, as well as other orchestras in Cuba and abroad. Among his works are *Obertura cubana* (1973), Concerto for flute and orchestra (1974), First symphony (1975), Second symphony (1978), *En la Plaza de la Catedral* (1980), and *Beat abruptio* (1981). He is currently a professor at the Higher Institute of Art.

López-Nussa, Ernán. Pianist. Born 10 September 1958, Havana. Made his early studies at the García Caturla Conservatory and his higher studies at the Amadeo Roldán Conservatory, where he took lessons from professors María Enma Botet, Vívian Lamata, and César López. López-Nussa later studied under Jorge Gómez Labraña at the Higher Institute of Art. In his career he has played Cuban concert music and, particularly, jazz. In 1977 he was a founder and the keyboard player of the Grupo Afrocuba, with whom he played for ten years. He also founded the Grupo Cuarto Espacio in 1989. He has performed as a soloist since 1993 and has toured throughout the Americas and in Europe.

Loyola, Efraín. Flutist and conductor. Born 18 January 1917, Cienfuegos. Began his career as a singer with the Septeto Los Naranjos in 1934; he later sang with other groups in his hometown. In 1939 he was a founder of the Orquesta Aragón, in Cienfuegos, in which he was a flutist. He founded the Orquesta Loyola in 1953, which he still conducts.

Loyola, José. Composer and flutist. Born 12 February 1941, Cienfuegos. Studied flute with professors Roberto Ondina and Emigdio Mayo at the National School of Art, where he graduated. He later studied composing at the Warsaw Higher School of Music in Poland, under professor Witold Rufzinski. Loyola was a member of the music section of the UNEAC's Brigada Hermanos Saíz and a member of the jury for the UNEAC's composition contest in 1975 and 1976.

He has taken part in international events, including the Symposium on Opera, Ballet and Musical Theater in Sofia, Bulgaria, March 1976; the Colloquium on Negro Civilization and Education, Lagos, Nigeria, 1977; and the Meeting of the Members of Governing Bodies of Composers' Associations of Socialist Countries, Moscow and Tbilisi, 1977. He was a member of the Organizing Committee of the Third Congress of UNEAC. He was the academic vice-rector of the Higher Institute of Art and a professor of composing and musical analysis. His main works are Music, for flute and strings, 1970; *Música viva no. 1*, for percussion instruments; *Tras imágenes poéticas*, for baritone, voice, and piano, 1972; *Música viva no. 2*, for symphony orchestra; *Monzón y el rey de Koré*, an opera in three acts, 1973; *Cantata a los mártires del 5 de septiembre*, for reciter, chorus, and orchestra, 1974; *Poética del Guerrillero*, for voice and orchestra, dedicated to Ernesto ("Che") Guevara, with texts by the Mexican poet Carlos Pellicer (a work that won him a prize in the 26th of July Contest held by the FAR in 1976); and *Homenaje a Brindis de Salas*, violin solo, 1975.

Lozano, Danilo. Flutist. Born 23 December 1956, New York. The son of the renowned flutist Rolando Lozano, Danilo Lozano took his first lessons from his father. He later graduated from the School of Music at the University of Southern California, and obtained a Master of Arts degree at the University of California at Los Angeles. He has performed as a soloist with the orchestra of the Opera of Los Angeles, the Symphony Orchestra of El Paso, the Symphony Orchestra of Mexico, and the Hollywood Bowl Orchestra. His repertoire includes Latin American and Afro-American music. He has performed as a soloist in various countries and has recorded several LPs. He is a notable musicologist and is a professor at California State Polytechnic University at Pomona, at Whittier College, and at UCLA. He plays with jazz ensembles and with Cuban popular-music groups.

Lozano, Rolando. Flutist. Born 27 August 1931, Cienfuegos. In 1950 he joined Orquesta Aragón. He later established himself in Mexico City, and then moved to Chicago, where he founded the *charanga* orchestra Nuevo Ritmo. Lozano subsequently played and recorded with various orchestras, including those of Mongo Santamaría, Tito Puente, George Shearing, and Cal Tjader. In Los Angeles, he played with the *orquestas típicas* Tropical and Antillana. As a flutist, he has played on various film soundtracks.

Luna, Manuel. Composer, guitarist, singer. Born 1887, Colón, Matanzas; died 1975, Havana. Was the author of boleros, most with texts by poets. "La cleptómana," with verses by Agustín Acosta, gained him great popularity. He also wrote the score and lyrics for "Secretos pasionales" and "Yo no soy tan bueno." As a performer of troubadour songs, he formed a duet with José Castillo in 1918, and later with Pablo Armiñán. In 1928 he sang in a trio with Antonio Machín and Armando Peláez. The renowned Cuarteto Luna was founded in 1939 by Manuel Romero (*tres*), José Chepín Socarrás, (guitar), Ramón Alvarado (lead vocals and maracas), and Manuel Luna (second voice and guitar). The quartet soon after performed in the Feria del Tabaco in Tampa, at the Cuban Pavilion of the New York World's Fair, and in several cities in the United States.

M

Macías, Orestes. Singer. Born 9 November 1934, Bejucal. When he was nine years old, Macías's family moved to Havana. He was a vocalist with the bands Casino and Rumbavana, and with the Hermanos Castro Orchestra. He has performed as a soloist on the radio, on television, and in nightclubs. He cultivates popular Cuban genres, especially the bolero. He has performed in various Latin American countries.

Machín, Antonio. Singer. Born 19 January 1904, Sagua la Grande; died 4 August 1977, Madrid, Spain. Began his singing career in his hometown. Widened his repertoire in Havana in 1926, by working with quartets and sextets. Machín sang with the Trío Luna, alongside Enrique Peláez (*tres*) and Manuel Luna (second voice and guitar), but is best remembered as the singer with the Orquesta de Don Azpiazu, with whom he recorded more than fifty records for RCA Victor. Some years later, he founded the Cuarteto Machín, along with Daniel (second voice and guitar), Mulatón (*tres*), and Fabelo (trumpet). He moved to Spain in 1936, where he became one of the most renowned exponents of Cuban music. He performed in several European cities.

Machito. Conductor, singer, percussionist. Born 16 February 1912, Tampa, Florida; died 16 April 1984, London. His given name was Frank Grillo. Machito's family moved to Havana when he was a child, and it was there he began his musical career. In 1937 he moved to New York and in 1940 he established his band, Machito y Sus Afrocubanos, in which he played maracas and sang and in which Mario Bauzá was lead trumpeter and an arranger. Machito's sister Graciela also performed with the group, joining him as one of its vocalists. Machito y Sus Afrocubanos successfully fused jazz and Cuban sounds in a style that came to be called Cubop, and the ensemble's popularity ultimately effected the musical trend that would eventually be known as salsa. The Afrocubanos' frequent collaboration with such notable jazz musicians as Dizzy Gillespie, Stan Kenton, and Charlie Parker in the 1940s resulted in a mutually influential relationship between Afro-Cuban music and jazz. In the late 1940s Machito was invited by the producer Norman Granz to perform in a jazz concert at Carnegie Hall. Machito's popularity rose with that of the mambo in the 1950s, and he continued to tour both in the United States and internationally into the 1980s. He won a Grammy Award in 1982.

Madrigalista, Coro. Choral group founded in 1960, in Santiago de Cuba; conducted by Miguel García. Their work in the dissemination of choral music has been very significant, particularly in the eastern provinces. They have also been influential in the training of singers.

makuta dance. A dance ritual performed by the Congo groups who arrived in Cuba starting in the sixteenth century. The dance is performed inside a *munanso bela* (sacred room) and is presided over by a king and queen. The three drums that accompany the dance are beaten with the hands. The drums are cylindrical and wide, with staves and hoops, and are adorned with symbolic figures of Bantu origin. A *reja*, or ploughshare, is also used. It is a couple's dance, in which a man and a woman are surrounded by a chorus.

Malcolm, Carlos. Composer. Born 24 November 1945, Guanabacoa. Began his studies of piano with Juan M. Quiñones and Sonia Montalvo. At sixteen years of age, Malcolm was a pianist with popular-music groups. He studied one year of composition under Federico Smith at the National School of Art in 1962, and later at the Amadeo Roldán Conservatory. He has composed incidental music for the theater, for stage dance, for the cinema, and for radio programs, and has received prizes in national contests. His compositions include Studies, for piano; *Marionetas*; *Allegro en son*, for wind quintet; Two canciones (with text by Martínez Villena); *Tonos de Orquesta*; Canción (with text by José Martí); *Montaje*; *Contornos*, for narrator, chorus, and orchestra; *Fragmentos*, for piano; and *Oposiciones-cambios*, for three pianos and percussion.

Mambí Army calls. The calls of the Mambí Army (independence fighters) were heard across the battlefields during the thirty years of Cuba's struggle for independence against Spanish colonialism (1868–

1898). The buglers who rode with the great generals were legendary, transmitting the generals' orders to the Mambí troops with their bugle calls. The initial calls were adaptations of popular *contradanzas*, since the Cubans did not want to use the calls the Spanish army used. Thus, fragments of pieces such as "La caringa," "La mano abajo," "Maria la O," and "El Obispo de Guinea" served for different orders and were heard on the battlefields and in the Mambí camps. So it was until Eduardo Agramonte, a musician and a Mambí soldier, composed specific calls to accompany the liberators in their glorious struggle: attention, reveille, cavalry saddle, fall in, march, halt march, fire, halt fire, take to the machete, retreat, guard relief, order, water, unsaddle, march of the flag, curfew, silence, right, left, and cavalry march.

mambo. Dance-music genre that also features singing. Its earliest roots were in the so-called *ritmo nuevo* made popular by Arcaño y Sus Maravillas. Arcaño's arrangements served as a stylistic framework for Orestes López when he composed his *danzón* "Mambo" (1938), in which syncopated motives taken from the *son* were combined with improvised flute variations. Other developments appeared in the *montunos* that Arsenio Rodríguez called "*diablo*." In the mid-1940s, the syncopated mode of the mambo became independent from the structure of the *danzón* in arrangements for jazz orchestra by both Bebo Valdés and René Hernández. Dámaso Pérez Prado experimented with all these elements, and from there emerged the type of big band mambos that brought the genre its universal fame. "Rico mambo," in 1951, was the first popular hit, and it reveals strong jazz influences. In mambo, the brass section—supported by the saxophones—achieves extraordinary effects with the melody, the harmony, and the rhythm, while the Cuban percussion provides a characteristic underlying rhythm.

Manfugás, Nené. Composer. Born mid-nineteenth century, Guantánamo; died (?). Learned to play the *tres* in the region of Baracoa, on the easternmost tip of the Island, and introduced the instrument in Santiago de Cuba toward the end of the century. Manfugás played primitive but very sonorous *sones* on the *tres*, in spite of the rusticity of his instrument. He was a bohemian, adventurous man.

Manfugás, Zenaida. Pianist. Born (?), Guantánamo. First studied with her mother, Andrea Manfugás, and later studied piano at the Havana Municipal Conservatory and in Spain under Professor Tomás Andrade de Silva. Manfugás graduated from the Royal Conservatory of Madrid. She performed concerts in the Peninsula and later studied under Walter Gieseking, in Paris. On her return to Cuba in 1959, she was appointed professor at the Alejandro García Caturla Conservatory. She gave many concerts and recitals in Cuba with the National Symphony Orchestra and also made tours of Europe and Asia. She has lived in Madrid for several years and has performed in the United States and Latin America.

maní dance. Argeliers León characterizes the *maní* as a pugilistic dance in which a man, dancing in a close circle of other men, moves to the rhythm of yuka drums and chanted singing. He attacks one of the men dancing in the circle around him with theatrical, aggressive blows. His victim, in turn, must then display an equal number of parries and counterattacks from his position in the circle, all the while continuing the dance. The *maní* dance seems to have spread among the slaves in the sugar mills during the nineteenth century (León, *Música folklórica cubana*, 67).

Maraca. *See* Valle, Orlando.

maraca. Although typically employed in Cuban music, the maraca did not have its origin in Cuba, for it belongs to a universal family of instruments and was used in various regions. The aborigines of the Antilles used maracas to make music. At the time of the arrival of the Spanish, the aborigines used them in their *areítos*. The word "maraca" is of indigenous, pre-Columbian origin. It consists of a closed receptacle made from the shell or skin of a

durable fruit or wood, containing seeds, small balls, or corpuscles of any other hard substance inside. The handle is typically made of wood. When shaken, the small hard objects inside the receptacle clash against one another and against the sides of the fruit or wood (Ortiz, *Los instrumentos de la música afrocubana*, 2:34).

maraca, aboriginal. A rattle that was present in the *areítos* of the Indo-Cubans. Made from two stems of *magüey* (a plant also called *pita*), fixed together; the heads contain small stones or seeds.

Maravillas de Florida, Orquesta. *Charanga* band formed in Florida, Camagüey, 1948. The orchestra has played in dance halls all over Cuba. Its repertoire includes *danzón*, *cha-cha-chá*, and other rhythms, and the ensemble has recorded LPs and performed on radio and television. It has also appeared in many European and African countries. Presently, its members are Eduardo F. Cabrera (bandleader and violin); Eladio Terry, Emil M. Castillo, and Enrique Alvarez (violins); Filiberto Depestre (viola); Orestes Calderón (cello); Orlando Beltrán (flute); José Boladeres (piano); Norberto Valdés (bass); Dalio Vento (timbales); Juan A. Tomás Espinosa and Rafael Villa (percussion); Juan R. Quintana (*güiro*); and Nicolás Mena, Lázaro Aparicio, and José Hernández Boza (vocalists).

Marcos, Daniel. Tenor. Born 27 October 1929, Havana; died 27 May 1984, Matanzas. Studied with Francisco F. Dominicis, Ana Talmaceanu, Kiril Krastev, and Iris Burguet. Marcos made his debut in 1961 at the Amadeo Roldán Theater in Verdi's *Rigoletto* and Gounod's *Faust*. He later sang in other lyrical roles. He was a founder of the Matanzas Lyric Group, with whom he staged many Cuban and Spanish works. He gave several recitals, almost always performing as a soloist.

Marcos, Hugo. Baritone. Born 7 October 1946, Havana. Studied music in his hometown. Marcos joined the chorus of the National Opera of Cuba in 1967. He studied singing in Sofia, Bulgaria, with professors Kiril Kravstev and Liliana Yablonska. Marcos made his debut as a soloist in 1971 and has sung in various operas and has given concerts. He sang at La Scala in Milan in 1981. He received several awards in Italy, including First Prize in the International Singing Contest of Alexandria. He has traveled to Bulgaria, Italy, and Mexico. He is a soloist with the National Opera of Cuba.

marímbula. An instrument used by *son* ensembles in Cuba. It is said to have evolved from the African *sansa* or *mbira* (thumb piano) and has also been used in other Caribbean countries. It is constructed of a wooden box with an opening on one side, into which steel rods are inserted. They are fixed at their center, with their ends loose. When pulsed, they produce vibrations in the sounding-body of the instrument. The player sits on the box and makes the sound by pressing on the rods with the tips of his fingers. Although sometimes it has five or even seven keys, generally only the tonic, the dominant, and the subdominant are played. The *marímbula* serves as a substitute for the double bass.

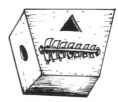

Marín, Víctor. Composer. Born 24 July 1924, Havana. Has lived most of his life in Santiago de las Vegas. Marín was a percussionist with the Naval Band, and in groups in his hometown. He has composed *sones*, *cha-cha-chás*, and *guarachas*, such as "A gozar la vida," "Baila Catalina con un solo pie," "Ritmo de azúcar," "Ponte en vela José," "Suena la flauta, Richard," "A bailar el minuet," "Yo no quiero onda," and "Ni tan sólo un instante."

Marín Varona, José. Composer, pianist, conductor. Born 10 March 1859, Camagüey; died 17 September 1912, Havana. Lived in Havana since his youth, and there he conducted the orchestra of the Albisu

Theater. His *zarzuela* El brujo was staged for the first time in 1896. Soon after, Marín Varona left for Key West, following his ideals of independence. In exile, he continued to perform, but also began to write as a journalist. At the inauguration of the Republic, he was organizer and first conductor of the staff band of the army. As a music critic, he founded the magazine *Cuba musical*. He was a professor at the Havana Municipal Conservatory. He conducted several orchestras, performing *zarzuelas*. He was a substantial composer, whose work began with the waltz "Consuelo," and includes *zarzuelas*, *romanzas*, piano pieces for children, potpourris, and *danzas*.

Marisela, Verena. Composer and singer. Born (?), Pinar del Río. Moved with her parents to the United States in early childhood, and established herself in Puerto Rico in 1971. There, she began her professional career. In 1976, Marisela moved to Madrid, where she gave recitals and recorded several LPs. She composed the songs "Mi corazón es un pueblo," "Amado de lejos," "Tu compañera," and "El águila de tus ojos."

Marquetti, José ("Cheo"). Singer. Born 26 April 1909, Alquízar; died 29 March 1967, Havana. Became popular in the 1930s during the peak of the *danzonete*, when he played with the orchestras Cuba, Cheo Belén Puig, and Ernesto Muñoz. He was also a member of *son* sextets, including Facenda and Habanero, and conducted the Hatuey Sextet. He sang with ensembles in the 1940s, and in the 1950s was one of the singers with the Orquesta Sensación. Marquetti cultivated the *guajira-son* and became quite popular as a result of the authenticity of his style.

Marquetti, Luis. Composer. Born 24 August 1901, Alquízar; died 29 July 1991. Was a primary-school teacher in his hometown for thirty-eight years and was highly respected by the community. Marquetti composed songs and popular-music pieces, among them the boleros "Plazos traicioneros," "Allí donde tú sabes," "Amor qué malo eres," "Deuda," "Llevarás la marca," "Entre espumas," and "Desastre."

Márquez, Beatriz. Singer. Born 17 February 1952, Havana. Began her studies of music at nine years of age. The daughter of the composer and singer René Márquez, she studied at the National School of Art.

She sang with the group Los Barba, and later became a soloist. Beatriz Márquez cultivates the international song repertoire. She toured Europe in 1971 with the musical *Ritmos de Cuba*, and received an award at the Sopot Festival, in Poland.

Márquez, Juanito. Composer, arranger, guitarist. Born 4 July 1929, Holguín. Studied music with his father, Juan Márquez Gómez, who was the conductor of the Municipal Band of Holguín. Juanito Márquez learned to play the guitar at an early age. He joined the Orquesta Hermanos Avilés in his hometown in 1948 and began to make arrangements for them and for Orquesta Riverside. He is the composer of the boleros "Alma con Alma," "Qué desesperanza," and "Como un milagro"; the *danzón-chá* "Dulce de guayaba"; the bolero-*chá* "Esos tiernos ojos"; the *pa'cás* "Pituka la bella," "Arrímate pa'acá," "Cuidado con la vela," "Joropero," and "Tengo ahora una chiquita"; and the *cha-cha-chá* "Naricita fría." In the early 1970s he moved to Spain, where he was very successful as a musician and arranger. He has recorded several LPs featuring his own compositions and those of other writers, directing a group of outstanding soloists. He currently lives in the United States, where he has made a brilliant career as a composer, arranger, and conductor.

Márquez, Ramón. *Trova* singer. Born 31 August 1908, Santiago de Cuba; died 27 June 1980. Sang second voice in duets and trios in his hometown. Márquez also performed with Angel Almenares and was a member of the Trío Azul. Right up until his death, he performed with various *trova* groups in Oriente.

Márquez, René. Composer, singer, guitarist. Born 9 September 1914, Remedios; died 23 December 1986. Learned to play the guitar so as to accompany himself as a singer. Márquez made his debut as a singer in 1930 with the Orquesta Cervantes, conducted by Bellín Domenech, in Remedios. He first appeared on the radio in Havana with Orquesta Paulín in 1937. He later joined the group Boufartique and the bands of Neno González, Antonio Arcaño, and Jorge Ánckerman. He was a member of the Julio Cueva Orchestra for ten years, and later performed with the Tanda de Guaracheros of the National Council for Culture. He wrote the *canciones*

"Ven junto a mí," "En el cíelo de mi vida," "Es la ilusión," "Espontáneamente," "La vida es un momento," and "Puede una flor," and the *guarachas* "Jícara," "El granito de maíz," and "Soltando chispas."

Márquez, Trío Hermanas. Made up of Trini, Cusa, and Olga Márquez, sisters who began their career in their hometown, Puerto Padre, and moved to Havana in 1940, where they appeared on radio and in theaters. They toured several countries in the Americas, performing a broad spectrum of Cuban genres. The sisters established themselves in New York in 1951, where they continued singing until their retirement as a trio in 1960. Trini continued a career as a composer and singer.

Márquez Gómez, Juan. Band conductor. Born 22 December 1883, Mayarí; died 31 August 1976, Holguín. Lived for several years in Puerto Padre, where he founded the Municipal Band. Márquez later moved to Holguín, where he was the conductor of the Municipal Band for seventy-five years, until a short time before his death. He was also a professor of guitar and gave recitals and concerts. Among the many musicians he taught were his children Eduardo, Aida, María, Amalia, Teresa, Ernesto, and Juanito. In his youth, he was a barber.

Márquez Lacasa, Juan. Composer. Born 8 February 1945, Havana. Began composing music for theater in 1968. Was an assistant conductor of the orchestra of the National Ballet of Cuba. Márquez Lacasa has composed scores for several films and since 1971 has been the musical adviser of the Cuban Institute for Movie-Making, Art, and Industry. His compositions include Suite, for piano; *Rimas*, for voice and piano (with text by José Martí); *Trío*, for trumpet, horn, and trombone; *Pequeña toccata*, for violin, viola, and cello; and *Sexta primera*, for bow instruments.

Marrero, Zoraida. Soprano. Born 19 September 1911, Bejucal. Began singing in her hometown at cultural events. Marrero acted with the Ernesto Lecuona Company, touring Latin America, and subsequently lived and worked in Argentina for five years. She sang in *zarzuelas* and musicals, as well as on the radio and on television. She moved to New Jersey in 1961.

Martí, Dúo Hermanas. Made up of the sisters Bertha and Amelia Martí, guitarists and singers. They began their career at the Corte Suprema del Arte in 1939. Since then, they have performed a repertoire of Cuban traditional songs on the radio, on television, on records, and in concerts throughout Cuba.

Martí, Virgilio. Composer, singer, percussionist. Born (?), Havana; died (?). Began his career playing and creating *guaguancós* in the barrios of Havana. Martí moved to New York toward the end of the 1940s and there continued to play the rumba and other rhythms from the Afro-Cuban folkloric repertoire. He accompanied the legendary dancer Yolanda Montes, known as "Tongolele." His compositions include "Alma mía," "Sonaremos el tambó," "Todos vuelven," and other *guaguancós*. He has made a substantial number of significant recordings and given memorable concerts of Afro-Cuban music and salsa with groups such as the Fania All-Stars and Grupo Folklórico y Experimental Nuevayorkino.

Martín, Agustín. Professor and conductor. Born 1867, Cataluña, Spain; died 1929, Matanzas. Was assistant conductor of the National Police Band in Havana in 1899. He and the band's conductor, Guillermo Tomás, organized a small symphony orchestra in 1910 and gave concerts at the Martí Theater. Martín later moved to Matanzas, where he taught many outstanding musicians.

Martín, Edgardo. Composer, professor, music critic. Born 6 October 1915, Cienfuegos. Completed his early study of music with his grandmother, and later, in Havana, with Jascha Fischermann and César Pérez Sentenat. Martín also studied composition with José Ardévol. After graduating in education from the University of Havana, he became a professor at the Municipal Conservatory and later at the National School of Art. He has taught numerous courses on various aspects of music in several parts of the country. He has published articles on music in Cuban periodicals and wrote the book *Panorama histórico de la música en Cuba*. Martín was part of the Grupo de Renovación Musical. He has composed, among other works, Fugues, for strings; Preludes, for piano; *Soneras*, for orchestra; Symphony no. 1, Concerto, for wind instruments; and Trio, for woodwind, as well as works for voice and piano, choral music, some incidental music, and, recently, *Canto de héroes*, a cantata.

Martín, Tamara. Musicologist. Born 10 January 1945, Cienfuegos. Studied piano, singing, and choral conducting at the Amadeo Roldán Municipal Conservatory, in Havana. He later graduated in musicology at the Higher Institute of Art. Martín has been a professor at various institutions. As a critic of music, he has published articles in several magazines and newspapers. He is author of the books *La música coral en Cuba* (1987) and *Música coral* (1990). He is currently the president of the musicology section of the Writers and Artists Union of Cuba.

Martínez, Alfredo. Composer and singer. Born 1938, Havana. Was a radio announcer on several radio stations until the end of the 1960s when he began a singing career on radio and television. Martínez has performed in nightclubs in Havana and toured in various European and Latin American countries. He composed the songs "¿Dónde está tu amor?" "Te quiero tanto," "Te espero," and "Acaba ya."

Martínez, Odaline. Orchestra conductor and composer. Born 31 October 1949, Matanzas. Moved to the United States at an early age, and in 1972 moved to London. Martínez has directed and conducted the Lontano Orchestra in works from a broad repertoire, but particularly those by twentieth-century composers. She has disseminated the works of Cuban and Latin American composers. Among her compositions are *Cantos de Amor*, songs based on poems by Federico García Lorca. She conducted the Orquesta Lontano at the Sixth Festival of Music of Havana in 1990.

Martínez, Orlando. Critic and musicographer. Born 17 October 1916, Havana. Studied at the Hubert de Blanck Conservatory, where he graduated as a professor of piano in 1936. Martínez gave some piano recitals, but later devoted himself entirely to research on the dissemination of music. For many years, he wrote the program notes for the Havana Philharmonic Orchestra and music reviews in magazines in Havana. He was the director of CMBF Radio Musical radio station. He has written *Mordentes* (1931), *Introducción a la crítica musical*

(1941), *La crítica musical en Cuba* (1941), and *Motivos del camino* (1956).

Martínez, Pedro Lugo ("Nene"). Singer. Born 1 August 1960. Began his career as a vocalist, working successively with various groups—La Monumental, Clave y Guaguancó, Conjunto Chapottín, El Quinteto de Tata Güines, and the Güniettes—until he reached Jóvenes Clásicos del Son, where he remains the lead singer.

Martínez, Raúl. Musicologist. Born 8 October 1937, Jaguey Grande. Began his studies of music in 1957 at the Havana Municipal Conservatory and continued at the School for Art Instructors and at the Ignacio Cervantes Conservatory. Since 1954 Martínez has performed traditional Cuban songs on guitar. He was a researcher and promoter of music in the province of Matanzas for ten years. He joined the National Museum of Music as a specialist in 1974. He has published articles and essays and given lectures and talks on Cuban music and is the author of "Benny Moré," a biographical essay.

Martínez, Rogelio. Singer, guitarist, director of ensembles of Cuban *típico* music. Born 7 September 1905, Matanzas. An early member of the Sonora Matancera ensemble, with whom he played guitar and sang second voice in the chorus. Martínez became the group's conductor in 1948 when Valentin Cané was forced to retire because of ill health. Because of his efforts the group has maintained its popularity for many years. He composed "Sunsún Babaé" and other Afro-Cuban themes. *See also* Sonora Matancera.

Martínez, Rolo. Singer. Born 15 May 1935, Havana. Has sung almost all genres of Cuban popular music. Martínez began his career in the conjunto of Félix Chappotín and later sang with the orchestras of Ernesto Duarte and Pachito Alonso. He has performed extensively on the radio and television and in theaters and nightclubs. He has been a soloist for several years and has made many popular records.

Martínez Corres, Cristóbal. Composer and pianist. Born June 1822, Havana; died 21 January 1842, Geneva, Italy. When he was nine years of age,

Martínez's family moved to France, where he began his studies of music; later he moved to Italy. He composed *romanzas*, a mass, and a Septuor. He was Cuba's first opera composer, but his two operas, El *diablo contrabandista* and Don *papanero*, were never staged and have been lost. Because of his premature death, his third opera, *Safo*, was never developed beyond the initial sketches.

Martínez Furé, Rogelio. Folklorist. Born 28 August 1937, Matanzas. Worked at the Institute of Ethnology and Folklore at the Academy of Sciences of Cuba, where he specialized in the study and dissemination of African cultural influences in America. In 1962 Martínez Furé founded the National Folkloric Ensemble with whom he has toured widely in Europe and Africa, and where he is currently an adviser and a librettist. He has worked ceaselessly at compiling Cuban folk music. He has occasionally sung Cuban, Brazilian, and Antillean folk music, as well as avant-garde musicals. He has published articles in periodicals in Cuba and abroad, as well as the book *Diálogos imaginarios*. His compositions include "La mulata" (*habanera*) and "Cómo cambia la gente."

Martínez Griñan, Lilí. Pianist, composer, arranger. Born 16 February 1917; died 17 September 1990, Havana. A self-taught pianist who later studied music, Martínez Griñan began a music career in his hometown and later moved to Havana. He joined Arsenio Rodríguez's group, for whom he also worked as an arranger. When Rodríguez moved to the United States and the group was taken over by trumpeter Felix Chapottín, he continued in both roles. He later played in Havana's nightclubs. He has composed the boleros "Eso sí se llama querer" and "Tú no puedes dejarme"; and the *sones* "Que se fuñan," "Mí son, mí son," "Sazonando," "Se acabaron los guapos en Yateras," "Alto Songo, se quema la Maya," and "Quimbombó." His individual piano style influenced many Cuban and Latin American pianists.

Martí Theater. *See* Irijoa Theater.

maruga. Also known as a *chench*. The *maruga* is made of two hollow cones of tin or metal, welded at their bases. The surface of the cones is perforated in entertaining shapes. The ends are truncated, and the handle, which is also made of tin, is attached to one of them (Castellanos, "Los instrumentos musicales de los afrocubanos," in Ortiz, *Los instrumentos de la música afrocubana*, 2: 312–13).

Matamoros, Miguel. Composer, guitarist, conductor of the famous trio named after him. Born 8 May 1894, Santiago de Cuba; died 15 April 1971. Worked in several trades—as a driver, carpenter, and painter—in his hometown while studying the guitar and learning to sing. With his guitar, Matamoros joined serenades in Santiago and thus became familiar with the world of the *trova* singers. He was a spontaneous and intuitive musician. He made his first public appearance at the Heredia Theater, in Santiago de Cuba, in 1912. In 1925 he joined Siro Rodríguez and Rafael Cueto, and the renowned Trío Matamoros was born. Two years later, the trio traveled to New York to make recordings of its songs, which became very popular. The guitar style of the Trío Matamoros was characterized by an expressive way of playing the melody and by the *tumbao* that Cueto created with his accompaniment, which imparted a polyrhythmic sound. To this was added the unique "street band" style and the exuberant Cuban flavor created by Miguel. The trio toured all of the Americas and many European countries. Matamoras wrote the boleros and *sones* "Lágrimas negras," "Juramento," "Reclamo místico," "Mariposita de primavera," "Mientes," "Triste muy triste," "Olvido," "Mamá son de la loma," "El que siembra su maíz," "Que te están mirando," and "Alegre conga." *See also* Cueto, Rafael; Rodríguez, Siro.

Matas, Antonio. Pianist and composer. Born (?), Mallorca, Spain; died 1984, Miami. Began his studies of music in Mallorca; later moved to Paris, and settled in Havana in 1940. He is known by the name of "El mago del Solovox." Matas gave numerous piano concerts. He composed the songs "Reflexión," "Hoy," "Una mirada," "Desesperación," "Llegaste tarde mi amor," and the well-known *guaracha* "Parece que va a llover."

Mateu, Alberto. Violinist. Born 31 January 1903, Guanabacoa; died (?). Studied music at the Mateu Conservatory, where his father José Mateu was the director. Alberto Mateu later went to Brussels to pursue further studies at the conservatory there. He gave concerts in several European cities, and performed extensively in Cuba, in recitals and as a soloist with the Havana Philharmonic Orchestra.

Mauri, José. Composer. Born 12 February 1856, Valencia, Spain; died 11 July 1937, Havana. The son of Cuban parents, Mauri lived in Cuba from early childhood. He studied violin, piano, harmony, counterpoint, fugue, orchestration, and composition. He composed numerous *zarzuelas*, among them El sombrero de Felipe II, El barberillo de Jesús María, Los amores de Eloísa, and Globos Dirigibles. Almost all were staged at the Alhambra Theater. He composed the three-act opera La esclava, with libretti by Tomas Juliá, which was premiered at the National Theater on 6 June 1921. Mauri traveled to several countries as the conductor of the National Band of Colombia. During those tours, he collected large sums of money for the cause of Cuban independence. He also composed various symphonic works—hymns, *contradanzas*, *danzones*, *canciones*, and some religious pieces. He was also a professor of music.

Mauri, Manuel. Orchestra conductor and composer. Born 28 December 1857, Havana; died 7 June 1939. The brother of José Mauri. Manuel Mauri performed in Mexico several times with a *zarzuela* company. He was the conductor of the orchestra of the Alhambra Theater for several years. He wrote the music for *zarzuelas* and composed popular-music pieces (*canciones*, *guajiras*, and *danzones*).

mayohuacán. An instrument used by the Indo-Cubans in their *areítos*. A xylophonic slit drum made

of the hollow trunk of a tree. There are grooves on the sides but no drumhead. It was beaten with rods and played by the *behiques* (priests).

Mazón, Jorge. Composer. Born 13 November 1923, Havana. Was a member of the *fílin* movement from its beginnings. Among his songs are "Rosa azul," "Indefinidamente," "La luna y tus ojos," "Niña ingenua," "Rey negro," and "Dame una vueltecita." Mazón also played guitar and was a bass singer with the National Chorus.

Mélendez, Mariano. Singer. Born 11 September 1886, Havana; died 15 October 1960. Sang mainly *habaneras*, as well as other styles of the *canción* repertoire. Meléndez made his debut in 1910 at a Havana theater. He was one of the artists promoted by Ernesto Lecuona.

Melis, Hilda. Pianist. Born 26 September 1948, Havana. Studied at the Higher School of Music in Warsaw, Poland. Melis has given recitals and concerts and is currently a professor at the Higher Institute of Art.

Melodias del 40, Orquesta. French *charanga* band formed by the piano player Regino Frontela Fraga in Havana, 1940. For thirty years, it has performed on radio and television and recorded many LPs. The orchestra appears mainly at festivals.

Membiela, Ñico. Singer. Born 3 December 1913, Zulueta; died 13 July 1998, Miami. At the age of seven, Membiela played the xylophone with a sextet, and, later, the *bongó*. He began singing at sixteen years of age, accompanied by guitar, in Sagua la Grande. He later lived in Cienfuegos and in Santa Clara, where he continued his career as a singer, mainly of boleros. He moved to Havana, where he sang on Radio Salas for five years, and in nightclubs. He gained sudden popularity with an LP of traditional boleros and made other recordings. He has performed in Latin American countries. He moved to the United States in the 1970s.

Méndez, José Antonio. Composer, guitarist, singer. Born 21 June 1927, Havana; died 9 June 1989. Made his initial foray into guitar playing and composing

in the 1940s. While still a high school student at the Institute of Havana, one of Méndez's compositions was sung at a celebration at the college. He later began performing at the Mil Diez radio station. He organized the group Loquibambia. Méndez traveled to Mexico in 1949, where he became well known by way of his performances in nightclubs and on the radio. While there, he recorded five LPs. He returned to Cuba in 1959 and continued a brilliant career. He was one of the main exponents of the *fílin* movement. He traveled to Europe and all of Latin America. He recorded an LP in 1965 with the piano accompaniment of Frank Emilio. His highly popular songs include "La gloria eres tú," "Novia mía," "Quiéreme y verás," "Ayer la vi llorar," "Si me comprendieras," "Sufre más," "Soy tan feliz," "Me faltabas tú," "Decídete," "Tú mi adoración," "Por nuestra cobardía," "Mi mejor canción," and "Ese sentimento que se llama amor."

Méndez, Silvestre. Composer and interpreter of Cuban popular music. Born 31 December 1921, Havana. Made his debut with folk-music groups in Havana, performing on radio and in shows. Méndez established himself in Mexico in the 1940s, where he performed as a percussionist and singer. He performed in several Mexican films. He composed the mambos "Yiri, yiri bon," "Mambeando," and "Tocineta"; the rumba "Tambó"; and the *guaracha* "El telefonito."

Mendive, Kiko. Singer. Born in Havana; died (?). Began his career singing *sones* and *guarachas* in the 1940s with orchestras in Havana. Mendive later moved to Mexico City, where he performed on the radio, in nightclubs, and in films, singing and danc-

ing Cuban music. He made several records. He moved to Venezuela in the 1970s.

Mendível, Joaquín. Pianist, arranger, conductor, professor of music, composer. Born 11 March 1919, Ciego de Ávila. When he was only months old, his family moved to the city of Camagüey. Mendível began his studies of music at seven years of age with Ángela Beltrán and Alberto Noriega. He later studied at the Peyrallade Conservatory with Professor Luis Aguirre, where he graduated in piano at seventeen years of age. He founded the Orquesta Tínima in 1932 and was later a pianist with the dance bands Morquesano and Hermanos González. Then, in 1940, he founded an eponymous orchestra that performed on radio, on television, and in clubs and nightclubs. He moved to Havana in 1959 and was a pianist with several orchestras, including Alí Bar, Julio Cueva, Sabor de Cuba, Capri, and Caribe. He studied with Gustavo Quirós, Armando Romeu, and Félix Guerrero. He was the arranger for many of Cuba's leading vocalists and orchestras and composed pieces in almost all genres: *danzones*, boleros, *guarachas*, Afro-Cuban music, *pregones*, *sones*, hymns, and marches.

Mendoza, Celeste. Singer. Born 6 April 1930, Santiago de Cuba; died 1998. Cultivated the *guaguancó* style and was known as the "Queen of Guaguancó." Mendoza made her debut as a singer on CMQ Television in the 1950s. She introduced the guaguancó style of singing with such songs as "Soy tan feliz," and "Que no me castigue Dios." She performed in nightclubs and on radio and television and made numerous recordings that were very popular. She has performed in Panama, Venezuela, Puerto Rico, the United States, Mexico, France, and the Soviet Union. She appeared in the Cuban film *Nosotros la música*.

Menéndez, Ana. Soprano. Born 1934, Havana. Studied with Carmelina Santana in the 1950s. Later traveled to Italy on two occasions, where she took lessons from Carla Castellani, an artist and repertoirist at La Scala in Milán. Menéndez has sung leads in various operas staged in Cuba and in Europe.

Menéndez, Ángel. Baritone. Born 5 July 1928, Cárdenas. Has sung leads in operas and zarzuelas staged in Cuba and performed in Bulgaria and Czechoslovakia. Menéndez is currently part of the National Opera Theater.

Menéndez, Nilo. Composer, pianist, dance-band conductor. Born 26 September 1902, Matanzas; died 25 September 1987, Burbank, California. Wrote the scores for many films. Menéndez performed with the Ernesto Lecuona Company. He composed many songs that were popular in the 1930s and 1940s, including "Perdóname," "Aunque no pueda vivir," "Tenía que suceder," and "Aquellos ojos verdes."

Menéndez, Pablo. Guitarist, composer, arranger. Born 21 June 1952, Oakland, California. Son of the singer Barbara Dane. Menéndez began his studies of music in his hometown and continued them in Havana after 1966, at the National School of Art. He later studied under Juan Elósegui, Federico Smith, and Leo Brouwer. He studied classical guitar at the Ignacio Cervantes Conservatory. After performing in the United States with his mother, playing blues and jazz, he joined the Grupo de Experimentación Sonora of the Cuban Institute for Movie-Making, Art, and Industry, with whom he remained for several years. He later joined the Grupo Síntesis, then Sonido Contemporáneo, and has been with Grupo Mezcla, as its conductor, since 1985. He has made several recordings as a guitarist and toured several countries, including the United States.

Menéndez, Ramón. Violinist and cellist, professor of violin. Born (?); died (?). Menéndez was prominent among young musicians in Havana in the late eighteenth century and came to be known as "El Maestro." His disciples included Tomás Buelta Flores, Secundino Arango, and many other outstanding instrumentalists. When he was already an old man, an accident disabled his left hand. Since music was his life, he reversed the strings of his violin, placed it on his right shoulder, took the bow with his left hand, and taught himself to play as well as he had when he was in top form. He was the composer of several contradanzas and other pieces.

Mercadal, Juan. Guitarist. Born 1925, Guanabacoa; died 1998, Miami. Began his studies of guitar with his father, Juan Ramón Mercadal, later took lessons from Professor Severino López, and then studied at the Mateu Conservatory, in Guanabacoa. After performing in various concert halls in Cuba, he traveled to the United States and South America in 1950. On returning to Cuba, he gave concerts and recitals, and then worked in the air transportation industry. Juan Mercadal moved to Miami in 1960, where he has worked as a professor of music at the School of Music of the University of Miami. He has played in concerts with various symphony orchestras in the United States.

Mercerón, Mariano. Composer, saxophonist, conductor. Born (?), Santiago de Cuba; died 26 December 1975, Mexico City. Studied music in his hometown. Mercerón founded his jazz-based orchestra in the 1940s, with whom he created a distinctive style and sonority while playing Cuban dance-music—particularly boleros, sones, and danzones. At the beginning of the 1950s the vocalists in his orchestra included Benny Moré, Pacho Alonso, and Fernando Álvarez. After several trips to Mexico, he moved to Mexico City at the end of the 1950s, and there continued to play Cuban music with his orchestra.

Metzler, Juan. Professor and composer. Born 1800, London; died (?), Havana. Moved to Havana in 1826, where he undertook the most diverse musical activities; he even founded a music journal. Metzler taught music and organized auditions. He traveled to New York in 1836 along with a number of other Cuban intellectuals, and there he met José Antonio Saco. He played a significant part in the creolization of the Spanish bolero. Among his songs are "El Misterio" and "Filis cantando."

Miari, Alfonso. Flutist and professor. Born 1830, Modena, Italy; died 31 March 1906, Havana. Arrived in Cuba in 1856 and settled in Camagüey, where he was a professor of music. Miari later moved to the capital and became lead flutist in the orchestras of the Tacón and Payret theaters, where he gained great renown. He was also a professor at the National Conservatory.

Milanés, Pablo. Composer, singer, guitarist. Born 24 February 1943, Bayamo. Essentially self-taught, in the 1960s Milanés introduced a new mode in Cuban *canción* that brought together elements of popular music from outside Cuba and genuinely Cuban forms. He sang with the groups Cuarteto del Rey and Los Bucaneros, and went solo in 1964. He has composed music for the theater and for documentary films. He has performed in theaters and in films. His lyrics are highly poetic and his melodies are exceptionally sensitive. He studied music under professors Federico Smith and Leo Brouwer and traveled to Italy and Chile. He was part of the ICAIC's Grupo de Experimentación Sonora. He is the author of "Tú mí desengaño," "Estás lejos," "Mís veintidós años," "Para vivír," "Su nombre puede ponerse en verso," "A Santiago," "La vida no vale nada," "Hombre que vas creciendo," "Los caminos," "Años," "Ya ves," "El breve espacio en que no estás," "Defiende el amor que te enseño," "Proposiciones," "Quiero ser de nuevo el que te amó," "Yolanda," "Soy del Caribe," and "Yo me quedo." His music has been sung the world over by the most renowned singers.

Milí, Néstor. Guitarist and composer. Born 18 February 1910, Havana; died 6 October 1967. A self-taught guitarist who began his musical career in 1930 in the Septeto Jóvenes del Cayo. Milí later founded Conjunto Cubanicay, Mamboletas, Cuarteto los Zafiros (in 1962), and Cuarteto Los Luceros (in 1964). He composed "Caminadora," "Rematando," "Sólo tengo un amor," "El yerberito," "Averígualo," and "Despacito." He has recorded several Gold Records.

Mirabal, Linda. Soprano. Born 9 January 1949, Havana. Began her career as a singer of lyrical song and Cuban songs, in the 1970s. Mirabal performed at the National Puppet Theater. She has toured many countries in the Americas and Europe and has performed in films and on television. She is a soloist with the Cuban National Opera.

Mirabal, Manuel ("El Guajiro"). Trumpet player. Born 5 May 1933, Melena del Sur. Studied music with his father, Luis Mirabal, the conductor of the band of Melena del Sur. Manuel Mirabel has played with the groups Universal and Rumbavana; the dance bands Swing Casino, Orquesta Riverside, and Orquesta Cubana de Música Moderna; and with radio, television, and cabaret orchestras. He was the lead trumpet in the Oscar D'Leon Orchestra. In the late 1990s he recorded with the Buena Vista Social Club and the Afro-Cuban All Stars, as well as with the splinter groups established by solo singers from those groups.

Miranda, Juan Pablo. Flutist and composer. Born 15 October 1906, Havana; died (?). Made his debut in 1927 with the French *charanga*–style orchestra of Silvio Contreras; later played with the Ismael Díaz orchestra. In the 1930s Miranda began composing *danzones* with lyrics, which were sung by popular singers of the day. He later joined Orquesta Sensación as a flutist, then founded his own band, Orquesta Riviera. He was conductor of the Orchestra Siglo XX. He composed the boleros "Mil congojas," "Seguiré sin ti," "Cielo y sol," "Qué difícil," and "Algo de ti."

(Los) Modernistas. Vocal quartet founded in 1960, in Havana, after two members of the quartet Los Faxas (Gilberto Aldanás and Eugenio Fernández) left and joined Miguel de la Uz and Yolanda Brito to form this new group. The quartet's debut appearance was on 24 April on *Show de Shows*, a program on Cuba's Channel 4 Television. Its subsequent success was achieved by way of radio and television, in theaters and cabarets, and on records. Los Modernistas has performed in Indonesia, Czechoslovakia, the Soviet Union, Bulgaria, Romania, and Hungary. Its current members are Lourdes Torres, Gilberto Aldanás, Miguel de la Uz, and Eberto Rodríguez.

Molina, Carlos. Guitarist. Born 15 February 1946, Havana. Studied at the Hubert de Blanck Conservatory and, later, at the Amadeo Roldán Conservatory. Molina studied with Professor Isaac Nicola, and was also tutored by Leo Brouwer, Abel Carlevaro, Alirio Díaz, and Alberto Ponce. He joined the Amadeo Roldán Conservatory as a professor in 1969. He was awarded First Prize in the National Music Contest in 1970. He gave numerous concerts and recitals in Cuba; he also performed in Martinique and in Europe. He played at the Metropolitan Opera House in New York in 1979. He was a professor at the Higher Institute of Art. He moved to the United States in 1982.

Molina, Joaquín. Violinist and professor. Born 1884, Mexico; died 1950, Havana. His family moved to Havana when he was two. Molina studied with his grandfather, Enrique Ramos, and with Tomás de la Rosa, and later with the outstanding violinist Juan Torroella. He gave violin concerts and played with the main theater orchestras in Havana. As a professor of violin, he had a long and significant career, especially in the Conservatory González-Molina, which he founded with his wife, the piano professor Matilde González.

Molina, Luis Manuel. Guitarist. Born 25 February 1959, Havana. Brother of the guitarist Carlos Molina. Luis Manuel Molina studied music at the Amadeo Roldán Conservatory and the Higher Institute of Art. He has made an outstanding career playing in concerts both in Cuba and abroad. He has participated in various guitar festivals and has been awarded several prizes. He took lessons from Alirio Díaz, Ichiro Suzuki, Costas Cotsiolis, Manolo Sanlúcar, Mónica Rost, and Leo Brouwer. He has conducted such groups as Géminis, Eclosión, Orfeo, and Metamorfosis, and has composed many pieces for the guitar.

Moncada, Grupo. Formed by a group of students from the University of Havana, this group made its debut appearance at a concert honoring Ernesto ("Che") Guevara. Its repertoire includes political and Latin American folk songs with elements of rumba and son. Its musicians are Julián Fernández (guitar and tres); Alberto Faya (vocalist and guitar); Manuel Calviño (vocalist, guitar, double bass); Pedro Trujillo (flute); Tomás Rivero (piano and double bass); and José A. Himely, Jorge Gómez, and Juan Gómez (percussion). The group has toured in Peru (1974), the German Democratic Republic, and Czechoslovakia (1976).

Montalván, María. Professor. Born 1865, Remedios; died 12 December 1947, Havana. Daughter of the conductor José María Montalván. With her husband, María Montalván trained noteworthy musicians in Remedios, at the Valdés-Montalván Academy. Her students included Alejandro García Caturla. Later she settled in Havana, where she continued her work and trained many outstanding instrumentalists and composers.

Montane, Carlos. Tenor. Born (?), Havana. Made his debut as an opera singer in 1970 at the New York City Opera and also sang at the Metropolitan Opera House. In 1973 Montane performed at the Opera Theater of Dusseldorf, Germany, and later in theaters in Hamburg, Barcelona, Budapest, Frankfurt, Stuttgart, Oslo, Bratislava, Belfast, Luxembourg, and other European cities. He has performed in thirty operas. He sings in six languages: Spanish, Italian, French, German, English, and Russian. He toured the Middle East in 1988. He is a professor of voice at the University of Indiana's School of Music.

Montaner, Rita. Singer. Born 20 August 1900, Guanabacoa; died 17 April 1958, Havana. Studied piano at the Peyrellade Conservatory. At thirteen years of age, Mantaner was awarded a Gold Medal. She made her debut as a singer on the radio in 1922, at the inauguration of the station PWX. She sang in theaters in Havana and performed in New York in 1926. In 1927 she made her debut in zarzuelas; in Niña Rita, she sang the congo-tango "Mamá Inés." The following year, she went to Paris for the first time, and performed at the Olympia Theater, and at the Palace Theater as a substitute for Raquel Mayer. A year later, she appeared in Josephine Baker's Revue. She then traveled to Madrid and Valencia. She returned to Cuba in 1930, but the following year traveled to the United States, under contract to Al Jolson for his musical Wonder Bar. In 1935 she performed at the Principal Comedy Theater in Havana, in a show by Gilberto Valdés, where she sang "Oggere Bembé," "Tambó," and "Sangre Africana." She acted in the film *Romance del palmar*. She was proclaimed Queen of the Radio in 1935. In 1938 she appeared in the film *Sucedió en La Habana*, and in the zarzuela, *Amalia Batista*. She acted in the film *María la O* in 1948. In 1949 she began a season with Bola de Nieve at the Mulgoba Cabaret; she later joined the Tropicana, where she sang for nine years. In 1954 she acted in the film *La única*. She sang in Menotti's *La Medium* at the Hubert de Blanck Theater. She was one of the most important figures in Cuban music.

Montero, Rolando ("El Muso"). Singer. Born 9 June 1952, Las Tunas. Began as a vocalist singing in the orchestras Nueva Ilusión, Gigante Miramar, and Jóvenes del Feeling, until he joined Roberto Faz's group, where he remained for fifteen years. Montero became popular singing virtually all styles of Cuban rhythm. In 1991 he formed his own group, Gran Sonora, which continues to perform in Cuba and abroad.

Montesinos, Rey. Guitarist, arranger, composer, conductor. Born 23 August 1944, Pinar del Río. Studied in Pinar del Río, where he took guitar lessons from the *trova* singer Che Tejera and lessons in harmony from René Pérez. Later played in popular-music groups. Montesinos was a guitar accompanist for Elena Burke and Ela Calvo. He was arranger and conductor for the orchestra of the Cuban Institute of Radio and Television. He has received guidance from Diez Nieto, Guyún, Jesús Ortega, Federico Smith, Italo Besa, Félix Guerrero, Víctor Zayas, Adolfo Guzmán, Armando Romeu, and Valdés Arnau. He has represented Cuba in various countries, including Peru, Spain, France, Italy, Mexico, the Soviet Union, Mongolia, Panama, and Angola. He has composed several songs.

montuno. The term "montuno" has a variety of meanings pertaining to Cuban music. "Montuno" translates literally as "from the mountains." When musicians speak of *son montuno*, they are usually referring to the older styles of rural *son* music played in the mountainous interior of the island and in eastern Cuba (Oriente). The term *montuno* alone, however, refers to the final section of *son*-based compositions that follows the *canto* or *tema* (verse); it is thus part of a given composition rather than a distinct

genre. A *montuno* constitutes a somewhat faster and more improvisational climax to the *son*, often incorporating call-response singing between a lead singer and a chorus. A number of other genres of Afro-Cuban music end in essentially the same way. *Montuno* improvisations occur over a short (usually two- or four-measure) repeated phrase that features relatively simple harmonies. Improvisations in this section can be instrumental as well as vocal. The apparent discrepancy in meaning between *son montuno* and *montuno* is partially explained by the fact that older *son montuno* pieces consisted primarily of call-response singing and improvisation, rather than precomposed verses. Finally, *montuno* can also refer to specific melodies and rhythms performed on the piano that accompany the *montuno* section of a *son* or salsa composition.

Morales, Carlos Emilio. Guitarist. Born 6 November 1939, Havana. Studied with Clara Nicola, García Gatell, Jesús Ortega, and Federico Smith. Morales began his career as a professional guitarist in 1959, on television and in jazz concerts. He played with the orchestra of the Havana Musical Theater and with Chucho Valdés's ensemble. Since 1967 he has played with Orquesta Cubana de Música Moderna, Noneto de Jazz, and with the Irakere Group, with whom he has traveled widely. He has been a professor at the Professional School. He is one of the best Cuban jazz guitarists.

Morales, Eduardo. Singer. Born 1940, Central Francisco, Camagüey. Known as "El Tiburón" (the Shark). A former baseball player, Morales began singing *sones* with the group Avance Juvenil in Camagüey, under the direction of Adalberto Álvarez, with whom he helped form the group Son 14 in 1980 in Santiago de Cuba. He remains with that group as a vocalist, having made many recordings and contrib-

Mo Fini

uted a particular vocal style and timbre within the arena of *son*.

Morales, Jesús. Musical eccentric. Born 17 November 1917, Havana. Plays the saxophone, clarinet, xylophone, accordion, kettle-drum, and a number of kitchen utensils converted into musical instruments. Morales has performed in theaters, recreation centers, and, most notably, in the circus. He has a son, who is also named Jesús Morales and who is also a musical eccentric, and he is the father of other musicians as well: Alexander (violinist), Ileana (pianist), and Noel (pianist). He has performed in Latin America and Europe.

Morales, Luisa María. Soprano. Born 25 August 1912, Havana; died 12 August 1973. Studied with Tina Farelli and Antonio Bovi. Morales sang with Ernesto Lecuona's Company and performed on radio, in the theater, and on records. Her repertoire included lyrical pieces, mainly by Cuban composers, and she also sang in operas. She performed internationally, in several countries.

Morales, Obdulio. Orchestra conductor and composer; also played the piano and violin. Born 7 April 1910, Havana; died 9 January 1980. At fourteen years of age, Morales was already performing. He presented his folk work *Batamú* in 1938. He conducted a folk chorus with the Havana Philharmonic Orchestra in 1942. A year later, he joined Radio Cadena Suaritos, where he conducted the station's in-house orchestra for many years. Under the auspices of Fernando Ortiz, he gave lectures on Afro-Cuban music at the Hispano-Cuban Culture Society and at the Society for Afro-Cuban Studies. He composed the music for the films *Rincón criollo*, *Una gitana en la Habana*, and *Yambaó*. He is also a music researcher. He has conducted the orchestra of the National Folkloric Ensemble. Among his works are "Enyoró," "La culebra," "Sube espuma," "Ecué," "Ochún," the *pregón* "Carretas," and also a more elaborate piece, *Ritmos*, for wind quintet.

Morales, Rafael. Pianist. Born 1905, Holguín. Studied music with his father, Agustín Morales; his brother, César Morales, is a piano accompanist. Rafael Morales finished his basic piano training at

twelve years of age. In 1917 he became choirmaster at the San Isidoro Church, in Holguín. He conducted the orchestra of the Cuba Theater in Santiago de Cuba between 1925 and 1929. He moved to Havana in 1930, where he became organist at the Encanto Theater until 1951. During that period he was also a pianist with the Havana Philharmonic Orchestra. He was a professor at the Havana Municipal Conservatory (today the Amadeo Roldán Conservatory) until 1971. He has accompanied the best Cuban singers and soloists, as well as many foreign artists who have performed in Cuba.

Morales, Zoraida. Soprano. Born 1927, Havana. Made her debut as a singer of the lyrical repertoire in the 1950s. Morales moved to Germany many years ago, but has performed in Cuba during visits to the country.

Moré, Banda Gigante de Benny. Jazz–dance band featuring Cuban percussion. Considered to be a Cuban *jazzband* because of its general musical structure and the composition and arrangements of its repertoire and pieces. It was formed by Benny Moré in Havana in 1953. At the peak of its popularity, the musicians were Lázaro Valdés (piano); Mauro Gómez, René Aillón, Roger Mena, Fernán Vincent, and Bebo Loredo (saxophones); Aníbal Martínez, Jorge Varona, Pedro Rodríguez, and Pedro Jiménez (trumpets); Generoso Jiménez (trombone); Ramón Caturla (double bass); Jesús González (drums); Clemente Piquero (*bongó*); Jesús López (conga); and Enrique Benítez, Gil Ramírez, and Delfín Moré (backup vocals).

Moré, Benny. Singer and composer. Born 24 August 1919, Santa Isabel de las Lajas; died 19 February 1963, Havana. Full name was Bartolomé Moré. Unanimously considered one of the greatest geniuses in

Cuban popular music, he excelled in all genres. He learned to play the guitar at an early age and sang enthusiastically, accompanied by his guitar, at parties and serenades in Las Lajas and neighboring towns, then moved to Havana in 1940. For several years, he sang, like a troubadour, in the cafés, streets, and parks of the city. He traveled to Mexico with the Miguel Matamoros group in 1945 and performed in nightclubs with the ensemble, until he met up with Pérez Prado and joined his orchestra. He remained with the "King of Mambo" for some time, making many recordings, acting in films, and singing. He later returned to Cuba and joined the Mariano Mecerón's orchestra, but some months later, he traveled back to Mexico, where he had an increasingly successful solo career. He returned to Cuba in 1953 and sang with the dance band of Bebo Valdés. Not long after, he founded his own orchestra, which would become internationally famous and earn him the devotion of his audiences. Moré's vocal style set a new standard in Cuban singing; in many ways, he can be seen as the culmination of the evolution of Cuban musical art. His voice covered a remarkable range of tonalities, tempos, and registers. He was an animated performer, dancing constantly while he sang and captivating his audience. Moré's versatility was a characteristic of his performances: he could change from a tender song to a *guaguancó*, almost seamlessly and without sacraficing the quality of either. Not having studied the formal technique of conducting, he nevertheless directed his vast orchestra (the Banda Gigante) in a manner that conveyed a deeply Cuban ethos. He was nicknamed "El bárbaro del ritmo"—the wizard of rhythm. With his "tribe," as he referred to his musicians, he toured the Americas. Tall and thin, he was an eccentric dresser and usually wore an enormous hat. He composed the

boleros "Ahora soy tan feliz," "Perdí la fe," "Dolor y perdón," "Preferí perderte," and "Amor fugaz"; the *sones* "Santa Isabel de las Lajas" and "Cienfuegos"; the mambos "Bonito y sabroso" and "Locas por el mambo"; and "Rumberos de ayer."

Morejón, Onofre. Composer and cellist. Born (?); died 1847, Havana. Continuously active in music in Havana in the nineteenth century. Morejón organized popular gatherings at his house that were attended by many. He did not possess outstanding skill as an instrumentalist, but his enthusiasm for music and his capacity to bring musical people together contributed to the development of the art of music at that time. He was much loved for his amiable nature. He composed many popular works, including *contradanzas*, *guarachas*, and the *danzas* "El colibrí," "Habanera," and "Carnaval."

Morón, Alonso. Vihuela (cithern, or ancient guitar) player. Born (?); died (?). One of the first musicians to arrive in Cuba from Spain, Morón lived in Bayamo from the time of the founding of the city in 1513. He developed musical activities among the population of Bayamo, until he left with Hernán Cortés for the newly conquered Mexico. There, he opened a school of song and dance in Colima.

Moya, Juan de. Pianist, organist, composer. Born (?), Santiago de Cuba; died 4 May 1896. Studied with his father, after whom he was named, and who was a professor of piano. Moya founded the Mozart Club in 1882. He was an organist at the Basilica of Santiago. Among his works arc Canción for voices and orchestra; the *danzas* "El plátano verde," "Hueso ná má," and "El sol de Cuba"; the waltz "Enrique"; the march *Heredia*; an Overture in D major; and several religious compositions.

Moya, Roberto. Guitarist and composer. Born 26 September 1897, Santiago de Cuba; died 27 January 1971, Havana. Began his music studies at an early age, and in 1923 he graduated as a professor of guitar. Moya traveled to Havana in 1928 with Valeriano Daugherty and Pepe Figarola and acted at the Teatro Campoamor. In 1932 he founded the Cuarteto Trovadores Líricos with Raúl Domínguez, Jorge Mauri, and Manuel Fontanals. With this quartet, he made his first trip to New York, where he later joined the Argentine Carlos Spaventa, and entered the world of tango. In 1933 he joined the group of guitarists that accompanied Carlos Gardel and performed in the singer's films *Tango Bar*, *El día que me quieras*, *El tango en Broadway*, and made many records. He returned to Cuba in 1937, and, two years later, traveled to South America on tour. He finally established himself in Cuba in 1946, and since then has devoted himself to teaching guitar. After the advent of the Revolution, he joined the School of Art as a professor, and continued performing as a guitarist and singer of Cuban traditional music. Among his compositions: the *sones* "Labios de amapola," "Mujer querida," "No intentes corazón," "Quisiera ser tu dueño"; and the *guajira* "Ranchito mío."

mozambique. Variety of rhythm which combines different musical elements, mainly the conga and certain ritual dances of African origin. Created by Pedro Izquierdo ("Pello el Afrokán"), this style enjoyed popularity during the late 1960s.

Muguercia, Alberto. Musicographer and lawyer. Born 22 February 1928, Santiago de Cuba. Made an extensive compilation of Cuban popular music, especially of the *son*, which he has arranged into valuable archives containing documents, interviews, and recordings. Muguercia is the author of the essay "Teodora Ginés: ¿Mito o realidad histórica?," which was published in the *Revista de la Biblioteca Nacional José Martí* in 1971, and which won him a prize in the Pablo Hernández Balaguer Musicology Contest in 1974. For years, he was a researcher in the music department of the José Martí National Library.

Mulens, Fernando. Pianist, composer, arranger, conductor. Born 29 September 1920, San José de los Ramos; died 10 November 1986, Puerto Rico. Began music studies with his father, and continued with the Catalan professor Mas Riera, at the Santa Cecilia Conservatory in Cárdenas. Mulens moved to Matanzas in 1934, where he worked as a piano accompanist in music programs at various radio stations. He settled in Havana in 1939 and continued the same work. In 1944, accompanying Pedro Vargas, he traveled to Puerto Rico, Venezuela, and Mexico City, and they later toured all of the Americas, returning to

Cuba in 1947, and then touring the United States. He returned to Cuba in 1949 and began performing with the singer María Luisa Landín, with whom he made an extensive tour of the Americas, returning to Havana in 1951, where he took up work as a conductor of several orchestras. He traveled to Spain and then Argentina with Esther Borja, and returned to Cuba in 1957. He founded Los Modernistas quartet. He conducted orchestras in nightclubs and on television. He made several recordings of piano, both solo and accompanied by string orchestras. Mulens traveled to Spain in 1966 and remained there for a number of years. He traveled to New York and finally settled in Buenos Aires. He composed the songs "Corazón a corazón," "Yo no sé qué me pasa," "Qué te pedí," "Romanza de la despedida," "Aquí de pie," "La noche quedó atrás," "Canción de estío," "Para ti," "Qué será el amor," and "A pleno sol." In Argentina, he composed *canciones* and tangos with lyrics by Roberto Lambertucci.

Munar, Alfredo. Conductor and composer. Born (?), Havana; died (?). At five years of age, he gave a piano concert at the Pro-Musical Art Society, in Havana, and at eighteen, conducted the Havana Philharmonic Orchestra. In the United States, Munar has conducted the symphony orchestras of Philadelphia, San Francisco, Chicago, Brooklyn, and has also conducted in Toronto. He has made concert tours of various Latin American countries. He has conducted Cuban *zarzuelas* in New York, Miami, and other cities.

Mungol, José Prudencio. Guitarist. Born 1837, Havana; died 1890. Studied in Barcelona and returned to Cuba a noteworthy guitarist. Mungol gave innumerable concerts. He composed studies and pieces for his instrument.

Muñequitos, Grupo Los. Rumba group that adopts an urban approach and plays mainly *guaguancó*. The composer Florencio Calle and the rumba singer Esteban Lantri, known as Saldiguera, established the band, along with Virulilla and Juan Mesa (vocalists); and Ernesto Torriente, Esteban Bacallao, Angel Pellado, and Gregorio Díaz (drums). The group's rumbas have a distinctive style, reflecting the way the rhythm is played in Matanzas, which is quite different from that played in Havana. The band has recorded many LPs.

Muñoz, Alfredo. Violinist. Born 20 June 1949, Havana. Studied at the Orbón Conservatory, at the National School of Art, and at the Higher Institute of Art. Muñoz joined the National Symphony Orchestra as a violinist in 1972. He has done outstanding work as a concert player and has been part of the Trío White. He has recorded LPs and performed abroad. He is a professor at the Higher Institute of Art and plays in concert with María Víctoria del Collado (pianist).

Muñoz, Ernesto. Pianist, composer, dance-band conductor. Born 24 November 1903, Havana; died (?). At fifteen years of age, Muñoz began the serious study of music. By 1929, the orchestra named after him was already popular, and one of the most active in playing the *danzonete*. For years, he was a professor of piano and also worked as a piano accompanist. His *charanga*-type orchestra made sporadic concert performances. He composed pieces such as the *danzón* "La flauta encantada" and the *pregón* "El viandero." *See also* Muñoz, Orquesta de Ernesto.

Muñoz, María. Choir conductor, professor, pianist. Born 27 September 1886, La Coruña, Spain; died 14 December 1947, Havana. Completed her studies at the Madrid Conservatory under Manuel de Falla. Muñoz was married to Antonio Quevedo. They moved to Cuba in 1919 and immediately became part of the Cuban music scene. María Muñoz co-founded the Cuban Society of Contemporary Music in 1929, and together with Quevedo, she promoted the journal *Musicalia*. She was a professor at her conservatory. In 1931 she opened up a new period in choral music in Cuba, when she founded the Havana Choral Society, but she also promoted other choral groups. She gave lectures in musicology and was a professor of folk music at the University of Havana's summer program.

Muñoz, Orquesta de Ernesto. *Charanga* band created by the pianist Ernesto Muñoz in Havana in the 1920s. At the beginning, its members were Eduardo Leal (flute), Jesús Muñiz (violin), Demetrio González (double bass), Gustavo Tamayo (*güiro*),

Justo Miranda (timbales), Ernesto Muñoz (piano), and Elena Li (vocalist). The band was very popular during the 1930s, when *danzonete* was at the forefront of Cuban music, and has been playing on and off ever since, performing at dances, on radio, and most recently, in concerts sponsored by the Ministry of Culture.

Muñoz Cedeño, Manuel. Violinist, composer, conductor. Born 1 January 1813, Bayamo; died 14 December 1885. Took music lessons from Julián Reinó and Francisco Señer. Founded, with relatives and musician friends, the first orchestra in Bayamo. Muñoz Cedeño was a choirmaster at the parish church of Bayamo. He orchestrated and interpreted, with his group, the patriotic song "La Bayamesa," by José Fornaris, Carlos M. Céspedes, and Castillo. On 11 June 1868, at the Te Deum and in the procession in the Corpus festivities, his orchestra played the National Anthem, composed by Perucho Figueredo, for which he also made the arrangement. It was later sung on 20 October. When the city of Bayamo was taken by the independence forces, he was appointed Alderman of the City Council. Later, when the city was taken by the Spanish colonialists, he was arrested and put on trial. Although the request was that he be condemned to death by firing squad, the defense obtained his acquittal. His orchestra played in many parties and festivities in the region of Bayamo. After his death, it was conducted by his son Joaquín Muñoz, and later by another son, Rafael Cabrera. Among his works were Theme with variations, for clarinet; *Homenaje, death-march; Ave María;* and the *canciones* "Elvira," "A la luna," and "Hermosa Rubia."

Museo Nacional de la Música Cubana. *See* National Museum of Cuban Music.

music in Cuban cinema. With the advent of the "talkies" in 1930, soundtracks began to be used in Cuban cinema. Ten years earlier, movie theaters had been using "sound machines" that synchronized music with the images on screen, along with incidental music that was suitable for all types of movies. In Cuba, ever since silent films were introduced, ensembles performed in the cinemas to make the films more enjoyable for the audience. With the advent of talking cinema, Cuban-made movies used either scores written by Cuban composers or classical pieces. With the creation of the Cuban Institute for Movie-Making, Art, and Industry (ICAIC) in 1960, incidental film music boomed. Because of the dearth of composers writing specifically for cinema, renowned musicians such as Harold Gramatges, Carlos Fariñas, José Ardévol, and Juan Blanco were asked to write incidental music to accompany motion pictures. The first motion pictures that were made after the Revolution were usually scored in a composer's distinctive style; eventually, however, composers began to craft their scores to suit the film rather than their own artistic tastes. Film soundtracks thus became less characterized by composers' individual aesthetics and became a more collective phenomenon. Harold Gramatges's music for *Historias de la Revolución*, the ICAIC's first motion picture in 1960, and for Joris Ivens's documentaries *Cuba, pueblo armado* and *Carnet de viaje* in 1961, conformed to his characteristic symphonic formation. The music he wrote for Sergio Giral's *El cimarron*, however, makes excellent use of new sound resources and suits the film's ambience and setting. Juan Blanco wrote the score for *El Megano*, a prototypical Cuban revolutionary film that was shot during the underground struggle against Batista, and later wrote the score for Tomás Gutiérrez Alea's documentary *Esta tierra nuestra* and for a long feature film by the same director, *Las doce sillas*. One of the foremost experimental musicians in Cuba in the 1960s, known in particular for his use of concrete space and aleatory music, Blanco's film scores were relatively more conservative and were composed according to the requirements of each film. Other Cuban composers who wrote music for the cinema industry include Leo Brouwer, Roberto Valera, Armando Guerra, Sergio Vitier, and Juan Márquez.

Cuban popular music also made its way into film soundtracks. Filmmaker Sara Gomez recruited not only art-music composers but also musicians who wrote popular music, such as Rembert Egues and Chucho Valdés, to score her films. For Tomás Gutiérrez Alea's film *Cumbite*, Sarah Gomez suggested that Haitian instruments be constructed and that the Cuban master percussionist Tata Güines be invited to play them on the soundtrack. The move to incorporate popular and traditional music into Cuban cinema gathered momentum with the estab-

lishment of the ICAIC Grupo de Experimentación Sonora. Some of the group's members, such as Eduardo Ramos and Emiliano Salvador, were closely tied to Cuban popular music and were involved with the soundtracks of a number of films. Popular songs by Pablo Milanés and Silvio Rodríguez were also included in the soundtracks of documentaries by Santiago Álvarez, Octavio Cortázar, Miguel Fleites, Manuel Perez, and other filmmakers. The emerging Latin American protest song (*nueva canción*) and new trends in Cuban film complemented each other, forging a close association between the two art forms. Although some composers no longer write scores for motion pictures, the others who have continued to do so include Leo Brower, Sergio Vitier, and Juan Márquez.

Cuban composers naturally have taken a distinctly individual approach to scoring films, even while film soundtracks have conformed to certain trends over the past several decades. Carlos Fariñas, for example, produces complex, heavy, dramatic scores that have suited long feature films such as *Mella* and *Aquella larga noche*, both directed by Pineda Barnet. Leo Brouwer, on the other hand, composes extremely simple, even economic, scores, such as those for *La última cena* and *Los sobrevivientes*. Vitier effectively scores pieces with a more antiquated sound, using lyrical passages of string instruments or melodies and rhythmic sequences that act as a leitmotif. Juan Márquez's scores evidence not only a musical acuity but an astute understanding of a film's setting, as well as an effective combination of symphonic and popular languages. In addition to writing film scores, Marquez has worked as a musical director with Manuel Duchesne Cuzán, the head of the ICAIC Music Department and director of the National Symphony Orchestra.

Cuban documentaries about music generally portray both aspects of and significant figures in popular music. Significant titles include: *Que bueno canta usted*, a tribute to Benny Moré by Sergio Giral; Juan Carlos Tabio's *Chicho Ibáñez*; Octavio Cortazar's *Hablando del punto cubano*; Hector Veitia's *La conga* and *Tonadas trinitarias*; *La rumba*, *Rompiendo la rutina*, about Antonio Arcaño's orchestra, and *A ver que sale*, about Juan Formell y Los Van Van, all by Oscar Valdés; Luis Felipe Bernaza's *Ignacio Piñeiro* and *De donde son los cantantes*; and Bernabe Hernandez's *Homenaje a la guitarra*. Hernandez has also made documentaries

about Cuban folklore and the *nueva canción* movement. Of the few musical comedies, Rogelio Paris's
Nosotros la música is particularly notable.

Musicalia. Specialist music magazine created by
María Muñoz and Antonio Quevedo in Havana in
1928. Many fundamental articles about Cuban and
international music are found in its pages. It informed people about aspects of current music and
could be described as Cuba's most important music
magazine. It ceased publication in 1942.

N

Nacional, Conservatorio. *See* National Conservatory.

Nacional, Septeto. Of all the many *son* septets and
sextets that flourished in the Havana of the 1920s,
only this one is still playing. Ignacio Piñeiro's Septeto Nacional achieved immediate success in 1927
for its repertoire, its quality, and the harmonies created in its vocal duets (tenor and baritone). The
members at that time were Ignacio Piñeiro (bandleader and double bass), Juan de la Cruz (manager,
lead vocalist, claves), Bienvenido León (backup singing and maracas), Abelardo Barroso (lead vocalist and claves), Alberto Villalón (guitar and backup
singing), Francisco González (*tres* and backup singing), José Manuel Incharte (*bongó*), and Lázaro Herrera (trumpet). The septet's original repertoire was
written by Piñeiro. Septeto Nacional was the first *son*
group with its own repertoire, and its example was
followed by Miguel Matamoros with his trio and by
Arsenio Rodríguez with his *conjunto*. When Piñeiro
formed the septet, he wanted it to be a vehicle for the
Cuban *son* and its variants, particularly the Oriente
son, which he enriched musically and lyrically.

The septet's long career is full of artistic achievements and important events. In 1927 it played at
the Academia Habana-Sport. Enrique Enriso substituted for Juan de la Cruz, and Eutimio Constantín, Alberto Villalón, and Alberto Rodríguez
substituted for José Manuel Incharte. In 1929 the
septet performed at the Cuban pavilion of the Ex-
posición Iberoamericana in Seville, Spain. At that
time, Eugenio Constantín replaced Alberto Villalón, and Agustín Gutiérrez, José Manuel Incharte,
and José Jiménez replaced Abelardo Barroso. The
septet signed a contract in Madrid with the recording company SEDECA. Back in Cuba, there were
more changes: Juan de la Cruz left, Miguel Angel Portillo replaced Agustín Gutiérrez, and Alfredo Valdés
(lead vocalist and claves) replaced José Jiménez. In
1933 it performed at the Chicago Exhibition-Fair, A
Century of Progress, where the group was awarded
the Gold Medal. In 1934 it performed in the musical documentary El *frutero*. Then Ignacio Piñeiro

left for economic reasons, and Lazaro Herrera led the septet from 1935 to 1937. The musicians then were Marcelino Guerra (backup vocals and *maracas*), Alfredo Valdés (lead vocalist and claves), Oscar Espinosa (double bass), Ramón Castro (*bongó*), Francisco González (*tres* and backup vocals), Eutimio Constantín (guitar and backup vocals), and Bienvenido Granda (lead vocalist and claves). Joseíto Nuñez and Pedro Rivero (lead vocalist and claves) also played with the septet. In 1954 Ignacio Piñeiro returned to the band and it appeared on the television show *Música de ayer y de hoy*, hosted by Odilio Urfé. This time, the musicians were Alfredo Valdés, Bienvenido León, Rafael Ortiz, Francisco González, Agustín Gutiérrez, Lázaro Herrera, and Oscar Vilarta. In 1959, new musicians joined: Marino González (*bongó*), with Alejandro Oviedo and Oscar Espinosa alternating on double bass. In 1962 the group participated in the First Popular Music Festival sponsored by the National Council for Culture. During the missile crisis of October 1962, it played at military bases and in the trenches. In 1963 the double bass player Charles Burke joined the septet and, in 1966, the *tres* player Hilario Ariza. The Army presented the Septeto Nacional with a certificate honoring its work. In 1968 the Arts and Education National Union awarded it with a medal for its contribution to Cuban music over the course of thirty years ("Septeto Nacional").

Nacional, Teatro. *See* Tacón Theater.

Nápoles, Dinorah. Singer. Born 26 June 1921, Santiago de las Vegas. Made her debut on the radio station RHC Cadena Azul in 1944 and later performed in other Havana stations, as well as in theaters and nightclubs. Nápoles recorded several LPs of Cuban and Mexican songs. She moved to the United States in the 1960s.

(Los) Naranjos. *Son* septet created by José Hernández in Cienfuegos, 1926. It made its debut at a dance celebrated on 3 April 1926 in that city. It has promoted a repertoire of traditional boleros and *sones*. It now features new musicians but has kept its distinctive sound.

National Concert Band. *See* Havana Municipal Band.

National Conservatory (Conservatorio Nacional). Founded in Havana by the professor and composer Hubert de Blanck on 1 October 1885. It was originally named after its founder and later renamed "Nacional." It was the first music school to provide higher education for Cuban musicians. It remained open until the late 1950s. Its curriculum was adopted by many other conservatories and music schools in Cuba.

National Folkloric Ensemble (Conjunto Folklórico Nacional). Formed on 7 May 1962, in Havana, under the leadership of Rogelio Martínez Furé and Rodolfo Reyes Cortés. Since then, it has fulfilled the task of compiling and spreading knowledge about Cuba's national dances and associated music, obtained from scientific research conducted throughout the country by its founder and folkloric adviser, Furé. The company's repertoire includes such pieces as *Ciclo Yoruba* (premiered on 25 July 1963), *Rumbas y comparsas* (premiered on 25 July 1963), *Ciclo Yoruba-Iyesá* (premiered on 8 July 1965), *Ciclo Abakuá* (premiered on 8 July 1965), *Ciclo de música popular* (premiered on 8 July 1965), *Alafin de Oyó* (premiered on 26 December 1974), and *Palenque*. The company has received many prestigious awards, trophies, and certificates, including the Golden Barrel and the Silver Necklace, 1975, at the Fall Games and Thirtieth International Vineyard Festivities, held in Dijon (the only competitive festival in which the company has participated); the Golden Sandal, a trophy awarded by Festidanza '74, in Arequipa, Peru; and the Silver Platter, awarded by the Billingham Folkloric Festival, England, 1976, among others. The company has made fifteen international tours and visited twenty-one countries: France, Belgium, Spain, the German Democratic Republic, Hungary, Czechoslovakia, Bulgaria, Poland, the Soviet Union, Romania, England, Yugoslavia, Algeria, Guyana, the Dominican Republic, Mexico, Jamaica, Barbados, Peru, Colombia, and the United States. It has performed at numerous festivals and cultural events: the Theater and Dance Festival, at the Sarah Bernhardt Theater of Nations in Paris (1964); the Sixth Festival of Latin American Theater, in Havana (1966); Carifesta 1972, in Georgetown, Guyana; the Festival of Cuban Popular Art, in Havana (1973); the Folkloric Festival at the Summit Conference of Non-Aligned Countries, in Algiers (1973); the Days of Cuban Culture in the

USSR, in Moscow, Leningrad, and Riga (1973); the Second International Cervantino Festival of Guanajuato, in Mexico (1974); Festidanza '74, in Arequipa, Peru (1974); the L'Humanité Festival, in Paris (1975); and festivities to mark the Fifth Anniversary of the Independence of Guyana, in Georgetown (1975). Reviews of the company's performances have appeared in the following publications: *La Suisse, France-Soir* (Paris), *Drapeau, Rouge, La Libre Belgique* (Brussels), *Le Peuple, Argel Republicaine* (Algiers), *La Gaceta del Norte* (Bilbao), *Baleares* (Palma de Mallorca), *La Prensa* (Barcelona), *La Republique* (Oran), FDGB *Magazine* (Berlin), USSR *Magazine* (Moscow), *El Sol de León* (Guanajuato), and others.

National Institute for Folkloric Research (Instituto Nacional de Investigaciones Folkloricas). Founded in 1949 by the pianist and musicologist Odilio Urfé, who was its director in subsequent years. The institute was first located in the building of the former Santa Paula church. Its initial aims were the compilation and analysis of Cuban musical works and their classification, based on the extensive and valuable collection of music scores, records, photographs, documents, books, instruments, and other materials that the Institute owned. Over the years, these objectives were achieved and contributed to shedding light on significant areas of Cuban music, especially the popular and folkloric genres, which had until then been either distorted or neglected by ill-informed or nonsystematic researchers. By the time it was renamed the Popular Music Research Center in 1962, the foundations had been laid for the institute to become the most important information center at the service of music researchers and musicians. Its present name is the Center for Music Research.

National Institute of Music (Instituto Nacional de la Música). Founded in 1950 by Enrique González Mantici. The symphony orchestra of the institute played a genuinely Cuban repertoire. Its performances, both educational and popular, had to confront the official institutions of the Batista tyranny.

National Museum of Cuban Music (Museo Nacional de la Música Cubana). Founded in 1971 under María Antonieta Henríquez, this museum houses valuable historical materials related to the development of music in Cuba, and also contains archival documents, books, records, scores, photographs, and journals. It promotes research on aspects of and figures in Cuban music history, and disseminates its findings through lectures, exhibits, publications, and concerts. It was directed by María Teresa Linares through the late 1990s. Its current director is Jesús Gómez Cairo.

National Polyphonic Choir (Coro Polifónico Nacional). Founded in 1960 and directed by Serafín Pro. It was modeled after the National Theater Choir, launched a year before. It has performed throughout the country, singing Cuban and foreign choral pieces. Its members are highly skilled vocalists. The present director is Digna Guerra.

National School of Music (Escuela Nacional de Música). Founded in 1962 as a branch of the National School of Art in the Cubanacán neighborhood of Havana. The school provides an intermediate-level training in music, offering instruction in string, wind, and percussion instruments, as well as in choral singing. It has its own orchestra, created by Nilo Rodríguez and continued by González Mántici, and a choral department directed by Carmen Collado.

National Symphony Orchestra (Orquesta Sinfónica Nacional). Created by a decree of the Revolutionary Government in 1960. Enrique González Mántici was its chief conductor and Manuel Duchesne Cuzán its deputy conductor. Later, Cuzán became first its chief conductor and then general conductor. The best Cuban musicians and some foreign instrumentalists have played with this orchestra, which had an annual concert season featuring Cuban and foreign conductors. Since its founding, the National Symphony Orchestra has promoted Cuban and international music. Among the many guest conductors of the orchestra are Alexander Gauk, Daniil Tiulin, Verónica Dudarova, Yuri Lutsev, Heinz Bongartz, Heinz Fricke, Václay Smetácek, Josef Wilkomirsky, János Sándor, Aran Jachaturiam, Luis Herrera de la Fuente, Blas Galindo, Camargo Guarnieri, Roberto Sánchez Ferrer, Félix Guerrero, and others. Among the soloists that have performed with this orchestra are Antón Guinsburg, Víctor Merzhanov, David Oistrag, Leonid Kogan, Halina Czerny-Stefanska, Emil Kamilarov, Yuri Boukof, Silvio Rodríguez Cárdenas, Cecilio Tieles, Evelio Tieles, Ramón Calzadilla, and Leo Brouwer. The National Symphony Orchestra gives concerts not only in Havana but also in the other Cuban provinces.

National Theater. *See* Tacón Theater.

Naya, Francisco. Tenor. Born (?), Spain. Moved to Cuba as a young man, and sang in operas, operettas, and *zarzuelas*. Naya made the first recording of the Cuban *zarzuela Cecilia Valdés* with the sopranos Rita Fernández and Marta Pérez, under the conduction of its composer, Gonzalo Roig. He has performed at the Metropolitan Opera in New York.

NG La Banda. An influential dance band from Havana that formed in 1988 under the direction of the flutist and composer José Luis Cortés, known as "El Tosco." More than any other ensemble, NG—New Generation—helped define the emergent sound of *timba* (modern Cuban dance music) in the early 1990s that fused elements of Cuban *son* and folkloric percussion with U.S. jazz, rock, and funk. NG emerged as an "all-star" group of sorts that drew many of its members from the most important bands of the 1980s. Singer Tony Calá had previously played violin in Ritmo Oriental; singer Isaac Delgado and the legendary *conguero* Juan "Wickly" Nogueras began their careers with Pachito Alonso; alto saxophonist Gérman Velazco played with Orquesta Revé; he, together with trumpeter José "El Greco" Crego, tenor saxophonist Carlos Averhoff, and trumpeter José Munguía had also played in Irakere. Cortés himself had performed previously in both Irakere and Los Van Van. Other initial members of NG included drummer Giraldo Piloto, *timbalero* Calixto Oviedo, bassist Feliciano Arango, and keyboardist Rodolfo "Peruchín" Argudín. Many of these individuals have since left the band to begin successful solo careers,

taking Cortés's new conception of dance music with them. Groups of the mid-1990s such as La Charanga Habanera, Klimax, Paulito F. G., and others owe much of their style to the creations of NG La Banda. Kevin Moore's timba website, www.timba.com, is a valuable resource for information on the group.

Nicola, Clara. Guitarist and professor. Born 1926, Havana. Daughter of Clara Romero and sister of Isaac Nicola. Clara Nicola gave guitar concerts in theaters and later devoted herself to teaching.

Nicola, Isaac. Professor and guitarist. Born 11 April 1916, Havana; died 14 July 1997. Studied with his mother, Clara Romero, and, later, in Paris, in 1939, with Emilio Pujol. Nicola conducted research on the *vihuela* (an early form of guitar) in Paris, London, Madrid, Barcelona, and New York. He gave concerts and lectures in Cuba and abroad. He joined the Havana Municipal Conservatory as a professor in 1951 and was later appointed director. He presided over the Scientific Technical Board for the Teaching of Music. He was the teacher of some excellent guitarists, including Leo Brouwer, many of whom are today important teachers in the Cuban school of guitar.

Nicola, Noel. Composer, singer, guitarist. Born 7 October 1946, Havana. From a family of notable musicians: Eva Reyes (violinist), Isaac Nicola, Cuqui Nicola (guitarist), and Clara Romero (guitarist). Noel Nicola began his career playing in various musical groups, and in 1967 joined the program of protest-song writing at the Casa de las Américas. He has written music for plays and cinema and to accompany the sung poems of José Martí and César Vallejo. He studied with Federico Smith and Leo Brouwer and was a member of the ICAIC's Grupo de Experimentación Sonora. He is currently the coordinator of the National Nueva Trova Movement. His compositions include "Por la vida juntos," "Diciembre tres y cuatro," "Para una imaginaria María del Carmen," "Comienzo del día," "Es más te perdono," and "Ámame como soy."

Nin Castellanos, Joaquín. Composer, pianist, professor. Born 29 September 1879, Havana; died 24 October 1949. Father of the pianist and composer Joaquín Nin Culmell. Nin Castellanos began his early studies in Spain and pursued them further in Paris at the Schola Cantorum. He lived in Germany for some years, and in 1910 came to Havana, where he founded a music society and published a newsletter for the promotion of music. Soon after, he moved to Brussels, where he gave concerts and lectures and devoted himself to research on and dissemination of Spanish music. He was a professor at the University of Brussels. He composed very Spanish music, using Spanish folk elements. Most of his outstanding works are pieces for piano and adaptations of Spanish Christmas carols and songs. He also composed three symphonies, one ballet, a mimedrama, and pieces for lute quartet. As a musicologist, he published the valuable piece "Pro-Arte: Ideas y comentarios." He returned to Havana in 1939 and took up the teaching of piano.

Noroña, Gilberto ("Carioca"). Musical eccentric and singer of décimas. Born 27 March 1917, Quemado de Güines; died (?), Havana. Held a diverse series of rural and urban jobs before becoming a professional musician in 1938. "Carioca" was awarded a prize at the Corte Suprema del Arte. He sang punto guajiro, parodies in the mode of décimas, and performed as an actor on various radio stations in Havana, Santiago de Cuba, and Guantánamo. He acted in the film Mulata, for which he composed the soundtrack, and performed in theaters, on streets, and in nightclubs throughout Cuba.

Nuestro Tiempo cultural society. Cultural society founded in 1951 and presided over by Harold Gramatges. Nuestro Tiempo gathered together young people interested in the development of Cuba's art and culture. It confronted the corrupt, exploitative, and proimperialist Batista regime through undertaking popular cultural work. Socialist in ideological orientation, it carried out a sustained struggle against the dictatorship. The society published the journal Nuestro Tiempo, which included a section on music criticism, until it was dissolved in 1960. Its music section carried out a sustained program for the promotion of works by Cuban composers, and it organized concerts by national musicians, lectures, concerts for discussions, and published music booklets and scores that included works by young composers. On its board were Juan Blanco, Manuel Duchesne Cuzán, María Antonieta Henrí-quez, Argeliers León, Edgardo Martín, Serafín Pro, and Nilo Rodríguez.

nueva trova. One of the most well-known forms of musical expression associated with revolutionary Cuba. Nueva trova might best be translated as "new song." The term "trova" derives from trovador, or troubadour, a name given to the early guitar player–composers who popularized the style. Nueva trova is a form of protest music incorporating stylistic influences from Cuban traditional and popular genres, jazz, rock, European classical music, and other sources. It emerged as a recognizable movement in the late 1960s among younger performers, although its direct antecedents can be found in compositions by Carlos Puebla, Eduardo Saborit, and those of traditional trova artists. Nueva trova represents part of the pan–Latin American song phenomenon that began in the late 1960s and was known as nueva canción, and also has links to protest song in the United States and Europe.

Lyrics of the nueva trova repertory vary in style but represent an attempt to escape from commercial banality and often make reference to political injustice, sexism, colonialism, and related issues. Pablo Milanés, Silvio Rodríguez, Noel Nicola, Sara González, Pedro Luís Ferrer, and other early figures performed informally, appearing on stage in street clothes and in other ways minimizing the divide between performer and audience. Far from being wholeheartedly embraced by the establishment, nueva trova artists through the mid-1970s maintained a tense relationship at times with government officials, who considered their long hair, "hippie" clothing, and interest in rock a manifestation of "capitalist decadence." By the late 1970s, however, many of the same artists had achieved strong official support and were transformed into international icons of socialism. Cuban protest singers emerging more recently (Carlos Varela, Amaury Pérez, Gerardo Alfonso, and others) play music more heavily influenced by rock, and in some cases more openly criticize government policies than their established counterparts.

Núñez, Arturo. Conductor, composer, pianist. Born 4 October 1913, Havana; died 1981, Mexico City. Studied at the Carnicer Conservatory in Havana, and performed as a pianist at the Alhambra Theater.

Núñez later played with various orchestras. He traveled to Mexico City and there founded a jazz-dance band, the first orchestra to accompany Benny Moré in that city. He performed with his group in various countries in the Americas. He composed "La cita" and other pieces.

Núñez, Joseíto. Singer. Born 13 December 1909, Havana; died 1979. Began his career singing in *son* sextets and later performed with ensembles and orchestras. Núñez sang with the orchestra of Belisario López at a great many dances. For some time, he conducted his own band, Modelo. He was an outstanding singer of boleros and *sones* while with the Septeto Nacional.

Núñez, Leopoldina. Guitarist. Born 1 November 1918, Santiago de Cuba. Began her piano studies with the Ibarra sisters in her hometown. Later, in Havana, she studied guitar with Clara Romero de Nicola, sang with Zoila Gálvez, and studied popular guitar styles with Roberto de Moya and then with Vicente González Rubiera ("Guyún"). Núñez joined the faculty of the School for Art Instructors in 1961, and in 1963 took a three-year course of harmony applied to the guitar, with Maestro Guyún, at the Popular Music Seminary. Soon after, she founded the Children's Workshop, which came to be very successful. She wrote a book on guitar harmony. Among her students were Miguel Porcel, Marta Valdés, Omar and Amed Barroso, and Carlos Montero.

Núñez, Tomasita. Soprano. Born (?); died 1980, Miami. Performed in theaters in Havana; sang pieces from the national repertoire of lyrical song since the 1920s and sang on radio and on many records, particularly those by Cuban composers.

O

Ochoa, Eliades. Composer and guitarist. Born 1946, Santiago de Cuba. Ochoa was the founder of El Quintetto de la Trova and later worked with the trio Ensueño. In 1978 he formed his own group, Quarteto Patria. In 1997, he achieved worldwide acclaim with the *Buena Vista Social Club* record.

O'Farrill, Chico. Trumpet player and arranger. Born 28 October 1921, Havana; died 2001. Given name was Arturo. He studied music (trumpet) first in the United States and then, back in Havana, studied composition and was taught by Félix Guerrero. O'Farrill played in several different dance bands in Havana; in 1946, he toured Europe with Armando Oréfiche's Havana Cuban Boys and then went to New York to take up work as an arranger. Over the next two years, he worked for Benny Goodman, Stan Kenton, and Dizzy Gillespie and Charlie Parker. He lived in Mexico, and then he and his orchestra moved to the United States. His arrangements for American and Cuban jazz musicians were recorded on a number of memorable LPs, including those by Glen Miller, Count Basie, and Gato Barbieri, and his own compositions were featured on Dizzy Gillespie's Afro-Cubop projects and were performed by Machito and Mario Bauza. In the 1970s and 1980s, he produced television jingles and even arranged jazz classics for Ringo Starr and David Bowie. In 1995, he recorded *Trumpet Fantasy* with Wynton Marsalis.

O'Farrill, Ela. Composer and instrumentalist. Born 28 February 1930, Santa Clara. Studied at the Pedagogical School in Santa Clara. Once in Havana, O'Farrill studied guitar with César Portillo de la Luz in 1950, and harmony and composition with Enrique Bellwer and Vicente González Rubiera ("Guyún") in 1964. She moved to Mexico City in the late 1960s. She is the author of "No tienes por qué criticar," "Ni llorar puedo ya," "Adiós, felicidad," and "Cuando pasas tú."

O'Farrill, Miguel. Flutist. Born 8 May 1922, Ciego de Avila; died (?). Started playing in Abelardito Valdés's Orquesta Almendra in Havana, 1942. O'Farrill traveled to Mexico in 1955 as part of Enrique Jorrín's orchestra and remained there until 1959, when he returned to Cuba. He continued playing with Jorrín while he performed with different bands such as Los Amigos. He has traveled to several countries.

O'Farrill, Pablo. Composer and double bass player. Born (?), Havana; died 1957, Mexico City. Played with different orchestras in Havana. In 1926 O'Farrill presented for the first time his *danzón* "Virgen de Regla," based on a *son* from the Septeto Habanero repertoire. Later, he composed "Milagros" and other *danzones*. He spent his last years in Mexico.

Ojeda, Grupo Campesino de. Formed and directed by the laud player Miguel Ojeda in the 1940s. It has traveled abroad promoting Cuba's country music style. At present, the band performs on the television show *Palmas y Cañas*.

Olga y Tony. Vocal duet formed by Olga Chorens and Tony Alvarez. It began singing in theaters and radio shows in the 1940s. During the 1950s, the duo performed on a show for Radio Progreso and also recorded several LPs. During the 1960s, Chorens and Alvarez moved to Puerto Rico where they continued their career. At present, they live in the United States.

olivas sonoras. Rattles worn as necklaces and used in Indo-Cuban ceremonies, chants, and dances. They are made by stringing small shells called *olivas* on a thread. Between 20 and 45 mm long and between 7 and 15 mm in diameter, measured at their widest part, these univalve shells are generally unadorned, but some are carved with geometrical figures or with faces. This carving often reveals the inner coil of the shell; a rattling sound is produced when the hanging *olivas* clash against one another (Morales Patiño, *Las olivas sonoras en Cuba y en México*). *Olivas sonoras*, according to studies conducted by various musicologists, have a dominant note, A natural. A pleasant, cheerful tinkle is heard when the *olivas* clash against each other as a result of body movement.

Ondina, Roberto. Flutist. Born 7 June 1904, Havana; died 1 July 1963. Received his first music lessons from his father, then studied flute with several teachers, but was for the most part self-taught.

At twelve, he played the flute as accompaniment to silent movies and in dance bands. Later, he was soloist in the Havana Municipal Band conducted by Gonzalo Roig. He played in radio orchestras. He was soloist in the National Symphony Orchestra. He was a respected flute teacher, training the best modern players, and is considered to be one of Cuba's greatest flutists.

opera, Cuban. The earliest opera performances in Cuba were at the end of the eighteenth century and the beginning of the nineteenth century when many Spanish, Italian, and French companies visited, performing mainly in Havana and Santiago de Cuba. Opera companies featuring Spanish singers began to appear in Havana in 1811. Many important European operas were staged during this early phase of opera in Cuba. *América y Apolo*, presented four years earlier, was the first work produced by Cuban lyrical writers; its libretto was by Manuel Zequiera and another anonymous author. The composers of the operas *Los apuros de Covarrubias*, with libretto by Diego Castillo, and *Las cuatro columnas del trono español* and *El mejor día de La Habana*, both with libretto by Luis Antonio Guerra and performed in 1814, are unknown. *Los apuros de Covarrubias*, a comic opera, premiered on 14 December 1811 at the Principal Theater and honored the *bufo* opera *Francisco Covarrubias*. *El sueño mágico o el hijo de la fortuna*, with libretto by Juan López Extremera, was presented on 14 November 1816. The following year, the Italian composer Stefano Cristiani, who lived in Cuba, presented the operas *Un loco hace un ciento*, *El vinagrero*, and *La Clarisa*. In 1823 the Spanish composer José Serrano, who also lived in Cuba, staged his opera *Quien bien ata bien desata* (or *El hermano Benito*). José Antonio Coccó, conductor of the orchestra at the Principal Theater, premiered *Fátima y Zelima* (or *Las dos prisioneras*) on 12 October 1825.

Cristóbal Martínez Corres might be considered the first Cuban opera composer. His operas were never publicly staged and were ultimately lost. It is known, however, that he wrote the comic operas *El diablo contrabandista* and *Don Papanero* (or *La burla del magnetismo*), and he finished the first act of his *Safo* (González, *La composición operística en Cuba*, 38–40). *Colón en Cuba* was presented at the Tacón Theater in 1848. That opera was the first lyrical work by the famous Italian composer Giovanni Battista Bottesini, with libretto by Ramón de Palma. The opera *Gulnara*, with libretto by Rafael María Mendive, based on the poet Byron's work, was premiered that same year at the same theater. The work also marked the debut of the outstanding Italian composer Luigi Arditi. On 16 May 1874 the opera *La hija de Jefté* was presented at the Reina Theater in Santiago de Cuba. It was composed by Laureano Fuentes Matons, with libretto by Juan Arnao. Fuentes Matons later made some additions to the opera and translated it into Italian. The Bracale Opera Company staged it at the National Theater in 1917, nineteen years after Matons's death. Gaspar Villate composed *Las primeras armas de Richeliéu* in 1871, an opera that has never been staged. While living in Paris, Villate attended the presentation of his operas *Zilia*, with libretto by Temístocle Solera, in 1877 and *La Zarina*, based on Armand Silvestre's book, in 1880. Both operas were later presented in Havana. In 1885 Villate composed a new opera, *Baltazar*, with libretto by Carlo d'Ormeville and based on Gertrudis Gómez de Avellaneda's drama. It was premiered at the Madrid's Real Theater, but was not performed in Havana until 10 March 1839. Hubert de Blanck wrote three operas: *Patria*, based on the nineteenth-century Cuban independence wars; *Actea*, about Nerón's time; and *Icaona*, about the indigenous Cubans. On 25 January 1901, the comic opera *Los saltimbanquis*, by the outstanding *danza* composer Ignacio Cervantes, was presented at the Albizú Theater in Havana. Eduardo Sánchez de Fuentes was a prolific Cuban opera writer. Besides his works on indigenous themes, including *Yumurí y Doreya*, which received an award at a national contest, he premiered *El náufrago*, *Dolora*, *Caminante*, and *Kabelia*.

Perhaps the most important opera composed in Cuba is *La esclava* (1918) by José Mauri. According to Alejo Carpentier, Mauri was a pioneer among Cuban musicians, the first composer to produce a well-conceived national opera that could be performed successfully in modern times. Besides its historical interest, the opera stood alone as a successful work of art (Carpentier, *La música en Cuba*, 285). *La esclava* was premiered on 6 July 1921 at the National Theater and has also been performed recently. Amadeo Roldán and Alejandro García Caturla, the most important composers of the 1920s, are credited with two operas: *Deirdre* and *Manita en el suelo*, which,

together with *El sombrero de yarey*, a three-act play by Ernesto Lecuona, have never been staged. Current trends in opera composition are reflected by such works as *S. XIV-69* by Sergio Fernández Barroso, which incorporates electronic instruments; *Ibeyi Añá* by Héctor Angulo, with libretto by Rogelio Martínez Furé and José Camejo and based on a popular short story by Lydia Cabrera; and *Van Troi* by Roberto Sánchez Ferrer, which is based on a Vietnamese hero of the same name. The Cuban National Opera was created in 1959; it is modeled on the institution created by the journalist Juan Bonich in 1938. It has played an important artistic role in Cuba.

opiabá. The first and largest of the set of three Abakuá drums known collectively as *enkomo*, the *opiabá* produces a deep tone. The other two drums are *kuchíyeremá* and *binkomé*. *See also* enkomo.

Oramas, Faustino ("Guayabero"). *Tres* player and composer. Born 4 June 1911, Holguín; died (?). *Trova* singer who played *tres* and sang about everyday events. Oramas began his career playing on radio shows in Holguín and in popular festivals in that western region. Based in Holguín, he is sponsored by the Cuban Ministry of Culture and travels around Cuba. He is the author of the *sones* "Tumbaíto," "En guayabera," "Como vengo este año," "Ay, candela!" "Mañana me voy," and others.

Orbón, Benjamín. Professor and piano player. Born 1874, Asturias, Spain; died 1914, Havana. Father of the composer Julián Orbón. Benjamin Orbón received his musical training in Spain and gave concerts in different Spanish cities. He came to live in Cuba in 1909 and turned to teaching. He established the Orbón Conservatory. He performed in Paris, to much acclaim.

Orbón, Julián. Pianist and composer. Born 7 August 1925, Aviles, Spain; died 22 May 1991, New York. Began his music training in the conservatory of his hometown and moved to Havana in 1940. There, Orbón studied harmony with Oscar Lorié and composition with José Ardévol, and gave piano concerts. He was a member of the Grupo de Renovación Musical of Havana. His relevant works are Sonata (honoring Soler) for piano (1942); Tocata, for piano (1943); Pregón, for voice, wind instruments, and piano (1944); Quintet, for clarinet and string quartet (1944); Capriccio concertante (1945); Symphony no. 1 (1945); and Suite, for guitar. In the 1960s he moved to the United States.

Ordaz, Everardo. Pianist. Born 6 January 1913, Havana; died (?), Mexico City. Began playing as a child with no formal instruction of any kind, then entered the Havana Municipal Conservatory, where he graduated in 1930. Ordaz was head of the theory and harmony department, where he worked for three years. At the same time, he performed popular music with the dance orchestras of Paulina Alvarez, Fernando Collazo, and Abelardo Barroso. He created his own band, La Típica de Ordaz, in 1942 and then went to Mexico in 1946, subsequently touring Central America. He moved to Mexico and became a popular exponent of Cuban music there. He recorded several LPs. He visited his homeland on many occasions and performed in theaters, and on radio and television shows.

Orefiche, Armando. Pianist, composer, conductor. Born 1911, Havana. Studied at the School of Education; also studied piano at a musical academy in Havana. Orefiche started his performance career with Ernesto Lecuona's company and traveled to Europe with the Orquesta Lecuona. When Lecuona returned to Cuba, Orefiche and the band continued touring. He became its conductor and the orchestra was renamed the Lecuona Cuban Boys. In 1939 he returned to Havana and the following year toured extensively around South America. In 1946, after a short period in Cuba, he went to Europe, returning in 1954, when he moved to Santiago de las Vegas. A year later, he reorganized the orchestra again, now calling it the Havana Cuban Boys, with whom he traveled around the world. He is the author of the songs "Cariñosamente," "Me estoy enamorando de ti," "Falsa herida," "Corazón para qué," "Mayarí," "Rumba blanca," and the afro song "Mesié Julián." He currently lives in Spain.

órgano oriental. Toward the end of the nineteenth century, Francisco de Borbolla introduced to the town of Manzanillo a mechanical organ operated by cranking or turning a handle. Its music was used for popular dances. The first organs were brought to Cuba from Paris, and they were soon being constructed on the island. Borbolla's descendants continued his work, and the popularity of the organ extended to the cities of Holguín (Varberena), Buenaventura (Ajo), and Bayamo (Labrada). Danzones, sones, polkas, and guarachas were soon played on the organ with the accompaniment of pailas criollas, a güiro or guayo, and the tumbadora. The órgano oriental is now present in all regions of the country and is considered an integral part of Cuban folk culture.

Oriental, Trío. Maximiliano ("Bimbi") Sánchez, the director, created this trio, together with Tico Alvarez and Feliú, in Santiago de Cuba. It was very popular during the 1940s and 1950s, mainly in Latin America. Known for its musicians' voices and guitar playing, the trio performed the best of the Cuban canción style.

Original de Manzanillo, Orquesta. French charanga band with modern new elements, created by the pianist Wilfredo Naranjo in Manzanillo, 1963. Its repertoire ranges from son and cha-cha-chá to more aggressive rhythms. At present, the orchestra plays mainly in dance halls. It has performed on many radio and television shows and has recorded several LPs.

Orovio, Helio. Musicologist, researcher, promoter. Born 4 February 1938, Santiago de las Vegas. Graduated in foreign relations from the University of Havana in 1966. Prior to his graduation, he studied guitar and percussion. Orovio played in many popular bands, such as Conjunto Jóvenes del Cayo, with whom he traveled to the United States. He was a researcher at the Institute of Ethnology and Folklore at the Academy of Sciences. Many of his reviews and essays have been published in Cuban magazines and newspapers, as well as in foreign publications. He has also written radio, television, and movie scripts on subjects relating to music. For many years, he was the host of the TV show Arte y Folklore. His remarkable work as a commentator on different Cuban television shows is noteworty. He is the author of Diccionario de la música cubana (1981; second edition 1993). This work has been a vital reference source

for all those interested in Cuban music. He has published a number of other books including *300 boleros de oro* (1991), *Música por el Caribe* (1995), and *El bolero latino* (1996), as well as poetry and an anthology of Brazilian poetry. He has been music adviser in several cultural institutions in charge of the promotion of popular musicians. (Zoila Gómez García)

Orozco, Danilo. Musicologist and professor. Born 17 July 1944, Santiago de Cuba. Studied music with Moraima Guash, then turned to choral activities. Orozco studied acoustics with Roberto Soto del Rey; mathematical analysis with Luis Estévez and Mario Vidaud; physics with Luis Aguilar; and the integrated and statisticalo analysis of composition with Federico Smith. He also received methodological training with Argeliers León. He worked with Sergio Fernández Barroso in 1971 and received technical guidance from the engineer Ricardo Llanes. From 1968 to 1972, he was a professor of musical acoustics at the National School of Art. He is a member of the advisory committee of the Cuban Libro Institute. His work *A propósito de la Nueva Trova* won the Pablo Hernández Balaguer award in a contest organized by the National Council for Culture in 1974. He is musical adviser to the Cultural Center in Santiago de Cuba, where he gives training courses and does promotion work through talks and lectures.

orquesta típica. Also known as a wind orchestra. The *orquesta típica* first emerged in the eighteenth century and reached its peak of fame in the nineteenth century. The earliest types of *orquestas típicas* played *contradanzas* and some hall dances; later they would play *danzones*. During the second half of the twentieth century the popularity of *orquestas típicas* waned, as audiences came to prefer *charangas*,

conjuntos, and *jazzbands*. The *orquesta típica* was composed of cornet, trombone á piston, ophicleide, two C-clarinets, two violins, a double bass, kettledrums (tympani), and *güiro*.

Orraca, Alina. Choral conductor. Born December 1957, Havana. Studied choral conducting at the National School of Art and later at the Higher Institute of Art. Orraca formed the chamber chorus at the National School of Music in 1979. In 1983 she created the Scola Cantorum Coralina. She has given concerts in Cuba and abroad.

Orta Ruíz, Jesús. *Décima* and *punto guajiro* singer. Born 30 September 1922, San Miguel del Padrón. Known as "El Indio Naborí." As a child, Orta Ruíz worked as an agricultural laborer and sang the *punto*. He also performed on radio and television shows. He graduated in journalism from the Manuel Marquez Sterling School in 1962 and has subsequently written books on the *décima*: *Guardarraya sonora* (1946), *Bandurria y violin* (1948), *Estampas y elegias* (1955), *Boda profunda* (1957), *Cuatro cuerdas* (1960), *El pulso del tiempo* (1966), and *Entre y perdone usted* (1973).

Ortega, Jesús. Guitarist. Born 15 September 1935, Guanabacoa. Studied guitar with Isaac Nicola and Leo Brouwer. Ortega gave his first concert in 1957. In 1959 he was head of the art section of the Oriente Army. He worked in the music division of the National Council for Culture. He is a professor at Amadeo Roldán Conservatory. His solo career is supported by the Ministry of Culture. He has made transcriptions for guitar. Among his works are Recitative and fugue, Three preludes, *Puntos* (for jazzband), and *Dos poemas de lucha*, based on a text by José Martí.

Ortega, Rafael. Pianist. Born 30 November 1917, Havana. Began his musical studies at the age of eleven but had to abandon them for economic reasons. He continued to study music without formal instruction. As a pianist, Ortega played popular music with different dance bands, including Típico Orquesta Paulin and later the Daiquiri Jazz Band. With the latter orchestra he traveled to Peru, Chile, and Argentina. In 1936 he left that band and traveled as a piano accompanist and with other orchestras to Uruguay and Brazil. In 1940 he returned to Cuba and began working as a director in Havana's theaters. In 1941 he traveled again to different Latin American countries, including Venezuela and Mexico. Back to Havana, he became the conductor of the Mil Diez radio orchestra. In 1948 he conducted the orchestra at the Sans-Souci cabaret, where he stayed for eleven years. In 1959 he conducted the orchestras of Garcia Lorca Theater and of the Capri Hotel. He has arranged and composed many songs.

Ortiz, Fernando. Ethnographer, lawyer, linguist, historian. Born 16 July 1881, Havana; died 10 April 1969. Went with his family to Menorca when he was one year old. Graduated from high school in 1895 and published his first article, "Principi y prostes," about the costumes of the people in Menorca. Back to Havana, Ortiz began studying law and finished his training in Barcelona, where he graduated. He received his Ph.D. in Madrid. In 1903 he became a Cuban diplomat. From 1917 to 1927 he was a representative in the Congress and was also a university professor. For many years, he was the president of the Economic Society of Friends of the Country. He founded the Folklore Society of Cuba (1923), the Hispano-Cuban Culture Society (1926), and the Society for Afro-Cuban Studies (1937). He always supported and defended any important scientific or artistic issues and movements of the day. He founded the magazines *Archivo del Folklore* (1924), *Revista Bimestre and Ultra* (1936), and *Revista de Estudios Afrocubanos* (1937). For many years, he was president of the National Board of Archeology and Ethnography. In 1955 he received an international tribute for the sixtieth anniversary of the publication of "Principi y prostes." He was nominated for the Nobel Peace Prize for his love for culture and humankind. Among his works, the following are commended:

Hampa afrocubana: Los negros brujos (1906), a book of great importance, which marks the first study of African culture in Cuba; *La clave xilofónica de la música afrocubana* (1935); *La africania de la música folklórica de Cuba* (1950); *Los bailes y el teatro de los negros en el folklore de Cuba* (1951); and *Los instrumentos de la música afrocubana* (5 vols., 1952–1955).

Ortiz, Juan. Cithern and viola player. Born (?); died middle of sixteenth century, Mexico. Known as "El Músico," since he was virtually the only musician in Cuba during the early days of Spanish colonization. He lived in Trinidad, where he began a music and dance school, the first on the island. His performances spoke to the island's small population. He followed Hernán Cortés in the conquest of the Aztecs and continued his work as a dance and music teacher.

Ortiz, Miguel Ángel. Tenor. Born 29 August 1922, Havana; died 31 May 1986. Began his career as an interpreter of Cuban songs on radio stations in 1939. Ortiz studied with Zanaida Romeu and Carlos Dalmau and took classes with Professor Antonioni in New York. He took part in operas and *zarzuelas*. He made many appearances in theaters and on television, as well as at cultural centers. He visited various countries, bringing the Cuban repertoire to the rest of the world.

Ortiz, Pura. Pianist. Born 3 March 1935, Havana. Studied in the Fischermann and Levy conservatories. Was a soloist on Channel 2 television. In 1963 Ortiz joined the National Symphony Orchestra, where he was a soloist. He was also a member of the Havana Chamber Orchestra, of the instrumental group Nuestro Tiempo, and of the Havana Trio. He has worked as a piano accompanist for many Cuban and other soloists. He has performed over fifty works for both piano and chamber music.

Ortiz, Rafael. Composer and guitarist. Born 20 June 1908, Cienfuegos; died 29 December 1994, Havana. Was a member of Ignacio Piñero's Septeto Nacional. He also played with other *son* groups, such as the Cienfuegos Septet and La Clave Oriental. Ortiz later joined the group Gloria Matancera. He is the author of the bolero-*sones* "Conciencia fria," "Muy junto al corazón," and "Amor de loca juventud"; of the *can-*

ciones "Tabernero" and "No me pidas"; of the *sones* "Un mensaje de amor" and "Cuatro paredes"; and of the conga "Uno, dos y tres."

Ovelleiro Carvajal, José. Composer. Born 1912, Pinar de Rio; died 3 January 1962, Havana. Author of the hymns "America inmortal" and "Canto rebelde," and of the *pregón* "Maracas."

Oviedo, Isaac. *Tres* player, singer, composer. Born 16 July 1902, Sabanilla, Matanzas; died (?), Havana. Directed the Septeto Matancero with Julio Govin in the 1920s. Oviedo formed the Quinteto Típico with Graciano Gomez, traveling with them in 1929 to Puerto Rico. In 1937 the group toured the United States. He is considered to have been one of the best *tres* players in Cuba. He composed pieces with a distinctly Cuban quality, including the *son montuno* "Engancha Carretero." In his last years he worked with a quintet he founded with Gomez, giving concerts of popular Cuban music.

Oviedo, Papi. *Tres* player. Born 1938. The son of the legendary Isaac Oviedo. Papi Oviedo is known as the number one *tres* player in Cuba. He was a member of a number of ensembles, including Conjunto Chapotín, Típica Habanera, Estrellas de Chocolate, and Orquesta Reve, before forming his own group, Papi Oviedo y Sus Soneros. His first album as a soloist was *Encuentro Entre Soneros* (1997), which has gained international acclaim.

Mo Fini

P

Pacheco, Jorge Luis. Baritone. Born 3 January 1941, Havana. Studied in the Soviet Union. Pacheco has given recitals in different concert halls and theaters. He has participated in operettas and operas. He is director of the National Opera Theater and a singing teacher at the Higher Institute of Art. He is a musical adviser at the Cuban Television Institute.

Pacheco Arias, Víctor. Clarinetist. Born 1835, Manzanillo; died 1910, Camagüey. Lived most of his life in the city of Camagüey, where he created a family of musicians. Pacheco was an instrumentalist and conductor at the Principal Theater and also established a music school there. He opened the first house of musical sound effects in Camagüey. He joined the Independence Army in 1895 and founded a band to perform on the battlefield. Captured and sentenced to death by the Spanish colonial regime, he was set free after agreeing duplicitously to join the Isabel La Católica Band; he then ran away to the battlefield. By the end of the war, he was a captain. His song compositions include "Tropical" and "Campamento" (waltzes), "La Aurora" (reveille), and "El Triunfo" (dance).

paila criolla. A percussion instrument that was traditionally made from large cooking pans and used in the street *murgas* (bands) of the nineteenth century. Later, it was introduced into the *danzón* orchestras as a substitute for the tympani. It has a hemispherical, closed, metallic-sounding body. The drumhead is tuned by tightening screws and nuts. The *paila criolla* produces high-pitched or low-pitched notes, depending on the dexterity of the musician, who plays it with two sticks.

Palanca, Alberto. Tenor. Born 14 August 1938, Santiago de las Vegas. His teachers were David Rendón, Ramón Bendoyro, Romano Splinter, Ramón Calzadilla, and Sergio Tulián. Palanca entered the world of popular song with the help of Isolina Carrillo. He began singing in the National Choir and, after 1962, became a member of the Lyric Theater. He is a graduate of the Higher Institute of Art. He has participated in operas and operettas.

Palau, Felipe. Organist, professor, composer. Born 1866, Camagüey; died 1937, Havana. Pupil of Ignacio Cervantes, Lico Jiménez, and Carlos Ánckermann. For forty-three years, Palau played the organ at the Havana Cathedral. He also taught music at the San Francisco de Sales College. He was subsequently a director at other music academies, and he composed works for organ.

Palau, Orquesta Hermanos. *Jazzband* created in Havana around 1930. It appeared on radio and television as well as at dances, for three decades. Its repertoire included American music, bolero, *son, guaracha,* and rumba. Many relevant musicians emerged from the Palau family, including the outstanding saxophonist Tata Palau, who continues to perform. The band's singer was Orlando Guerra ("Cascarita"). The group performed on CMQ radio.

Palau, Rafael. Orchestra conductor and composer. Born 1864, Catalonia, Spain; died 1906, Havana. When still a child, Palau moved to Camagüey with his father, who was also a musician but who worked as a merchant. He composed operettas, comedies, one-act farces, piano pieces, songs, and religious music. He conducted the orchestras that accompanied Cuban comic operas (*bufos*). His brother Felipe was for many years an organist at the Havana Cathedral. He participated in the struggle for independence and his song "La Palma" became a revolutionary symbol for the fighting patriots.

Palma. *See* Reyes, Ernesto.

Palma, Néstor. Violinist. Born (?), Santa Clara; died 1896. Studied violin in Paris with Jean D. Alard and gave concerts in various Cuban cities. According to Anselmo López, Palma "mastered the bow, had impeccable harmony, and a mighty soul." He died in combat during the War of Independence.

palo dance. This dance is one of the rituals of the Congos (the Afro-Cuban liturgy). The word *"palo"* derives from the Ki-Kongo *mpali,* meaning "witchcraft." The dance is known as the *regla de palo* and is accompanied by chants and *toques de palo.* The name derives from Congo mythology, according to which the dance is performed to celebrate an important function, the *palos del monte.* It is performed by couples, who make rapid forward motions with their arms and chests, along with alternating motions of the arms and feet, as if they were slipping, in time with the rhythm of the drums.

Pancho Majagua. *See* Salazar, Francisco Albo.

(Los) Papines. Vocal and percussion quartet founded in Havana in 1957 by the Abreu brothers: Luis, Alfredo, Jesús, and Ricardo. Its repertoire consists of Afro-Cuban music, with particular emphasis on rumba, but played in quite an original way with innovative elements. The quartet has performed in many countries, including France, Japan, the Soviet Union, Canada, and the United States and has made numerous records and appeared on several radio and television shows.

Pardo, Enrique. Clarinetist and orchestra conductor. Born 26 April 1905, Caibarién. Began studying harmony and music theory with his father and acquired the clarinet with the guidance of José María Montalván. For thirty-two years, Pardo was the lead clarinetist in the Havana Philharmonic Orchestra, where he performed many concerts as a soloist under Pedro Sanjuán, Amadeo Roldán, Massimo Freccia, Erich Kleiber, Igor Markóvich, and Frieder Weissman. He was also a solo clarinetist in the National Police Band. He played in several chamber music groups, in opera and ballet orchestras, and in radio and television orchestras. He studied with Jan Constantinescu and Alexander Frolov to become a conductor and has conducted the symphony orchestras in the provinces of Oriente, Camagüey, Las Villas, and Matanzas. He was a professor at the García Caturla and Amadeo Roldán conservatories and in the music department of the National School of Art. He has trained several outstanding Cuban clarinetists.

París, Juan. Composer. Born 1759, Barcelona, Spain; died 10 July 1845, Santiago de Cuba. In 1805 París was appointed choirmaster at the Santiago de Cuba Cathedral. He kept alive the music of Esteban Salas in that city. He gave the first performances of Beethoven's music in Cuba, and also played works by Pergolesi, Haydn, Cherubini, Paisiello, and Cimarosa. He was a piano professor. His own compositions include Three masses, Introit, Psalms, *Lección primera de difuntos*, *Oficio de difuntos*, Christmas carols, and Motets. He organized concerts and stimulated the music scene in the capital of Oriente Province.

Párraga, Graciela. Composer. Born 10 March 1905, Havana; died 7 October 1971, United States. Born into a well-to-do family, Párraga sang to guitar accompaniment and also played piano. She is the author of "Como mi vida gris," "Te besaron mis ojos," and other songs. Her music was used in American movies and recorded by different labels. She performed in the theater and on radio and television shows.

paseo. A *contradanza* step. The man puts his arm around his partner and guides her to where the couple before the pair was dancing. He then leads her forward again until the couple is standing between the two facing lines of dancers (Pichardo, *Diccionario provincial casi razonado de voces cubanas*).

Pastor, Rafael. Composer and professor. Born 1870, Alicante, Spain; died 14 May 1947, Havana. Came to Cuba in 1896 and began teaching music and composition. Founder of the National Academy of Arts and Literature. Pastor composed symphonies, chamber music, several dances for piano, religious music, and other pieces such as Serenade, Mimetto in A major, and *Tres danzas cubanas*.

Patterson, Miguel. Clarinetist, bassoonist, arranger, orchestra conductor. Born 23 September 1948, Holguín. Played the clarinet at the Oriente Symphony Orchestra from 1962 to 1964. Patterson studied music at the National School of the Arts. In 1968 he moved to Havana, where he joined the orchestra of the Cuban Broadcasting Institute and became its conductor in 1973. He has conducted orchestras both in Cuba and abroad and has also participated in music festivals.

Payret Theater. Opened in 1877 with a concert, followed by an opera season. Its founder, Jaime Payret, lost the theater two years later when he could not repay its mortgage to the government. Dramas and operas were presented there. The theater fell into the hands of many different owners over the years and would eventually become a movie theater. The original structure was demolished, with no consideration of its status as a national monument, in order to construct the current Payret Theater. The new building is suitable only as a cinema: it lacks the proper acoustics for a theater. It may be considered a curiosity that the theater continues to be called the Payret.

Pedroso, Andrés. Composer and double bass player. Born 6 September 1942, Ciego de Avila. Studied music in his hometown, then joined a series of different dance bands, first as a percussionist and then as a double bass player. Pedroso went on to study at the National School of the Arts. In 1971 he was a cofounder of the group Manguaré, which worked out of Chile for some time. He composed such *sones* as "Junto a mi fusil mi son," "En la casa del licenciado," "Tonada y feeling para un caminante," among others. At present, he is the leader of Manguaré.

Pedroso, César. Pianist, composer, orchestrator. Born 24 September 1944, Havana. Studied at the García Caturla Conservatory in Marianao. Pedroso performed with the Orquesta Unión Juvenil, the Orquesta Fascinación, and the Orquesta Revé. He left Revé, along with Juan Formell, with whom he cofounded Los Van Van. He has stayed with Los Van Van for thirty years. He made a notable contribution to the creation of the musical style known as *songo*. He is the author of "Ya tu campana no suena," "El buena gente," "Azúcar," "Calla," and "Hoy se cumplen seis semanas."

Peichler, Clemente. Spanish pianist and songwriter. Born (?); died (?). Moved to Cuba and settled at first in Camagüey. After moving to Havana, he founded the magazine *Revista Musical* together with Salvador Palomino in 1843. His compositions are varied, but particularly notable are the *contradanzas* "La Peñalver," "La preciosa Lolita," "La benéfica Merlin," "La chalupa," "La Bruja," and several waltzes. He also taught piano, harmony, and composition and gave piano recitals in Havana and Camagüey.

Pello El Afrokán. *See* Izquierdo, Pedro.

Pena, María Elena. Singer. Born 4 May 1949, Havana. Began singing in music groups in 1964 and subsequently became a soloist. Pena studied the art of singing at the Ignacio Cervantes School. She has toured Germany, Bulgaria, Colombia, and Venezuela. At first, she sang pop ballads, but several years ago she turned to boleros.

Peña, Orlando. Composer and double bass. Born 7 December 1932, Havana; died (?). Worked as a double bass player in several popular dance bands. Peña is the author of the bolero "Misterio de amor," the *sones* "A Don Nadie" and "Tremendo cumbán," among others, and the rumba "Muriéndome de risa."

Peña, Orquesta de Enrique. The composer and cornetist Enrique Peña founded this band, at the beginning of the twentieth century, as a *típico*, or wind, orchestra. Besides Enrique Peña (cornet), its musicians were Antonio González (trombone), Féliz González (ophiclenic), José de los Reyes (timbales), José Belén Puig (first clarinet), José Urfé (second clarinet), Julián Barreto (violin), Alfredo Sáenz (violin), and Rufino Cárdenas (*güiro*). The orchestra split up in 1922, when the leader, Peña, died. Over the two decades of the group's existence, it was very popular in dance halls.

Peñalver, Armando. Composer. Born 13 March 1920, Havana; died 8 June 1994. Linked to the so-called *filin* movement since 1945, Peñalver is the author of "Si me dices que sí," "Coincidencia de amor," "Cuando estoy junto a ti," "Me parece mentira," and many other songs. He worked at the National Copyright Center.

Peñalver, Josémaría. Pianist. Born end of the eighteenth century in Havana; died (?). Peñalver made

the *contradanza* familiar to music lovers, giving numerous concerts in the Cuban capital during the early years of the nineteenth century.

Peraza, Armando. Percussionist, congas, *bongós*. Born May 1924, Havana. Worked extensively in Havana with various singers and in 1948 traveled to New York and joined a group doing backups for the bebop singer Slim Gaillard. Peraza moved to the West Coast of the United States and played on many hit records in the orchestras led by such greats as Pérez Prado (Peraza performed on the international hit "Cereza Rosa"), Carl Tjader, Dave Brubeck, George Shearing (with whom he worked until 1963), and Mongo Santamaria. He played for almost twenty years in the band of the Mexican-American guitarist Carlos Santana. In the 1980s he played with the San Francisco–based group Machete. He is one of the most outstanding Cuban percussionists of all time.

Pereira, Tata. Flutist. Born 21 August 1874, Matanzas; died 17 May 1933, Havana. His real name was Juan Francisco. At the age of fourteen, Pereira began studying music in Havana and made his debut two years later as a flutist at the Santa Teresa Convent. He studied with the professor Luciano Raluy. He played the double-bass tuba in the bands of the Santa Cecilia Society and the fire department. In 1896 he joined the Independence Army, where he founded Maceo's Marksmen Battalion and, together with Chencho Cruz, set up a band whose music was heard all over the battlefield. With the founding of the Republic, he launched Havana's Police Band, which subsequently became the Municipal Band. In 1914 he began manufacturing the first Pianola rolls in Cuba. He won First Prize in a music competition sponsored by Havana's City Hall. In the 1930s he chaired the Society of Freelance Authors. During the first two decades of the twentieth century, he led a *charanga* orchestra, playing an outstanding role as the flutist. He also wrote *danzones* and arranged pieces for his orchestra.

Pérez, Amaury. Composer, singer, guitarist. Born 26 December 1953, Havana. This self-taught musician took his first steps within the *nueva canción* movement in 1972. His best-known songs include "Andes lo que andes," "Acuérdate de abril," "Vuela pena," "Noticias," "Por siempre Puerto Rico," and

"Uruguaya." Pérez has performed in Poland, Bulgaria, the German Democratic Republic, Western Germany, and Spain, and he has recorded one LP. He gives recitals in theaters and performs on radio and television. His music has been used in Cuban films.

Pérez, Jesús. Drummer. Born 1915, Havana; died 5 April 1985. Student of Pablo Roche. In 1936, alongside Pablo Roche and Agueda Morales, Pérez played the *batá* drums for the first time at a public concert, when Fernando Ortiz presented a show at the University of Havana. He continued to play the drums for many years and became an expert on Cuban folklore. He worked with the National Folkloric Ensemble.

Pérez, Lucrecia. Singer and pianist. Born (?), Havana. Graduated in classical piano from the Higher Institute of Art and gave classical performances before turning to popular music and becoming the vocalist in the all-female group Anacaona. In 1993 Pérez moved to Barcelona, Spain, and became a soloist. She enjoys success in the international piano arena, playing *guaracha, son,* salsa, bolero, and pop.

Pérez, Manuel. Cornetist. Born 1863, Havana; died (?), New Orleans. When he was young, Pérez left Havana for New Orleans, where he studied music. He was an outstanding cornet player and one of the pioneers of jazz at the end of nineteenth century. Around 1890 he was a member of the Robichaux Band. Then, in 1898, he set up his own band, called at first the Imperial and later known as the Onward Band. When jazz began its exodus to the north of the United States, he and his musicians made successful road trips to Chicago and other cities. Had his music been recorded, he would have been recognized as a true pioneer of jazz. When his tour of the north ended, early in the twentieth century, Pérez returned to New Orleans, where, to everyone's surprise, he bought and ran a grocery store, virtually casting himself into oblivion, and died in that line of work.

Pérez, Marta. Mezzo-soprano. Born (?), Havana. Began singing Spanish songs at the age of seven. Pérez studied the art of singing with Marila Granowska. She was a soloist in the Havana Philharmonic Orchestra and sang for the radio station CMQ for seventeen years. In 1946 she embarked on a tour of several American cities with Ernesto Lecuona. Later, she performed in Mexico City. In 1954 she sang at La Scala in Milan. She also toured several Latin American countries and the United States. She was invited to appear on the *Steve Allen Show* in 1957. She toured Europe, where she sang on the BBC in London in 1959. In 1961 she performed on the *Ed Sullivan Show*. In the mid-1960s she settled in the United States, where she continued her career.

Pérez, Ricardo. Composer. Born 27 September 1923, Havana. Pérez was linked to the so-called *fílin* movement and worked for the publishing house Musicabana. A version of his first bolero, "Tu me sabes comprender," was released by Benny Moré in 1954. Later songs were "Qué te hace pensar," "Demanda el corazón," "Ofensa," "Al presentirte," "Tenemos que vivir así," "Sorpresa," "Algo en mí," "Tu falta de calor," "No sabrás de mí," and "Guacha-mambo." He was honored at the International Bolero Festival in 1989.

Pérez Chorot, Pablo. Composer and double bass player. Born 18 November 1911, Cárdenas. Began his musical career playing in different bands in his hometown of Cárdenas. After moving to Havana, Pérez Chorot played double bass in Cheo Marquetti's orchestra. In 1940 he went to Paris, where he played in several groups. He returned to Cuba by the end of that decade and joined the Orquesta Almendra. In 1959 he traveled to Mexico City, and then settled in Los Angeles playing in various bands. He wrote the boleros "Punto negro," "Alma blanca," and "No sufras corazón." He is the creator of the *bereguá* rhythm.

Pérez de Alaix, Lucas. Singer and guitarist. Born in the seventeenth century in Burgos, Spain. By the middle of the century, he had settled in Santiago de Cuba, where he stood out as a guitar player. It is known that around 1680 Pérez de Alaix sang in the music chapel at the Santiago Cathedral. He died in Santiago at the end of the seventeenth century.

Pérez Fernández, Rolando. Cellist and musicologist. Born 1947, Santiago de Cuba. Studied at the Esteban Salas Conservatory in his hometown. In 1962 he joined the Oriente Symphony Orchestra, playing cello. The following year, in Havana, he studied under Ernesto Xancó. In 1969 he joined the National Symphony Orchestra. In 1981 he graduated as a musicologist from the Higher Institute of the Arts. He has presented several papers to different symposia dedicated to the art of music. He has carried out research in Angola and Grenada on the basic elements of Afro-Cuban musical expression. His writings have been published in magazines in Cuba and abroad. He is the author of *Proceso debinarización de los ritmos ternarios africanos en América Latina* (1987).

Pérez Pérez, Alfredo. Conductor, arranger, composer. Born 29 December 1944, Havana. Began his studies of piano with the professor Carmen González and completed them at the García Caturla Conservatory. Pérez Pérez studied orchestration with Félix Guerrero; and Manuel Duchesne Cuzán and Roberto Valdés Arnau shaped his abilities as a conductor. He began his career as a piano accompanist. In 1975 he became the conductor of the orchestra of the Cuban Radio and Television Institute. He has composed music for theater, movies, and television shows, but has also consistently worked as an arranger and has written songs.

Pérez Prado, Dámaso. Pianist, composer, conductor. Born 11 December 1916, Matanzas; died 14 September 1989, Mexico City. Studied with María Angulo and Rafael Somavilla. Pérez Prado started out as an orchestra pianist in his hometown. In 1942 he came to Havana, where he worked in the orchestra of the Pennsylvania Cabaret, on Marianao Beach. One year later, he joined the Orquesta Casino de la Playa. At the same time, he was also playing in the dance bands Hermanos Palau, Cubaney, and Pilderó and on radio CMQ. In 1944 he carried out his first musical experiments, trying to incorporate elements of American music, mainly jazz, into Cuban rhythms and melodies. In 1948 he traveled to Mexico, where he joined several bands. In 1949 he finally established his famous orchestra and, that same year, wrote his first mambo, using mambo rhythms created by other Cuban musicians and developing one of the most universally popular genres in Cuban music. "Rico mambo," his first hit, was followed in rapid succession by a series of immensely popular pieces, such as "Mambo no. 5," "Pianolo,"

"Caballo negro," "El ruletero," "Mambo en sax," "Mambo no. 8," "Lunita," "Cerezo rosa," and "Patricia." His arrangements are distinguished by the use of the Cuban percussion, which gives a foundation for the counterpoint between the saxophones and trumpets. The notable influence of American jazz, mainly the style of Stan Kenton, and the time he spent in several North American bands is evident in most of his mambos, which have been described as "semi-grunts" or "semi-screams." In the wake of the mambo's success, Prado created new rhythms, such as the *dengue*, that were the basis of several songs. A more ambitious project was his *Suite de las Américas*.

Pérez Puente, José A. Guitarist and composer. Born 20 September 1951, Havana. Studied at the Amadeo Roldán Conservatory and at the Higher Institute of Art. He gave guitar concerts both in Cuba and abroad. Among his compositions are Tocata for violoncello and piano (1979), *Oda al sol* (1981), and Divertimento (1981). He is a professor at the Amadeo Roldán Conservatory.

Pérez Sentenat, César. Professor, pianist, composer. Born 18 November 1896, Havana; died 4 May 1973. Studied music theory and harmony with professor José Molina, and also studied and practiced piano with Antonio Saavedra, Rafael Serrano, and Hubert de Blanck. From 1913 to 1922 Pérez Sentenat studied in Paris with professors Joaquín Nin Castellanos and Saint-Requier at the Schola Cantorum. He returned to Cuba in 1922 and was employed as a professor of piano and harmony at the National Conservatory. At the same time, he assisted Gonzalo Roig and Ernesto Lecuona, who were founding the Havana Symphony Orchestra, and subsequently became its general secretary. In 1924 he joined Amadeo Roldán shortly after Havana's Philharmonic Orchestra was founded. He worked for fifteen years as a professor of piano at the Havana Municipal Conservatory, and in 1931 was appointed its director. He founded Havana's Normal School of Music with Amadeo Roldán. In 1945 he was designated as provincial music inspector, and in 1949 was chosen as general music inspector of the Ministry of Education, a post he held until 1952. In 1961, after the Revolution, he began work as a piano teacher and also became director of the Guillermo Tomás Conservatory in Guanabacoa. In 1965 he was appointed general music director at the National Council for Culture and chair of the Commission on Reforming Musical Education. He gave piano recitals. He is not remembered as a composer of music; rather his career had an educational orientation. His compositions were structurally simple and always nationalistic, with an emphasis on rural traditions. His piano compositions include Cuban suite in G major; Preludes in all tones; *Cuatro estampas para un pinero*, for singer and piano; *Martianas*; *Tres canciones campesinas*; and *Tríptico de villancicos cubanos* (Cuban Christmas carols).

Periódico Musical. Published for the first time in Havana in 1822. The editors were Enrique González (Spanish) and Santiago Lessieur (French). The newsletter was printed at Lessieur's Litografía de La Habana. It proudly claimed to publish "useful pieces for music lovers," written by Cuban and foreign authors.

Pessino, Enrique. Guitarist and composer. Born 22 January 1922, Havana. Made his debut performance on radio in 1929. In 1930 Pessino was one of the most popular *trova* singers, alongside Guyún, Panchito Carbó, Joaquín Codina, and Roberto García Pessino. He was one of the first musicians to use harmonies that were considered too modern for the time, a technique he developed without actually knowing anything about musical theory. He founded a duet called Los Cancioneros Modernos, which later became a trio. He is a member of the Society of Cuban Composers. In 1968 the National Trade Union for the Performing Arts decorated him with the National Order for his contribution to the arts for over thirty years. He worked at the Center for Artistic Engagement. His compositions include

"Corazón en cristal" (1940), "Qué desesperanza," and "Cuando termine la noche."

Peyrellade, Carlos Alfredo. Professor and pianist. Born 1840, Camagüey; died 1908, Havana. Brother of the musicians Eduardo, Emilio, and Federico. Carlos Alfredo studied piano with Ruiz Espadero. On the advice of the composer Louis Gottschalk, his father sent him to Paris, where he studied piano with Stamat and harmony with Maleden. Shortly afterward, he gave several concerts in Paris. In 1865 he returned to Cuba, where he set up music schools in Camagüey and Havana. He wrote several songs.

Peyrellade, Eduardo. Professor. Born 1846, Camagüey; died 1930, Havana. Studied piano with Antonio Cosculluela and with his brother Carlos Alfredo Peyrellade. In 1869 Eduardo Peyrellade graduated as a dental surgeon, but he decided to teach music and he gave a few piano recitals. His students included Rita Montaner, Ernesto Lecuona, and Catalina Larrazábal.

Pichardo, Adolfo. Pianist, conductor, arranger, composer. Born 11 October 1939, Havana. Studied piano at the Havana Municipal Conservatory. In 1954 Pichardo joined the band Conjunto Casino Juvenil as a pianist. Later, he appeared at different clubs in Havana. In 1959 he began working as a conductor of popular bands. He has written and arranged popular songs and music for the theater. As a solo pianist, he recorded five LPs of Cuban instrumental music. He has conducted different orchestras in other countries. He is currently a producer for EGREM, in Havana.

Pichardo, Luis. Bass player. Born 1925, Havana. After studying and making his first performances in Cuba, he moved to the United States, where he improved his technical skills. He played in many different venues, including New York's Metropolitan Opera House and La Scala, in Milan. He has lived mostly in the United States.

Pico, Armando. Tenor. Born (?), Havana. Pico's career began in the 1950s with Cuban lyrical songs. He appeared on television shows, performed in operettas and light operas, and sang popular songs.

He recorded several LPs. He moved to Spain in 1981 and now lives in the United States.

Piloto, Giraldo. Drummer. Born 5 June 1962. Studied in the National School of Art, Havana, and was a member of Havan Son, NG La Banda, and Isaac Delgado's group. Piloto is currently the director of the group Klimax.

Piloto, Giraldo, and Alberto Vera. Composers of popular Cuban songs. Giraldo Piloto (1929–1967) and Alberto Vera (1929–1996) composed both music and lyrics in a very successful partnership. Their songs were covered by many other artists in the 1950s. Among their most successful songs were "En ti y en mí," "Sólo tú y yo," "Ni callar ni fingir," "Mambo infierno," "Añorado encuentro," "Fidelidad," "Perdóname conciencia," "Debí llorar," "Duele," "Mi guajira de hoy," "Qué es esto que llega," and "Digan lo que digan." Giraldo Piloto died in an air crash on his way back from Canada. Alberto Vera was music director for the Cuban Institute of Radio and Television. After Piloto's death, Vera continued writing songs, which include "Lo que me queda por vivir" and "Amigas."

Piñeiro, Ignacio. Composer. Born 21 May 1888, Havana; died 12 March 1969. While still a child, Piñeiro's parents moved from his native district of Jesús María, to Pueblo Nuevo, where he began his musical career by singing in the children's choirs. His primary education started at the Niño Jesús School and ended at another public school. As a young man he worked in many different jobs, including as a barrel maker, foundryman, port worker, cigar maker, and mason. At the same time, he was absorbing the African dances and chants he heard in his local neighborhood. In 1906 he joined the clave and guaguancó group Timbre de Oro, where he improvised and sang décimas. Later on, he directed the group Los Roncos, for which he wrote several choral compositions, such as "Cuando tu desengaño veas," "Mañana te espero niña," and "Dónde estabas anoche." Shortly afterward, he joined another group called Renacimiento. In 1926 he began playing the double bass with the Sexteto Occidental, founded by María Teresa Vera. He traveled to New York with this group, and after returning to Cuba in 1927 he set up the Septeto Nacional, which actually began as a septet. The group participated in several international events. In 1932 the American composer George Gershwin came to Havana and visited the radio station CMCJ, where the group was recording. Gershwin made friends at the station and took some notes on the works of this brilliant Cuban composer. Those notes gave birth to *Cuban Overture*, in which Gershwin uses elements from Piñeiro's son-pregón "Échale salsita." Piñeiro was a prolific songwriter, and he worked with many different rhythms and rhythmic combinations including *son, son-montuno, guaguancó-son, canción-son, afro-son, conga, guajira-son, guaracha, guaguancó, canción, guajira, villancico, danzón, son-campesino, rumba, son-pregón, guaracha-son, rumba-son, tango-congo, plegaria, lamento, pregón,* and *preludio.* Of approximately 327 compositions, his most popular include "Cuatro palomas" and "Esas so son cubanas" (1927), "No jueges con los santos" (1928), "Suavecito" (1930), "Buey viejo and "La cachimba de San Juan" (1931), "Mentira" and "Salomé" (1932), "Bardo," "Entre tinieblas," and "Échale salsita" (1933), all of them *sones. See also* Nacional, Septeto.

Piñeiro, José. Musical researcher. Born 5 January 1931, Havana. One of the founders of the National Museum of Music. Piñeiro studied music with Carmelina Muñoz and Rita María Castro. He has given lectures at cultural centers and organized exhibitions of various artists. He has worked as a presenter of radio and television shows and published pamphlets and articles on many of Cuba's outstanding musicians.

Piñera, Juan. Composer. Born 18 January 1949, Havana. Began studying music with César Pérez Sentenat, then became a pupil of pianist Silvio Rodríguez Cárdenas and Margot Rojas. Piñera was a student at the Higher Institute of Art. He has written piano, vocal, chamber, choral, symphonic, and children's music, as well as incidental compositions for the theater. He has set to music several poems by Cuban and foreign poets. He has won prizes at the 13th of March and the Golden Age contests and at the International Children's Festival.

Pla, Enrique. Percussionist. Born 22 May 1949, Santa Clara. Studied at the National School of Art and at the Ignacio Cervantes Conservatory. He was a drummer with the Orquesta Cubana de Música Moderna. He joined the band Irakere in 1972 and has also performed with several jazz quintets. He is a professor of percussion and has traveled around the world.

Pla, Luisito. Composer and troubadour. Born (?), Havana; died (?). In 1939 Pla founded a trio with Senén Suárez and Manolito Menéndez, performing boleros, *sones*, and *guarachas* on the radio and at theaters. In 1947 the trio made a tour of the Americas, and during the 1950s, it performed extensively in the United States and also made several records. Pla is the author of "Jacarandosa," "La canción del caminante," "El madrugón," and "Perico sordo." He moved to the United States in 1948.

Planas, Raúl. Singer. Born 8 August 1924, Camagüey; died 2001. Began singing mostly *sones* and boleros in the province formerly known as Las Villas, then moved to Havana, where during the 1950s, he sang with La Sonora Matancera, Rumbavana, and Tropicabana. Planas has recorded several records of traditional and modern *sones*. He sang on the Buena Vista Social Club's recording.

Ponce, Daniel. Percussionist. Born 21 July 1953, Havana. Played the *tumbadora* and *batá* drums in several folkloric groups in Havana, and in 1980 moved to New York. Ponce made a sensational impact on the New York Latin Jazz scene. He performed at concerts and on records with such distinguished musicians such as Jerry González, Paquito Rivera, MacCoy Tyner, Eddie Palmieri, Herbie Hancock, Mick Jagger, Ginger Baker, Celia Cruz, Mario Bauzá, Dizzie Guillespie, and Tito Puente. He recorded a solo LP and several dance singles, and cultivated Afro-Cuban music, jazz, and salsa.

Ponce Reyes, Tomás. Composer, double bass, clarinetist, pianist. Born 18 September 1886, Sagua la Grande; died 10 September 1972, Mexico City. When he was very young, he moved to Mexico, where he worked as a double bass player in several popular bands. Ponce Reyes studied at Mexico's National Music Conservatory with professors Julián Carrillo and Gustavo E. Campa, and also learned how to play the clarinet and the piano. He wrote the *danzones* "El cisne," "Salón México," "Yo soy el árbol," "Posada

mexicana," "Arcoíris," and "Mérida carnaval"; the song "Eloísa"; and the march "General Sandino." He also arranged Mexican traditional tunes and wrote symphonic pieces.

Ponciano, Emiliano. Guitarist and popular composer. Born 1920, Manzanillo; died 1977, Havana. Ponciano is the author of the boleros "Muelle de luz" and "Rosa marchita"; the *canción* "Bardo gentil"; and his best-known piece, the bolero-*son* "Oriente, cuna florida." He was a typical *trova* singer, roaming the streets of Havana, strumming his guitar, and singing *canciones* and *sones*.

Porras. Singer. Born (?); died (?). He arrived in Cuba at the beginning of the Spanish conquest, in the early sixteenth century. He was one of the first musicians on the island and later moved to Mexico, where he died.

Portabales, Guillermo. *Trova* singer and composer. Born 6 April 1914, Cienfuegos; died 1961. Began singing serenades and at parties with his guitar. Portabales sang *canciones*, boleros, tangos, and *guajiras*. He is the creator of the so-called *guajira de salón*. In 1937 he went to Puerto Rico and, shortly afterwards, toured Venezuela, Ecuador, Colombia, and Panama. In 1940 he returned to Cuba and, back in Havana, sang at the radio station RHC Cadena Azul. He traveled to the United States and Puerto Rico several times, where he sang on different radio stations and in theaters. He died in Cuba in a traffic accident on Isla Verde.

Portal, Otilio. Composer and guitarist. Born 1915, Camajuaní. Started his musical career in different trios, including one led by Servando Díaz. Portal is the author of such popular pieces as "Me lo dijo Adela," "A romper el coco," "Tú no son lubia," and "Bayoya" and the boleros "Ya me despido" and "Enferma del alma." He has lived in the United States for several years.

Portela, Paquito. Composer, guitarist, double bass player. Born 24 February 1889, Santiago de Cuba; died, 24 July 1975. Since he was a carpenter, Portela used to make his instruments. He worked in several popular music bands. Among his compositions are the bolero-*son* "El fiel enamorado."

Portillo de la Luz, César. Composer, singer, guitarist. Born 31 October 1922. When he was nineteen years old, Portillo de la Luz began singing nonprofessionally, accompanied by his guitar. For a time, economic constraints forced him to work as a house painter. He also worked as a guitar teacher. In 1946 he made his debut as a professional artist, appearing on two radio stations: Radio Lavín and Mil Diez. He continued working at the latter for some time, eventually hosting his own music show. In 1956 he performed at the Sans-Souci club, leading a group composed of Frank Domínguez (piano), Alfredo León (contrabass), Gastón Laserie (drums), and Luis Ortellado (trumpet); Portillo played guitar.

Later on, he played at the cabarets Karachi, Chateau Piscina, Gato Tuerto, and St. John's. Several of his songs have been used in films. He has given recitals and conferences on the development of Cuban music, especially of the *fílin* movement (he was one of its initiators) all over Cuba. For several years, he hosted a show called *Cita a las Cinco* on Radio Progreso. He would sing his own songs and those of other authors. His music has been recorded by many non-Cuban orchestras. Since 1938 he has composed his own material, including "Ave de paso" and "Más allá de tus ojos." In 1950 he composed the melody "Contigo en la distancia," then, one after another, "Noche cubana," "Nuestra canción," "Delirio," "Canto a Rita Montaner," "Perdido amor," "Sabrosón," "Realidad y fantasía, canción de un festival," "La hora de todos," "Oh, valeroso Vietnam," "Al hombre nuevo," "Amor es eso, canción de los Juanes," "Interludio," "Son al son," and many other high-quality compositions.

Portillo Scull, Gerardo. Singer. Born 24 September 1929, Havana. Portillo Scull lived for several years in Matanzas Province, where he began singing in various bands. In 1957, in Havana, he joined the Orquesta Cubaney and subsequently sang with the Revé and Senén Suárez orchestras, before going solo. He has performed on radio and television, in theaters, at nightclubs, and on records. He sings Cuban *canción* and *son*.

Portuondo, Omara. Singer. Born 29 October 1930, Havana. Studied for a bachelor's degree at the Havana Institute. Portuondo made her debut as a singer on an amateur show on Radio Cadena Habana, where she won second prize. Frank Emilio invited her to sing with his group Loquibambia, which then performed on radio Mil Diez, and from there she appeared in a series of choreographed shows, with the quartets of Alberto and Rodney Alonso and Orlando de la Rosa, and also with the all-women band Anacaona. In 1952 she became a member of the Cuarteto D'Aida, directed by Aida Diestro. The original lineup was Elena Burke, Moraima Secada, and Omara's sister Haidée Portuondo. She sang with this group for fifteen years and then became a soloist, performing on radio and television, at theaters, and on records. Her specialty is the *fílin* style and the ballad. She has traveled to the United States, Haiti, Mexico, several South American countries, the former Soviet Union, and Poland. In the late 1990s she sang on the *Buena Vista Social Club* album and also with the Afro-Cuban All Stars, and her career was transformed as she toured the world with these musicians. She received a Grammy award for her contribution to these recordings, and also recorded her own solo LPs, and toured with her own band.

Pourcel, Mike. Composer and singer. Born (?), Havana. Pourcel is the author of *canciones* that include "Diálogo con un ave," "Esa mujer," and "La canción murió sin conocerte." He also set to music some of José Martí's writings. In 1978 his song "En busca de una nueva flor" was selected as the theme for the Eleventh World Festival of Youth and Students. He lives in Spain.

Poveda, Donato. Composer and singer. Born 18 September 1960, Havana. Started out as a *trova* singer in 1978, having come out of the *nueva canción* movement. In 1986 Poveda's song "Como una campana" received a prize at the Sopot Festival. Then came "Cambiando el tema," "El eslabón perdido," "Alguien llama," and "Agua dulce, agua salá." He has written music for plays and television. In the late 1990s he moved to the United States, where he formed a duet with the Colombian singer Estáfano.

Poveda, Manuel. Guitarist and composer. Born 11 June 1903, Santiago de Cuba; died (?), Havana. Cousin of the poet José Manuel Poveda. Manuel Poveda was a self-taught musician. His parents were also musicians and encouraged him to develop an artistic career. He worked as a cigar maker but eventually began singing with Siro Rodríguez, Rafael Cueto, his brother Rafael, and others. He was a member of the Septeto Matamoros and wrote the *canciones* and *sones* "Mi Teresa," "Ojos profundos," "La vieron pasar," "La sanluisera," "También la tumbé," "Compay calambuco," "Majá pintón," and "Criolla del Guaso," among others.

Pozo, Chano. Singer, dancer, conga drummer, composer. Born 7 January 1915, Havana; died 2 December 1948, New York. His full name was Luciano Pozo González. When Pozo was very young, he got involved in popular music and fell under the spell of African rhythms. He built a great reputation in 1940 through his performances in a show at the Sans-Souci Cabaret called "Congo Pantera." He would go on to compose hits in the style of *guaracha-rumba*, including "Blen-blen-blen," "Pin-pon-pan,"

and "Nagüe"; and rumbas such as "Anana baroco tinde," "Ariñañara," "Wachi-wara," and "Rumba en swing," all of which earned him a great deal of money. In 1946 he emigrated to New York, where his fame soared. It was there he composed his famous "Manteca." On 29 September 1947 he was introduced to a New York audience by Dizzy Gillespie at a jazz concert at Town Hall. His performance, characterized by drumming and vocal interpretations of the musical style that combined West African and Cuban elements, caused quite a stir among the audience. He introduced new Afro-Cuban elements, rhythms, and voices to Gillespie's big band, and in the process contributed to the creation of the new jazz style they called "Cubop." Pozo was shot to death in a Harlem café.

Pozo, Chino. Percussionist. Born 10 April 1915, Havana; died 1977, Las Vegas, Nevada. In 1937 Chino Pozo took up residence in the United States. He played *bongó*, conga drums, and timbales with Machito y Sus Afrocubanos, as well as in the ensembles of José Curbelo, Noro Morales, Tito Puente, Tito Rodríguez, Enric Madriguera, Pérez Prado, Stan Kenton, Herbie Mann, Jack Cole, Xavier Cugat, René Touzet, and Billy Taylor.

Prats, Jaime. Composer, conductor, flutist. Born 29 March 1883, Sagua la Grande; died 3 January 1946, Havana. Prats also played the clarinet, the violin, the double bass, and the piano. He began studying music at the age of seven with professor José Márquez. In 1897 he moved to Cienfuegos, where he continued his musical activities and took a bachelor's degree at seventeen. In 1899 he went to the capital and got a job as the leading flutist with the orchestra of the Azzali Opera Company, with which he toured several Latin American countries. Upon his return, he became the conductor of the Municipal Band in Sagua La Grande. He graduated from the Peyrellade Conservatory in 1904. Shortly afterward, he founded a music school in Santa Clara, attached to the Carlos Alfredo Peyrellade Conservatory. By 1906, he was performing with the orchestras of different theater companies and once again traveled with them to Central America. In 1913 he earned a doctorate in pharmacy from the University of Havana. A year later, he gave a Cuban music concert with ensembles from New York. In 1922 he founded the Cuban Jazz Band; made up of Cuban musicians, it was the first of its kind in Cuba. He composed music for several plays. One of his most outstanding compositions is a bolero, "Ausencia." He devoted the last years of his life to teaching the history of music at the Iranzo Conservatory. At the same time, he taught harmony and composition at the Ramona Siscardó Conservatory.

Prats, Jorge Luis. Pianist. Born 3 July 1956, Camagüey. Began studying the piano in 1963 at the Fernández Vila Conservatory with Professor Bárbara Díaz Alea. In 1970 he entered the National School of Art, where he was painstakingly trained by Margot Rojas until his graduation in 1976. He has continued improving his skills with the assistance of the pianist Frank Fernández, and at the same time, has given recitals at halls and theaters all over Cuba. In 1977 he won the First Piano Grand Prix at the Margueritte Long–Jacques Thibaud Contest in Paris, an important event, in which he was also selected as Best Player; received the Ravel Award; and performed to acclaim from critics and audience alike. In 1979 he was awarded the Gold Medal at the Katia Popova Music Festival of Winning Contestants, in Pleven, Bulgaria.

Prats, Rodrigo. Composer, violinist, pianist, conductor. Born 7 February 1909, Sagua la Grande; died 15 September 1980, Havana. Began studying music at the age of nine, with his father Jaime Prats and Professor Emilio Reynoso. Rodrigo Prats later finished his basic training at the Orbón Conservatory. He made his debut as a violinist, when he was just thirteen years old, with the Cuban Jazz Band, directed by his father. Almost simultaneously, he joined the Havana Symphony Orchestra, founded by maestro Gonzalo Roig. His first stint as a conductor was with the Arquímedes Pous Theater Company. He later conducted and directed several orchestras. He was the founder and director of the Symphonic Wind Orchestra and of the Chamber Orchestra of the Fine Arts Circle; deputy director of the Havana Philharmonic Orchestra; musical director of the radio station RHC Cadena Azul; conductor of the Ministry of Education's Symphony Orchestra, after winning an audition; musical director of TV Channel 4; founder and director of the Jorge Ánckermann theater group at the Martí Theater; and musical director of Ha-

vana's Lyric Theater. He also produced music for theater. When he was fifteen, he wrote the tune "Una rosa de Francia," which is often regarded as a classic in the traditional style. He composed numerous operettas, including La perla del Caribe, María Belén Chacón, La Habana que vuelve, Amalia Batista, Guamá, and Soledad. He also wrote the canciones "Así como sus canciones," "Aquella noche," "Miedo al desengaño," "Espero de ti," "Tú que no sabes mentir," "Creo que te quiero," and "Eres rayo de sol"; and pregones, such as "El heladero," "El tamalero," and "El churrero."

pregón cubano. The Cuban street-vendor's cry. This genre of music was born in the towns and cities of countries where the climate favors street sales and was quite common some time ago. The songs were based on the cries of street vendors as they sought to promote their goods. In Cuba, such songs emerged, with highly defined characteristics, in the nineteenth century. Today, because of the country's social development, pregones have disappeared from the streets and have rather become elements of folkloric and ethnological importance. Miguel Barnet notes that metric innovations and stanzaic combinations appear in Cuban pregones. Many pregones borrow heavily from rural music or popular genres such as sones or guarachas; musicians simply modify the son or guaracha verses and sing them as if they were pregones. On the same note, composers of popular or classical music, using a line or two from a street vendor's cry, have created well-known pregones, such as the famous "El manisero" by Moisés Simons, "Frutas del Caney" by Félix B. Caignet, and "El botellero" by Gilberto Valdés. The pregón's musical structure, Barnet explains, comprises two main characteristics. One identifying aspect of the pregón is a melisma, typical of the pregones used by mango vendors, which may perhaps be most closely compared to flamenco singing, the use of the falsetto, or similar singing innovations. Similarly characteristic of the pregón is an appoggiatura, like that so popular in the pregones used by peanut, tamale, and other vendors; the appoggiatura functions as the "closing" of the pregón, in which the first syllables of a word break up (Barnet, "Pregones Cubanos," 73–75).

Principal Theater. Opened on 2 February 1850 in the city of Camagüey, with the José Miró Company's production of the opera *Norma* by Bellini. During the 1868 war, Spanish troops took possession of the theater to retaliate for the patriotic activities that took place there. Its architect was Juan Jerez. *See also* Coliseo Theater.

Pro, Serafín. Choirmaster, professor, composer. Born 30 July 1906, Havana; died 1978. Pro studied the ins and outs of composition with José Ardévol and, together with María Muñoz, concentrated on choral activity at the Havana Choir (Havana's choral school). He worked as a professor in several schools and conservatories. He was a member of the Grupo de Renovación Musical. He founded the Choir of the Municipal Conservatory and, after the Revolution, founded the Rebel Army Choir. He wrote piano and chamber music, tunes for voice and piano, and, particularly, choral pieces. He was the director of the National Polyphonic Choir.

Pro-Arte Musical. The publication of the Pro-Musical Art Society. It played an important role in promoting Cuban music from 1924 to 1958. It included essays, criticism, news of important events in the world of music, and reviews of concerts, mainly those promoted by the institution.

Pro-Musical Art Society. This musical art society was founded in 1918 by María Teresa García Montes. Even though it made a remarkable contribution to the cultured music of Cuba, it was limited to the minority population of wealthy people. García Montes hired world-famous musicians from outside Cuba who were performing in Havana and for many years also published a music magazine.

Provedo, Lucy. Soprano. Born 29 May 1946, Havana. Studied at the García Caturla Conservatory, in Marianao, where she graduated in 1965. Provedo continued her studies at the Amadeo Roldán Conservatory, in Havana, completing her training in 1969. A year later, she received First Mention in the singing category of a music contest sponsored by the Writers and Artists Union of Cuba; in 1973, she won First Prize. Since 1970 she has performed all over Cuba in concerts and on radio and television. Her repertoire includes vocal works created by preclassical as well as contemporary composers.

Provincial Conservatory of Oriente (Conservatorio Provincial de Oriente). Founded by Dulce María Serret in Santiago de Cuba, 1927. It played an important role in providing musical education for students in the province of Oriente. It gave many instrumentalists a solid professional training. In the 1960s it became part of the National Council for Culture and continued its activities in the province. It was renamed the Esteban Salas Conservatory.

Puebla, Carlos. Composer, guitarist, singer. Born 11 September 1917, Manzanillo; died 12 July 1989, Havana. Puebla had a number of different occupations before starting a professional career as a musician. He studied harmony and theory of music. In 1962, with his own *típico* quartet, he livened up the afternoons and evenings at the Bodeguita del Medio Restaurant, in Havana. He also cut records and performed on radio and television programs. In 1959 he began to work for the National Council for Culture. He traveled with his quartet to several Latin American and European countries. He composed the soundtracks for the films *Nuestro hombre en La Habana*, *Alba de Cuba*, *Estado de sitio*, and his own songs, recorded with his group, have been heard in other films as well. Many of his songs have also been recorded and performed by non-Cuban artists. His successful songs include "Quiero hablar contigo," "Este amor de nosotros," "Serenata cubana, canción definitiva," "Qué sé yo," and "Parábola," but his most famous songs are "Llegó el Comandante" and "Hasta siempre."

Puerto, Carlos del. Double bass player. Born 14 February 1951, Havana. Studied at the Amadeo Roldán Conservatory. Puerto joined the group Los Anónimos, set up by Felipe Dulzaides. Later on, he entered the Orquesta Cubana de Música Moderna. In 1972

he became one of the founders of Irakere. He has been a professor of double bass and has also written a manual for this instrument and for bass guitar. He has performed in many countries.

Puig, Gladys. Soprano. Born in Havana; died (?). Daughter of the pianist and composer Cheo Belén Puig. Gladys Puig began studying the art of singing in the 1950s. After the Revolution, she performed in several different operas and operettas presented by the Cuban Lyric Theater. She has worked in radio and on television, and has given recitals at different concert halls in Havana. She performs a lyrical repertoire that includes mostly Cuban material.

Puig, José Belén ("Cheo"). Pianist, composer, dance-band director. Born 29 December 1908, Havana; died 15 May 1971. Son of the *danzón* musician José Belén Puig. When Cheo was eight years old, he began studying music under the influence of his family. In 1925 he took a job as a pianist at one of Havana's movie theaters, playing to silent movies. A little later, he worked in several *charanga* orchestras and in other jazz-style bands. In 1934 he founded his own orchestra, which became very popular with dancers. He began a degree in medicine, but gave it up shortly afterwards. He graduated from a Civil Law School in 1940. He wrote the *danzones* "Flor de trébol" and "San Lázaro te acompañe," and worked as an arranger. He participated as a pianist in several music shows and was a member of the group led by Joseíto Fernández. *See also* Puig, Orquesta de Cheo Belén.

Puig, Orquesta de Cheo Belén. French *charanga* created by the pianist José Belén Puig in Havana, 1934. José Belén Puig, known as "Cheo," was named after his father, also a musician. The band was very popular from the outset because of its singer, Pablo Quevedo. Other founding members were José Antonio Díaz (flute), Salvador Muñoz (violin), Julio Safora (double bass), Daniel Reyes (timbales), Francisco Vergara (*güiro*), and Cheo Belén Piug (piano). Later musicians who joined were Rodolfo O'Farrill (cello), Domingo Vergara (timbales), and Odilio Urfé (piano). After Quevedo's death in 1936 the band featured a succession of new singers: Alberto Aroche, Alfredito Valdés, Vicentico Valdés, Oscar Valdés, and Paulina Alvarez. The band still played in some festivals in Havana during the 1950s.

Puig, Orquesta de José Belén. *Charanga* band created by the composer and clarinetist José Belén Puig in Havana at the beginning of the twentieth century. In its final years, its musicians were Julián Fiallo (flute), Carlos del Castillo (violin), Rufino Cárdenas (*güiro*), Juan García (timbales), and José Belén Puig (clarinet). It disbanded in the 1930s.

punto guajiro. Also known as *punto cubano.* Vocal genre that emerged in the countryside in the seventeenth century. Its Hispanic roots were implanted in Cuba by immigrants from the Canary Islands, who themselves had assimilated elements of Andalusian music. Although *punto guajiro* remains true to its Iberian origins, there is no doubt that it is truly Cuban music, as it fused with elements of Cuba's African heritage. *Punto guajiro* is played by a group, using a variety of Cuban guitars—the "Spanish" guitar, the *tres*, the *tiple*, and the *laúd*—plus three percussion instruments, the claves, the *güiro*, and the *guayo*. Singers divide themselves into different "teams" and improvise their lines. Two styles prevail in the *punto guajiro*: the free style and the fixed style. The free style, *pinareño*, comes from the western Pinar del Río province and has a fluent, melodic line, a slow tempo, and a flexible meter. The instruments perform strumming patterns or follow the singer's voice, with some picking. Once the singer finishes the stanza or the first lines of a stanza, the musicians start in a second beat of a 3/4 bar, playing in *tempo giusto*. In the "fixed" style, native to the Las Villas and Camagüey provinces, the singer maintains the same pace and a precise meter. The guitar and the *laúd* continue to accompany him or her without a break, and the claves play continually as well. The "fixed" style is often called *punto en clave*. Other variations of the *punto guajiro* include *punto espirituano* (from central Sancti Spiritus province) and *punto matancero* (from western Matanzas province). Another common style is a hybrid version of the fixed style, which consists of syncopated singing over instrumental accompaniment. Yet another style, one not often performed today, is the *seguidilla*, which consists of several stanzas sung without interruption, to a tune that can at any moment break off a lyric mid-sentence. The accompaniment here ranges from tonic to dominant and results in a modal sound in which the singer also participates (León, *Música folklórica cubana*, 53–54).

Puyans, Emilio. Flutist. Born 22 May 1883, Santo Domingo; died 1957, Paris. Puyans was born in the Dominican Republic to Cuban parents. After spending his early years in Cuba, he left to study at the Paris Conservatory. In 1903 he won the conservatory's First Prize in the flute category, a recognition that launched a brilliant career, placing him among the best flute players in the world. He was a student of the prominent Professor Taffanel. He performed all around the world and in Cuba. He was also, for many years, a diplomat in Europe.

Q

Querol, Carlos. Singer, guitarist, composer. Born 15 May 1920, Máximo Gómez; died 24 October 1991, Havana. At the age of ten, when he was still living with his family in the city of Matanzas, Querol joined the Nuevo Mundo Septet, playing the claves and singing second voice. After that, he sang with different groups, until 1940, when he set up the Trío Matancero with Elías Castillo. The trio performed on several radio stations in Havana. In 1945 he joined the Conjunto Kubavana, directed by Alberto Ruiz, and in 1949, the band Diablo Rojo. As of 1955, he sang in the Conjunto de Luis Santí. In 1960 he joined Los Bocucos, founded by Pacho Alonso, and traveled through Mexico, Venezuela, France, Czechoslovakia, and the Soviet Union. He cut several records of duets with other singers. His song compositions include "Delirio de grandeza," "El amor me hizo poeta," and "Mi castigo."

Quevedo, Antonio. Entertainer, writer, critic. Born 18 March 1888, Spain; died 3 February 1977, Havana. Settled in Cuba in 1919. Quevedo gave up his profession as an engineer to pursue an active musical and artistic career. He married María Muñoz, with whom he founded the significant magazine *Musicalia* in 1928. Later, he published the magazine *Pro-Arte Musical*. He also wrote for other Cuban publications and was a musical adviser at the Cuban Broadcasting Institute.

Quevedo, Pablo. Singer. Born 19 September 1907, Union de Reyes; died 10 November 1936, Havana. Quevedo worked both as a baker and a cigar maker. As a young troubadour, guitar in hand, he would sing and play at parties and family gatherings in his hometown. When he was twenty years old, he moved to Havana. He promptly formed a duo with Panchito Garbó, with whom he performed on various Havana radio stations. He later joined the *orquesta típica* Los Caciques, and Cheo Belén Puig's orchestra, where he became immensely successful. He was known for singing the *danzonete*, a popular form at the time.

quijada. A primitive instrument made from the lower jaw (with all the teeth left in) of a horse, mule, or burro. When shaken, rubbed, or beaten, the loose teeth make a rattling sound. It is still occasionally used by some Cuban musical groups.

Quintana, Alfonsín. Singer. Born 28 January 1923, Havana. Quintana sings boleros, canciones, and *guarachas*. In 1940 he joined the band Conjunto Jóvenes del Cayo, which he would lead until 1963. With this orchestra, he cut several records and hosted various radio and television shows, and also took their Cuban music abroad. He later turned solo. He has performed many times in the United States.

Quintana, José Luis ("Changuito"). Percussionist. Born 18 January 1948, Havana. Plays kit drums, timbales, congas, the *bongó*, and other drums. His father, Pedro, was a percussionist who worked in bands and orchestras, and who recognized his son's special musical ability at an early age. José Luis Quintana worked in several groups until 1969, when he joined Los Van Van, with whom he would stay for over twenty years. He contributed a distinctive rhythmic scheme that turned out to be central to the creation of the *songo*, a version of the *son* promoted by the group through its leader, Juan Formell. Presently, he works as a soloist and has made guest appearances on many significant records. He is also a teacher of percussion, giving master classes in universities and music centers in Europe and the United States.

quinto. A Cuban instrument of African origin, it acts as a chimer in popular-music groups, particularly those playing rumba and conga. Smaller than the *tumbadora* or the conga drum, it produces a high-pitched sound. It was formerly tuned using fire, but today keys are used. When playing the drum while walking, the player carries it hanging from a strap around his shoulder. It is also called a *requinto*.

Quiñones, José Dolores. Composer. Born 1910, Havana. Author of "Los aretes de la luna," "Camarera del amor," "Que me haces daño," and other boleros. Quiñones has lived in Paris for many years.

R

Rabí, Rolando. Composer of popular songs. Born 17 April 1916, Baire, Oriente; died (?). In 1934, in Santiago de Cuba, Rabí played the guitar with Reinaldo Henriquez in the duo Rabí-Henriquez. He studied music with professor Arturo Arango, popular guitar with Angel Almenares and Guillermo Duforneau, piano with the Argentine Pascual Oliván, and technique with Felo Bergaza, Frank Emilio, Pedro Jústiz, and José Oxamendi. He was a piano accompanist and a member of the Orquesta Chepín-Chovén. He composed the boleros "Humo y espuma," "Aquí estoy," "Cada noche que pasa," "Serenata de Haiti," and others. He also has a doctorate in education.

Raffelín, Antonio. Composer. Born 1796, Catalonia, Spain; died 1882, Havana. Studied violin, cello, and double bass with maestro Gregorio Velázquez and later, counterpoint and fugue with Antonio Coccó. Reffelín set up a prestigious orchestra. He was a teacher and established the Christian Philharmonic Academy. He went to Paris in 1836, where his music was already well known. In 1849 he returned to Havana and continued his career. Some years later, he traveled to Philadelphia, where he edited *La lira católica*, a musical magazine, and also composed mainly religious music. He visited Rome, Madrid, and the United States in 1862. In 1867 he returned to Cuba and was honored for his work. He composed three symphonies, a quartet, masses, motets, and antiphonic hymns.

Rafols, Félix. Composer and professor. Born 1894, Spain; died 1961, Camagüey. Studied with Enrique Granados. When Rafols arrived in Cuba, he settled in Camagüey and founded the Catalán Choral Society. He also founded an eponymous conservatory. He promoted musical events in Camagüey and conducted choral groups. He composed pieces for piano and orchestra, as well as choral songs.

Ramírez, Serafín. Historian and music critic. Born 1833, Havana; died 11 May 1907. Studied music and mastered the cello; studied piano with Manuel Saumell. Ramírez played an important part in promoting musical events. He was a founder of the Classical Music Society in the music division of the Havana Lyceum. As a critic, he published polemical articles in many Cuban magazines. He wrote "Prontuario del dilettante" and "La Habana artística," in which he depicted the musical life of the bourgeois salons of the Cuban capital. He is acknowledged as the first Cuban music critic.

Ramos, Eduardo. Composer, arranger, guitarist, double bass player. Born 20 October 1946, Havana. Received his musical training with Juan Elósegui and studied double bass with Silvio Vergara, and later, counterpoint, form, and composition with Leo Brouwer. In 1968 Ramos joined the band Sonorama 6 on double bass. He subsequently performed with other bands and in programs for the Political Song movement. He traveled to the German Democratic Republic and the Soviet Union and performed at festivals. He has composed *canciones* including "Canción de los CDR," "La batalla empezó," "Siempre te vas en las tardes," the music for ballets such as *Sikanekue*, and other works. He was a member of the Grupo de Experimentación Sonora of the Cuban Institute for Movie-Making, Art, and Industry.

Ramos, Miriam. Singer and guitarist. Born 6 May 1946, Havana. Studied at the Popular Music Seminary and joined the National Polyphonic Choir in 1963. In 1964 Ramos made her debut as a soloist, singing pieces from the international repertoire. She performed at the International Song Festival in Varadero in 1967. She traveled to Bulgaria in 1969. She has also studied at the Ignacio Cervantes Conservatory. She has sung on radio and television and in theater concerts. She represented Cuba at international festivals in Bulgaria, Poland, the Soviet Union, and Japan. Her repertoire includes traditional Cuban songs and songs from the *nueva trova* repertoire.

Ramos, Severino. Instrumentalist, pianist, composer of popular music. Born 1903, Matanzas; died 2 November 1965, Havana. Ramos and Luis Reyes together wrote such boleros as "Luna yumurina" and "Vendrás," and also *guarachas*. His main contribution lies in his instrumentation of popular Cuban music. He made one LP, recording some of his compositions, for EGREM records.

Ramos Saavedra, Eduardo. Conductor. Born 1 April 1928, Guanabacoa. Ramos Saavedra also plays horn, ophicleide, and trumpet. His musical training began at the Guanabacoa Municipal Academy with maestro Gerardo Guanche. Then, in 1942, he joined a hometown band as a trumpet player. In 1948 he joined the National Police Band, playing ophicleide, and three years later, became a member of the Banda del Estado Mayor del Ejército. He founded a new band in Guanabacoa in 1960. He traveled to the Soviet Union to study conducting at the Kiev Conservatory. He has conducted the National Symphony Orchestra and orchestras from the Cuban provinces, and also the orchestra of the Cuban National Ballet.

Raventós, José. Professor. Born 24 September 1894, Tarragona, Spain; died 1937, Havana. Began his musical training in Spain. Settled in Cárdenas in 1915 and founded a music academy. Raventós later moved the academy to Havana and renamed it Peyrellade. He accumulated an important collection of musical books and documents, which today reside in the archives of the National Library. He composed several pieces, including *Canción de cuna*, for piano; *Amor güajiro*; *A través de la isla*, for chorus and orchestra; *Suite española* and *Amanecer*, both for orchestra; and the *canciones* "Yo se" and "Cabellera Bruna."

Recio, Mario. Singer, guitarist, composer. Born 22 February 1914, Camagüey; died 21 October 1961, Havana. Arrived in Havana in 1939 and performed with the Conjunto Kubavana. Recio later worked with the Conjunto Casino. He joined Servando Diaz's trio in the 1940s (along with Servando and Otilio Portal), and some years later formed an eponymous trio. He is the author of "Llegaste tarde" and "Vive corazón" (boleros); "Soy de Jaronú" (*son*); "En el tiempo de la colonia" (Afro-Cuban); "Kilimanjaro" (*pachanga*); "Las trompetas" (*cha-cha-chá*); and other popular pieces.

Reina, Félix. Composer, instrumentalist, violinist. Born 21 May 1921, Trinidad, Las Villas; died 10 February 1998, Havana. Received his musical training from his father, and also from Isidro Cintra, who taught him to play the violin. After working in *orquestas típicas* in Trinidad, Reina moved to Havana in 1946 and performed with the *charanga* bands of José Antonio Díaz and Antonio Arcaño, and with Fajardo

Tomás Casademunt

y sus Estrellas and Orquesta América. He is author of the *danzones* "Angoa," "Los jóvenes del silencio," and "El niche"; the *cha-cha-chás* "Muñeca triste" and "Pa'bailar"; and the *canciones* "Y se llama Cuba," "Si no estas tú," and "Si te contara." Reina was a remarkable instrumentalist and led the orchestra known as Estrellas Cubanas.

Reina Theater (later, the Cuba). Opened on 13 June 1850 in Santiago de Cuba with the official name of Teatro de la Reina Isabel II, but it was known by everyone as Teatro Reina. On opening night, the orchestra played the overture that announced the entry of the José Robreño Company. Its architect was Manuel Heredia Ivonet, from Santiago de Cuba; Francisco Becantini was the designer and he also painted the theater's backdrop. The Reina was later renamed the Cuba Theater.

Reineri, Laura. Pianist and professor. Born 4 April 1885, Havana; died (?). Developed a remarkable career as a performer, both in Cuba and abroad. Reineri was also a professor of piano, harmony, and composition, and president of the Pro-Musical Art Society.

Reinoso, Aurelio. Singer. Born 5 October 1924, Havana; died 4 January 1985. Reinoso received only a basic music education and began his singing career on radio shows. From 1948 to 1955 he was a member of the Orlando de la Rosa quartet. He traveled to many Latin American countries and to the United States. He turned solo in 1961 and sang romantic pieces. He performed on television shows and in theaters and recorded a number of LPs.

Reinoso, Nicolás. Flutist and saxophonist. Born 1 May 1939, Havana. Studied at the Centro Especial de Música No. 1, then at the Havana Muncipal Conservatory, and later continued studying by himself. After performing with different dance bands, Reinoso joined the orchestra that played at the Hotel Capri as a saxophonist. He later played with several other nightclub bands in Havana and in other provinces. He is a proficient jazz performer who has recorded with many different orchestras. He led the Lobo Band, which played international and Cuban music. Later, he joined the Grupo Afrocuba. He lives in Montevideo, Uruguay.

reja. A rudimentary instrument used in street congas. Made from a ploughshare, it is hit with a nail, usually one of the sort used in railroads. There are two or three *rejas* in every conga.

Remolá, María. Soprano. Born 7 December 1930, Barcelona, Spain. Moved to Cuba in 1952. In 1956 Remolá received singing lessons from Francisco Fernandez Dominicis. She sang in the *zarzuela Doña Francisquita* at the Payret Theater in 1961. Later, she performed lead roles in *zarzuelas* and operas staged in Cuba. She has given solo concerts with the National Symphony Orchestra, sung on radio and television, and recorded three LPs. She has traveled to the Soviet Union, Bulgaria, Korea, Mongolia, Vietnam, and Mexico. She improved her singing skills with the Bulgarian Liliana Yalenska. She was part of the Grupo Lírico Gonzalo Roig. She lives in Spain.

Renovación Musical, Grupo de. Founded by José Ardévol in Havana in 1942, the group was made up of young musicians who had studied with Ardévol at the Municipal Conservatory. The members of the group included Harold Gramatges, Edgardo Martín, Julián Orbón, Argeliers León, Hilario González, Serafín Pro, Gisela Hernández, Juan Antonio Cámara, Dolores Torres, and Virginia and Margot Fleites. According to Ardévol, the group's composers played a great part in the introduction of popular universal styles into Cuban music and incorporated stylistic Cuban elements into their compositions more subtly and creatively than their forebears, such as Roldán and Caturla (Ardévol, *Introducción a Cuba: La música* 84).

Repilado, Francisco. Composer, guitar and *tres* player, clarinetist. Born 18 November 1907, Santiago de Cuba; died 13 July 2003, Havana. Known as "Compay Segundo." Repilado played in the Municipal Band of Santiago de Cuba, which was conducted by his teacher Enrique Bueno. He later performed in a quintet that included Ñico Saquito. He moved to Havana in 1934 and joined the Municipal Band there as a clarinetist. During the 1950s, he and Lorenzo Hierrezuelo formed the duet Los Compadres. He is the composer of the *sones* "Sarandonga," "La calabaza," "Macusa," "Hey caramba," "Chan-Chan," and "Saludo Compay." He directed his own trio, in which he played an *armonico*—a variation of the *tres* guitar that he created—along with Juan Enrique Coquet (lead vocalist and guitar) and Adolfo Peñalver (double bass). He currently leads his own group, which includes his son Salvador Repilado (double bass), Benito Suarez (guitar), and Julio Fernández (lead vocalist and maracas). He played a leading role in the recording of the *Buena Vista Social Club* album, working alongside the American blues guitarist Ry Cooder. He subsequently toured the world and received a Grammy for his work. He has made several records as a result of that success.

Revé, Elio. Percussionist, composer, bandleader. Born 23 June 1930, Guantánamo; died 23 July 1997, Havana. Revé began his career in his hometown in 1947, then in 1955, formed his own band in Havana, which is still popular both in Cuba and abroad. His ensemble's specialty was *changüí*, a variant of *son*. He composed many popular songs, including "Samá," "Changüí campanero," "Salgado," "Rumbero latinoamericano," and "Changüí clave."

He played mainly the timbales. With his orchestra, he visited many American, European, and African countries. He was killed in a traffic accident while on tour in Cuba.

Revé, Elio, Jr. Pianist. Born 25 October 1963. He studied piano and joined his father's band, the Orquesta Revé. After his father's death in 1997, Elio Jr. took over as director of the band.

Revé, Orquesta. French *charanga* band formed in Havana in 1956 and directed by the popular Guantanamero percussionist Elio Revé. It became popular in 1967 due to the arrangements and creations of the double bass player and composer Juan Formell. He enriched its sound by combining different musical elements such as the *changüí*, *cha-cha-chá*, and many other traditional rhythms with non-Cuban popular musical elements.

Reverón, Ricardo. Composer and pianist. Born 1895, Havana; died 1847. Author of many of the *danzones* that were essential in the repertoires of *charanga* bands in the 1920s, including "Reminiscencia," "Irimo Maco-Irimo" (folkloric), "Primavera," "Trigueña del alma," "El misterioso," "El canto del guajiro," and "El limonero."

Revista de Música. Edited by the music department of the José Martí National Library. It was published quarterly beginning in 1960 and lasting until October 1961. It included articles about different aspects of Cuban music, including studies of dance and folk music, and it also published news about musical events at the library and at other Cuban institutions. Musicologists and Cuban scholars were among its contributors; the editor was Argeliers León.

Rey de Latorre, José. Guitarist. Born 9 December 1917, Gibara; died 1944, San José, California. Settled in Havana when he was a child and received his first music lessons from Severino López. At age fourteen, Rey de Latorre moved to Spain and studied guitar with Miguel Llobet, receiving additional musical education at the Granados Conservatory in Barcelona. At sixteen, he gave a successful concert in that city. He returned to Cuba in 1934 and gave concerts and recitals. In 1937 he moved to New York,

although he traveled abroad extensively to give guitar concerts. He worked as a professor and finally settled in California.

Reyes, Ángel. Violinist. Born (?), Havana. His father is the professor Ángel Reyes. Ángel Reyes Jr. graduated from the Paris Conservatory in 1935, receiving First Prize for violin studies. He has played with the best conductors and as a soloist with the most important orchestras. He has always lived abroad and has performed in Cuba for short periods of time.

Reyes, Ernesto ("Palma"). Bassist. Born 25 July 1967. Studied bass and guitar at the University of Santiago de Cuba and later moved to Havana, where he joined the bands of Celina Gonzalez, Albita Rodríguez, and Candido Fabré, as well as the group La Nueva Trova. Reyes is currently the director and bassist with the band Jovenes Clasicos del Son, which he cofounded.

Reyes, Jorge. Double bass player. Born 1951, Havana. Studied at the National School of Music. Reyes was a member of the Orquesta Riverside and of Perspectiva and Irakere. He has performed in jam sessions (*descargas*) and at many Latin jazz festivals.

Reyes, Orlando. Singer. Born 9 November 1933, Palma Soriano. Began his career with Conjunto Supremo in his hometown. Later joined the Orquesta de Ventura Calzado. Once in Havana, Reyes joined the *conjuntos* Kubavana, Casablanca, Casino, Roberto Faz, Los Latinos, and Los Chuquis. He sings all Cuban music genres.

Reyes, Pablo. Composer. Born 7 June 1928, Havana. Reyes is a member of the *filin* movement and author of "Oh, mi amada," "Gemelos," "Tu razón," "Por ser obstinado," and other pieces.

Reyes, Pepe. Singer. Born 1927, Santiago de Cuba; died (?). Began his career in his hometown, then moved to Havana in the 1940s and began singing modern songs. At first Reyes performed at Radio Mil Diez, then at CMQ and RHC Radio Cadena Azul. He premiered many of the best Cuban songs of the 1940s and 1950s. Years later, he moved to Colombia, then to Venezuela and other South American countries, and only sporadically visited Cuba.

Reyes, Walfredo de los. Drummer and percussionist. Born 16 June 1933, Havana. Son of the trumpet player and singer of the same name from Casino de la Playa. Reyes excelled at playing the drums and Cuban percussion, and beginning in the 1950s, he could be heard on the Cuban Jam Sessions series organized by the bass player Cachao. He worked for years with the Parisién Cabaret orchestra at the Hotel Nacional. Reyes recorded with Nat King Cole in Havana in the 1950s. He settled in Puerto Rico in the early 1960s and played with different orchestras. Later, he moved to Las Vegas, Nevada. He is widely acknowledged as one of the most outstanding Cuban percussionists. In 1985 he was a member of the recording group WalPaTaCa, a Miami-based group of Cubans from the *descarga* era. The group's name was formed by the first syllables of the names of the musicians involved: Reyes, Paquito Echavarría, Tany Gil, and Cachao. Reyes's son, named after him, is one of the best drummers in the U.S. Latin music scene.

Reyes Camejo, Ángel. Composer and professor. Born 1889, Matanzas; died (?). Studied in Cienfuegos with César Bonafú and in Havana with Pedro Sanjuán, then traveled to Mexico, where he was taught by Julián Carillo. Reyes Camejo settled in Paris during the 1930s. He composed Symphonic poem, for orchestra; Suite and Concerto, for violin and orchestra; Tambó, for quintet; Yemayá, for violin and piano; and Fantasía, for harp.

Ribot, Agustín. Singer, guitarist, composer. Born (?), Havana; died 1987. Ribot played with Conjunto Casino from 1945 to 1951. In 1951 he formed his own band and performed on radio and at dance halls. He is the author of the *guarachas* "Viejo verde," "El sordo," "Pelú pélate," "Pancho Tabaco," "Don Fo," "Perico perejil," and "Con la lengua afuera."

Rigual, Trío Hermanos. Pituko, Carlos, and Mario Rigual formed this trio in the 1940s. It performed both Cuban and Latin American songs. Some years later, the trio moved to Mexico, where the musicians appeared in films and recorded many LPs. The trio toured many Latin American countries and visited Cuba sporadically. It is remembered particularly for its popular songs "Corazón de melón," "Te adoraré más y más," and "Cuando calienta el sol."

Río, Elizabeth del. Singer. Born (?), Havana. Rio built a reputation as a singer of *nueva canción* in the 1940s. She performed on radio and television, in theater and cabarets, and also appeared in the films *Siete muertos a plazo fijo* and *Tiros, locuras y mambo.* In 1946 she was elected Queen of Cuban Radio, and in 1947 and 1953 was honored as most outstanding singer by the Association of Cuban Critics. She lives in the United States.

Ríos, Efraín. *Tres* player and composer. Born 1958. With his brother Luis Ríos (author of "Que manera de quererte" and other songs) Efraín Ríos founded the group Agüere in the Isla de Pinos during the 1980s. The two brothers also founded the excellent group Raisón, dedicated to traditional Cuban *son.* With Luis as vocalist and Efraín as *tres* player, the brothers are at the forefront of the *nuevo son* movement.

Riset, Panchito. Singer. Born 21 October 1911, Havana; died 9 August 1988, New York. Made his debut with Sexteto Atarés during the 1930s, then moved on to Sexteto Cauto and other *son* bands such as Esmeralda and Habanero. Riset went to New York in 1933, where his original style was very influential. His recordings were widely featured on the radio there and he was very popular among the Latin community in the city, singing with Cuarteto Caney and with Pedro Flores. He recorded with the band of Puerto Rican composer Rafael Hernández and with Luis Lija Ortiz's *conjunto.* He made his name with the bolero "El cuartico."

Ritmo Oriental, Orquesta. *Charanga* band that incorporated changes in the conventional harmony and timbre. It was created in Havana in 1958. Its repertoire includes *son, danzón, guaracha,* bolero, and conga, all given a modern musical treatment. At the peak of its popularity, the band members were Humberto Perera (bandleader and bass); Raúl Ríos, Jorge Hernández, Humberto Legat, Antonio Calá, and Sergio David Calzado (violins); Rubén Alvarez (cello); Luis A. Peñalver (piano); Policarpo

Tamayo (flute); Daniel Díaz (drums); Juan C. Bravo (conga); Enrique Lazaga (*güiro*); and the vocalists Juan Crespo Maza, Samuel Pérez, and Jorge Quiala.

Rivera, Niño. Composer and *tres* player. Born 18 April 1919, Pinar del Río; died 27 January 1996, Havana. His full name was Andrés Echeverría. Rivera began his career with Sexteto Caridad. In 1934 he moved to Havana and played with Sexteto Boloña. Later, he joined Sexteto Bolero, and in 1945 formed his own band. He also worked by writing scores, but his more important role was as an instrumentalist. His most popular work is the *son* "El jamaiquino," but he composed other relevant pieces, including "Carnaval de amor," "Eres mi felicidad," and "Fiesta en el cielo"; as well as the *son* "Monte adentro" and the *cha-cha-chá* "Cherivón." He traveled to Italy, Spain, Czechoslovakia, the Soviet Union, and the German Democratic Republic. He led his band and played *sones* with his *tres* for many years.

Rivera, Paquito. Saxophonist, clarinetist, arranger, composer, bandleader. Born 4 June 1948, Marianao. One of the most outstanding Cuban jazz musicians. His father, the saxophonist Tito Rivera, introduced him to the world of music, and he has played the saxophone since he was a child. Paquito Rivera entered the Havana Municipal Conservatory in 1960, at the age of twelve. He played with the orchestra of the Havana Musical Theater and later with the Orquesta Cubana de Música Moderna. He was a founding member of Irakere in 1973. He settled in New York in 1980 and continued his career. He founded the Havana/New York Ensemble, and was a leading member of Dizzy Gillespie's pan-Latin jazz band, the United Nations Orchestra. He became the band's director after Gillespie's death. He has recorded many excellent LPs with the most highly rated Latin soloists working in the United States and Latin America. In 1989 he produced *Forty Years of Cuban Jam Sessions*, which featured three generations of Cuban musicians. He has also recorded with both Arturo Sandoval and Chucho Valdes, the founding members of Irakere. He has composed many remarkable pieces.

Rivero, Cuca. Choral professor. Born 17 June 1917, Candelaria, Pinar del Río. When she was a child, Rivero moved to Guanajay and studied at a music academy there. She studied guitar with Clara Romero in Havana. She obtained a Ph.D. in pharmacology. She was a member of the Havana Choir. She formed choral groups for Cuban television in 1953, and conducted the chorus of the Lyric Theater. She traveled to Finland. At present, she works on a music education program for the Ministry of Education and at the Cuban Institute of Radio and Television.

Rivero, Facundo. Pianist and composer. Born 1910, Havana. Started his career playing with the *charanga* bands led by Raimundo Pía and Belisario López. Then played with other orchestras and also worked as a piano accompanist. Rivero formed a vocal quartet in the late 1950s. He is the author of the *son* "No me quieras"; the lullaby "Lacho"; the Afro-Cuban piece "Obatalá"; and the *cha-cha-chá* "Oyeme mamá." He has lived abroad for many years.

Rivero, Olga. Singer. Born 28 April 1922, Havana. Began her career in Havana during the 1940s. Rivero immediately gained a reputation for her distinctive style of singing boleros and *sones*. She recorded many classic pieces in the Cuban repertoire and also sang in the *fílin* style. She performed on radio and traveled to Panama, Venezuela, and Colombia. She moved to Mexico City during the 1950s.

Riverside, Orquesta. *Jazzband* created by Enrique González Mántici in Havana, 1938. It performed on radio shows as a backup band for different singers. Pedro Vila was its leader in 1947; he was then replaced by Adolfo Guzmán, and more recently, by Nelson Arocha. At the peak of its fame, the musicians were Nelson Arocha (bandleader and piano);

Jorge Lavin and Raúl Nacianceno (saxophones); Mario del Monte, Mayía Martínez, and Abel Fernández (trumpets); Roberto Morell (trombone); Jorge García (bass); Rolando Piloto (drums); Pedro Soroa (conga); and Braudilio Carbonell (*bongó*); with Tito Gómez and Orlando Reyes (vocalists). The ensemble has recorded many LPs and singles and has toured all around the Americas.

Rizo Ayala, Marco. Pianist. Born 30 November 1920, Santiago de Cuba; died (?). Began his concert career in his hometown in 1938 with the Havana Philharmonic Orchestra in a duet with Ernesto Lecuona. In 1940 he studied at the Juilliard Academy in New York, and settled in that city. He was arranger and pianist for the *Bob Hope Show* and later was musical director for the television series *I Love Lucy*, featuring Lucile Ball and Desi Arnaz, his childhood friend. He composed the show's theme song, and also music for films for MGM, Paramount, and Columbia Pictures. He gave many piano concerts and played a significant role in the promotion of Cuban music in the United States.

Roch, Pascual. Guitarist, professor, and an important guitar maker. Born (?), Valencia; died 1921, Havana. Roch arrived in Cuba in 1911 and devoted his time to guitar teaching. He published *Método moderno para guitarra*.

Roche, Pablo. *Batá* drummer. Born end of the nineteenth century in Havana; died around the 1940s. Known as "Akilakua" (the powerful arm). Pablo Roche was the son of the famous drummer Andrés Roche, who played African drums in Cuba in the nineteenth century. He taught Raúl Díaz.

Rodríguez, Adriano. Baritone. Born 27 September 1924, Guanabacoa. Rodríguez has given many concerts and recitals all over Cuba with the Grupo de Trovadores Cubanos of the National Council for Culture. He has a select repertoire consisting of works by mainly Cuban composers.

Rodríguez, Albita. Singer, guitarist, songwriter. Born 6 June 1962, Havana. Studied at Ignacio Cervantes Conservatory, although she was mainly self-taught. Born into a family of musicians, Rodríguez learned to play *guajira* from her parents, the singers Martín and Minerva Rodríguez. She began her career as a singer of *trova* on the television show *Palmas y Cañas*, which also featured Celina Gonzalez. She had her own show at the Vedado Hotel in Havana, playing modern Cuban country music. In 1989 she and her band went to Bogotá, Colombia, where they were very successful. In 1993 she settled in Miami. There, she has performed in nightclubs, theaters, and on radio and television. She has gained a worldwide reputation playing a modern Cuban style based on the *punto* and *son*. Her most successful songs include "Qué culpa tengo yo," "Raíces," "La parranda," "Habrá música güajira," and "No se parece a nadie."

Rodríguez, Aldo. Guitarist. Born 8 July 1955, Havana. Studied at Amadeo Roldán Conservatory and at the National School of Art with the professor Marta Cuervo. Later studied with the professor Isaac Nicola at the Higher Institute of Art. In 1979 Rodríguez won First Prize at the Festival of Young Interpreters, in Hesztergom, Hungary. A few months later, he won Third Prize at the Alirio Díaz Competition, in Venezuela. He has given concerts in Czechoslovakia and the Soviet Union, including one at Tchaikovsky Hall in Moscow. His repertoire includes Cuban and Latin American classical pieces.

Rodríguez, Alfredito. Singer and songwriter. Born 29 November 1951, Marianao. Since the 1970s, Rodríguez has sung ballads and pop music on radio and television and in concerts all over Cuba. He has also made some international tours. He has recorded six LPs and won many awards for his own hit songs.

Rodríguez, Alfredo. Pianist. Born 25 October 1936, Havana. At the age of seven Rodríguez began his studies of the piano with his mother. Later, he studied classical piano at the Peyrellade Conservatory, and was also taught by Juan Jauma and Orlando de la Rosa. He moved to New York in 1961 and studied at the Settlement School of Music. He specialized in jazz under Roland Hanna, Albert Dailey, and Bill Evans. Beginning in 1966, he played with different orchestras and *conjuntos*, and later formed his own jazz quartet. He has worked with some of the most significant Latin musicians. In 1983 he based himself in Paris, and from there he has toured all over the world. He recently recorded an LP in Cuba.

Rodríguez, Antonio. Composer and guitarist. Born 13 June 1924, Las Villas, Santo Domingo. Began his career singing in trios and performing in theaters and on the radio in Santa Clara. Later, he began a solo career and worked in Havana. Rodríguez was the guitarist accompanying the Los Idaido duo. He wrote the bolero "Qué motivos," among many others.

Rodríguez, Arsenio. Composer, bandleader, *tres* player. Born 30 August 1911, Güira de Macurijes; died 31 December 1970, Los Angeles, California. Known as "El Ciego Maravilloso" (the marvelous blindman), since he lost his sight at the age of thirteen. His full family name is Ignacio Loyola Scull Rodríguez. He began playing when he was an adolescent in his hometown. Rodríguez moved to Havana during the 1930s, where he joined other *soneros* playing in the capital. He played the *tres* with Sexteto Boston and later with Sexteto Bellamar. Around 1940 he formed his own *son conjunto*, which was radical and became very popular. During the 1940s, he was very popular among the dancers at the Tropical Gardens, where he performed every Sunday afternoon. In the late 1950s he went to New York to see an eye specialist, and though he did not regain his sight, he stayed, playing there with his *conjunto*. He was phenomenally successful and influential. His compositions include the *sones* "Bruca Maniguá," "Güira de Macurijes," "Triste lucha," "Matanzas," "Fuego en el 23," "Laborí," "Tumba palo cocuyé," "No me llores," "Vacuno," and "Lo dicen todas"; and the boleros "Cárdenas," "Zenaida," "En su partir, Camagüey," "La vida es sueño," "Feliz viaje," "Acerca el oído," and "Nos estamos alejando."

Rodríguez, Conjunto de Arsenio. Created by the composer and *tres* player Arsenio Rodríguez in Havana, 1940. Its earliest musicians were Miguelito Cuní, Arsenio ("Scull") Rodríguez, and Pedro Luis Sarracent (vocalists); Marcelino Guerra (guitar); Lilí Martínez (piano); Nilo Alfonso (double bass); Rubén Calzado, Benitín Bustillo, and Félix Chapotín (trumpet); Antonio Suárez (*bongó*); and Israel Rodríguez (conga). In the 1950s Arsenio moved to New York and was replaced as leader by the trumpet player Félix Chapotín, who then named the orchestra after himself. Rodríguez was the first to play the *son* style with a *conjunto* band and not in a septet, as before.

Rodríguez, Edesio. Composer, singer, guitarist. Born 28 March 1958, Havana. Rodríguez studied guitar at the García Caturla Conservatory. He has given concerts of his songs and music in the rock and electro-acoustic styles. He has composed for plays, films, and television. He has won several awards in Cuba and abroad.

Rodríguez, Ezequiel. Musicographer and promoter of popular music events. Born 10 April 1913, Havana; died (?). Rodríguez began his career as a musicographer by researching and compiling information at the National Institute for Folkloric Research in 1958. In 1962 he was put in charge of the popular music section at the Havana Province Coordinating Agency of the National Council for Culture. He has published articles, booklets, artists' profiles, and monographs about Cuban musicians and musical genres. He was director of the Casa de la Trova in Havana.

Rodríguez, Evelio. *Guajira* singer and composer. Born 26 January 1921, Sancti Spiritus. Rodríguez began his career in his home region and moved to Havana in 1943, where he sang *guajiras*, *puntos*, and *sones* on radio shows. With Ramón Huerta, he formed the duo Espirituano. Later, he performed on television and recorded many LPs and singles. He is the author of "Mi guayabera" (*punto espirituano*); and "Vida guajira" and "Camina para el chapea'o (*son montuno*). He still performs on country music programs on radio and television.

Rodríguez, Javier. Guitarist. Born 1 August 1964. Rodríguez studied the guitar and is currently the lead guitarist of the rock band Rock Extraño Corzon.

Rodríguez, Nilo. Composer. Born 19 September 1921, Jagüey Grande; died 23 January 1996, Havana. Studied at Havana Municipal Conservatory and was a leader in the Nuestro Tiempo cultural society. Rodríguez worked as a music promoter and ran the music department at the National Printing House. He was director of the García Caturla Conservatory and, subsequently, of the Cubanacán Music School. His compositions include *Son entero*, for orchestra; Sonata; Fugue, for strings; Divertimento, for chamber orchestra; *Elegía por Manuel Ascunce* (cantata); and *Triplum, Continuidad, Contrastes*. He worked at the Cuban record company EGREM.

Rodríguez, Osvaldo. Composer, singer, guitarist. Born 9 June 1949, Los Arabos. At the age of five he and his family moved to Havana where he studied at the Abel Santamaría, a special school for visually impaired children. Rodríguez and three school friends formed the quartet Voces del Trópico. Two years later, he formed the 5U4 band along with Jorge Antonio Aguilera Tejeda and José Leonardo Fernández Pérez, among others. With this band, he experimented with a fusion of Cuban rhythms and rock music. He studied elementary music with the help of the Braille system. He is the author of "Son ideas," "En cinco minutos," "Se me perdió el bastón," and "Canción del Vigésimo Aniversario"; as well as the boleros "El amor se acaba," "Enhorabuena," "De lo simple a lo profundo," and "Canción a mi compañera." In 1979 he won First Prize at the International Youth Song Festival in Sochi, Bulgaria. He also won the Adolfo Guzmán Contest.

Rodríguez, Silvio. Composer. Born 29 November 1946, San Antonio de los Baños. Rodríguez began by singing, to his own guitar accompaniment, original pieces of a high musical and melodic standard. In early 1967 he made his debut performance at the Palace of the Fine Arts at a poetry and music concert organized by the magazine El Caimán Barbudo. Later he performed on the Sunday television show Mientras tanto. In 1968 he participated in the Meeting for the Political Song Movement, an international song festival organized by Casa de las Américas. His songs were broadcast on radio and television, and he also performed them at concerts at Cuba's cultural institutions. In 1970 he joined the Grupo de Experimentación Sonora of the Cuban Institute for Movie-Making, Art, and Industry. He is the author of "Mientras tanto," "El barquero," "La víspera de

siempre," "La canción de la trova," "Hay un grupo que dice," "La era está pariendo un corazón," "Canción del elegido," "El papalote," "Mariposas," "El Mayor," "Rabo de nube," "En el claro de la luna," "Sueño con serpientes," "Peueña serenata diurna," "Te doy una canción," "Testamento," "Unicornio," "Por quien merece amor," "Son desangrado," "La maza," "Resumen de noticias," "Oleo de una mujer con sombrero," and "Ojalá." He is one of the most remarkable composers in the Latin American nueva canción genre and has recorded a number of significant LPs of his songs and performed in many countries.

Rodríguez, Siro. Songwriter, singer, maracas and claves player. Born 9 December 1899, Santiago de Cuba; died 29 March 1981, Havana. As a child, Rodríguez showed a gift for singing and performed at parties and family gatherings. In 1915 he made his debut at a theater in Santiago de Cuba, in a performance in honor of the trova singer Leopoldo Rubalcava. His earliest work was as a blacksmith; then, in 1925 he sang with Cueto and Miguel in the premier of what would become the hugely popular Trío Matamoros. In 1927 the trio traveled to the United States and recorded their first LPs there with great success. That same year, Rodríguez sang a Mexican song in a duet with the famous tenor José Mujica.

Rodríguez, Víctor. Pianist. Born in Havana. Studied at García Caturla and Amadeo Roldán conservatories and later with Frank Fernández at the Higher Institute of Art. Rodríguez has given concerts in Cuba and performed in many Latin American and European countries. He has received several awards at international and national contests. He is a professor at the Higher Institute of Art.

Rodríguez Cardenas, Silvio. Pianist. Born 6 January 1930, Banes. As a child, Rodríguez Cardenas began studying piano with Carlos Avilés and Dulce María Serret, then with Barcel Ciampi at the National Conservatory in France, and with Maestro Layonet at the Beethoven Conservatory. Later, he took advanced classes for five years with Professors Feimberg and Nátanson in the Soviet Union. He has given concerts in many European countries, including Poland, Bulgaria, Czechoslovakia, Austria, France, Belgium,

England, and Peru. He has performed solo all over Cuba and as a soloist with the National Symphony Orchestra. He was a professor at the National School of Art.

Rodríguez Ferrer, Antonio. Composer and conductor. Born 23 August 1864, Havana; died 22 October 1935. Began writing music when he was an adolescent. At the end of the Cuban War of Independence, Rodríguez Ferrer moved to Guanabacoa. There, he conducted the Cuba Libre Band and performed the patriotic song "La bayamesa," which later became the Cuban national anthem. He composed the song's introduction. He was a professor and a choir conductor, and he composed ensemble pieces, including two symphonic pieces, Thematic prelude and Fantasía, as well as a series of *danzas cubanas* for piano.

Rodríguez Fife, Guillermo. Composer and guitarist. Born 10 February 1907, Mayarí; died c. 2000, Miami. Began his career singing and playing the guitar in *típico* bands such as Trío Criollos. Rodríguez Fife is the author of the *guaracha* "Bilongo" and other popular pieces such as "Ofrenda Lírica."

Rodríguez-Ojea, Arturo. Composer. Born 22 October 1908, Havana; died (?). A doctor of education, he also studied violin and piano. Rodríguez-Ojea devoted many years to teaching and he also made music for children. In the 1930s he was the leader of several theater orchestras and dance bands. He is the author of "Negro de sociedad" and other songs.

Rodríguez Rojas, Bernarda. Singer and harpist. Born 1786, Santiago de Cuba; died (?). She married the musician Leonardo González Abreu, who was born in the Canary Islands, and they performed at music events in the eastern provinces during the first two decades of the nineteenth century.

Rodríguez Silva, Humberto. Composer. Born 14 August 1908, Guatánamo; died 3 April 1952, Havana. Majored in law at the University of Havana and worked as a judge in Yateras. During the 1930s, Rodríguez Silva became a popular composer. He wrote *afro* songs and *guarachas*, including "Se me rompió el bongó," "A caridad le da santo," and "La

negra Cacha." His music was used in both Cuban and foreign films.

Rogel, Gustavo. Singer and music professor. Born (?), Madrid; died 27 October 1924, Santiago de Cuba. Nephew of the Spanish composer José Rogel. Gustavo Rogel arrived in Cuba in 1890 and settled in Camagüey, where he worked as a singer. Later, he moved to Santiago de Cuba and continued his career singing lyric song. He taught singing and piano at the Municipal Academy of Fine Arts in Santiago de Cuba. He published a book and some articles about music. He is the author of the *zarzuela Acuarela criolla* (lyrics by Mariano Corona Ferrer).

Roig, Gonzalo. Composer, band conductor. Born 20 July 1890, Havana; died 13 June 1970. In 1902 Roig began studying piano, theory, and harmony with Agustín Martín Mullor, and later with Gaspar Agüero Barreras at the Association of Dependents of Commerce in Havana. He studied violin with Vicente Alvarez. He received advanced musical training at Carnicer Conservatory. In 1907 he joined, as pianist, a trio that performed at the Monte Carlo movie theater and began his professional career. That same year, he wrote his first musical work and the song "La voz del infortunio," for voice and piano. Two years later, he started playing violin at the Martí Theater. He began studying double bass without a teacher in 1911. The tenor Mariano Meléndez premiered Roig's *criolla*-bolero "Quiéreme mucho" in Havana. He traveled to Mexico in 1917 and worked with María Guerrero, returning to Cuba the same year. In 1922 Roig founded the National Symphony Orchestra with Ernesto Lecuona, César Pérez Sentenat, and others. He was the orchestra's conductor and also played a key role in promoting the work of the most renowned Cuban composers. He is consequently considered to be the pioneer of symphonic music in Cuba. In 1927 he was appointed director of the Havana School of Music and the Municipal Band (now known as the National Concert Band). He held that position until his death. As director of the band, he arranged numerous works by Cuban and foreign composers, and his individual style of conducting gave an innovative sound to the band, which even provided accompaniment for singers, a first in Cuba. In 1929 he formed Orquesta Ignacio

Cervantes and a year later was invited by the Pan-American Union to conduct a series of concerts in the United States. He made a successful tour as a conductor of such bands as the U.S. Army Band, the U.S. Soldiers Home Military Band, the U.S. Marine Band, and the U.S. Navy Band. He contributed to the universal recognition of the rhythmic richness of Cuban music. In 1931 he and Agustín Rodríguez formed a *bufo* company at the Martí Theater, which lasted for five years and five months. In 1932 he premiered the work *Cecilia Valdés*, internationally acknowledged to be the most representative Cuban *zarzuela*. He founded and worked as conductor of the Cuban National Opera in 1938, and that same year composed the soundtrack for the film *Sucedió en La Habana*, which was premiered in 1939. During his lifetime, he was actively involved with the unions, particularly those involving musicians, and he was the founder of the Society of Cuban Composers, the Cuban Authors National Federation, the Cuban Authors National Union, and the Cuban Authors National Society, among others. He wrote essays and articles about Cuban music, and composed some of the most important Cuban *zarzuelas*.

Rojas, Francisco. Flutist, composer, instrumentalist. Born 1887, Havana; died 11 September 1943. Rojas made valuable arrangements of Cuban and international compositions, particularly those by Gonzalo Roig. He was a founder of the army's staff band. He composed "Mosaico cubano," "Estampas africanas," "En el batey," "En el palmar," and "A pie, a danzón."

Rojas, Jorge Luis ("Rojitas"). Singer. Born 8 February 1965, Havana. From 1974 to 1979, Rojas lived in London, where his parents were diplomats. On his return to Cuba in 1980, he joined the group Tampa as a singer, and then moved on to the group Oasis. He later worked with Alfredo Hernández in the *trova* duo Evocación. In 1991 he joined Adalberto Alvarez y Su Son. In 1995 he formed his own group, specializing in interpretations of ballads, salsa, and *son*. He is the author of "Regálame tu encanto," "Pégame a tu cintura," and "Mi salsa esta buena."

Rojas, Margot. Pianist and professor. Born 24 March 1903, Veracruz, Mexico; died 1 November 1966, Havana. Rojos lived in Cuba from 1912 and studied at the National Conservatory, where she received several awards. She later studied harmony and the history of music in New York, and piano with Alexander Lambert. She gave concerts and was the first soloist with the Havana Philharmonic Orchestra, in 1924. She was a teacher at several music academies, including the Amadeo Roldán Conservatory and National School of Art, where she trained several brilliant pianists.

Rojas, Martín. Composer, guitar and double bass player. Born 23 February 1944, Havana. Studied guitar with Professor Isaac Nicola and Roberto de Moya. Later continued to study independently. In 1959 Rojas started playing professionally with Los Antares, singing Latin American music. In 1964 he started playing double bass for a dance band and also played in Frank Domínguez's group. In 1966 he founded and directed the Sonorama 6 combo. Beginning in 1968 he was the piano accompanist for Omara Portuondo. His song compositions include "Cuento para un niño," "Mi montuno son," "Romance de la alondra y el quetzal," "Siempre es 26," and "Preludio por la soledad."

Rojas, Ñico. Guitarist and composer. Born 3 August 1921, Havana. Rojas was a civil engineer who also composed music inspired by his family, friends, and popular characters in the town of Matanzas, where he lived for many years. Examples of this music include "Guajira a mi madre," "Homenaje a Bebo," "Saldiguera y Virulilla." He also wrote "Mi ayer," "Esta dicha nuestra," and "Ahora sí sé que te quiero." He teaches urban hydrology at the José Martí Institute.

Rojas, Orquesta de Perico. A *típico*, or wind, orchestra formed by the trombonist Pedro Rojas, known as Perico, in Güines, 1884. Besides Rojas, its first musicians were Patricio Valdés and Andrés Rojas (violins); Martín Caraballo and Miguel Rojas (clarinets); Jesús Urfé (cornet); Ambrosio Marín (trombone); Anacleto Larrondo (ophiclenic); Juan R. Landa (double bass); Pedro Hernández (timbales); and Leopoldo Castillo (*güiro*). This orchestra continued to play in dance halls well into the twentieth century.

Roldán, Alberto. Cellist. Born 1902, Madrid; died 24 May 1942, Havana. Started studying music with his mother in 1907, then entered the Conservatory of Music and Recitation in Madrid, where he graduated in 1918, with First Prize for cello. Roldán continued his studies in Paris under professors André Hekking and Vincent d'Indy. In 1920 he arrived in Cuba with his brother Amadeo and they began performing music. He was a member of the Chamber Music Society, the Havana Philharmonic Orchestra, the Havana Quartet, and the Havana Trio, and he also worked as a soloist. He also played in several significant orchestras in the United States and Venezuela.

Roldán, Amadeo. Composer, professor, violinist, conductor. Born 12 July 1900, Paris; died 2 March 1939, Havana. Mother was Cuban, father was Spanish. Though born in France, Roldán adopted Cuban citizenship. His sister Maria Teresa (a mezzosoprano) and his brother Alberto (a cellist) were born some years later. It was Amadeo's mother, the pianist Albertina Gardes, who initiated him to music. In 1908 he entered the Conservatory of Music and Recitation in Madrid. His violin teachers were Agustín Soler and, later, Antonio Fernández Bordas. In 1913 he started studying harmony and composition with Conrado del Campo and continued with Benito García de la Parra. In 1916 he graduated from high school. One of his first compositions was the Suite in G minor. In 1917 he won the Sarasate Prize in Violin and joined the Philharmonic Orchestra of Madrid as a violinist. He appeared in concerts in several Spanish cities. In 1919 he arrived in Cuba and worked as a professor in a conservatory in Havana. In 1921 he played the viola with the Chamber Music Society, conducted by Alberto Falcón (pianist), with Casimiro Zertucha on violin and his brother Alberto on cello. In 1922 Amadeo started working as a violinist with the Havana Symphony Orchestra, conducted by Pedro Sanjuán. For economic reasons, he also played the accompaniment for silent movies and played in restaurants and cabarets in Havana. In 1925 he composed the *Obertura sobre temas cubanos*, using elements of Cuban folk music. In 1926 he organized, with Alejo Carpentier, a series of new music concerts, which allowed the Cuban people, for the first time, to hear the outstanding pieces of Cuban contemporary music that had already been heard by music lovers around the world. The following year, he played first violin with the Havana Quartet, joining with the Spanish pianist and composer Joaquín Turina in a concert in Cuba. He also composed *Tres pequeños poemas*. In 1928 he conducted the premiere of *La rebambaranba*, and in 1929, *Milagro de Anaquillé*, both accompanied by the Havana Philharmonic Orchestra. At the same time, he was in contact with avant-garde musicians from Cuba and abroad, and he gave several lectures and presentations on the subject. In 1930 his *Rítmicas* was premiered. The following year, with César Pérez Sentenat, he founded the Havana Normal School of Music. In 1932 he was appointed conductor of the Havana Philharmonic Orchestra, a position he held until his death. In 1934 Nicolás Slonimsky premiered Roldán's "Motivos de son" at New York's Town Hall. The fact that his works had been played in different cities of the world contributed to his reputation as an innovator and a creative force. He also directed the Havana Municipal Conservatory, which today carries his name. He was in close contact with the experimental artists of his time, including Grupo Minorista. He also joined Fernando Ortiz in promoting Afro-Cuban folk music, which had been ignored by the reactionary ruling orthodoxy. In his defense of both Afro-Cuban and Spanish music as a part of Cuban music, he followed in the same path as García Caturla. The two men are considered to be the pioneers of Cuba's modern symphonic art. He died at the peak of his creative capacity.

(Amadeo) Roldán Conservatory. *See* Municipal Conservatory of Havana.

Roloff, Julio. Composer. Born 27 December 1951, Havana. Studied at the Amadeo Roldán Conservatory and the Ignacio Cervantes Conservatory. Roloff is the author of *Masa*, for mixed choir and instruments (1974); Trio for flute, cello, and piano (1975); Sonata, for flute (1977); and Variations for percussion (1980). He also composed electro-acoustic pieces. A graduate of the Higher Institute of Art, he worked as a musical adviser at EGREM records. He lives in the United States.

Romero, Clara. Guitarist and professor. Born 6 January 1888, Havana; died 5 April 1951. After giving some concerts, Romero worked as a music teacher. She founded the modern Cuban school of guitar, where she trained her children Cuqui and Isaac Nicola. In 1939 she founded the Guitarists' Society of Cuba. She published several research findings on guitar techniques.

Romero, Eloy. Improviser, *décima* singer. Born 1 December 1907, San Antonio de Cabezas; died (?). Worked in agriculture since childhood and later was a barber. Romero started singing *décimas* at country dances and in serenades. In 1940 he moved to Havana, where he performed in country music shows on several radio stations, including Cadena Roja, Mil Diez, DMQ, Radio Rebelde, and Radio Progreso.

Romeu, Antonio María. Composer, pianist, bandleader. Born 11 September 1876, Jibacoa; died 18 January 1955, Havana. When he was eight, Romeu started studying music under the supervision of the priest Joaquín Martínez. At the age of ten, he studied piano by himself. Two years later, he played at his first dance and composed his first work, a mazurka. On 22 January 1899 he moved to the capital, where he found a job playing piano, accompanied by the *güiro*, at the Café La Diana. By introducing the piano into Leopoldo Cervantes's *danzón* orchestra, he created what came to known as the French *charanga* style. The band had featured flute, violin, double bass, timbales, and *güiro*. In 1911 Romeu created his own orchestra, which made him very popular and which would last for over fifty years. He traveled to the United States to play at Cuban parties, and he made several recordings for the RCA Victor Company. He wrote more than five hundred *danzones*, the most

popular of which are "Marcheta," "Alemán prepara tu cañón," "Eva," "Siglo XX," "La danza de los millones," "El servicio obligatorio," "Cinta azul," "El mago de las teclas," "Jibacoa," "Ay que me vengo cayendo," "Los frescos," and, above all, "La flauta mágica," in collaboration with Alfredo Brito. He also made successful arrangements for a number of Cuban songs for *danzón*. These included "Guarina," by Sindo Garay; "Me da miedo quererte," by Alberto Villalón; "Mares y arenas," by Rosendo Ruiz Sr.; "Mercedes," by Manuel Corona; "Perla Marina," by Sindo Garay; "Aquella boca," by Eusebio Delfín; and "La cleptómana," by Manuel Luna. Romeu also orchestrated such operas as *The Barber of Seville*, by Rossini. His most famous work was the song "Tres lindas cubanas," which he composed out of an old *son* and premiered in 1926. He was a pioneer in the creation of a particular style of playing *danzón*, which was a turning point in the future of the genre. He was an outstanding pianist and won several prizes during his career. He was awarded the Gold Medal at the Great Exhibition in Seville in 1928, a Silver Medal at the Philadelphia Exhibition, the Medal of the Fiftieth Anniversary in Cuba, in 1952, and the Carlos Manuel de Céspedes Medal. In 1950 he ceased working as a pianist, but continued as a songwriter and orchestrator. *See also* Romeu, Orquesta.

Romeu, Armando. Conductor, bandleader, composer. Born 22 October 1890, Jibacoa; died 14 October 1990, Houston, Texas. Studied piano with his brother Antonio María and also with Angel Planas and Benjamín Orbón, and harmony with Juan M. Sabio y Farnós. Romeu directed the municipal bands of San Antonio and Regla. In 1915 he became the director of the Artillery Band, and in 1925, of the staff band of the army of Marina de Guerra, a job he held until 1960. With the latter, he won two band contests in the United States. He gave concerts in different American cities. He composed *Tres fantasías* for band and orchestra, and *Tres valses* and *Danzas cubanas* for piano.

Romeu, Armando, Jr. Conductor, arranger, composer, saxophonist, flutist. Born 17 July 1911, Havana. From a family of musicians; received his first music lessons from his father, Armando Romeu Marrero. When Armando Romeu Jr. was eight, he played the flute in the military band. In 1926 he began playing with the American jazz bands that performed in Havana's nightclubs. In 1932 he went on tour in Europe with Orquesta Siboney, playing saxophone. A year later, in Havana, he founded his own *jazzband* and toured with it in several South American countries. The band took up residency at the Tropicana Cabaret in 1941 and continued playing there for more than twenty-five years. In 1967 Romeu was appointed conductor of the Orquesta Cubana de Música Moderna. He has composed several mambos, including "Bop City Mambo," "Mambo a la Kenton," and "Mocambo," all of which exhibit clear jazz influences.

Romeu, Gonzalo. Conductor and professor. Born 1945, Havana. A member of the family that produced several outstanding musicians. Gonzalo Romeu studied with José Ardévol, Edgardo Martín, and Leo Brouwer at the Amadeo Roldán Conservatory in Havana, and specialized in conducting with the Soviet professor Daniil Tulin. He later studied in the USSR, at the Rimsky-Kórsakov Conservatory in Leningrad, and at the Tchaikovsky Conservatory in Moscow. He also worked with I. A. Musin and O. A. Dimitriadi. For three years, he conducted the Symphonic Orchestra of Oriente, during which time he premiered works by contemporary Cuban composers. He also played, for the first time in Cuba, the most significant pieces from the international symphonic repertoire. He has conducted provincial orchestras. Since 1975, he has frequently conducted the National Symphony Orchestra, and has given concerts in Poland, Hungary, and the Soviet Union. He is the head of the teaching department for chamber ensembles and practical orchestras at the Higher Institute of Art, where he teaches conducting.

Romeu, Mario. Pianist. Born 27 April 1924, Regla. From a family of musicians, Mario Romeu grew up in a musical environment. He started studying with his father Armando Romeu and his sister Zenaida Romeu (pianist), and improved his skills with the pianist Jascha Fisherman. In 1938 he won a scholarship to the United States. He made his debut performance at the Encanto Theater, where he performed both as a soloist and with his sister Zenaida. Later, he was presented as a soloist with the CMZ radio orchestra, and in 1940 at the great hall in the Museum of Fine Arts. In 1951 he performed with the Symphonic Orchestra of Venezuela, conducted by Thomas Mayer. He has also been a conductor and has performed as a piano accompanist.

Romeu, Orquesta. French *charanga* created by the composer and pianist Antonio María Romeu in Havana around 1910. The musicians in the first lineup were Alfredo Brito (flute), Feliciano Facenda (violin), Rafael Calazán (double bass), Remigio Valdés (timbales), José de la Merced (*güiro*), and Romeu (piano). Later, new musicians joined the orchestra: Francisco Delabart (flute); Augusto Valdés (clarinetist); Juan Quevedo (violin); Aurelio Valdés and Félix Vazquéz (*güiro*); Antonio María Romeu Jr. (violin); Pedro Hernández (violin); Dihígo (trumpet); Regueira (trombone); and José Antonio Díaz (flute). The singers Fernando Collazo and Barbarito Diez performed with Romeu at different times. During the 1930s, the orchestra incorporated more instruments and became a giant orchestra. It combined elements from the *charanga* and the *típico* style. Antonio María Romeu died in 1955, but the orchestra continued playing under the leadership of his son and with Barbarito Diez as singer. Years ago, the orchestra was renamed after Barbarito Diez.

Romeu, Zenaida. Pianist. Born 5 June 1910, Havana; died 21 September 1985. From a family of important musicians, Zenaida Romeu gave some solo concerts but worked mainly as an accompanist. She composed a few pieces for piano and some songs.

Roncona. *See* González, Benito.

Rosa, Orlando de la. Composer and pianist. Born 15 April 1919, Havana; died 15 November 1957. Started studying piano with his mother when he was nine. He was taught harmony by Panchencho. Rosa attended secondary school at the Havana Institute. For years, the vocal quartet carrying his name was very popular. He worked as an accompanist for many popular singers. His first composition was the bolero "Yo sé que es mentira," which was premiered in 1940. He followed with "Tu llegada," and over the next fifteen years wrote boleros and *canciones* that developed a new style of Cuban music. Among the most outstanding were "Cansancio," "Vieja luna," "Mi corazón es para tí," "Qué emoción," "No vale la pena," "Nuestras vidas," "Para cantarle a mi amor," and "La canción de mis canciones."

Rosa, Trío La. Created in Santiago de Cuba during the 1940s by Juan Francisco de la Rosa (director), Julio León, and Juan Antonio Serrano. The trio made several recordings, and its boleros, *sones*, and *guarachas* were very popular in Cuba and Latin America.

Rosell, Electo. Composer, violinist, bandleader. Born 7 November 1907, Santiago de Cuba; died April 1984. He was known as Chepín. When Electo Rosell was fourteen, he started studying music with his father, José Rosell, a guitarist. He joined the Municipal Academy of Fine Arts in Santiago de Cuba, studying harmony, theory, and violin with Professors Ramón Figueroa and Angel Castilla. When he was seventeen, he traveled to Puerto Rico, the Dominican Republic, Venezuela, and Panama, playing violin with the theater company Arquímides Pous. In 1925, when he returned to Cuba, he dedicated himself to composition. In 1932, with Bernardo Chovén, he organized the successful dance band Chepín Chovén, which he would direct for the next twenty-five years. He composed the boleros "Murmullo" and "Elba"; the *danzones* "Bodas de oro," "Diamante negro," and "Reina Isabel"; and the *guaracha* "El platanal de Bartolo."

Rosell, Rosendo. Radio/TV host, writer, composer. Born (?), Placetas. Author of popular songs, including "Calculadora" and "Caimitillo y marañón" (*cha-cha-chás*) and the bolero "Cobarde." Rosell has lived in the United States for many years. He is the author of the book *Vida y milagros de la farándula cubana*.

Ross, Harry. Pianist. Born 15 August 1901, New York; died (?). His parents were Cubans, and they emigrated during the War of Independence in Cuba. Ross studied with his mother but mostly with his uncle Laureano Fuentes Pérez, a pianist and composer. Later, he took advanced studies with Argelina Sicouret. He spent his childhood and early youth in Cuba and then went to New York where he worked with Hoffmann, Leopold Stokowski, and Pachmann. He gave concerts in several European and Latin American cities. Finally, he settled permanently in the United States.

Ross, Lázaro. Akpwón (singer of Afro-Cuban lucumí or arará songs). Born 1925, Havana. Ross has made a significant contribution to groups performing this kind of music. He has made recordings in Cuba and for the Chant du Monde label in Paris. He was a founding member of the National Folkloric Ensemble, with whom he has traveled to many countries.

Rubalcaba, Gonzalo. Pianist and composer. Born 27 May 1963, Havana. Grandson of Jacobo Rubalcaba and son of Guillermo G. Rubalcaba, the pianist and director of his own *orquesta típica*. Gonzalo Rubalcaba studied piano and percussion at the National School of Art. He was a member of the Orquesta Cubana de Música Moderna, and of the group Sonido Contemporáneo. In 1983 he founded his own band, Proyecto, with whom he has performed a repertoire of Afro-Cuban jazz in Cuba and abroad. He has made many quality recordings of other composers' works, as well as his own contemporary jazz compositions with an emphasis on the Cuban elements. He is one of the most outstanding and virtuoso jazz pianists in the world, as is revealed on his first solo album, *Inicio*, released in 1987. He lives in the United States and tours with a band comprising key figures in Cuban and American jazz.

Rubalcaba, Guillermo. Pianist and orchestra conductor. Born in Pinar del Rio; died (?). Father of the pianist Gonzalo Rubalcaba. Studied music with his own father, Jacobo Rubalcaba, and joined Pedrito Ruiz's orchestra in his hometown. After moving to Havana, Guillermo Rubalcaba played in several orchestras, until he entered the National Concert Charanga, which he would later conduct. Today, he runs and directs his own *danzón* orchestra named after him, in which he is also the pianist. He is the composer of *danzones* and *cha-cha-chás*. In the 1990s he became a member of several touring groups of veteran musicians who emerged in the wake of the success of the Buena Vista Social Club.

Rubalcaba, Jacobo (González). Composer, professor, trombonist, trumpet player, conductor, bandleader. Born 28 November 1960, Sagua la Grande. When he was fifteen, Rubalcaba began working as a tailor and, at the same time, studied music at the Municipal Academy of Sagua la Grande with Antonio Fabre. When he was eighteen, he started playing trombone with the Santa Clara Music Band. In 1915 he moved to Pinar del Rio, where he worked as a trombonist in the Military Band. From then on, he was an important figure in the promotion of music and in music education. He founded municipal bands in Mantua, San Juan Martínez, San Luis, and Pinar del Rio. In 1918 he became the conductor of his own *orquesta típica*, which helped spread the *danzón* around the West of Cuba. His compositions include "Los pinareños," "Linda Mercedes," "Ulpiano y su contrabajo," and "Hay que echar manteca," but his most important contribution was "El cadete constitucional." Almost all of his children have followed in the family musical tradition: José Antonio is conductor of Metropolitan Orchestra of Pinar del Río, and Guillermo leads the *charanga típica* of the Ministry of Culture. Rubalcaba died in a traffic accident while he was traveling from Havana to Pinar del Río.

Rufino, Cuarteto Los. Founded in 1950, in Havana, by Mercedes and José I. Rufino, along with their children July and Carlos. The quartet sang and played the guitar and performed a repertoire of Cuban and Latin American music on television, in theaters, and in cabarets. During the mid-1950s, the musicians settled in Mexico City and later moved to the United States.

Ruiz, Alberto. Singer. Born 14 September 1913, Havana; died 6 April 1978. Began his career singing in *típico* orchestras during the late 1930s, and in the 1940s founded and led the band Kubavana, which set a pattern that was followed by many other dance bands. Ruiz also pioneered a new and peculiar style of singing boleros that was imitated by other well-known singers. He was a member of the *conjuntos* Casino and Tropicana. As well as boleros, he had hits with *guarachas*.

Ruiz, Candito. Pianist and composer. Born 1914, Havana; died 1980. During the 1940s, Ruiz was a popular piano accompanist and composed successful *canciones* and boleros, including "Ya es muy tarde" and "Sin tu amor." For many years, he played interpretations of traditional Cuban works at the Lincoln Hotel in Havana.

Ruiz, Magaly. Composer. Born 1941, Santa Clara. Magaly studied piano with César Pérez Sentenat and composition with José Ardévol. She graduated from the García Caturla Conservatory and the Higher Institute of Art in Havana. Her tutor was Roberto Varela. Her compositions include Three preludes, for piano (1968); Three pieces, for violin and piano (1976); Concerto, for oboe and orchestra (1986); *Tres ambiente sonoros*, for symphony orchestra (1981); and Movemento for string quartet, no. 2 (1980). She is a teacher at the Higher Institute of Art.

Ruiz, Orquesta de Pedrito. *Charanga* band formed by the pianist Pedrito Ruiz. The founding musicians were Simón Hernández (flute); Luis Domínguez and Guillermo González Rubalcaba (violins); Pedrito Ruiz (piano); Armando Silva (double bass); Carlos Madam (timbales); Feliciano Chamizo (*güiro*); Raúl Hernández (conga); Roberto Díaz (trumpet); and Enrique Madam (vocalist). They played *danzón* and other Cuban rhythms. The band is still playing, nowadays with new musicians, and led by Pedrito Ruiz.

Ruiz, Rey. Singer. Born (?), Marianao. Started singing in Havana's nightclubs and in 1992 moved to

New York, where he made his first record. Ruiz is known for his *salsa romantica* style and has become very popular and widely known. He has performed on radio and television, and at concerts and festivals, both in the United States and in other countries. His several CDs have been very successful.

Ruiz, Rosendo. Composer. Born 1 March 1885, Santiago de Cuba; died 1 January 1983, Havana. Started out in music as a *trova* singer in the capital city of the eastern region. In 1902 Ruiz wrote his first song, "Venganza de amor." In 1911 José Parapar sang Ruiz's famous *criolla*, "Mares y Arenas," at the Martí Theater in Havana. In 1917 Ruiz composed the worker's anthem "Redención," which is perhaps the first of its kind in Latin America. When he was still a young man, he moved to Cienfuegos, where he wrote a great many of his works. He later settled in Havana. Together with Sindo Garay, Alberto Villalón, and Manuel Corona, he is one of the greatest representatives of the Cuban *trova* genre. He led the Cuba Quartet, which featured Ruiz, Matas, and Corso. In 1934 he directed Trío Azul with Guillermo Rodríguez Fife and Vals. He was also a guitar teacher. Among his most popular works are "Rosina y Virginia" (also known as "Dos lindas rosas"), "Falso juramento," "Confesión," "Cuba y sus misterios," "Terina," "Naturaleza," "Prestigio triste," the *guajira* "Junto a un cañaveral," the *son* "La chaúcha," and the *pregón* "Se va el dulcerito." He was awarded the Certificate of Honor at the Seville Exhibition in 1929. He is the author of a guitar manual which is in its third edition. In 1963, he presided over the Trova Cubana Forum.

Ruiz, Rosendo, Jr. Composer. Born 17 October 1918, Havana. Ruiz studied music for a short time at the Municipal Conservatory, but the greatest impact on his music education came from his father and his friends. He cultivated almost all popular genres. The rumba "Rataplán-Plán-Plán" was one of his first creations. In 1945 he composed the song "Hasta mañana vida mía," which was widely broadcast both in Cuba and abroad. He was a pioneer in the *filin* movement and wrote the *guaracha* "Saoco." During the 1950s, he composed some very well known *cha-cha-chás*, including "Rico vacilón," "Los marcianos," "Cha-cha-chá del cariñoso," and "Los fantasmas." His works have been recorded in Holland, Austria, Germany, the United States, Spain, Italy, and some Latin American countries. Some of his music has been used in films. He studied at the Popular Music Seminary of the National Council for Culture from 1964 to 1967. He has traveled to Mexico, Venezuela, Czechoslovakia, Spain, and France. He has received awards for some of his records. He was elected vice-president of the Society of Cuban Composers.

Ruiz, Tomás. Composer. Born 1834, Havana; died 1888. Studied music at Liceo Artístico y Literario in Havana. Ruiz wrote some very popular *contradanzas*, including "Usted dispense," "El dedo de Landaluce," and "Toma Perico." He was also a piano and singing teacher.

Ruiz Castellanos, Pablo. Composer. Born 26 June 1902, Guantánamo; died (?). In 1922 Ruiz joined the band which performed on the cruise ship "Cuba." He later became a member of the army staff band. He also worked as a teacher. He composed such works as "Rumba en rapsodia," "Río Cauto," "Mito," "Sinfonía heterodoxa cubana," "El gran changüí," "Campiña," "Concierto negro," and his most successful piece, "Monte Rus." He has also written music for chamber orchestra and for ballet, as well as a musical.

Ruiz Espadero, Nicolás. Pianist and composer. Born 15 February 1832, Havana; died 30 August 1890. Studied piano with his mother and with the professors Miró and Fernando Arizti. Ruiz Espadero was a close friend of the composer Louis Gottschalk, who initiated him and helped him to promote his work in Europe. He was a piano virtuoso, yet spent many years away from concert halls, working as a teacher.

Among his students were Angelina Sicouret, Cecilia Arizti, and Ignacio Cervantes. He played at Fernando Arizti's house for soirées there, and he also performed at the Society of Classical Music. He composed music for piano (more than fifty pieces), violin and piano, and also chamber pieces. His most outstanding works are: Elegy, for violin and piano; Trio, sonata for piano; Andante, for violin, viola, cello, and piano; *Vals satánico*, for piano; *Tarantela furiosa*; Scherzo; *La queja del poeta*; *Sobre la tumba de Gottschalk*; Quintet; and his best-known works, *Canto del guajiro* and *Canto del esclavo*, which both involve Cuban elements. He died in an accident.

rumba. A musical song and dance genre, driven by drums. Of African-Spanish origin, with special emphasis on African influences, mostly with regard to rhythm. Rumba originated in the poor, black sectors of the urban centers, where the people lived crowded together in the run-down neighborhoods that had been established around the sugar mills. The rumba is played with drums (*tumba*, *llamador*, and *quinto*) or simply with wooden boxes (particularly those that were traditionally used to carry cod or candles), accompanied by claves and, sometimes, spoons. The term "rumba" also applies to a party at which the rumba is danced. Rumba has no religious significance.

According to the musicologist Argeliers León, rumbas begin with an expressive singing section that is followed by a choral section, during which the spectators-participants start to dance. The rumba is danced in pairs in the *guaguancó* and *yambú* rumbas. The *columbia* variety, however, is inspired by rituals observed by Abakuá and Ñáñigo secret brotherhoods and is performed by a man who dances alone.

There is also a series of ancient rumbas dating back to the Spanish colonial era; these consist of a brief solo singing section and then a *capetillo*, or turn, during which the soloist alternates with the chorus. The instrumentalism of the rumba is quite particular: the claves set the rhythm, the bass drum then adds depth, the *quinto* builds a richer and richer rhythmic filigree, and finally the spoons join in.

In the *yambú* rumba, the dancers imitate the elderly and pretend to have difficulty moving. *Yambú* dancers do not move the pelvis in the aggressive way (*vacunao*) that characterizes the *guaguancó*; the *yambú* is, rather, a slow tempo mimetic dance. Indeed, *yambú* dancers sing the phrase "En el yambú no se vacuna" (In *yambú* there is no "vaccination"). The vocalization of the *yambú* is characterized by a short singing section; there may also be a *tarareo* or *lalaleo*, known as the *diana*, that is the beginning of the chorus section. The *guaguancó* is the better known rumba, having become popular among an international audience. It is a faster and far more aggressive variety of rumba: its steps are sexually charged, as the man pursues the woman in a stylized sort of conquest. León notes about the *guaguancó* that its initial singing section is long and descriptive and tells the story of a person or an event. Its melody is smooth, with some long, tense notes. *Pareados* (prose sections) are often part of the singing. The movements of the *guaguancó* are free and unarticulated; the couple feign with their dance steps an attraction and a rejection, a game of offering and taking away. Finally the man makes a dramatic forward pelvic motion, and the woman submits to his advances, no longer making the hiding gesture that is the basis of most of her steps. The *columbia*, unlike the *yambú* and the *guaguancó*, is not a couple dance. It is a virtuoso dance

performed by a male soloist, whose steps are stylized evocations of íremes or *diablitos abakuás*, the little devils in Abakuá rituals. It is danced in front of the *quinto* drum, and dancer and instrument perform a kind of rhythmic dialogue (León, *Música folklórica cubana*, 78–80). Rumba was adapted, in a sophisticated style, by the Cuban *bufos*, or comic musicals.

Rumbavana, Conjunto. Popular band formed by the leader Tomás Martínez in Havana, 1956, and later, by his replacement, José González. It became very popular in the late 1960s and performed on radio and television and at dances. It has recorded many LPs. Its success is due to the new instrumentation created by the artistic director and pianist Joseíto González. His innovative work is founded in traditional Cuban music. At the peak of its popularity, the singers were Guido Pérez, Fernando González, and Orestes García; later, Ricardito and Onelio Pérez joined the band. They have all toured throughout Latin America.

S

Sabín, José. Composer, singer, guitarist. Born end of the nineteenth century, Guantánamo; died middle of the twentieth century, San Antonio de los Baños. Worked as a cigar maker, dedicating his free time to music. He also lived in Cárdenas. Sabín wrote the very popular clave songs "Maceo y Martí" and "Oriente y La Habana," and other pieces.

Saborit, Eduardo. Composer and guitarist. Born 14 May 1912, Campechuela; died 5 March 1963, Havana. Moved to Niquero and studied music under Crescencio Rosales, and later learned the guitar and the flute. In 1934 Saborit became a member of Trío La Clave Azul, which also included Teodoro Benemelis and Luis Raga. The trio was active for over five years. In 1939 he joined the Trío Ensueño. In the 1940s he began to work as a guitarist, promoting country music on Radio CMQ. He composed many hit songs, *guajiras*, and *guarachas*, such as "Qué linda es Cuba," "Despertar mi," "Tengo miedo de ti," "La guayabera," and "Conozca Cuba primero."

Sacasas, Anselmo. Pianist. Born 23 November 1912, Manzanillo. Began his music studies in his hometown and continued them in Havana, where he learned harmony and composition under Pedro Sanjuán. Sacasas worked as a pianist in several dance orchestras, including Orquesta Hermanos Castro. In 1937, along with most of the musicians from that band, including the singer Miguelito Valdés, and Guillermo Portela, he set up the Orquesta Casino de la Playa. His piano solos and innovative arrangements were very influential. In 1940 he left for New

York, joined Xavier Cugat's band, and also led his own for many years. Later, he moved to Puerto Rico.

Sahig, Ñola. Pianist. Born 11 January 1924, Ciego de Ávila; died 29 October 1988, Havana. Began studying piano in her hometown and continued in Camagüey. Sahig later attended the Havana-based Orbón Conservatory. Around 1950 she moved to New York, where she improved her skills as a pianist at the Juilliard School of Music for five years. She also studied in Paris, Rome, and Chicago. She then began a series of performances in different foreign cities. On returning to Cuba, she gave numerous concerts and also worked as a soloist with the National Symphony Orchestra. She promoted Cuban music and wrote articles for newspapers and magazines.

Salakó, Eduardo. Conga drummer. Born (?); died 1914, Havana. Famous *olú-batá* drum player. Salakó was born in Cuba was of Lucumí ancestry. According to those who heard his music, he seemed to speak in the Lucumí language with his *iyá* drum: he could ask for water, cigars, or anything he chose with his drum's "voice," as was the custom with West African talking drums. He would beat out phrases that were answered vocally in the Lucumí language by his elders.

Salas, Esteban. Composer. Born 25 December 1725, Havana; died 14 July 1803, Santiago de Cuba. Little is known about his life and work while he lived in Havana. At the age of eight, Salas joined the choir of the main parish church as a boy soprano, and there he also began his studies of plain-song, organ, and violin, as well as counterpoint and composition. At fifteen, he entered the San Carlos Seminary to study philosophy, theology, and canonic law. He spent much of his life teaching and writing music for the different parochial churches run by the Western government. In February 1764 he moved to Santiago de Cuba, carrying with him a document in which Morell de Santa Cruz designated him a stand-in teacher. In compliance with the established rules, he performed for the town council, as a demonstration of his abilities, an Ave María Stella that has been preserved to the present day, and a Salmo de Completas that has not yet been found. On 12 March, the town council, as a sign of approval, gave him the provisional title. To receive the full title, he required

a Royal Certificate issued through Mexico, which he actually received on 12 March 1769. He began to reorganize the Chapel of Music at the Cathedral, which, in spite of being the third chapel, was the only one to last. The chapel had fourteen musicians: three trebles, two altos, two tenors, one harp, two lead violins, one backup violin, one organist, and two bassists (or musicians who played the general bass part, a cello and a bassoon). Salas used the term *baxon* for his bassoon parts, but some of his works that have been preserved only contain one part for this instrument, and there is evidence that Matías Alqueza, the first person to run a printing shop in the city, was his cellist for some time.

On 20 March 1790 Salas was ordained as a priest in a ceremony held at Dolores Church. For that occasion, he composed a non-Christmas carol called "¿Quién es ésta cielos?" and a Stabat Mater in fourteen movements. During those years, he struggled to improve the economic conditions of the musicians at the chapel. Apart from working as a composer, this cultivated man also wrote music for all the parish churches under the eastern government, which included Puerto Príncipe, and was responsible for the Eucharistic service at the Cathedral and its subordinate, the Carmen Church. He was a professor of plain-song, philosophy, and ethical theology at the San Basilio Seminary, though he was paid only for his work as choirmaster. He was a poet, and wrote lyrics for his own secular songs. He composed his last carol for Christmas 1801. His music embodies elements of the last stages of the baroque style, with remarkable ingredients of classicism. It was naturally influenced by Italian and Spanish musicians, but Salas also displays, unambiguously, a truly Latin American sensibility.

The catalog of his works comprises seven masses, five hymns, seven sequences, twelve antiphons, five psalms, one Passion songbook, three canticles, two litanies, eight lessons, seven invitatories, two motets, twenty-nine hallelujahs, one evensong, one terce, and one none; in addition, he wrote the Christmas carols "Pues la fábrica de un templo," "Toquen presto a fuego," "Quién ha visto que en invierno," "Sobre los ríos undosos," "Una noticia alegre," "Escuchen el concento," "Vayan unas especies," "A Belén José y María," "Como la luz ha nacido," "El que impera soberano," "O que anuncio tan plausible," "Vengan todos presurosos," "Resuenen armoniosos," "Que dulce melodía," "Preparaos o mortales," "Claras luces," "Qué niño tan bello," "Los cuatro elementos," "O los tiempos," "Oigan una nueva," "Al niño muy hombre," "Una nave mercantil," "Quién es ésta, cielos," "Ya en el apacible puerto"; the cantatas such as "Saltando viene," "Silencio," "Por si dormido," "Unos pastores," "Astros luminosos," "El cielo y sus estrellas," "Respirad, o mortales," "O que noche," "Resuenen armoniosos," "Tú mi dios entre galas," "Vengan a ver," "Son la de Jacob," and "Nace el sol"; and the *pastorelles* "O niño soberano," "Pastores por un angel prevenidos," "Unos pastores de lo alto avisados," and "Lleguen en buena hora."

Salazar, Francisco Albo. *Trova* singer. Born 1876, Regla; died 1966. His nickname was Pancho Majagua. As a boy, Salazar traveled throughout South America and Spain. At the age of eighteen, he sang with the choir of Havana's House of Charity, and then moved to the Cathedral choir in the capital. He next joined a lyric theater, singing tenor in several operettas. He later became a full-time *trova* singer, and with Tata Villegas set up a duo that would perform for over half a century.

Salazar, Parmenio. Composer. Born 1902, Santiago de Cuba; died (?). Double bass player. Salazar played in several different popular music groups and composed songs, including "Yo soy el son cubano," "Se olvidaron de Santiago," "Como le gusta a Chana," and "Suena tu bongó."

Salcedo, Rafael. Composer and pianist. Born 23 October 1844, Santiago de Cuba; died 15 April 1917. Studied music with his father and, later, with Casamitjana and with Isidro Matón, an organist at the Cathedral in Santiago. In 1856 Salcedo was sent to Paris to study at Le Coupey, where he learned harmony, counterpoint, and composition, and became a pianist and a conductor. He returned to Cuba in 1865 and a few years later founded the Beethoven Music Society. He worked as a music critic and a professor, and established his own orchestra in Santiago de Cuba, performing religious music, piano compositions, and several symphonies. He was influenced by classicism, French romanticism, and Rossini.

salsa. Musical genre that emerged in New York's Latin American community in the 1970s. Its origins lie in the Cuban *son*, *guaracha*, and rumba, with influences also drawn from the Puerto Rican *bomba* and *plena*. Salsa also incorporated elements from Colombian *cumbia*, Dominican *merengue*, African American jazz and soul, and rock-and-roll. It includes some offshoots, such as the *pachanga* and the *boogaloo*, which were also launched in New York. Salsa as an expression, a style, a sound, was born in 1971, when the band the Fania All-Stars performed a legendary show at the Cheetah Club; another memorable all-star line-up performed at Yankee Stadium two years later, in 1973. The energy of the Latino *barrio* marked this style forever. The list of the composers, arrangers, orchestras, soloists, and vocalists who were involved in those events illustrates the best moments of this cultural phenomenon, which has now spread all over the world. "Heavy" or "classic" salsa (*salsa dura*) has today given way to what is known as romantic, erotic, or limp salsa (*salsa romantica, salsa erotica, salsa gorda*), with an emphasis on sentimental, love-related themes and repetitive, formulaic music. The term "salsa" currently encompasses all varieties of Afro-Latin, Spanish-language popular dance music.

Salvador, Emiliano. Pianist and composer. Born 19 August 1951, Puerto Padre; died 22 October 1992, Havana. Studied at the National School of Art, and was also trained by professor María Antonieta Henríquez. Salvador played with the Grupo de Experimentación Sonora of the Cuban Institute for Movie-Making, Art, and Industry. Shortly afterwards he joined Pablo Milanés's group, as both director and pianist. He participated, with his own band Nueva Visión, in jazz festivals in Cuba and abroad. His songs include "Puerto Padre," "El montuno," "Angélica," and "Post-visión." He was one of the most

celebrated pianists in the last decades, with a very distinctive and personal style.

Sánchez, Agustín. Clarinetist. Born 28 August 1860, Cienfuegos; died 1950. Sánchez organized and directed the Municipal Band of Cienfuegos, with whom he won, in 1911, the National Band Contest. He directed an eponymous *orquesta típica*, which continued to play for many years, mainly in Las Villas Province.

Sánchez, Alfredo. Guitarist and composer. Born 15 1878, Remedios; died 6 July 1959, Havana. In 1895 Sánchez moved with his family to Caibarién, where he began his musical studies, in harmony, singing, and piano, with the Bueno sisters. Immediately afterwards, he joined the El Clavel Choir, which was then very popular in Caibarién. He began to study guitar under the supervision of professor Carlos Bravé, and around that time, began composing pieces, including "Ojos indefinibles," "En el mar," and "La luna en Manhattan." A little later, he wrote music for the poems of Pedro Revuelta: "Pena de amor," "Más allá," and "El perdón." He joined the local band in Caibarién, conducted by maestro Jarque Gómez, as a saxophone player and clarinetist. In 1934 he moved to Havana, where he worked as a guitar professor, and later took up teaching music in public school no. 13.

Sánchez, Alina. Soprano. Born 5 September 1946, Havana. Studied with María de Gonitch and Carmelina Santana, then became a pupil of Gonzalo Roig. Sánchez began as an amateur singer at the University of Havana, where she was studying at the School of Literature and Art in 1965, when she took the lead role in Roig's operetta *Cecilia Valdés*. She subsequently starred in the role of Cecilia Valdés in a documentary film about the work produced by the Cuban Institute for Movie-Making, Art, and Industry. She also played the lead in the film *El otro Francisco*. She has traveled through Europe and to Mexico with a repertoire of preclassical songs, romantic operas, lieder, Negro spirituals, and Cuban and Latin American folk songs. She lives in Spain.

Sánchez, Antonio ("Musiquita"). Composer, violinist, pianist. Born 20 April 1916, Pinar del Río. Studied with his father, the clarinetist Fernando Sánchez, and then with Jacobo González Rubalcaba and the violinist Rafael Berroa. Antonio Sánchez played in his father's *orquesta típica*, then joined the bands of Rubalcaba and Fernando Luis in Pinar del Río. In 1936 he moved to Havana, where he played with Sport Antillano, Paulina Alvarez, Arcaño y Sus Maravillas, América, and Fajardo y Sus Estrellas. He played the violin with the CMQ Orchestra and later with the orchestra of the Cuban Institute of Radio and Television. His compositions include the *danzones* "Felicidades," "Los sitios llaman," and "Por un cerro mejor," and the *cha-cha-chás* "Poco pelo" and "Yo sabía."

Sánchez, José ("Pepe"). Composer and guitarist. Born 19 March 1856, Santiago de Cuba; died 3 January 1918. Father of the Cuban *trova* song style and the bolero. "Pepe" Sánchez taught the troubadours who emerged in Santiago de Cuba, including Sindo Garay, with whom he launched a group toward the end of the nineteenth century. He had a remarkable artistic intuition, and even though he was not technically trained, he created remarkable melodies. Most of these were composed in his head and never written down and thus, unfortunately, have been lost forever. Sánchez had a baritone voice, which he used mainly in serenades and in parties thrown in Santiago de Cuba. He was also a competent guitarist. He was often praised by established musicians, who were surprised at his impressive sense of melody and rhythm despite his lack of any formal knowledge of the rules of composition. Among the *canciones*, boleros, and *guarachas* that have been preserved by friends, the most memorable are "Pobre artista," "De profundis," "Rosa I," "Rosa II," "Rosa III," "Cuando oí la expresión de tu canto," "Cuba, mi patria querida," "Elvira," "Caridad," "Esperanza,"

"Naturaleza," "Adan y Eva," and "Tristeza." He also wrote "Himno a Maceo."

Sánchez, José Ramón. Guitarist, troubadour, singer of *decimas*. Born 9 December 1901, Consolación del Norte; died (?). Sánchez was a farmer who, for ten years, hosted a radio show of country music on RHC Cadena Azul. Since the show was usually broadcast at dawn, he was nicknamed "El Madrugador" (the early riser). Apart from *décimas*, he also wrote *sones* and *guarachas*. His *guajiras* "El madrugador" and "Noche serena" were extremely popular. Toward the end of his life he performed at the Cucalambé House and Museum, in the city of Victoria de Las Tunas.

Sánchez, Roberto. Singer. Born 26 August 1934, San Cristóbal. Began his musical career singing *punto guajiro*. In 1961 Sánchez appeared on radio and television in Havana singing boleros. Between 1966 and 1980 he was a vocalist with Gloria Matancera. He has recorded LPs and several singles. He went solo in 1981, and is now one of the most famous singers of traditional bolero.

Sánchez de Fuentes, Eduardo. Composer. Born 3 April 1874, Havana; died 7 September 1944. Born in a family of artists: his father, Eugenio, was a playwright, and his mother, Josefina Peláez, was a pianist and a singer. Eduardo Sánchez de Fuentes conducted a great deal of research into Cuban folk music. He was a pupil of Ignacio Cervantes and Carlos Ánckermann and studied at the Hubert de Blanck Conservatory. He earned a degree in civil law. In 1911 he was a Cuban delegate at the International Music Congress held in Rome. He conducted the first concerts of traditional Cuban music at the National Theater in 1922. He traveled throughout Mexico, Italy, France, and the United States. In 1929 he joined Alejandro García Caturla at the Ibero-American Festival in Barcelona. In 1939 he and Gonzalo Roig attended the International Music Congress, hosted in New York. He became president of the School of Arts and Letters at the Society of Cuban Songwriters. He won several prizes as a composer and also for his work in Cuban music. His books on Cuban music include: *El folklore en la música cubana, Cuba y sus músicos, Influencia de los ritmos africanos en nuestro cancionero, La contradanza y la habanera, Ignacio Cervantes, Consideraciones sobre la música cubana, Viejos ritmos cubanos, La última firma de Brindis de Sala, La música aborigen de América*, and *Folklorismo*. Among his compositions that have been preserved are the operas *Yumurí, El náufrago, La dolorosa*, and *Doreya*; the ballet *Dioné*; the oratorio *Navidad*; the cantata *Anacaona*; and the songs "Mírame así," "Corazón," "Vivir sin tus caricias," "Linda cubana," "Silenciosamente," "Por tus ojos," and "La volanta." He also wrote the well-known *habanera* "Tú."

Sánchez Ferrer, Roberto. Conductor. Born 31 December 1917, Havana. Began his study of music at the Conservatory of the Edison Institute, with professor José Ardévol, and at the same time learned the clarinet. Sánchez Ferrer later studied harmony and composition with Félix Guerrero, and conducting with Jan Constantinescu and Enrique González Mántici. He has worked as an instrumentalist and conductor on radio and television shows. Since 1961, he has many times conducted the National Symphony Orchestra. He wrote the opera *Van Troi* and the cantata *Jatín*. He has worked as a professor. He chaired the music department of the Writers and Artists Union of Cuba.

Sandoval, Arturo. Trumpet player. Born 6 November 1949, Artemisa. Began his studies in his hometown, then studied at the National School of Art, where he graduated in 1967. Sandoval played in the Orquesta Cubana de Música Moderna. In 1974 he joined the band Irakere, with whom he cut several records and appeared as an extraordinary trumpet soloist. He also participated in some of the band's international tours, until leaving in 1980 to set up his own group. He played and sang in a jazz-scat style. In 1990 he toured Europe with Dizzy Gillespie's United Nations Orchestra. He subsequently

moved to the United States, where his career has since flourished.

San José, Alberto. Singer. Born 7 August 1944, Camagüey. Studied singing with various teachers and at the Higher Institute of Art. San José was a member of the Havana Musical Theater, and has given lyrical concerts and performed with various symphony orchestras. He also teaches singing.

Sanjuan, Pedro. Composer, professor, conductor. Born 1887, San Sebastián; died 1976, United States. In Madrid and Paris, Sanjuan studied violin with Julio Francés and composition with Joaquín Turina. He conducted dance bands and orchestras. In 1924 he traveled to Cuba, where he founded, directed, and conducted the Havana Philharmonic Orchestra. He taught Amadeo Roldán, García Caturla, and other young musicians. In 1930 he composed his well-known *Liturgia Negra*. He is the author of several symphonies inspired by Hispanic themes. He and García Caturla represented Cuba at the Second Festival of North American, Mexican, and Cuban Music, which was organized by Nicolás Slonimsky. According to Alejo Carpentier, his "work as a musician and his prolonged stay among us make him almost a Cuban citizen" (*Carteles*, 12 July 1931). In 1932 he returned to Spain, but was back in Cuba in 1937, and in 1939 he settled in the United States for good. He has authored compositions which incorporate Afro-Cuban folk elements, including "Invocación a Ogún" (1942), "Canción Yorubá" (1942), "La Macumba" (1945), "Poema antillano" (1945), and "Sketch Caribe" (1946).

sanmartín. A well-tempered iron sheet, about 30 or 40 centimeters long and 20 or 25 centimeters wide, curved into a near-closed cylinder. It is held with the left hand and struck with a small iron rod held in the right hand. The *sanmartín* produces two notes. The Iyesá negros usually play the *sanmartín* in their ceremonies. It is of Nigerian origin (Ortiz, *Los instrumentos de la música afrocubana*, 2:206–7). The *sanmartín* is used by street conga groups.

Santa Cruz y Montalvo, María de las Mercedes. Soprano. Born 5 February 1789, Havana; died 31 March 1852, Paris, France. Was the Countess of Merlín, a title she obtained after marrying Cristóbal Antonio, Count of Merlín, with whom she lived in Paris. Santa Cruz y Montalvo studied singing with the Spanish professor Manuel García, father of María Malibrán, with whom she sang on several occasions. She was also acquainted with such outstanding composers as Franz Liszt, Frédéric Chopin, Gioacchino Rossini, and Giacomo Meyerbeer, who praised her voice and style. In 1840 she sang in Havana's concert halls and theaters. She was also an exceptional writer.

Santamaría, Mongo. Percussionist. Born 7 April 1922, Havana. His given name is Ramon. Santamaría was a percussionist from childhood. He went to Mexico in 1948, and then, in 1949, he moved to New York. There, he joined the *charanga* band of flutist Gilberto Valdés, and then worked with Tito Puente, with whom he made several albums of classic Afro-Cuban percussion throughout the 1950s. In 1955 he recorded his first solo album of drums and chants, entitled *Changó*, and in 1958 he joined up with the vibraphonist Cal Tajader, working out of San Francisco. In 1959 Mongo composed his best-known piece, "Afro Blue." His 1962 record "Watermelon Man" was a sensational worldwide hit. He would perform again in Havana, and also in New York, producing both Cuban jazz and also many popular "crossover" recordings. His own bands would, over the years, feature many celebrated musicians, including many Cubans who by then lived in the United States. His records also featured guests such as the pianist Chick Corea, the trumpeter Dizzy Gillespie, and the flute player Hubert Laws. Santamaría was one of the most significant promoters (and purveyors) of the fusion between jazz and Afro-Cuban rhythms. In the 1990s he performed a series of concerts in Cuba.

Tomás Casademunt

Santana, Hilda. Singer of traditional Cuban songs. Born 22 December 1920, Sagua la Grande. Santana began her career in her hometown and then moved to Havana. She participated, on different occasions, in duets with Antonio Machín, Justa García, Ana María García, Luz Mustelier, and Gina del Valle. She sang with Armando Valdespí's orchestra. She belonged to the Tanda de Guaracheros of the National Council for Culture. She now performs solo, in concerts of Cuban traditional music, and on radio and television.

Santana, María de los Angeles. Singer and actress. Born 1914, Havana. Santana has had a remarkable career as an international cabaret artist, with great success in Spain for many years. She has appeared in Mexican, Argentinian, American, and Cuban films and has also sung in operettas. She currently works mostly on television.

Santana, Ramón. Baritone. Born 23 March 1937, Matanzas. Began studying music in Cuba and improved his vocal techniques in Romania. He has sung operas, operettas, and the repertoire of Cuban and universal popular songs. He is a member of the National Lyric Theater and also performs solo recitals all over Cuba.

Santana Reyes, Carmelina. Lyric soprano and professor. Born 18 February 1907, Havana; died 22 November 1981. Studied piano, theory of music, and harmony at the Falcón Conservatory and sang at the Havana Municipal Conservatory under Francisco Fernández Dominicis, who tutored her in singing skills and schooled her in a repertoire of operatic songs. With Luisa Lepa Ves, she learned how to sing German lied, and with Joaquín Nin, Spanish traditional songs. Santana Reyes made her debut as a soloist with the National Opera Company under Gonzalo Roig in Havana in 1938, and subsequently performed at all of Cuba's theaters and cultural societies and also in the United States at private recitals. She sang with the Havana Symphony Orchestra and the Philharmonic Orchestra. She performed in Spanish, French, English, Italian, German, and Portuguese, and also in several dialects. She worked as a teacher of music theory at the Hubert de Blanck Conservatory for a year beginning in 1944, and taught singing, theory, and harmony at the Levy Conservatory from 1948 to 1960, when she retired. In her last years, she taught courses on singing technique.

Santí, Luis. Pianist and director. Born 10 December 1931, Havana. Studied guitar with professor Digna Soler and with José Bolivia, and piano with his mother. His father was a flute player. In 1948 Santí founded an orchestra bearing his name. It played mostly boleros, *sones*, and *guarachas*. Since 1970 he has lived in Miami, Florida, where he continues to play piano in nightclubs with his own group. His songs include the bolero "Con sinceridad," the *son montuno* "Te estoy vigilando," and the *merengue* "El bigote."

Santos, Orestes. Composer, trombone player, conductor. Born (?), Havana; died (?). From the 1940s, Santos played with his own *jazzband* for dances and parties, performed on the radio, and made several records. He settled in the United States many years ago. He wrote a number of boleros, including "Lágrimas de hombre," "Señora," "Amor de media noche," "Burbujas," and "Furia de amor."

Saquito, Ñico. *See* Fernández, Antonio.

Saratoga, Conjunto. Created by the trumpet player Pedro Balseiro in Havana, 1952. Its repertoire included boleros and *guarachas*. It has performed on radio and television, at nightclubs, and in dance halls. The band has also accompanied such remarkable singers as Ñico Membiela, Lino Borges, and Jesús Navarro. It has recorded many LPs.

Sardiñas, Israel. Singer. Born 16 October 1949, Havana. Began his singing career with the group Neosón and later joined Los Yakos. In 1981 Sardiñas became a member of Los Van Van, with which he stayed until 1983, when he moved to New York to work as a soloist. He traveled to Mexico City and then to Miami, where he currently lives. He runs his own band, which performs in Miami nightclubs. He has cut several LPs containing his popular songs.

sartén. An instrument made from two small frying pans fixed to a wooden frame that acts as a support. It hangs from the player's neck and reaches his waist. It is played with two metal rods and produces various tones. The *sartén* is still used in congas as a sonorous and rhythmic instrument.

Saumell, Manuel. Composer. Born 19 April 1818, Havana; died 14 August 1870. Often regarded as the pioneer of Cuban nationalist music. Saumell studied piano with Juan Federico Edelmann and harmony, arranging, counterpoint, and fugue with Maurice Pike, director of an Italian opera company that visited Cuba. He played the organ in several churches in Havana. He interpreted Beethoven's music for trios with Toribio Segura and Enrique González. He organized musical meetings, made orchestrations and arrangements, and taught classes. His active life left little time for composing, and he also suffered from many hardships during the course of his life. He was a great worker, sensitive and extremely demanding of himself. In 1839 he came up with the idea of writing an opera around a Cuban theme, with a plot that would unfold on the island and feature elements of everyday life in Cuba. Indeed, three years after Glinka premiered *Life for the Czar*, which inaugurated musical nationalism in Russia, Saumell had already envisioned a Cuban nationalistic opera (Carpentier, *La música en Cuba*, 103).

Saumell's rhythmic and melodic invention was astonishing. He was the father not only of *contradanza* but also of the *habanera* (first movement, "La amistad"), the *danzón* ("La tedezco"), the *guajira* (second movement, "La Matilde"), the clave song ("La Celestina"), the *criolla* (second movement, "La nené"), and certain variants of Cuban music (second movement, "Recuerdos tristes"). After Saumell's visionary work, all that was left to do was develop his innovations, all of which profoundly affect the history of Cuban nationalist musical movements. His work was the first to portray the true Cuban spirit; he arguably singlehandedly created the particular ambiance, melodic atmosphere, and rhythmic harmony that have come to characterize Cuban music. As a result of Saumell's influences, the diverse aspects of the Cuban spirit were finally established, refined, and recognized, and thanks to his illuminating work, popular musical effects were galvanized into a Cuban musical identity (Carpentier, *La música en Cuba*, 110–11). The catalog of Saumell's compositions includes *Plegaria*, for soprano and organ; *Idilio*, for violin and piano; *Ave María*, for voice and orchestra; *Melopea*, set to a poem by Francisco Blanché; and the *contradanzas* "La niña bonita," "Recuerdos tristes," "Lamentos de amor," "Toma, Tomás," "La territorial," "La Josefina," "La Luisiana," "El somatén," "La Tedezco," "La amistad," "La Matilde," "La Nené," "Los chismes de Guanabacoa," "La dengosa," "La suavecita," "La caridad," "Los ojos de Pepa," and many others.

Sauto Theater. The Matanzas Lyceum sponsored the building of this new theater with funds provided by Ambrosio Sauto. The architect was Daniel Dall'Aglio, an Italian. Construction was finished in 1873 and the theater opened on 26 April with two plays, *A buena hambre no hay pan duro* by Pablo Milanés and *El hombre del mundo* by Ventura de la Vega, accompanied by music. The theater's original name was the Esteban Theater, after Brigadier Pedro Esteban, the governor of Matanazas, but sometime after 6 May 1899, under Spanish control, it was renamed the Sauto. Many significant events in the history of Cuba's musical theater took place there. After a period of renovation, it was reopened on 27 July 1969.

School of Professional Achievement (Escuela de Superación Profesional). Founded by the National Council for Culture in Havana, 1966. It provided technical and cultural training and enabled senior soloists and instrumentalists from popular music bands to upgrade their skills.

Secada, Jon. Singer. Born 1962, Havana. Nephew of Moraima Secada. At the age of nine Jon Secada left for Miami, Florida, with his parents. He studied music at the University of Miami. He began to sing jazz and taught singing at Miami Dade Community College. He briefly sang with the group Miami Sound Machine, backing Gloria Estefan, but left in 1992 to launch his solo career. His specialties are ballads and pop songs with African American influences. He has won many awards, including a Grammy for his excellent CDs, which feature songs such as "Otro día más sin verte," "Angel," "Sentir," and "Si te vas."

Secada, Moraima. Singer. Born 10 September 1930, Santa Clara; died 30 December 1984, Havana. Secada began singing with the all-woman Orquestra Anacaona, then joined the Cuarteto D'Aida, together with Elena Burke, and Omara and Haideé Portuondo. She then joined Memé Solís's quartet. Begining in the 1960s she had a remarkable career as a soloist, singing a repertoire of romantic songs, especially in the *fílin* style, of which she was one of the pioneers. She performed on radio and television and in theaters and also made many records and toured abroad.

Segundo, Compay. *See* Repilado, Francisco.

Segura, Toribio. Composer and violinist. Born (?); died 1860, Havana. Born in Valencia, Spain, and moved to Havana in 1816. Segura was an editor of music. In 1822 he opened a music and dance hall. In 1832 he organized concerts and shows with Antonio Raffelin and promoted musical events in the capital. He composed waltzes and mazurkas.

Seminario de Música. *See* National Institute for Folkloric Research.

Sensación, Orquesta. *Charanga* band created by the guitarist and singer Rolando Valdés in Havana, 1953. It played *cha-cha-chá* and *son*. Abelardo Barroso, Luis

Donald, and Mario Tabenito were the vocalists at the peak of its popularity, and Juan Pablo Miranda was the band's outstanding flutist. It has recorded many LPs and has performed on radio and television. Since 1964, it has been led by Eduardo Egües.

Serrano, Jorge. Clarinetist. Born 1952, Havana. Studied at the National School of Art with Professors Juan J. Junco and Roberto Sánchez. He then improved his technique in Bulgaria and the Soviet Union. Serrano presented concerts in Cuba and abroad. With the pianist Alberto Joya he worked as a duo called Concertante. He has received prizes both in Cuba and the Soviet Union. He has given lectures and offered master classes.

Serret, Dulce María. Pianist and teacher. Born 1898, Santiago de Cuba; died (?). Received her first music lessons from Gustavo Rogel and Ramón Figueroa in her hometown and later on in Havana attended the conservatory directed by Hubert de Blanck. Serret received a grant from the Cuban government to study at a conservatory in Madrid, then spent several years in Paris, where she was taught by Risler. She gave some brilliant concerts in Madrid and Paris. In 1926 she returned to Cuba, where she was a resounding success in a recital at the National Theater. In 1927 she settled in Santiago de Cuba, where she ran the Provincial Conservatory. She has taught many renowned musicians.

Serviá, Estanislao. Double bass player, composer, band director. Born 1895, Matanzas; died 1966, Havana. Serviá came to Havana in 1920 with his brother and Julio Govín, with whom he set up a trio. In 1930 he founded his own *charanga*-style orchestra called Habana, which was active for nearly a decade. He is the author of the *danzones* "El tremendo cumbán," "Chévere más con chévere," "Sota, caballo y rey"; the *son* "Bombolaye"; and some very popular *guarachas*, including "Agua pa' mi."

sexteto. Type of music group that was born around 1920 in Havana to sing a repertoire of *son* songs. It is made up of the following instruments: guitar, *tres*, double bass or *marímbula*, *bongó*, maracas, and claves. In 1927 a trumpet was added, and the configuration became known as a *septeto*.

Shueg, Silvano ("Chori"). Percussionist. Born 6 January 1900, Santiago de Cuba; died April 1974, Havana. A highly popular showman, Shueg began playing in *son* groups in eastern Cuba and arrived in Havana in 1927. He played congas, timbales, and cowbells at cabarets and nightclubs in Marianao Beach. His technique was very original. He appeared in the movies *Un extraño en la escalera* and *La pandilla del soborno*. He composed the *sones* "La choricera" and "Hallaca de maíz." As part of a personal promotional campaign, he painted his nickname, "Chori," on walls, doors, and sidewalks all over Havana. In 1963 he joined the music group Los Tutankamen, which featured older musicians. Every Sunday, he joined in on a music show hosted by the famous musician Sirique, his performance accompanied by peculiar gestures and vocal style.

Siaba, Serbio G. Composer, singer, guitarist. Born 31 July 1915, La Coruña, Spain; died 5 July 1989, Havana. Came to Cuba at the age of six with his parents. Siaba joined the Trío Moya and Los Trovadores del Caney. From 1935 he sang as a troubadour on the radio stations CMQ, CMK, and RHC Cadena Azul. He toured Cuba with the Mexican singer Lorenzo Barcelata. During the 1960s and 1970s he directed his own trio, which later became a group. Among his most notable compositions (interpreted by various popular singers) are "Oyelo bien corazón" and "Perdóname vida"; the *guajiras* "Mi monona" and "Guasabeándome"; and the *guarachas* "Ave María Lola," "El cuarto de Tula," "Pedacito de mi vida," and "Mi manzanita."

Sicardó, Ramona. Pianist and teacher. Born 1878, San Juan, Puerto Rico; died 1945, Havana. At fifteen, Sicardó went to Cuba, formalizing her musical studies at the National Conservatory and in classes from Hubert de Blanck and Ignacio Cervantes. In 1900 she went to Madrid, where she studied at the Royal Conservatory to refine her piano technique. She also took music lessons with Pedrel, Tragó, and Marmontel. She gave concerts in Spain. She returned to Cuba in 1914 and became a teacher.

Sicuoret, Angelina. Pianist and teacher. Born 1880, Havana; died 1945. Sicouret first began to study the piano with her mother and shortly afterward became a pupil of José Fornells and Fernando Arizti. She also took classes with Ruiz Espadero and a few lessons in harmony with Ignacio Cervantes. She gave some memorable concerts in Havana at the beginning of the century, then became a teacher.

Sierra Maestra, Septeto. A nine-piece *son* band formed in 1976 by Juan de Marcos Gonzalez, who directed it until 1996. Sierra Maestra specializes in reviving the traditional *sones* of the 1920s, 1930s, and 1940s.

Silva, Chombo. Saxophone player and violinist. Born 1923, Baracoa; died 199(?), New York. His given name was José. After playing with several orchestras in the eastern Cuba, he moved to Havana, where he joined different big dance bands, including Benny Moré's Banda Gigante. Through the 1950s, he participated in the now historic jam sessions—*descargas*—that were also recorded. He moved to the United States, where he joined the bands of Machito, César Concepción, René Touzet, and Eddie Palmieri, and also played with the bands that recorded for Fania Records. He was a popular member of many salsa and jazz programs and performed on many significant records.

Silva, Electo. Choirmaster and composer. Born 1 November 1930, Santiago de Cuba. At the age of eight, Silva began to study the violin in Haiti, where he had moved with his family. A little later, he was already playing in bands and small orchestras and he also joined several choirs. In 1952 he went to Paris on a scholarship to expand his musical knowledge. He studied education and psychology at the University of Oriente, where he became a professor in those subjects. Since 1957 he has been linked to the promotion of choral groups. After the Revolution, he founded the Santiago Choral Society and the University Choir. He has put to music works by Spanish-speaking poets, which he has also arranged for choir. He has composed several pieces for the piano, violin and piano, and for children, and has also adapted them for choral performance. He has worked with large choirs and received awards for his work.

Silva, Gonzalo de. Havana's first music professor. From 1605, Silva gave organ and singing lessons to the people living in the Cuban capital.

Silveira, Eliseo. Composer and *tres* player. Born (?), Havana; died (?). Silveira's family was extremely poor but he developed a sense for music and became one of the reformists of *son* in the 1930s. As a *tres* player, he joined some of Havana's *son* sextets. His creations developed the line of that time and represented a breakthrough in thematic and harmonic structure. He introduced many original rhythmic expressions into the genre. He is the author of the boleros "Borrando el pasado" and "Antes de partir"; and of the bolero-*sones* "Alma sensible," "La choza de guano," and "Así terminó el amor." He used lines from poetry in his songs.

Simonet, Manolito. Pianist, composer, director. Born 1962, Camagüey. Began in the groups Inspiración, Lágrimas Negras, and Maravillas de Florida in the area of Cuba where he was born. In 1993 Simonet formed his own group, Trabuco, which he dedicated to a new interpretation of *son* with original elements, excellent arrangements, and a magnificent orchestral sound. He wrote "El águila" (which he performed accompanied by a dance that represented the eagle of the title), "Que te váya bonito," and "Y todavía no." His repertoire consists of catchy melodies with strong and often humorous lyrics, interpreted by his lead singer "El Indio." He has toured America and Europe.

Simons, Moisés. Composer, pianist, conductor. Born 24 August 1889, Havana; died 28 June 1945, Madrid. Son of Leandro Simons, a Basque musician. At the age of five, Simons began his musical studies under his father's guidance. When he was nine, he became an organist at the church in the Jesús María District and choirmaster at the Pilar Church. At fifteen, he undertook more rigorous studies with the Professors Tellería, Carnicer, Palau, and Mauri. Later, he worked as a concert pianist and as musical director of lyrical theater companies. As a conductor at the Martí Theater, he was involved in the premiers of many of his own operettas, variety shows, and lyrical comedies. He conducted academic research into Cuba's musical folklore, and his reviews were published in magazines and newspapers. As a dance-band director in the 1930s, he introduced the *danzón* to this type of group. He wrote the score for several movies. He was the chairman of the Cuban Association of Musical Solidarity and the technical director of the Society of Wind Orchestras. Several of his songs are world famous, including the *pregones* "El manisero" and "Chivo que rompe tambó"; the *canción-habanera* "Marta"; and other romances and capriccios.

Sinfonica de La Habana, Orquesta. *See* Havana Symphony Orchestra.

Sinfónica Nacional, Orquesta. *See* National Symphony Orchestra.

Sintesis, Grupo. *See* Alfonso, Carlos.

Sirique. *See* González, Alfredo.

Smith, Federico. Professor and composer. Born 1929, New York; died 1977, Matanzas. A self-taught musician, but did study music for a while when he was in Mexico studying mathematics at the Autonomous University. Smith arrived in Cuba in 1962. He worked as a professor of composition at the music department of the National School of Art. He actively participated in encouraging many young people in a creative musical life. He wrote scores for radio and television and for films. During his last years, he did much valuable work in the province of Matanzas. His compositions were characterized by constant experimentation and innovation. His most memorable works are Music for orchestra; Trio for oboe, guitar, and percussion; and Music for two saxophones and orchestra; as well as the score for the variety show *Oh, la gente!*

(Los) Sobrinos del Juez. Band created in 1967 by a group of Cubans living in New York, led by keyboards player Carlos Oliva. A year later, the musicians moved to Miami and continued playing there. The band has achieved a distinctive sound by combining Cuban dance rhythms with electric rock.

Socarrás, Alberto. Flutist and conductor. Born 18 September 1908, Manzanillo; died 26 August 1987, New York. His mother taught him to play flute, and he also studied at the conservatory in Santiago de Cuba. Along with his entire extended family, he was a member of the Socarrás Family Orchestra. In 1928 Alberto Socarrás went to New York, where he performed with many dance bands. He worked in the

Harlem Opera House and as a studio session musician for Columbia Records. He reportedly recorded the first flute solo in the history of jazz, in 1929. He also worked as an arranger for such greats as Cab Calloway and Miguelito Valdés. As a solo flute player and saxophonist, he played in a variety of jazzbands and Afro-Cuban dance orchestras. He traveled to Europe with the Cuban all-women band Anacaona, and with the variety shows Blackbirds and Black Rhapsody. He directed his own band at the Cubanacán Club and at the Campoamor Theater, in New York. In 1933 he played with the Benny Carter Orchestra. Afterward, he joined the Sam Wooding Orchestra. He performed with the most outstanding jazz and Latin musicians of his time, including Tito Puente and Dizzy Gillespie, and he taught Cuban rhythms.

Solís, Meme. Composer, pianist, director of vocal groups. Born 1943, Mayajigua; died (?). His full given name was José Manuel. Solís began to study the piano when he was six years old, and at fifteen he graduated from the Santa Clara Conservatory. At seventeen he went to Havana to work as a piano accompanist. In 1960 he founded a quartet bearing his name, which broke up nine years later. With Elena Burke, he cohosted a radio show called A solas contigo. His songs include "Otro amanecer," "La distancia," "Traigo mi voz," and "Contigo." He has cut seven LPs. In 1987 he traveled to Madrid, then moved to the United States, where he continues to lead a quartet.

Solís, Ramón. Flutist. Born 1854, Sagua la Grande; died 1891. He began studying music in his hometown with professor Oriol Costa and continued in Madrid, where he received many prizes and much praise. He made tours of Europe and Latin America and was considered the top flutist of his time. His concerts in major U.S. cities were phenomenally successful. He was a friend of José Martí and organized and presented concerts to raise funds for the patriotic cause.

Somavilla, Rafael. Conductor, director, professor. Born 15 January 1899, Matanzas; died 1973. Father of the pianist and composer Rafael Somavilla Jr. Rafael Somavilla studied with Félix Cobarrubias, whose orchestra hired him as a cornet player. In 1918 he founded the Jovellanos Music Band. Then he played trumpet in and directed the Matanzas Band. In 1923 he organized a dance band that was active until the 1960s. He was the director of the José White Musical Academy in Matanzas Province. He wrote music for the bands in which he participated and also for the theater. After the Revolution, he was appointed director of the Amateur Music Movement and became a professor at the Provincial Music School in Matanzas. He directed and conducted the Matanzas Symphony Orchestra.

Somavilla, Rafael, Jr. Pianist, arranger, composer, conductor. Born 1927, Matanzas; died 20 January 1980, Havana. Studied with his father and began work as a pianist in several music groups in Matanzas. During the 1950s, Somavilla Jr. moved to Havana, where he played piano and conducted several orchestras. He was an important arranger of popular music. He composed several works, including a Requiem. He promoted Cuban music in his tours of many countries. He worked at the Cuban Institute of Radio and Television.

son. Vocal, instrumental, and dance genre that is one of the basic forms of popular Cuban music. It retains elements from Spanish and African (Bantú) music, blended in a particularly Cuban style. Its rhythmic variations, refrains, percussion techniques, intonations, and sonorities reveal both original sources. It is danced by couples holding each other close. A wide range of instruments is used to produce the music, including, in its most basic form, a tres or guitar, and sometimes a marímbula, a güiro, and bongó drums. The earliest groups to popularize the son were sextets and septets that featured these instruments. Larger and more complex groups of instruments are often used today. According to Odilio Urfé, the son is the most syncretic sound component of Cuba's national cultural identity. Its origins can be traced back precisely to the end of the nineteenth century in the suburbs of such eastern Cuban cities as Guantánamo, the birthplace of changüí; Baracoa, where, according to Sindo Garay, the Cuban tres originated; Manzanillo, which is famed for its mechanical organs; and Santiago de Cuba, which is well known for its different styles of folk music. The history, characteristics, and social significance have made the Cuban son an extremely popular means of expression, particularly among the poorer sectors of the country. The *son* has also been tremendously popular in the Caribbean, Latin America, Europe, and other parts of the world.

The *son* moved from eastern Cuba to Havana around 1909. It was carried to the capital by soldiers of the Permanent Army, as part of the process of cultural exchange that allowed the rumba to enter the eastern zones. The incorporation of elements of the *son* by *danzón* orchestras followed José Urfé's innovative addition of a *son* motif to the final part of his *danzón* "El bombín de Barreto" in 1910. The legendary Sexteto Habanero, which emerged in 1920, and the Septeto Nacional shortly afterwards, also brought the Cuban *son* great fame. Initially danced in street-level rooms, tenements, and popular dance schools, it was rejected by the bourgeoisie and prohibited by the government on grounds of immorality, but its popularity forced most ballrooms in Havana and other major cities to open their doors to it, and the major record labels released unlimited editions of *son* records. Classical *son* writers such as Bienvenido Julián Gutiérrez, Ignacio Piñeiro, and Arsenio Rodríguez, and musicians like trumpeter Félix Chapottín and the brilliant singer Benny Moré, were key to the progressive development of the *son* and its incorporation into almost all strata of Cuban music. They influenced—and still influence—music in many different parts of the world.

Emilio Grenet characterizes the structure of the *son* as consisting of a repeated refrain of no more than four beats (originally called a *montuno*), sung against a contrasting solo motif of no more than eight beats ("Música cubana," 82). Initially, the groups that performed the *son* were formed by guitar, *tres*, *bongós*, a *botija* or a *marímbula* (and later replaced by a double bass), claves, and maracas; one or more trumpets were added later. The format used today is almost limitless, and there are numerous variations, some with almost independent personalities. Urfé refers to several types of *son*: *son montuno*, *changüí*, *sucu-sucu*, *ñongo*, *regina*, *son de los permanentes*, *bachata oriental*, *son habanero*, *guajira*, *guaracha*, *bolero*, *pregón*, *afro-son*, *son guaguancó*, *mambo*, and *cha-cha-chá*. The Cuban *son* is usually included as part of the *son* complex found in the Caribbean region. Based on an analysis of the essential aspects of the genre, Rosendo Ruiz Jr. and Vicente González Rubiera (Guyún) write: "One of the fundamental features that defines the character of the Cuban *son* is the peculiar distribution of the different timbres of its percussion and its rhythmic and harmonic complex which together create a unique polyrhythm. By examining old *sones*, and also on the basis of aural experience, it can be said that the *son* (the classical form represented by the Sextets and Septets in Havana in the 1920s) breaks down into three clearly defined sections based on the timbre of the percussion and the particular rhythmic-harmonic design. The double bass playing *pizzicato* and the guitarist's typically semi-percussive strumming converts both instruments into percussion sources and adds to the percussion weave executed by the other—true percussion—musicians. A constant pattern executed in *pizzicato* by the double bass establishes the rhythmic-harmonic basis of the *son* in what specialists call an anticipated (syncopated) bass and summarizes the rhythmic and expressive essence of the primitive *son* from eastern Cuba, as played by the so-called *bungas*, small groups featuring a *tres*, a guitar, and singers. While the *tres* plays a melody, the guitar maintains a steady accompanying pattern by means of semi-percussive strumming. Its 2/4 rhythm corresponds, in musical terms, to two groups of four semi-quavers. Playing the guitar in this way requires a distinctive change of emphasis that only those musicians familiar with the genre can master thoroughly. The maracas and the *bongó* drums duplicate the guitar rhythmically. The rhythmic module of the clave presents a two-beat design. In the 2/4 beat, the first beat (strong) is occupied by the so-called Cuban triplet, while the second beat (weak) is formed by quaver rest-quaver-quaver-quaver rest. To sum up, the instrumental complex of the *son* (sextet or septet) shows a constant and contrasting juxtaposition of three rhythmic sections that have an independent dynamic projection. The first line (syncopated) is represented in the anticipated bass; the second includes at the same time the accompanying guitar, the maracas, and the *bongó* drum (the latter, only during the first part of the *son*, because in the refrain the *bongó* drum abandons its constant rhythmic hammering and plays different variations and free rhythmic improvisations). Both sections, mentioned earlier, adapt themselves and submit to the two-beat metric module of the claves" (González Rubiera and Ruiz, "Música popular cubana"). The presence of this Cuban genre is important, and increasingly so around the world, within today's most genuine and valuable musical expressions.

Son 14, Conjunto. Formed in Santiago de Cuba in 1978. It made its debut on 11 November of the same year. The group plays popular music, mainly bolero, *guaracha*, and *son*. Its innovative versions of these styles have contributed to the development of contemporary music. Its first singer was Tiburón ("The Shark") Morales, who, now an old man, is still an outstanding and original *sonero*. They have many LPs and have traveled abroad.

Mo Fini

Sonora Matancera. Sextet created by Valentín Cané in Matanzas, 12 January 1924. Its first name was Tuna Liberal. Its musicians moved to Havana in 1927 and performed in dances at the academies and social clubs and on Radio Progreso shows. The ensemble has played all the popular Cuban dance music styles and have accompanied the most important Cuban and foreign singers. The guitarist Rogelio Martínez became the group's leader in the 1940s. Founding musicians were Ismael Governa (trumpet), Pable Vázquez (double bass), José Manteca Chávez (timbales), Carlos Caíto Díaz (vocalist and maracas), and Valentín Cané (bandleader). Later musicians included Rogelio Martínez (vocalist and guitar), Calixto Leicea and Pedro Knight (trumpets), Angel Yiyo Alfonso (conga), Simón Esquijarrosa and Papaíto Muñoz (timbales), Lino Frías and Javier Vázquez (piano), and Elpidio Vázquez (double bass). More than a hundred vocalists have sung with the band; among them have been Bienvenido Granda, Celio González, Laito Sureda, Raúl Planas, Rodolfo Hoyos, Alberto Pérez Sierra, Jorge Maldonado, Justo Betancourt, Yayo El Indio, Roberto Torres, and Welfo Gutiérrez, as well as Daniel Santos, Celia Cruz, Nelson Pinedo, Mirta Silva, Bobby Capó, Reinaldo Hierrezuelo, Carlos Argentino, Leo Marini, Víctor Piñeiro, Miguelito Valdés, Carmen Delia Dipiní, and Vicentico Valdés. Band members settled in New York in 1960 and have subsequently traveled all over the world and recorded many LPs of their repertoire of Caribbean music. Sonora Matancera has influenced many bands in the United States.

Sosa, Nelo. Singer. Born (?), Guanabacoa. Began singing in groups in Havana, and in the 1940s joined Orquestas Kubavana and Casino. During the 1950s, Sosa set up his own dance band called Colonial. His repertoire consisted of boleros and other Cuban rhythms. In 1981 he moved to the United States.

sostenido. A *contradanza* step, executed by two couples holding each other close. After the fourth beat, or half-figure, the couples remain joined and crossed at the center after a turn, rather than releasing the hands. The dancers maintain that formation, moving only their feet and turning around in a circle for the other four beats or the remaining half-figure (Pichardo, *Diccionario provincial casi razonado de voces cubanas*).

Soto, Arístides. Percussionist. Born 30 June 1930, Güines. One of the most outstanding conga drummers in Cuban music. His famous nickname is "Tata Güines." At the age of twelve, he made his debut playing *bongós* at a dance party, with the group Ases del Ritmo in his hometown. At eighteen, he moved to Havana, where he was unable to find work as a musician and was forced to take different jobs for over four years. During that time, he lived in a poor district called Las Yaguas. From time to time, he was hired as a substitute in some bands. In 1952 he joined the *charanga* Fajardo y Sus Estrellas, with whom he traveled to Venezuela in 1956. In 1957 he went to New York, where he stayed for two years, performing at the Waldorf Astoria and various nightclubs. He returned to Cuba in 1959 and was given a solo slot in the Caribe Cabaret at the Habana Libre Hotel. He performed on the experimental recording *Cuban Jam Session in Miniature* in 1957, with bass player Cachao. In 1960 he recorded with Chico O'Farrill's band. He was also a member of Frank Emilio Flynn's memorable *jazzband*, Los Amigos, making an invaluable contribution as he infused its sound, as Chano Pozo had done earlier, with Cuban rhythms. He has recorded with Jesús Alemány's Cubanismo. He currently directs a percussion group bearing his name.

Soto, Titi. Composer. Born 5 June 1944; died 7 August 1992, Miami, Florida. His given name was Aníbal. In the mid-1960s, Soto settled in Puerto Rico, where he wrote his first songs. Later he moved to New York, where he took different jobs and worked as a dancer in several shows, particularly those promoted by his uncle Julio Gutiérrez. In the late 1980s, he moved to Miami, where he led a busy artistic life. He is the author of "Lo que está pa' ti," "Colgando de un hilito," "San Sarabanda," "Esquina habanera," and other songs in which he combines the modern *son* with pop.

Sotolongo, Oscar. *Bongó* player. Born 11 October 1900, Havana; died 1974. Sotolongo was one of the first *bongó* players in the Cuban capital, because in 1913 he was already playing some rudimentary *bongó* drums he had made himself. In 1920 he was a founding member of Sexteto Habanero. From there, he pursued his own career, directing the Septeto Típico

Cubano, which was associated with the National Council for Culture.

Sotolongo, Ramón ("Longo"). Tenor. Born 1830, Havana; died (?). Sotolongo had become very popular by the middle of the nineteenth century. He wrote several authentically Cuban songs. Sometimes he sang with the second harmony voice behind Mariano Soto.

Strada, Marta. Singer. Born in Havana; died (?). She began her studies singing with professor Mariana Gonitch and also studied guitar. Strada made her debut appearance as a singer at the Habana Libre Hotel in 1963. A year later, she offered her first recital at the Idal concert hall. She has performed on radio and television, in cabarets and nightclubs, and in theaters, and has made several records. A few years ago, she moved to the United States.

Suárez, Caridad. Soprano. Born (?), Jagüey Grande. Studied at the conservatory run by Tina Farelli and Arturo Bovi, and later worked with Alfredo Grazziani. Suárez started singing in the United States while still a student. She made her Cuban debut in 1923, in concerts organized by Ernesto Lecuona. Later, she took part in Cuban operettas and variety shows, some of them premieres. In the 1960s, she moved to the United States.

Suárez, Humberto. Pianist, arranger, composer, conductor. Born 20 November 1920, Havana. Suárez began studying the piano at the age of nine, with his mother, and then was placed with a professor from western Pinar del Río Province, where he lived as a teenager. He performed on the radio as a pianist. After returning to the capital, he took a doctorate in civil law at the University of Havana and practiced as a lawyer. In 1940 he joined the Orquesta Cosmopolita, which he would later conduct. He composed the songs "Ahora," "Yo no sé qué pasa contigo," "Sombras y más sombras," "Atardecer," and, most famous of all, "Con mi corazón te espero." In 1960 he moved to Puerto Rico, where his musical career has continued.

Suárez, Juan José. Guitarist. Born 19 March 1948, Santa Cruz del Sur. Started his music studies in Camagüey and continued them in Havana in 1966, with Isaac Nicola. Also studied arranging with Félix Guerra. Suárez has performed throughout the country. His repertoire includes his adaptations for guitar of popular songs. He currently lives in Colombia.

Suárez, Senén. Guitarist and composer. Born 30 July 1922, Manguito. In his hometown Suárez played with several popular music groups. In 1941 he moved to Havana. In the 1950s his band's songs were heard on radio and television and in nightclubs. During the 1960s, he founded another group, which became very successful for its mix of new musical elements with traditional Cuban rhythms. In 1967 he performed with his group at Expo-67, in Canada. He issued a new record in the late 1990s. His compositions include the boleros "Divina imagen" and "Eres sensacional"; plus "Sandunguéate," "Reina rumba," "Tres temas para guajira son," "Regreso feliz," "Qué sabroseao," and many others.

Sublime, Orquesta. *Charanga* band formed by the flutist Melquiades Fundora in Havana, 1956. It played *danzón*, bolero, and *cha-cha-chá*. It premiered the famous piece "La pachanga," written by Eduardo Davidson. At the peak of its popularity, its vocalists were Marcos Perdomo, Máximo Gómez, and Miguel Agramonte. The group still plays at festivals around Cuba. At present, with new musicians, it is led by the violinist Gerardo Chapellí.

Sucarich, Narciso. Composer and pianist. Born 29 October 1881, Havana; died 1952. When he was very young, Sucarich moved to Santiago de las Vegas, where he was musically very active. For most of his life he was a piano accompanist. For some time, he was a member of Ernesto Lecuona's Company, with whom he traveled to New York and other places. He was a professor at Havana's Municipal Conservatory. He is the author of "La casita cubana," "Mi bohío," "Viene el cabildo arrollando," and a few other pieces.

sucu-sucu. Variation of the *son*, the origins of which stretch back to the nineteenth century on the Isle of Youth. The term *sucu-sucu* describes a dance, a musical form, and the party at which this song and dance is performed. As a musical form, *sucu-sucu* is played in a distinctive style. María Teresa Linares notes of the *sucu-sucu* that its music is similar, in its formal, melodic, instrumental, and harmonic structure, to

that of a *son montuno*. A soloist alternates with the chorus; the two sing the same lines to the accompaniment of the musicians. The *sucu-sucu* is preluded by a soloist's improvisation of either an octo-syllabic quatrain or a country ballad; then comes an introduction in which each instrument joins gradually, after the *tres*. This eight-beat introduction is followed by a choral refrain that alternates continually with the soloist's singing. When the body of the song begins, the *tres* and the guitar both strum a bass part over a tonic, both dominant and subdominant, or in descensions falling toward the tonic. The maracas beat a regular rhythm based on semi-quavers, the drum and *bongós* are allowed free rhythmic schemes, and a *machete* is used against a knife as a scraper to create a regular rhythm pattern. All the while the clave keeps the time. The *sucu-sucu* is danced in groups, and the couples hold each other close. The man puts one arm behind the woman's back and both dancers extend the other arm and clasp hands. The shoulders and hips remain stationary. The *sucu-sucu* is danced as if it were a *son* (Linares, El *sucu-sucu de Isla de Pinos*). In the 1940s Eliseo Grenet based several songs on the *sucu-sucu* style, helping to diffuse this new style all over Cuba and abroad.

Superacion Profesional, Escuela de. *See* School of Professional Achievement.

Sureda, Laíto. Singer. Born 7 May 1914, Cienfuegos; died 7 September 1999, Havana. In 1935 Sureda joined the Cienfuegos Jazz Band as a vocalist. From 1944 he sang with a variety of musicians' groups in Havana, including Kubavana, Ernesto Grenet, Senén Suárez, Sonora Matancera, Orquesta Casino, and Orquesta América. He has made numerous records and toured widely. In the 1990s he worked with his band Sonora and revealed that he was a master of all styles of Cuban music.

T

Tabranes, Baz. Born 10 July 1922, Havana. Composer, guitar player, singer with trios. Tabranes first sang with Penabad and Landa, and later with Landa and Llerena. He studied harmony with Professor Vicente Gonzalez Rubiera ("Guyún"). In 1947 he joined the Trío Taicuba. His song compositions include "No importa si mentí," "Y te perdí," "Cada vez que me acuerdo de ti," "Si digo," and "Y no estás conmigo." An LP with his songs was recently released.

Tacón Theater (Later, the National; currently, the Garcia Lorca). The wealthy Francisco Marty y Torrens, a fishing magnate, aided by the unpopular Captain General Miguel Tacón, originally built this large theater on the Isabel II promenade between San José and San Rafael Streets. Tacón provided slaves and funds for the construction work and the theater opened in 1838 with six carnival dances. Later, a Spanish theater company occupied it. In 1846 it replaced Principal Theater as the home of Italian and French opera composers, and Spanish zarzuela companies. At the beginning of the so-called pseudo-republic period (1902–1959), it was renamed the National, despite the fact that its owners were not Cuban nationals; it had been sold to the Society of the Centro Gallego of Havana (a Spanish society) in 1909. The building that today houses the National Theater was built at that time around the pre-existing theater. In 1962 the theater was nationalized and renamed the García Lorca. Today it is the headquarters of the Cuban opera and ballet companies.

tahona. A kind of tambourine, made from a small barrel, with goatskin covering one end. There were

traditionally groups with the same name, similar to the ancient claves. This drum is used to accompany a type of rumba.

tahona. Variety of rumba. This folk music was originally performed in Santiago de Cuba and later carried to the Alto Songo, La Maya, and Ti Arriba regions. It was introduced into Cuba by the slaves who arrived from Haiti with their owners after the Haitian Revolution. Structurally, it is related to *tumba francesa*, but it also features a mocking singing style performed by a ridiculous character. The *tahona* (or *tajona*) has two main dance rhythms: one slow, for "walking," and the other fast, "de tajona." Today, this music is only performed by folkloric groups working within the Ministry of Culture.

Taicuba, Trío. Baz Tabranes, Alfredo Cataneo, and Héctor Leyva created this trio in Havana in 1947. Its debut performance was on the radio on 15 August 1947, and it has continued performing boleros and *sones* ever since. Taicuba has, more than once, been voted Best Cuban Trio. Heriberto Castro would eventually replace Leyva. Over the years, the trio has toured in Panama, Venezuela, and the United States, and has also given concerts and performed in entertainment centers and on radio and television in Cuba. Its recorded albums reveal a distinctive style that is quite different from the one created by the Mexican trios. It has been imitated by other Cuban groups.

Tamayo, Gustavo. *Güiro* player. Born 5 September 1913, Havana; died (?). Tamayo has been a member of the most popular and superior *charanga* orchestras in Havana. He played in Quinteto de Música Moderna, conducted by Frank Emilio, and also was part of the Los Amigos group. The rhythm he played formed the basis of the *cha-cha-chá* dance style that was developed by Enrique Jorrín.

tambores. *See* Arará drums.

tango-congo. A variety of *canción* that contains rhythmic influences from other genres, particularly the *son*. It was developed in the 1920s within the Cuban *zarzuela* style. The tango-*congo* is a song that characterizes the Negro. "Mamá Inés" (in *Niña Rita* by Lecuona) and "Popopó" (in *Cecilia Valdés* by Roig) are classic examples.

Taño, Tony. Composer and conductor. Born 20 April 1938, Caimito. Started as a trumpet player in a dance band, and later studied harmony with Félix Guerrero, composition with Carlos Fariñas, and conducting with Manuel Duchesne. Taño also studied in Europe. He is an outstanding arranger and composer. He conducted orchestras at the Havana Musical Theater and at the Cuban Institute of Radio and Television. Among his compositions are "Te autorizo para amar," "Sin tu permiso," "Sube un poquito más," and "La batea." He also wrote more elaborate works, including his Preludios. He composed the music for the play *Mi solar and Manuela* and the soundtrack for the film *De tal Pedro tal astilla.*

Tariche, Augusto. Composer. Born 1918, Havana. His *canciones* and boleros, including "Qué noche aquella," "Al encontrarte," and others were widely broadcast during the 1940s.

Tarraza, Juan Bruno. Composer and pianist. Born 1912, Caibarién. Studied trumpet at the age of ten and then moved on to the piano. After working as a composer and pianist, Tarraza traveled extensively around the Americas. In the 1940s he went to live in Mexico, where he has performed in theaters and nightclubs and on radio. He has played in several movies. Among his significant songs are "Alma libre," "Besar," "Penumbra," "Sentir," "Soy tuyo," "Mi corazón," "Eso y más," "Cantar y llorar," "Soy feliz," "Por eso estoy así," "Palabras calladas," and others well known in Latin America. As a piano accompanist, he has worked with the most important Spanish-speaking singers. He has lived outside Cuba for many years.

Tata Güines. *See* Soto, Arístides.

Tejedor, José. Singer. Born 7 August 1922, Havana; died 2 November 1991. Tejedor began his singing career with Luis Oviedo in amateur shows, at parties, and at public performances. In 1959 he recorded his first boleros, which revealed his very distinctive style. From 1962 on, he was backed by the Orquesta Musicuba. He has recorded several LPs.

Tejera, Tony. Composer and guitarist. Born 23 June 1969, Vueltas. Studied at the Havana Municipal Conservatory. Tejera joined *La Corte Suprema del Arte* and has also been a member of the Trío Avileño and Nelo Sosa's band. He has traveled around Latin America with several groups. His main works include "Invierno y Navidad," "Te miro en la copa" (boleros); and "Y no tenía corazón," "Vuela la paloma," and "Filtra un mazo" (*guarachas*).

Téllez, Héctor. Singer. Born 15 August 1945, Santa Clara. Téllez started singing and played the guitar at the age of thirteen, with Trío Venus from Santa Clara. He then joined other trios and moved to Gustavo Rodríguez's quartet, where he was also a soloist. By now living in Havana, he became a member of the Trío Voces de Oro and Meme Solís's quartet. He studied with Francisco García Caturla. He has been a soloist for many years, has recorded several LPs, and has appeared in documentary films. He wrote the songs "Búscame," "Vive," "Me preguntarás," and "Viviré soñando," among others.

Tieles, Cecilio. Pianist. Born 5 August 1942, Havana. Started studying piano when he was seven, with Professor Cesar Perez Sentenat. In 1952 Tieles went to Paris to study with M. Berthelier, J. Benvenutti, and M. Ciampi, and in 1958, to Moscow, with S. Feimberg and L. Roschina. He graduated in 1963 and attended postgraduate courses until 1966. That same year, he was ranked fourth at the Vienna Da Molta Contest in Portugal. In 1969 he won Eighth Prize at the international Margueritte Long–Jacques Thibaud Contest in France. He has given concerts in France, Spain, the Soviet Union, Portugal, Germany, and Czechoslovakia and has recorded in Cuba and abroad. He was a teacher at the National School of Art. He lives in Spain.

Tieles, Evelio. Violinist. Born 8 August 1941, Havana. Started studying violin at the age of seven with his father. In 1952 Tieles went to Paris to study with Jacques Thibaud and René Benedetti. In 1959 he went to the Moscow Conservatory, where he graduated in 1963. Three years later, he finished his postgraduate studies with David and Igor Oistrav. He was a finalist in the Tchaikovsky Contest (Soviet Union) and in the Wieniawsky Contest (Poland). He has performed in Mexico, the Soviet Union, France, Spain, Poland, Romania, and Czechoslovakia. He was a teacher at the National School of Art. He lives in Spain.

Tieles Soler, Evelio. Composer. Born 28 August 1904, Pedro Betancourt; died (?). Father of Cecilio and Evelio Tieles. Evelio Tieles Soler started studying music in his hometown and continued in Matanzas. He played violin and saxophone in several bands. He also studied violin with Jaoquin Molina, Pedro Sanjuán, and Ernesto Xancó. He graduated in dentistry from the University of Havana and combined music with his professional career. He composed a Sonata for viola and piano; Elegy for voice, chorus, and orchestra (from one of Neruda's poems); Concerto for piano and orchestra; and the lyric drama *Yerba hedionda* (with words by Paco Alfonso), as well as works for voice and piano and *danzas* for piano.

timba. In present-day usage, "*timba*" is the name for the contemporary Cuban dance music that has emerged on the island since the late 1980s. It is similar in certain respects to New York and Puerto Rican salsa but also differs in important ways. As opposed to salsa, the roots of which are with the Cuban *conjunto* bands of the 1940s and 1950s and, to a lesser extent, in *bomba* and *plena*, *timba* represents the synthesis of a wider variety of popular and folkloric sources. *Timba* bands draw heavily from international influences (jazz, rock, and funk) and local folklore (rumba, *guaguancó*, *batá* drumming, and the sacred songs of *santería*). The North American drumset is heard in all *timba* bands, further distinguishing the sound from that of *saleros*. Use of synthesized keyboard is also common. Talking to the audience for an extended period over a musical groove is typical as well, as is the inclusion of rapped vocals. Each *timba* band strives for a unique sound distinguishing it from others in the form of characteristic "signature breaks," innovative *montuno* patterns, and other musical elements. *Timba* songs tend to sound more innovative, experimental, and frequently more virtuosic than salsa pieces for this reason. Horn parts are usually fast, at times are bebop-influenced, and stretch to the extreme ranges of all instruments. Bass and percussion patterns are similarly unconventional. *Timba* lyrics generated considerable controversy in Cuba in the 1990s because of their use of vulgar street terminology, and also because they made veiled references to public concerns, including prostitution, crime, and the effects of tourism on the island, which had only rarely been addressed by other musicians. Well-known *timba* artists and bands include NG La Banda, Adalberto Álvarez, Isaac Delgado, Paulito y su Élite, la Charanga Habanera, Bamboleo, and Klimax.

timbal criollo. Made of two drums whose heads are attached to a metal structure on a tripod. They were originally tuned with heat, but today tuning keys are used. They evolved from the tympani and were used in the *charangas* that played the Cuban *danzón* in the late nineteenth and into the twentieth century.

Timor, Leonardo. Trumpet player. Born 18 October 1933, Havana. Having studied music with his father, a well-known orchestra conductor, Timor made his debut with the Hermanos Palau band. Later he joined Orquesta Riverside, where he remained until founding his own band. In 1967 he started playing in Orquesta Cubana de Música Moderna. Later, he played in the orchestra of the Cuban Institute of Radio and Television. He is also a jazz soloist. He has lived in the United States for a number of years.

tingotalango (or tumbadera). A flexible twig, stuck in the ground, that when arched tenses a wire or cord tied to a vegetable (dried palm-tree leaf) or tin sheet. The sheet is fixed to the ground, covering a hole that has been dug at a certain distance from the tensing arch. The musician, who either sits or stands according to the size of the instrument, faces the tensed vertical cord and hits it with a stick; with his other hand he manipulates the tension in the arch and achieves various pitches (León, *Del canto y el tiempo*, 72). The *tingotalango* is of Congo origin.

tiple. Instrument brought to Cuba from Spain and widely used in the *campesino* music of Cuba. It is a type of small *bandurria* (a small Spanish plucked chordophone) with five double strings and a very high-pitched sound. It is also used in other types of Spanish-influenced Latin American music.

Toledo, Armando. Violinist. Born 1950, Holguín. In 1962, Toledo joined the National School of Art in Havana and continued his studied at the Odessa Conservatory with Professor U. N. Porin. His repertoire includes works by classical, romantic, and contemporary composers. He has worked as a teacher at different music schools in Havana and Holguín. He is the author of *Presencia y vigencia de Brindis de Salas* and *José White*. He has conducted research on the violin.

Tomás, Guillermo. Orchestra conductor, teacher, musicologist, composer. Born 10 October 1868, Cienfuegos; died 30 October 1933. His father, Tomás Tomás, initiated him in music. In 1888 Guillermo

Tomás went to New York, where he studied and gained a doctorate in Music. With his wife, Ana Aguado, he organized several events to raise funds for the Cuban War of Independence. In 1899 he founded the Aguado Tomás Vocal Institute, and later, the Police Band, which gave its first concert on 1 September. The concert featured Wagner's Rienzi overture. The band played 188 works during its first year. In 1901 the band played at the Buffalo Pan-American Exhibition and also performed in various cities across the United States. When it returned to Havana, the band was renamed the Havana Municipal Band. On 2 October 1903 Tomás established the O'Farrill School of Music, with the aim of training musicians who could then become part of the band. In 1910 the school was renamed the Havana Municipal School of Music, but it was not opened as such until 19 April 1911, by Gaspar Agüero, the founder-secretary. Tomás organized a series of eight concerts of music from the eighteenth and nineteenth centuries, in a cycle titled Great Epochs in Music. He prepared a first series of four concerts (1905), with music from Germany, Italy, France, and Russia, and a second in 1906, with music from England, Scandinavia, Spain, and the Americas. The orchestra played works by forty-eight composers including the Cubans Laureano Fuentes Matons, Nicolás Ruiz Espadero, Ignacio Cervantes, Gaspar Villate, and Lico Jiménez. Between 1908 and 1909, he organized more concerts around the theme of the Great Tone Poets, which included thirty-nine composers from Bach to Debussy.

Tomás founded the magazine *Bellas Artes* in 1908. Felipe Padrell, Henry T. Fink, and Joaquín Nin all worked for it. A single series of concerts called Orientations of Modern Tonal Art was performed in 1912 and featured music by sixty-nine composers. In 1913 he staged a concert to celebrate Wagner's one-hundredth birthday. It included three songs set to poems by Matilda Wesendonck and sung by Ana Agüado. In 1914 he conducted five concerts in a series called Women and Art, which included the best composers from Italy, Germany, France, the United Kingdom, Belgium, Holland, Cuba, Norway, Spain, and Sweden. Cuba was represented by Cecilia Arizti and forty-four musicians. In 1917 he organized another cycle, as an extension of the Orientations of Modern Tonal Art series, which he called Epochs of Contemporary Symphonic Art. He also organized concerts around such themes as Heroic France and Its Military, Martial, and Patriotic Music (1918) and The Music of the United States in Peace and in War (1919). His great technical knowledge and his admiration for Wagner and Richard Strauss are always evident in his works, which include *Suite Lírica*, *Dos impresiones*, *Solitude*, *Esbozo de mi tierra*, and *Rondó*. He also composed for brass bands, including the *Serenata cubana*, *Rapsodia*, and Cantata for voice, chorus, and band, as well as for piano.

Tomás, Tomás. Composer. Born 1820, Cienfuegos; died 1888. Father of Guillermo Tomás. Tomás Tomás studied piano, harmony, and composition in the United States. Around 1841, he returned to Cuba and established an orchestra in his hometown. From that time, he was exceptionally active on the Cuban music scene. His musical compositions were fundamentally romantic and very Cuban. His *contradanzas* for piano were widely performed in the second half of the nineteenth century.

(Guillermo) Tomás Conservatory. Founded in 1960 in Guanabacoa by the National Council for Culture. Its antecedents are found in other music schools that already existed in that municipality. Many significant Cuban musicians were trained in those schools. Its first director was César Pérez Sentenat.

tonada trinitaria. A rhythm created in Trinidad, in the province of Las Villas; also called *fandango*. It is a mixture of Spanish, African, and probably Latin American music. It has been said that *tonadas*, or *fandangos*, were sung in Trinidad after that island's War of Independence (1868–1878), and that Patricio Gascón was the founder of the genre since he played the African *cuña* drums. *Tonada* groups consist of a lead singer, a mixed-voice chorus, three *cuña* drums, a *quinto*, a bass drum, a spade, and a *güiro*. Augusto Suero observes of the structure of the *tonada trinitaria* that the solo voice begins by singing the *tonada*, or theme, then the percussion instruments join in and continue playing until the end. After a specific amount of time, the chorus answers the *tonada*. The lead soloist enters for a second time, improvising around the theme, and the chorus answers the initial *tonada*. A characteristic of the *tonadas*' themes is that they all start with anacruses of one and two tempos, played to 6/8 or 2/4 rhythms. There are *tonadas* in both major and minor tonalities (Suero, "Tonadas trinitarias"). The *tonada trinitaria*'s themes include patriotism, love, and religion. The groups performing them would go out onto the streets and assemble downtown, where they would engage in their *controversias* contests. This musical tradition is still carried on in Trinidad; today, groups of players and singers are sponsored by the Ministry of Culture.

Torre, Marta de la. Violinist. Born 29 July 1888, Camagüey; died 29 July 1988. Studied at Brussels Conservatory with Professor Thomson and was awarded First Prize in 1909. Torre returned to Cuba and played in the main cities. She later went to the United States and visited several Latin American and European countries. She composed some works for piano and a piece titled *Rapsodia Cubana*.

Torregrosa, Trinidad. Drummer, singer, lute player. Born 28 May 1893, Havana; died 20 April 1977. Torregrosa started working with Fernando Ortiz and was a valuable source of information for researchers of music of African origin. He traveled to Haiti, the Dominican Republic, Jamaica, and the United States. He made records and performed in films. He was a member of the National Folkloric Ensemble of Cuba.

Torres, Dennis. Percussionist. Born 10 October 1962. Torres was the director of Grupo Clave and as a vocalist he has accompanied Alina Izquierdo and Pablo Milanes, among others.

Torres, Doris de la. Singer. Born 18 January 1933, Santa Clara. Torres started singing in the 1950s in her hometown and later moved to Havana, where she joined Felipe Dulzaides's group Los Armónicos. As a soloist, she performed on television and in nightclubs in Havana. During the late 1960s she moved to the United States, where she continued her career. She is a member of the *fílin* movement.

Torres, Juan Pablo. Trombonist, bandleader, instrumentalist. Born 17 August 1946, Puerto Padre. Studied with his father. When Torres was fifteen, he played the tuba (a kind of ophicleide) in the Municipal Band of his hometown. He later took up the trombone and played in several popular music bands. He studied at the National School of Art. In

1967 he entered the Orquesta Cubana de Música Moderna as a trombonist. In 1976 he set up the band Algo Nuevo, which was a vehicle for researching and experimenting with Cuban music. In 1979 he produced the five-LP series entitled Estrellas Areíto, a great Cuban descarga (jam session), that was reissued by the U.K. label World Circuit two decades later. He performed in the Soviet Union, Bulgaria, Romania, Canada, and Spain. He also worked at EGREM records, where he compiled his own works and some arrangements of other sones made by Cuban authors on the records Superson and Con todos los hierros. He has lived in the United States for several years, where he has a full and successful career as a performer and record producer.

Torres, Lourdes. Singer and composer. Born 29 April 1940, Guanabacoa. Torres studied at Havana Municial Conservatory. She started as a lyrical singer in 1953 and later sang in radio shows and theaters. She performed at Ernesto Lecuona's concerts. She was also a soloist with the Cuarteto Anaya and sang in Havana nightclubs. She was a member of the Cuarteto Los Astros, directed by Felo Bergaza, and in 1961 joined the Cuarteto Los Modernistas, where she remains. She has traveled extensively. She has composed many songs, including "Fue así que te olvidé," "Yo sé que esa mujer," "Canción a esa señora," and "Un nuevo sentimiento me sorprende." She has won awards in both national and international festivals.

Torres, Roberto. Singer. Born 10 February 1940, Güines. Started as a singer at Orquesta Swing Casino in his hometown. Afterwards, Torres was a member of Conjunto Universal. In 1959 Torres moved to New York and performed with José Fajardo's band and was a founder member of Orquesta Broadway. He also spent some time as a singer with Sonora Matancera. After turning solo, he had success with records for the SAR label, which he co-owned, and after moving to Miami, on his own Guajiro label. He has produced many LPs of Cuban and Caribbean music with a range of well-known Cuban musicians. In the late 1980s he had a series of hits with a hybrid style called charanga vallenata, which he created from a fusion of Cuban charanga and the Colombian folk style vallenato, which is led by a solo accordion.

Torroella, Antonio ("Papaíto"). Pianist. Born 17 May 1856, Matanzas; died 9 July 1934, Havana. In the early years of the twentieth century, Torroella introduced the piano into the French charanga in Havana. He was one of the most outstanding danzón players in the capital. He composed some danzones, as well as waltzes and danzas. He was the director of a popular charanga that played in Havana then.

Torroella, Juan. Violinist and professor. Born 1874, Matanzas; died 1938, Havana. Began his studies with his father and immediately afterward entered the Liceo de Matanzas, where he began studying violin with Ricardo Diez. In Havana, from 1885, Torroella studied with Anselmo López. In 1893 he went to study at the Madrid Conservatory, where he won First Prize for violin. He later studied with José White in Paris. Over the following years, he gave concerts in France, the United States, and Canada. He returned to Cuba in 1899 and gave a memorable concert at the Sauto Theater in his home city. In 1900 he started teaching in Havana; Diego Bonilla, Virgilio Diago, and Joaquín Molina were among his students. He was a member of the National Academy of Arts and Letters.

Torroella, Orquesta. French charanga created by the pianist Antonio Torroella at the turn of nineteenth century. The original musicians were David Rendón (violin), Faustino Valdés (flute), and Evaristo Romeu (double bass). It is considered to be the first band of this kind ever heard in Havana.

Tosca, Alberto. Composer and trova singer. Born 12 March 1955, Havana. Tosca studied singing, guitar, and piano at the Ignacio Cervantes School. He is the author of many songs that are well known in Cuba and abroad, among them, "Sembrando para ti," "Canción a un viejo trovador," and "Palia." He has performed in Curaçao, Mexico, and in some European countries.

Touzet, René. Pianist and composer. Born 1916, Havana. Touzet started studying piano as a child. In 1930 he created his own orchestra. He worked as a piano accompanist both in Cuba and abroad. He is the author of such canciones and boleros as "No te importe saber," "Tu felicidad," "Parece mentira," "Cuando tú quieras," "Anoche aprendí," "La noche de anoche," "Estuve pensando," "Me contaron de ti," and "Déjame creer en ti." In 1961 he went to live in Mexico City. Several years thereafter he met the jazz bandleader Stan Kenton, who invited him to play on his recording of "El Manicero." He later moved to New York, where he continued working as a pianist and composed many new works.

Travieso, Mario. Tenor. Born 16 April 1942, Agramonte. Studied singing with Mariana de Gonitch. In 1962 Travieso gave his first concert at the Habana Libre Hotel. For three years he worked as a soloist at the Office of Culture in Matanzas and later joined the Cuban National Opera. In 1970 he won First Prize at the National Singing Contest. Nowadays, he sings in concert halls, theaters, and on radio and telelvision.

tres. A traditional Cuban string instrument. It is closely related to the guitar, from which it is derived. The wooden body and neck are strung with three double steel strings, which are tuned in unison— two in a high octave, the other one octave lower, in D minor. It is plucked with a tortoise-shell plectrum. The *tres* is used mainly in *punto guajiro* and *son* groups. According to research conducted by Alberto

Muguercia in Oriente, where the instrument originated, the earliest versions were made from wooden boxes, the neck from a stronger kind of wood, and the strings from waxed fishing-line. Nené Manfugás, a nearly legendary figure, brought the *tres* back from Baracoa and played it in the streets of Santiago in the late nineteenth century.

Trespuentes, José. Professor and composer. Born 1798, Logroño, Spain; died 1862, Havana. In 1830 Trespuentes settled in Havana at the Colegio San Cristóbal as a professor of music, algebra, and geometry. He played the organ at the Havana Cathedral. He was knowledgeable in literature and languages. Beginning in 1844 he was president of the music section at the Liceo de la Habana and director of the music journal *Revista Musical*, in which he published articles on music. He founded two academies for the teaching of harmony, counterpoint, and composition, in 1823 and 1842. He composed several *romanzas*, duets, a Stabat Mater, a mass, and the two operas, *Gonzalo de Córdova* and *Le baccanale di Roma*, among other pieces.

trova. Also known as *trova tradicional* or *vieja trova*. This is the term for a body of Cuban music written primarily by working-class singer-songwriters on the guitar in the late nineteenth and early twentieth centuries. The *trova* movement originated in Santiago, primarily among black and mulatto men. Many of its early protagonists were barbers, tailors, or artisans who gathered together informally in their shops to entertain each other. Though a style of music that developed among performers with little formal training, traditional *trova* demonstrates a surprising degree of influence from international romantic song traditions and opera arias. It is typically sung with two voices in harmony accompanied by a guitar. The tempo of the songs is relatively slow, with some rubato, and the chord progressions tend to be complex, with extended harmonies and frequent modulations. Lyrically, most songs allude to romantic themes, though because performers of the early days of *trova* became involved in the Wars of Independence against Spain, patriotic themes are also not uncommon. José "Pepe" Sánchez (1856–1918) and Sindo Garay (1867–1968) represent two of the earliest protagonists of Santiago's *vieja trova* movement. The *vieja trova* repertoire is that in which the Cuban bolero first emerged, becoming internationally recognized within the space of only a few decades.

trío. A kind of musical group that emerged during the second half of the twentieth century. Its members play *canciones*, boleros, *sones*, and *guarachas*. As the name indicates, it is composed of three members; they play guitar and maracas, or simply guitar.

tumbadora. A drum with a barrel-shaped body, made of staves fixed together by metal hoops, and with a skin on one of its ends. It was formerly tuned using heat; now tuning keys are used. It is placed on a stand between the legs of the player or, if he is moving with a conga procession, is hung from his shoulder by a strap. It is beaten with the hands.

tumba francesa drums. Percussion instruments used by musical and social groups of the same name, to accompany singing and dancing. They were introduced in Cuba toward the end of the eighteenth century by Haitian immigrants who arrived with the families of French colonizers in flight from the Haitian slave revolution. The slaves were considered to be French, which is how the drums earned their name. The drums are called *premier*, or *redoublé*; *second*; *bulá*, or *bebé*; *catá tambora*; and *chachá*, or rattle. They are usually painted. The skins of the drumheads are tuned by means of cords and hook-shaped wedges; some cords are tied to the hoop, from which they descend diagonally and pass below a stick or wedge and again ascend to the drumhead, forming angles. To tighten the cords and tune the drumhead, the wedges are hammered to make them penetrate deeper into the one-piece, cylindrical wooden body. They are beaten with both hands. They are still played in Santiago de Cuba and Guantánamo, in the easternmost region of the country, and it is said that there were formerly *tumbas* in other parts of the

country, too. The dance steps and dance genres associated with *tumba francesa* are the *babú*, the *grasimá*, the *jubá*, and the *masón*. The festivities of the *tumbas francesas* are placed under the protection of virgins or saints; portraits of Cuban patriots are hung on the walls, since some of them would have participated in such events before going to war. The houses of *tumba* players were also used for conspiracy. The *tumba francesa* is traditionally not only a musical phenomenon but a social one as well.

tumbao. Also *marcha*. The term *tumbao* is perhaps best translated as "groove." It refers most often to the basic pulse of a composition, with characteristic aggregate rhythms, pulses, emphases, and syncopations. Rafael Cueto of the Trío Matamoros is said to have developed a *tumbao*—in this case a unique strumming pattern—on the guitar that he used to accompany *sones*. It proved highly influential with later generations of performers. Alternately, *tumbao* can refer to the most typical patterns played on particular instruments, especially the conga drum. *Tumbao* in this sense is the most fundamental rhythm of the instrument that the performer will repeat in endless variation throughout the course of a composition.

Tuzio, Guillermo. Pianist. Born 14 June 1946, Havana. Tuzio started playing at the Peyrellade Conservatory and finished his studies at the Guillermo Tomás and Amadeo Roldán conservatories. He has worked continuously as a piano accompanist and soloist. He has performed on radio and television, as well as in theaters. He has given concerts all around the country and traveled to Russia, Hungary, Czechoslovakia, Bulgaria, Korea, Angola, Argentina, and Spain. He is the composer of several songs and instrumental works. He has recorded three LPs.

U

Ubeda, Manuel. Composer, professor, pianist. Born 1810, Spain; died 1891, Havana. Ubeda settled in Havana during the nineteenth century and taught singing and piano. He was the teacher of José Mauri. He composed vocal music—including an aria that was awarded during the Juegos Florales at the Liceo de la Habana in 1846—and a religious work, a Stabat.

Ulloa, Leopoldo. Composer. Born 21 October 1931, Havana. When he was eight, Ulloa moved with his family to Catalina de Güines. During the 1950s, many leading singers sung his boleros. He wrote "Sùplica," "En el balcòn aquel," "Como nave sin rumbo," "Moriré de amor," and "Por unos ojos morenos." EGREM recently released a compilation album of his greatest boleros. He received awards at the international festival Boleros de Oro, in 1988.

Urbay, José Ramón. Trumpet player and conductor. Born 31 August 1934, Caibarién. Studied with his father, Roberto Urbay. José Ramón Urbay entered the Municipal Band of Caibarién and later played with other dance bands. In 1956 he went to Havana and joined Orquesta Cosmopolita. In 1959 he became a member of the staff band of the Rebel Army, later becoming its conductor. In 1961 he started playing with the orchestra of the Cuban Institute of Radio and Television. He has conducted orchestras for opera and ballet, as well as orchestras in Latin America and Europe.

Urbay, Marcos. Trumpet player. Born 21 October 1928, Caibarién. Father of the pianist Roberto Urbay and brother of the conductor José Ramón Urbay. Marcos Urbay began playing with the Hermanos Farach jazzband in his hometown, then joined the Orquesta Riverside in Havana. For many years he has played trumpet with the National Symphony Orchestra. He teaches at the National School of Art, where he has trained many notable players.

Urbay, Roberto. Pianist. Born 1953, Havana. Urbay began studying piano in 1962 at the García Caturla Conservatory. In 1968 he continued his studies at the National School of Art, and in 1973 won the piano award at the Second National Music Contest, sponsored by the Writers and Artists Union of Cuba. Presently, he is a teacher at the Amadeo Roldán Conservatory.

Urfé, José. Composer, clarinetist, professor, conductor of orchestras and dance bands. Born 6 February 1879, Madruga; died 3 November 1957, Havana. Urfé's sons, Odilio, Orestes, José, and Esteban, were also musicians, and his brother Jesús Urfé was also a clarinetist. In 1894 José Urfé started studying music with Professor Domingo Ramos in his hometown, then a year later, went to Havana where he continued studying, with Hipólito Rodríguez and with Professor Carnicer, who taught him harmony. When he joined the Payret Theater orchestra, he was coached by Pedro Pablo Díaz. In 1902 he was a founding member of Enrique Peña's *orquesta típica*, where he played second clarinet to José Belén Puig. Later, they both left to join Félix González's band. He composed *habaneras* and *criollas*, but is particularly remembered for his *danzones* and religious music. He traveled to Mexico and the United States as a member of theater orchestras. In his works, he incorporated elements of the *son* into the *danzón*, and his contribution influenced the way *danzón* is played today. He gave a new structure to the last trio, a variation which was heard for the first time in his song "El bombín de Barreto" (1910). His most popular *danzones* are "Fefita," "Nena," "El churrero," "El dios chino," "El progreso," and particularly, "El bombín de Barreto" (named for the bowler hat worn by a friend, the musician Julían Barreto).

Urfé, José Esteban. Composer and conductor. Born 1910, Madruga; died 23 December 1979, Havana. A doctor of education, Urfé began his musical studies with his father and other teachers. Although primarily a pianist, he worked mainly as a conductor of theater orchestras, and he also composed choral works, pieces for clarinet and piano, and *danzas*, preludes, and songs for voice and piano. He composed music for ballet and *zarzuela*.

Urfé, Odilio. Musicologist, pianist, professor, dance-hall orchestra leader. Born 18 September 1921, Madruga; died Havana. Son of José Urfé. His father guided him during his early musical studies, and his first job was as a member of the Madruga Music Band. Odilio Urfé later founded a dance band, which he led for many years. He also studied with his mother, Leonor González, and Professor María Josefina Padiñas, who taught him piano. He expanded his knowledge of piano with Professor Luisa María Chartrand at the Havana Municipal Conservatory from 1938 to 1947. For many years, he played piano with several different groups, and in 1931 founded and conducted the Orquesta Ideal. From 1942 to 1950 he was a flutist in Cheo Belén Puig's orchestra; also in 1945 he played piano with the chamber orchestra of the Municipal Conservatory. Encouraged by Leopoldo Stokowski and others, he founded the National Institute for Folkloric Research in a former church, the Saint Paula Church, with other outstanding personalities in Cuban culture at that time. In 1951 he was appointed general coordinator of cultural missions at the Ministry of Education, but he renounced that role in March 1952. On 10 October 1959 he organized and directed the Cuban Folk Festival. In 1960, the General Office of Culture assigned him to work as musical director on the film *Cuba canta*, directed by Julio García Espinosa.

In 1962 Urfé organized and directed the First Cuban Popular Music Festival. All genres and styles that had developed over the previous three centuries were represented at this important event. The second festival took place in 1963. Urfé was the general director of the music division of the National Council for Culture (CNC). In 1966 he was a member of the jury for the Sopot song festival in Poland, and in 1969 was a delegate to the First Pan-African Culture Festival, held in Algiers. He was the organizing secretary of the music section of the Writers and Artists Union of Cuba in 1970; the general secretary for the CNC Cuban Committee at UNESCO; and a delegate, representing Cuba, at the Seventh Assembly and Congress of the Council of International Music, in Moscow in 1971. A member of the UNEAC national board, he also attended the Union of Composers Congress in the German Democratic Republic in 1974 as a representative of the CNC. He participated in UNESCO's Seventh Assembly of the Council of International Music, in the World Week of Music, in Canada, and in the Arabian Conference on Music, held in Iraq in 1975. He also conducted the National Concert Charanga and has delivered countless courses and lectures, in Cuba and abroad. In addition, he was director of the Research Seminar on Cuban Music and has published articles on Cuban music in newspapers and magazines.

Urfé, Orestes. Teacher and double bass player. Born 30 October 1922, Madruga; died 9 March 1990, Havana. After having studied in Cuba with his father José Urfé, in 1974 Orestes Urfé obtained a two-year scholarship to the Berkshire Music Center in the United States, where he was a student of George Edmund Moleux. He later played with the Boston Philharmonic Orchestra. Sergei Koutssevitzky gave him double bass lessons. In a concert to honor his professor, given by the Boston orchestra at the Waldorf Astoria in 1949, Urfé performed a double bass solo. In 1936 he began playing double bass with the Havana Philharmonic Orchestra. In 1961 he joined the Orquesta de Teatro y Danza. He was a teacher at the National School of Music of Cubanacán, was the national adviser for double bass education, and was also a member of the the Ministry of Culture's National Concert Charanga.

Uriola, Ramón. Composer, double bass player, cornetist, dance-band leader. Born 1840, Santiago de Cuba; died (?). In 1855 Uriola was conducting his own *orquesta típica*, which was very popular in Oriente Province. He composed the waltzes "Los campos de Cuba" and "El desengaño," and the overtures *El genio* and *Sinfonía.*

Urquiza, Gilberto. Composer and singer. Born (?), Havana. In 1943 Urquiza went to Mexico to sing in a trio and settled in Mexico City, where he became very successful. Among his most popular songs are "Tonterías," "Engáñame otra vez," "Hola que tal," "Habladurías," "Si me atreviera," and "Humillación." He still lives in Mexico City.

V

Vaillant, Rodulfo. Composer. Born 8 May 1939, Santiago de Cuba. Studied trumpet in his hometown. Vaillant was producer at Radio CMKC and the musical director of Oriente Province. He later worked at the Cuban Institute of Radio and Television. He is the composer of the *sones* "La escoba barrendera," "El lápiz no tiene punta," "El teléfono frío," "Tiene vida limitada," "Malé Malé," "Quién dice que la gorda," "Si te dejé," "Se muere de sed la tía," and some other popular pieces. He is president of the musical branch of the Writers and Artists Union of Cuba in Santiago de Cuba.

Valdés, Abelardito. Composer and leader of a *charanga* band. Born 7 November 1911, Havana; died 9 December 1958. Valdés received his first classes in melody, theory, and flute from José M. Arriete and started his career playing *güiro* with the dance band led by Luis Carrillo, where his father played double bass. He also performed with the *charangas* directed by Tata Pereira and Tata Alfonso and the López-Barroso *charanga*. He played double bass with the band Hermanos Contreras. In 1938 he composed the classic and most famous *danzón*, "Almendra." In 1940 he formed the popular Orquesta Almendra and toured with it in Colombia, the Dominican Republic, and around Latin America. His other compositions include the *danzones* "Horchata," "Salvaje," and "Penicilina."

Valdés, Alfredito. Singer. Born 1908, Havana; died (?). Brother of the ballad singer Vicentico and the Irakere percussionist and vocalist, Oscar, and father of the pianist Alfredo Jr. Alfredito Valdés began his career singing with *son* bands; in 1930 he joined Septeto Nacional, with which he developed a distinctive style. He later played with other popular bands, and moved to the United States, where he was a member of Tito Puente's first band, the Picadilly Boys, on its first record, *Encanto cubano*.

Valdés, Alfredo, Jr. Pianist. Born 31 May 1941, Havana. Son of the singer Alfredito Valdés and the guitarist and singer Ana María Purmuy, who performed with the all-woman band Anacaona. In 1956 Alfredo Jr. moved to New York to live with his father and developed a remarkable career there playing with many salsa bands, beginning with the band his father had formed with Arsenio Rodríguez and then with Machito. In the early 1960s he played piano for Ray Barretto's band. He later worked on successful records with Roberto Torres, Paquito D'Rivera, and many other celebrated musicians. He was a key player on the records made in the late 1990s by Estrellas Caimán.

Valdés, Amadito. Timbales player. Born 14 February 1946, Havana. Son of the famous saxophonist Amado Valdés, who played with the Armando Romeu band at the Tropicana nightclub. Amadito Valdés began his musical studies with his father and subsequently studied percussion with Walfredo de los Reyes. He has been a member of many groups, including Tres Más Uno, Eddy Gaytán, Samuel Téllez, Las Estrellas d'Areito, and the Afro-Cuban All Stars, and has played sessions with many different bands, including the band led by Bebo Valdés. He has played a key role in many important recordings, both in Cuba and abroad, most notably with the *Buena Vista Social Club*, which won a Grammy award in 1998, with the Afro-Cuban All Stars, and with the touring band led by bass player Cachaito.

Valdés, Bebo. Composer, arranger, pianist, bandleader. Born 9 October 1918, Quivicán. Father of the pianist Chucho and the singer Mayra. Bebo Valdés studied with Moraima González in his hometown. In Havana, he studied harmony and composition with Oscar M. Boufartique. In the 1940s he played with bands led by Ulacia, García Curbelo, and Julio Cuevas, and with Armando Romeu's band at the Tropicana nightclub. He recorded several LPs with Afro-Cuban jazzbands. In 1952 he founded his own Orquesta Sabor, which created the short-lived *batanga* dance style, a variation on the mambo. One of his singers was Benny Moré, who later left to found his own band. In 1960 Valdés traveled to Mexico City and then to the United States, and later went to Spain with the Havana Cuban Boys, eventually settling permanently in Sweden in 1963. He composed the mambos "Rareza del siglo" (for Romeu), "Infierno," and "Wempa." In 1994, after a long silence, he recorded the LP *Bebo Rides Again*,

under the direction of Paquito D'Rivera and featuring an ad hoc group of important Cuban musicians living in the United States. He subsequently recorded with a group that included his son Chucho, once again directed by D'Rivera. Bebo Valdés is considered one of the most prolific musicians to emerge from Cuba.

Valdés, Carlos ("Patato"). Percussionist. Born 4 November 1926, Havana. Started his career playing rumba in Havana's neighborhood of Los Sitios. Valdés studied *marímbula* and *tres* guitar, but in the early 1940s he played congas with Conjunto Kuvabana, later joining Conjunto Casino. He settled in New York in 1954, and in 1959 recorded the first of many LPs with flute player Herbie Mann. He would subsequently record with the likes of Machito, Mongo Santamaría, the Fania All Stars, Tito Puente, Machito's Afro-Cubans, Johnny Pacheco, Cal Tjader, Dizzy Gillespie, and many others. He has made a notable career as a conga player who has a distinctive, melodic style, and he has made many lasting recordings of Afro-Cuban music.

Tomás Casademunt

Valdés, Carmen. Professor and musical activist. Born 17 April 1915, Havana; died 1987. Studied piano with Ramona Sicardó and Alberto Falcón. Studied theory at the Havana Municipal Conservatory. Valdés was devoted to teaching and to the promotion of Cuban music on radio and television and in various periodicals. She has taught music at all educational levels. She wrote articles for music education and was a professor at the School for Art Instructors, since its founding in 1961. She was deputy director of music at the National School of Art.

Valdés, Ester. Soprano. Born 15 September 1927, Havana. Received singing lessons from Mariana de Gonitch and made her debut at the Corte Suprema del Arte, performing lyrical Cuban songs as a soloist. Valdés sang with the National Concert Band (formerly the Havana Municipal Band), conducted by Gonzalo Roig. She has performed in many countries. She sang the lead role in Roig's *Cecilia Valdés* at the Opera Theater in Leipzig. She is currently a member of the National Lyric Theater and performs on radio, television, and in theaters all over Cuba.

Valdés, Felipe. Trumpet player, composer, orchestra leader. Born in the second half of the nineteenth century in Bolondrón; died (?). Valdés founded the *orquesta típica* that bore his name in 1899, and it became very popular with Havana's dancers. He composed the *danzones* "La africana," "Lamentos," "Yeyé Olube," and others.

Valdés, Gilberto. Composer and bandleader. Born 21 May 1905, Jovellanos; died 1971, New York. Valdés was a student of Pedro Sanjuán. He settled in Havana in his early youth and would introduce African music into the symphonic style. In 1937 he gave a series of concerts of his own music based on Afro-Cuban elements. He performed with Rita Montaner at Havana's Municipal Amphitheater. He was musical director of Katherine Dunham's Afro-American Ballet. He led many bands in Cuba. Among his main pieces are "Rumba abierta," "Evocación negra," "Likó-ta-irube," "Baró," "Sangre africana," "Danza de los braceros," "El botellero" (*pregón*), "Yo vengo de Jovellanos," "Tambó," "Bembé," and the lullaby "Ogguere." He incorporated Congolese, Yoruba, and Arará percussion instruments into his music.

Valdés, Jesús ("Chucho"). Pianist, composer, instrumentalist, organist, bandleader. Born 9 October

Mo Fini

1941, Quivicán. Jesús Valdés was taught to play piano by his father, Bebo. At the age of nine, he started formal music training with Angela Quintana at the Havana Municipal Conservatory, and later studied with Zenaida Romeu and Rosario Franco. Before he was twenty years old, he was a masterful pianist. He gave some piano concerts and then played with jazzbands. In 1963, with Paquito D'Rivera and Carlos Emilio Morales, he founded the band at the Havana Musical Theater, which performed innovative works. In 1967 he joined Orquesta Cubana de Música Moderna. With the key soloists from that group, he founded Irakere in 1973. He wove new expressive elements drawn from classical, rock, and jazz music into Cuba's traditional music, creating a unique sound. He is internationally acknowledged as one of the four greatest jazz pianists in the world. His compositions include "Mercy cha," "Niña," "Por la libre," the danzón "Valle Picadura," Prelude for piano, Misa negra, Alamar, and many others. His main contribution to Cuban music is the original instrumentation of his popular pieces. He has toured in many countries, received two Grammy awards, and made many records, including solo works.

Valdés, Marta. Composer, guitarist, singer. Born 6 July 1934, Havana. Valdés studied philosophy and letters at the University of Havana. She received her musical education from Francisqueta Vallalta, Guyún, and Leopoldina Nuñez. She studied harmony and composition with Harold Gramatges. She has sung on radio and television and at cabarets. She has written music for the plays El perro del hortelano, Pasado a la criolla, El alma buena de Se-Shuan, El becerro de oro, and La casa de Bernarda Alba, and for such films as Lucía and Desarraigo. She was deputy president of the Society of Cuban Songwriters. She has written about popular music. At present, she is the music adviser

to the Theater Studies Group. She has written many well-known songs, including "En la imaginación," "Tú dominas," "No es preciso," "Tú no sospechas," "Si vuelves," "Hay mil formas," "Toma esta flor," "Canción de la Plaza Vieja," "Llora," "Canción difícil," "Aida," "Y con tus palabras," "Deja que siga sola," "Tengo," and "José Jacinto."

Valdés, Merceditas. Singer of folk and popular music. Born 24 September 1928, Havana; died 13 June 1996. Began her career at Corte Suprema del Arte, then began to perform mostly works from the Afro-Cuban repertoire. In 1951 Valdés performed in Rapsodia negra, directed by Enrique González Mántici at Radio CMQ. She traveled abroad with Ernesto Lecuona's Company and with the Zunzún Dan Baé show. She was subsequently directed by Obdulio Morales on Radio Cadenas Suaritos's Sunday show. She served as the vocalist for Fernando Ortiz's lectures about African music. She recorded many LPs and often performed on radio and television. She belonged to the artistic staff of the Cuban Institute of Radio and Television. She performed with the Los Amigos band and also gave many solo recitals.

Valdés, Miguelito. Singer. Born 16 September 1912, Havana; died 9 November 1978, Bogotá, Colombia. Started his career with a youthful sextet, playing guitar, tres, double bass, maracas, and singing vocals. Valdés then moved into Sexteto Jóvenes del Cayo as lead singer. Later, he performed with the orquestas típicaos of Ismael Díaz, and with the bands Habana and Gris. In 1933 he joined María Teresa Vera's Sexteto Occidente. The following year, he went to Panama with a Cuban orchestra and performed there in theaters and cabarets for three years. Back in Cuba, he joined Orquesta Hermanos Castro and stayed with them until 1936. In that same year, with a group of musicians, he formed the band Orquesta Casino de la Playa, which would become very popular for its interpretations of Cuban rhythms and songs, including a version of Arsenio Rodríguez's "Bruca Maningá" and some of Valdés's own compositions. Almost all of his songs were congas and bolero-*sones*. They include: "Ya no alumbra," "Negro," "Dolor cobarde," and "Qué tal te va." In 1940 he moved to New York and joined Xavier Cugat's orchestra at the Waldorf Astoria, introducing his conga style to that city. He became very popular and within a few years founded his own band, with whom he toured the world. He was very famous for many years. He recorded many LPs and sang in several films. He was known as "Míster Babalú."

Valdés, Oscar. Percussionist and vocalist. Born 12 November 1937, Havana. Born into a family of musicians: his father Oscar, a percussionist; his uncles, Marcelino, percussionist, and Alfredo and Vicente, both vocalists; and his son, Oscar, a percussionist. Oscar Valdés Sr. has performed with the CMQ radio and the Cuban Institute of Radio and Television orchestras, with the Banda Gigante de Benny Moré, and with the Orquesta Cubana de Música Moderna. He was Irakere's percussionist and vocalist throughout the golden era of that band and performed with them in many countries. He currently plays with the Diákara Band.

Valdés, Vicentico. Singer. Born 10 January 1921, Havana; died 25 June 1995, New York. In 1930 Valdés joined Cheo Belén Puig's orchestra. Later, he performed with Septeto Nacional, in which his brother Alfredito was lead vocalist. Years later, he traveled to Mexico and New York. In 1947 he joined the band of pianist Noro Morales. In 1953 he settled in New York and was contracted to sing with Tito Puente's Orchestra. He would gain a great reputation as a singer. He is widely acknowledged as one of the most popular Latin vocalists, due to his personal style, which is especially evident in the boleros that contributed to his reputation. His repertoire included mainly Cuban pieces. His recordings with the most outstanding bands and most brilliant arrangers have been heard around the world.

Valdés Arnau, Roberto. Violinist and conductor. Born 23 July 1919, Havana; died 15 December 1974.

Played with the Havana Classical Quartet, the Chamber Orchestra, the Philharmonic Orchestra, and with the orchestra of the National Institute of Music. Valdés Arnau later conducted the resident orchestras of the radio stations Mil Diez and CMQ and the staff band of the Rebel Army. Finally, he directed the orchestra of the Cuban Institute of Radio and Television. He represented Cuba in many international festivals.

Valdés-Brito, Alfredo. Clarinetist. Born (?), Havana. Valdés-Brito studied at the Amadeo Roldán Conservatory and graduated from the Higher School of Music in Berlin. In 1970 he joined the National Symphony Orchestra. He has performed as a soloist and has given concerts in many European cities.

Valdés Costa, Mario. Composer. Born 11 October 1898, Isabela de Sagua; died 1930, New York. Studied music in Cuba and broadened his knowledge in the United States. Valdés Costa was a promising talent who died very young. He left behind the compositions *Rapsodia cubana*, *Suite cubana*, Symphonic prelude, Quartet, *Capricho cubano*, *Añoranzas*, and Suite for flute, violin, and violoncello.

Valdés Miranda, Concha. Composer. Born (?), Havana. Valdés Miranda moved to Miami in the 1960s and suddenly became popular for her interpretations of aggressive and daring songs, which have become her repertoire. Her compositions include "Déjame ser," "La mitad," "Las cosas buenas de la vida," "Tápame contigo," and "Orgasmo."

Valdespí, Armando. Composer and pianist. Born (?), Havana; died 1967, Puerto Rico. Studied at the Havana Municipal Conservatory. In 1930 Valdespí formed his own orchestra and wrote and recorded many boleros sung by some of the most celebrated Cuban and Puerto Rican vocalists. He lived for many years in New York and later settled in Puerto Rico. He is the author of the boleros "Sola y triste," "Alma de mujer," "No tienes corazón," "Como una rosa," "Quiero saber," "Fuiste mía," "Soñé contigo," "Sólo por ti," and "Duerme corazón."

Valdés Rodríguez, Francisco. Composer and guitarist. Born 1838, Havana; died (?). During the 1860s, Valdéz Rodríguez formed a *bufo* company in Havana. He possessed a warbling falsetto voice and alternated lyrics with music in a very typical Cuban style of vocalizing. He composed *canciones*, *contradanzas*, and *guarachas*, the most outstanding of which are "La joven moribunda" (*canción*); "Guataqueando" (*contradanza*); "El negro bueno," "Los ñañigos," "La negra tomasa," and "El ferrocarril" (*guarachas*); and "A los frijoles," whose lyrics were written by the *trova* singer Ramitos, who popularized it. He was also a satirical journalist.

Valdés Torres, Armando. Composer and pianist. Born 3 March 1898, Havana; died 1 May 1953. Started his piano career playing in a series of Havana-based bands. When he joined Septeto Collazo, led by Fernando Collazo, in the 1920s, Valdés Torres became the first pianist to perform in a *son* band. He was later the piano accompanist with Septeto Cuba on its tour of Spain. In the 1930s, he formed the Orquesta Gris. He wrote many popular *danzones*, including "El sinsonte gris," "Eskimo Pie," "Sentimental," and "Ritmo suave."

Valenzuela, Orquesta. Created by the trombonist and composer Raimundo Valenzuela in Havana, 1877. Valenzuela used to play with Juan de Dios Alfonso's orchestra, but after Alfonso's death, he became the leader and renamed the group after himself. It was the most popular *típico* orchestra of its day. At various times, its musicians have included Félix de la Cruz, Enrique Pastor, Tomás Olivera, Manuel Hernández, Ramón Quirós, Julián Vargas, Dionisio Romaguera and his brother, the outstanding cornetist Pablo Valenzuela. Pablo became the leader when Raimundo died in 1905. In 1926 Pablo died and the orchestra split up. Since the orchestra was in great demand at many dance halls, Valenzuela operated three or more groups to perform in different places at the same time.

Valenzuela, Pablo. Cornetist and orchestra leader. Born 2 March 1859, San Antonio de los Baños; died 25 December 1926, Havana. Brother of Raimundo Valenzuela. Pablo Valenzuela received his first music lessons from his father, Lucas Valenzuela. When he was young, he was taken to Havana to play the cornet with Manuel Espinosa's orchestra, and his original sound made him very popular. He subsequently joined his brother's *orquesta típica*. When Raimundo died in 1905, Pablo became the leader of the orchestra, where he stayed for over twenty years. He composed *danzas* and *danzones*.

Valenzuela, Raimundo. Dance-band leader, composer, instrumentalist, trombone player. Born 23 January 1848, San Antonio de los Baños; died 27 April 1905, Havana. His first music teacher was his father, Lucas Valenzuela. As well as the trombone, Raimundo Valenzuela also learned to play viola, piano, and percussion. He played trombone during the long operatic seasons in Havana. He composed *canciones*, *contradanzas*, *guarachas*, rumbas, and *danzones*, and some classical pieces, religious pieces, and chamber music. He also composed some zarzuela, including *La mulata María*. He adapted to the *danzón* style some passages from Italian operas, such as *Rigoletto*, *Tosca*, and *Madame Butterfly*. In 1864 he joined the orchestra of Juan Dios Alfonso and became its leader when Alfonso died. From then on, the band was called the Orquesta Típica de Raimundo Valenzuela, and it was at the forefront of popular Cuban music in the late nineteenth and into the twentieth century. He was personally involved with and contributed funds for the War of Independence from Spain.

Valera, Roberto. Composer. Born 21 December 1938, Havana. Studied at the Havana Municipal Conservatory with Leo Brouwer, José Ardévol, and Edgardo Martín. Valera earned a doctorate in Education at the University of Havana. He worked in the music department at the Cuban Institute for Movie-Making, Art, and Industry. In 1965 he went to Poland on a scholarship granted by the Revolutionary government and studied for two years at the Higher School of Music in Warsaw. On returning to Cuba, he was appointed deputy director at the García Caturla Conservatory. In 1968 he became head of harmony and contemporary technique at the National School of Art. He has composed *danzas* for orchestras, chamber music, and pieces for voice and chorus, such as *Devenir*, *Conjuro*, and *Jitanjáfora*.

Valiente, Ángel. Singer of *punto guajiro* and *décima* songs. Born 1916, San Antonio de los Baños; died 1987. Valiente became popular on radio and television as an improviser of *punto* songs. He had an extensive knowledge of versification and a personal style of harmonizing. He influenced many other Cuban *décima* singers.

Valiente, Consejo. Percussionist and orchestra leader. Born 16 April 1899, Santiago de Cuba; died 6 June 1987, Mexico City. Known as "Acerina." Valiente learned to play percussion instruments, mainly timbales, as a child. In 1913 he traveled to Mexico and performed there in *danzón* orchestras. He formed his own *orquesta típica* in 1948, and performed on radio and television, and in films and cabarets. He is the composer of the *danzones* "La bruja," "El arete de Mariles," and "A mi porros." He appeared in several movies.

Valladares, José. Composer and singer. Born 15 March 1947, Havana. In 1970 Valladares joined the band Los Reyes and was later the vocalist with Franco Lagana's band. He turned solo in 1974. He composed the songs "La casa ni yo," "Amor de miedo," "Me pides demasiado," "Prefiero ser algún recuerdo," and the *vallenato* "La parranda." He has received awards for his songs at many competitions and festivals.

Vallalta, Francisqueta. Professor and guitarist. Born (?), Havana; died (?). Daughter of Professor José Vallalta. Francisqueta Vallalta gave guitar concerts in theaters and dance halls during the 1920s, 1930s, and 1940s, and also led guitar bands. She also gave guitar lessons at different centers around Cuba.

Vallalta, José. Guitarist and professor. Born in Spain; died (?), Havana. Vallalta was a pupil of Francisco Tárrega and he gave many concerts in Spain. In 1901 he visited Cuba and began to work as a music teacher. He was a mentor for his daughter, Francisqueta, who continued her father's educational work. In Havana, José performed in different concerts.

Valle, Manolo del. Singer. Born 7 May 1947, Manzanillo. Vocalist with the Orquesta Original de Manzanillo. In the late 1960s, Valle turned solo and was popular for his romantic boleros. He has performed on radio, television, and in theaters and nightclubs, and has recorded many LPs of boleros by different composers.

Valle, Moises ("Yumurí"). Singer. Born 29 July 1964. Valle studied economics at the University of Havana. He has sung with Imagen Latina and Orquesta Revé, and is currently the director and singer of his own band called Yumurí y Sus Hermanos.

Valle, Orlando. Flutist. Born 1966, Havana. Known as Maraca. Valle studied in the Manuel Saumell and Amadeo Roldán conservatories and at the Higher Institute of Art. He was a member of the groups led by Bobby Carcassés and Emiliano Salvador in the late 1980s, and played in Irakere from 1988 to 1994. He currently directs his own group, Otra Visión, a Cuban *jazzband* incorporating elements of jazz-fusion, and also works on projects with other Cubans, including Jésus Alemany's Cubanismo, Frank Emilio, Tata Güines, Chucho Valdés, the Puerto Rican saxophonist David Sanchez, and his French wife, the flutist Céline Chauveau. He has given many significant performances in Cuba and abroad.

Valle, Vilma. Singer. Born 16 September 192, Matanzas; died 29 March 1998, Havana. In 1940 Valle made her debut at La Corte Suprema del Arte and later performed at the Tropicana. She traveled to Mexico, where she performed frequently, as well as to many other Latin American countries. She returned to Cuba in the 1950s and performed at the Pico Blanco in the St. John's Hotel, accompanied by Enriqueta Almanza on piano. She moved to New York in 1959 and worked there for a year, then in 1960 went back to Cuba and continued singing in Havana nightclubs. She also appeared on radio and television and in theaters.

Vallejo, Orlando. Singer. Born 30 April 1919, Arroyo Naranjo; died 20 January 1981, Miami. Vallejo grew up in Santiago de las Vegas and began his career singing tangos at the Popular Theater and as a vocalist with the Orquesta Ritmo Alegre. He later joined Septeto Progreso, and the orchestras Paulín, Quintana Melody Boys, and Havana Casino, and the *conjuntos* Casino and Kuvavana. He became a soloist, performing on radio and television and in nightclubs, and recorded many LPs. He is acknowledged as one of the greatest Cuban bolero singers. He moved to Miami in 1965 and continued singing and recording popular boleros.

Valoy, Félix. *See* Baloy, Felix.

Vandertgucht, José. Violinist. Born at the turn of the eighteenth century in Belgium. Vandertgucht came to Cuba with his father Juan and his brother Francisco, both violinists. Years later, his father and brother went back to Belgium and José settled in Havana. He was director of the Musical Association for Mutual Aid in Havana. He performed in orchestral concerts in Havana in the 1850s, and was a member of the Classical Music Society. He was considered an outstanding violinist.

Van Van, Orquesta. Formed by the composer and double bass player Juan Formell in 1969. It plays a variant of *son* which Formell called *songo*. Its rhythm is based on a mixture of *tumbaos*, *son* with jazz elements, and some influences from rock and Caribbean music. The original members were Orlando Canto (flute); Jesus Linares, Fernando Leyva and Gerardo Miro (violins); Cesar Pedroso (piano); Juan Formell (double bass); José L. Quintana (timbales); Yulo Cardenas (conga); Julio Noroña (*güiro*); and Lele Raspal (vocalist). Later members included José Luis Cortés (flute); Edmundo Pina, Hugo Moregón, and Lázaro Gonzáles (trombones); Samuel Formell (timbales); Manuel Labarrera (conga); and Pedro Calvo, Lazaro Morua, Israel Sardiñas, and Mario Valdes (vocalists). The group's successful career has made Van Van one of the most important dance bands in the history of Cuban music.

Varela, Carlos. Born 11 April 1963, Havana. Played percussion and guitar in rock bands until 1980, when he joined the *nueva trova* movement. Since a 1986 tour in Spain with Silvio Rodríguez, Varela has gained an international reputation. In 1967 he founded his own group. His song compositions include "Guillermo Tell," "Monedas al aire," "Como los peces," "Jalisco Park," "Muros," "Memorias," and "Boulevard." His songs reflect everyday life in a critical way.

Varona, Calixto. Clarinetist and composer. Born beginning of the nineteenth century, Camagüey; died at the turn of the nineteenth century in Santiago de Cuba. Varona settled in Santiago. He was a notable clarinetist and he also composed religious and secular music. His works include *Salve Regina* for piano and voice; *Adriano waltz*; *A Cuba*, a *canción*; *Danza* for piano; and March for a brass band.

Varona, Jorge. Trumpet player. Born 3 July 1932, Camagüey; died 1989, Havana. Varona played with many jazz and dance bands, including Benny Moré's Banda Gigante and the Orquesta Cubana de Música Moderna, and was a founding member of Irakere. He developed a perfect trumpet technique and a very sensitive playing style, and his many recordings are memorable.

Varona-Puig, Duo. Duo formed in Sancti Spiritus in the 1930s by the composer and guitarist Alfredo Varona and Juan Manuel Puig (lead vocalist). Varona also performed with Rafael Teofilito Gómez and Miguel Companioni. The duo had a repertoire of *trova* songs. They split up in 1972.

Vázquez, Javier. Pianist, arranger, composer. Born 8 April 1936, Havana. Son of Pablo Vázquez, double bass player with La Sonora Matancera, and brother of Elpidio Vázquez. Javier Vásquez studied at the Municipal Conservatory. He played the piano with Orquesta Jóvenes del Cayo and Orquesta Saratoga. In 1964 he moved to the United States, where he made several important recordings and performed with different salsa bands. In 1976 he joined La Sonora Matancera. He is a leading instrumentalist and arranger, and author of "Estoy loco," "Psicología," the *merengue* "Toitico tuyo," and of boleros and *guarachas*.

Vázquez Millares, Ángel. Professor and musicographer. Born 4 October 1937, Havana. Has a bachelor's degree in Spanish language and literature from the School of Arts and Letters at the University of Havana. Vázquez began his musical training with Edgardo Martin and is a self-taught musicographist. He was director of music for the province at the

Havana Delegation of the National Council for Culture. He writes music reviews for the concert programs of the National Symphony Orchestra, and he writes scripts for and directs radio and television music shows.

Vega, Aurelio de la. Composer. Born 28 November 1925, Havana. Began his music studies in Havana and finished them with Ernst Toch in Los Angeles, California, in the late 1940s. Vega also studied composition with Harold Gramatges. During the 1950s, the Havana Philharmonic String Orchestra played some of his works, including Two movements for a string orchestra (1945), Quartet no. 1, Tríptico for a string orchestra, and *Leyenda del Ariel Criollo* for cello and piano (1953). His compositions were based on different styles of musical structure: dodecaphonic atonalism, serialism, and, latterly, electronic music. He moved to New York in 1959 and has continued producing music. His pieces have been played at concerts in many cities. He has been a professor at different California conservatories.

Vega, Justo. *Punto guajiro* singer. Born 6 August 1908, San Antonio de Cabezas; died 13 January 1993, Havana. Vega moved to Havana when he was fifteen; he began his career in 1934 on the radio with the quartet Trovadores Cubanos, alongside Pedro Guerra, Alejandro Aguilar, and Bernardo Guerra. For many years, he sang in the style of *décima guajira* and performed on the Sunday television show *Palmas y Cañas*. He participated in music festivals in Cuba and Latin America and appeared in documentaries about Cuban culture.

Vega, Pedro. Composer and sculptor. Born 1920, Havana. A member of the 1950s artistic movement, Vega worked with the publishing house Musicabana, and later founded a record printing company. He is author of the boleros "Hoy como ayer," "Herido de sombras," and "Bellos recuerdos," among others.

Vega Caso, Rafael. Composer and professor. Born 1901, Gibara; died (?). Studied with Conrado del Campo in Madrid. Vega Caso composed symphonic poems, a cantata dedicated to the victory at Playa Girón (Bay of Pigs), and some traditional pieces. He later switched to teaching and musical research.

Velázquez, Miguel. Born at the beginning of the sixteenth century in Santiago de Cuba; died (?). He is the first notable musician born on the island. His mother was an indigenous islander and his father a relative of Diego Velázquez. Miguel Velázquez studied music in Seville and Alcalá de Henares, while training for the seminary. He returned to Cuba and was placed in charge of the ruling council in Santiago de Cuba. He played the organ and conducted songs in the style of plain-song. He was a professor of music and of grammar.

Veloz, Ramón. Singer of *guajira* and *son montuno*. Born 16 August 1927, Havana; died 16 August 1986. Veloz began his career in 1950, performing mainly on radio shows. He premiered many pieces from the indigenous Cuban repertoire, and also performed on television, mainly on the Sunday *Palmas y Cañas* show. He recorded LPs accompanied by different *guajira* and *son* bands. He is the father of the singer and actor with the same name.

Vera, Alberto. *See* Piloto y Vera.

Vera, María Teresa. Singer, guitarist, composer. Born 6 February 1895, Guanajay; died 17 December 1965, Havana. One of the most important singers in the history of the Cuban *trova* song style. Vera's first guitar professor was the cigar roller José Díaz. At age fifteen, she performed in a musical homage to Arquímides Pous at Havana's Politeama Grande Theater, and around the same time, set up a duo with Rafael Zequeira, with whom she traveled on many occasions to New York to record albums. When Zequeira died in 1924, Vera performed solo or sometimes accompanied by a troubadour. In 1926 she joined Miguelito García, and the same year traveled to New York with García's Sexteto Occidente to record a selection of *sones*. In 1937 she formed another duo, this time with Lorenzo Hierrezuelo. Its popularity

would last for twenty-five years. They went to Mexico in 1974 and performed in nightclubs. Vera promoted Cuban music on Havana's radio stations. She composed the songs "Por qué me siento triste," "No me sabes querer," "Yo quiero que tú sepas," and the ultimate classic "Veinte años." She received certificates and medals from different Cuban institutions for her work, and retired in 1962 at age sixty-seven.

Vergara, Rolando. Composer. Born 19 February 1926, Havana. Vergara is the author of the popular boleros "Hermosa Habana" and "La nada nada inspira," of the *cha-cha-chás* "Calle 22" and "Yo bailo con Chana," and of "Rumba como quiera."

Vergara, Silvio. Double bass player and composer. Born 2 November 1940, Placetas; died 17 February 1996, Havana. Began his musical studies in his hometown, then performed with several local bands. In 1962 Vergara played the double bass with the Santa Clara Symphonic Orchestra. He was the leader of Orquesta Aliamén. He moved to Havana in 1965 and studied at the García Caturla Conservatory. He joined the orchestra of the Cuban Institute of Radio and Television and also played with Orquesta Cubana de Música Moderna and then with the National Symphony Orchestra. He was a professor at the Ignacio Cervantes Conservatory. Later, he joined Conjunto Rumbavana and Septeto Raisón. He is the author of "Y sabes bien," "Siempre hay una forma," "Bajo con tumba'o," "Llegó el malembe," and "Es tu recuerdo."

Verges, Dominica. Singer. Born 19 September 1918, Tapaste. In her early career, Verges performed with a *son* septet, then after moving to Havana, she joined Alicia Seoane's orchestra, and Orquesta Imperio. She also played with Justa García's quartet, Orquesta Siglo XX, and Orquesta Almendra. She is an outstanding *danzón* and *danzonete* interpeter. She was the vocalist with Charanga Típica Cubana.

Vidaurreta, José Luis. Professor and composer. Born 25 May 1912, died 1975. Studied music first in Havana, then continued in New York. Vidaurreta conducted choral groups and orchestras. He was a member of the National Academy of Arts and Letters and he wrote about the history of music. He is the author of several works for orchestra, some choral pieces, some chamber music, and other pieces.

Vilató, Orestes. Timbales player. Born 12 May 1944, Camagüey. Moved to New York in the 1960s, and played with José Fajardo and then Ray Barretto's band. He was a founding member of the Fania label, for whom he played on many successful records. He has played the timbales with famous Latin orchestras, given memorable concerts, and made excellent recordings, including those with Roberto Torres, Alfredo de la Fe, and Johnny Pacheco. In 1980 he moved to San Francisco and joined the band of Latin rock guitarist Carlos Santana, alongside Cuban *bongó* player Armando Peraza. In the 1990s, after leaving Santana, he joined Jon Santos's Machete Ensemble, playing more *típico* Cuban music, and through the 1990s, also recorded with Cachao, Patato Valdez, and Changuito.

Villa, Ignacio ("Bola de Nieve"). Singer, pianist, composer. Born 11 September 1911, Guanabacoa; died 2 October 1971, Mexico City. Rita Montaner nicknamed him Bola de Nieve, or Snowball, in consideration of his round shape and, ironically, his dark skin. He began his career playing piano accompaniment at silent movies in his hometown. He had studied music from the age of eight, starting at the Mateu Conservatory in Guanabacoa, then moving on to other musical institutions in Havana. In the 1930s he studied at the capital's School of Education. He was an outstanding pianist. He joined Gilberto Valdés in the La Verbena Cabaret. In 1933 he traveled to Mexico to work as accompanist to Rita Montaner. As a singer, he had a distinctive style, a personal way of singing very close to that of the French *chansoniers*. He traveled extensively. Among the songs he composed are "Si me pudieras querer," "Ay amor," "Tu me has de querer," and a lullaby, "Drumi mobila." He sang in many languages—Catalan, English, French, Italian, and Portuguese. He died in Mexico City during a South American tour. His body was taken back to Cuba and buried in his hometown.

Villafruela, Miguel. Saxophonist. Born 27 January 1955, Holguín. Villafruela started his musical studies in his hometown and continued them at the National School of Art. In 1980 he studied with Daniel Deffayet at the Paris Conservatory. He won First Prize at the National Saxophone Contest in France in 1982. He has performed in concerts in Cuba and abroad. He currently teaches saxophone at the Higher Institute of Art in Havana.

Villalón, Alberto. Composer, guitarist, *trova* singer. Born 7 June 1882, Santiago de Cuba; died 16 July 1955, Havana. One of the greatest musicians in the Cuban *trova* style. Villalón studied music with his sister América and guitar with Pepe Sánchez. At fourteen, he composed his first *canciones* and boleros. In 1908 he led a quartet and played guitar with Adolfo Colombo (tenor), Claudio García (baritone), and Emilio Reinoso (mandolin). He moved to Havana in 1900 and there continued his career as a troubadour. In 1904 he directed the Teatro de Variedades de Palatino, and two years later, premiered his musical El triunfo del bolero. He was a professor of guitar. In 1907 he recorded LPs of Cuban *canciones*. He toured in Mexico and the United States many times. Villalón founded Sexteto Nacional with Ignacio Piñeiro and Juan de la Cruz in 1927. In 1951 he was awarded the Commemorative Medal of the First Centenary of the Cuban Flag for his work. He composed *canciones* and boleros of a high standard, including "La paloma," "Yo reiré cuando tú llores," "Penas y flores," "Me da miedo quererte," "Martí," "La palma herida," "Los muertos de esta tumba no están tan muertos," "El ocaso," "Boda negra," and "Con cuánto amor." He also composed *guarachas, guajiras*, and rumbas.

Villanueva Theater. Built by Miguel Nins y Pons at Zulueta Street between Colón and Refugio Streets. It was opened in 1847 with a masked dance billed as the "Circo Habanero" (Havana circus). In 1853 it was named the Villanueva after Claudio Martinez Pinillo, Count of Villanueva. Dramas, operas, and *zarzuelas* were staged there, but it is best remembered for its politically sensitive *bufo* (comic) works. The first Cuban bufo company performed in this theater in 1868. The theater is enshrined in Cuba's revolutionary history because of an incident in 1869: during a performance of the work El perro huevero, as the Flor de Cuba Orchestra was playing, a group of Spanish volunteers shot at the audience. Miguel Nin was sentenced to death for that episode, but he escaped

to Mexico. The theater was closed down and, much later, demolished.

Villar, Manuel. Music researcher, director, adapter, music critic for radio and television. Born 25 February 1930, Havana. Villar has worked at the radio stations CMK, García Serra, Continental, CMBY, CMBF (Radio Musical), CMQ, Rebelde, and Taíno. He has been a critic and a television host and has worked as a consultant on music shows. He has presented research papers and given lectures at musicological conferences.

Villate, Gaspar. Composer. Born 27 January 1851, Havana; died 9 October 1891, Paris. At the age of sixteen Villate composed the opera Angelo, tirano de Padua, based on Victor Hugo's work. In 1868, at the start of the War of Independence, he moved to the United States, returning in 1871, after the war. He then composed the opera Las primeras armas de Richelieu. He traveled to Paris and studied with Bazin, Jonncieres, and Danhauser and became a friend of Giuseppe Verdi. In 1877 he saw the premier of his opera Zilia, with libretto by Solera, at the Italian Theater in Paris. In 1880 he staged his opera La Zarina at The Hague, and in 1885 the opera Baltasar, based on Avellaneda's drama, was premiered at the Real Theater in Madrid. It is said that there is no Cuban theme in Villate's plays, but this is not the case with his *criolla* works "La virgen tropical" and "Adiós a Cuba," and his *contradanzas*, which are considered to be his most important pieces. He also composed eight waltzes, Soirées Cubaines, and many *romanzas*.

Villegas, Tata. *Trova* singer and guitarist. Born 2 March 1886, Sancti Spiritus; died (?). His full name was Carlos Díaz de Villegas. Villegas began to become acquainted with the songs of the Cuban troubadours while still in his hometown. In 1899 he and his family moved to Havana. Once there, he began singing with relatives and friends. He went to study in the United States and sang there, first with a religious choir and then with a quartet, where he began to refine his style. Back in Cuba, he set up a duo with Alvaro Moreno, a tenor in the Arquímides Pous Company. He later sang as a duo with Pancho Majagua and became very popular. That partnership lasted over fifty years and only ended with

Pancho's death. During his last years, he participated in gatherings of trova singers.

viola. A percussion instrument, not to be confused with the orchestral string instrument of the same name, that evolved from the ancient Ethiopian lyre and made its first appearance in Cuba toward the end of the nineteenth century. It is a hoop with a body 8 centimeters high and 30 centimeters in diameter at its drumhead. From one of its sides, two wooden rods protrude and penetrate the body from side to side. These rods are adorned with ribbons of various colors. When playing the viola, the musician is seated; with the instrument leaning against his shoulder, he hits the viola with both hands. The musician may also sometimes play the viola when standing. It is played in the clave choruses; sometimes a banjo with no strings is used as a substitute.

Vitier, José María. Pianist and composer. Born 7 January 1954, Havana. Studied at the Amadeo Roldán Conservatory, under Margot Rojas and César López. Vitier has written music for plays, films, and television. With his brother Sergio, he composed the soundtrack for the television serial En silencio ha tenido que ser. He has also written music for children, as well as chamber and choral music. He was the founder of the band Síntesis, which combined elements of popular music (including fusion jazz) and classical elements, and he has also composed popular songs. He was piano professor at the National School of Art and studied composition at the Higher Institute of Art. His compositions include Trio for flute, cello and piano, Contextos, and Variaciones.

Vitier, Sergio. Guitarist and composer. Born 18 January 1948, Havana. Studied with Elías Barreiro and Isaac Nicola. Later, worked with Leo Brouwer, Federico Smith, and José Ardévol. Vitier has performed in halls and theaters all over Cuba and played with the National Symphony Orchestra as well as with the Conjunto Instrumental Nuestro Tiempo. He has written scores for films. His best-known soundtracks were for the films Girón, El programa del Moncada, De cierta manera, and La tierra y el cielo. He has also composed for the stage plays Divinas palabras and De la risible y trágica ascensión de Rubén Acíbar, and for the ballets Palanque, Iroko, and El dúo de siempre. His classic pieces include the symphonic work Desprendi-

mientos, and the chamber and electro-acoustic music Raíces, Danzaria, and Nacimient-vida, as well as some pieces for piano (Destiempos), for flute (Zonas con algo de son), and for percussion (Pequeña sesión de ritmo). Among his popular pieces are Siete bachianas populares cubanas, Corales, and El danzón. With his brother, he composed the music for the successful television serial En silencio ha tenido que ser. He is director of the Cuban National Dance company.

Vivar, Alejandro. Trumpet player. Born 1923, Havana; died 1979, Miami. Was known as "El Negro." Vivar played trumpet in the most sophisticated and successful Cuban jazz dance bands, including the Banda Gigante of Benny Moré, and he also contributed to the first descargas, organized in 1952 by Bebo Valdes, and the 1956 descargas recorded as Cuban Jam Sessions (his performance is still used as a model by students of the Cuban trumpet style). In the 1970s he moved to the United States, where he continued playing trumpet with both jazz and Latin American musicians.

W

Y

White, José. Composer, violinist, professor. Born 1 January 1836, Matanzas; died 12 March 1918, Paris. Was taught first by his father and, later, by other professors. White learned to play sixteen instruments: cello, double bass, guitar, piano, flute, clarinet, valve trombone, cornet, horn, clavichord, ophicleide, piccolo, *busccon de vara*, *altoviolo*, tympani, and, particularly, violin. When he was fifteen, he composed a Mass for voice and orchestra, and he gave his first violin concert at the age of nineteen, with Gottschalk accompanying him on piano. In 1855 he went to France to take advanced studies in violin, harmony, and composition at the Paris Conservatory. A year later, he won First Prize in the violin category. Some time later, he was teacher to Enesco and Thibaud. He returned to Cuba and gave concerts in Havana and Matanzas. In 1860 he returned to Paris, where he stayed for some time and gained a reputation, after having been accused of plotting against the government. In 1875 he went to Havana; he left hastily for Mexico, however, when he was accused of allying with the independence movement. From Mexico, he traveled to Venezuela and Brazil, where with Arthur Napoleao he founded the Classic Concert Society, and also worked as a conductor at the Imperial Conservatory. He visited other cities before settling in Paris in 1888. Among his most important works are Concerto for violin and orchestra, Six brilliant studies for violin, Quintet, Bolero for violin and orchestra, *Marcha cubana*, and *Danzas*. He also wrote Variations on an original theme, for clavichord and orchestra, and the universally popular *La bella cubana*.

yambú. *See* rumba.

Yáñez, Luis. Composer. Born 14 February 1920, Havana; died 24 November 1993. Was part of the *fílin* movement since its inception in the 1940s. Yáñez composed such boleros as "Nuestro sentimiento," "Me miras tiernamente," "Otra vez mi canción," and the hit "Oh, vida." He also composed the *cha-cha-chá* "Átomo," and the Afro-Cuban piece "Congo." Almost all his works were written in collaboration with Rolando Gómez. He was an editor at EGREM records.

Yolí Raymond, Lupe Victoria. Singer. Born 1938, Santiago de Cuba; died 28 February 1992, New York. Started singing in her hometown, and later moved to Havana, where she continued her career. Yolí Raymon became a member of Trío Tropicuba and then left to perform solo. She had a very distinct way of singing and performing. She was very popular during the late 1950s at the Club La Red in Havana. She performed on television and made several records. In 1960 she traveled to Mexico City to sing and then moved to New York. She made important recordings in the United States, especially those with Mongo Santamaria and with Tito Puente's orchestra. Her singing style and performances were very dynamic and rhythmic, and she mixed singing and free-form gestures with humor and grace. She was known as the "Queen of Latin Soul," and called herself "La Yiyiyi."

Yoruba, música. Includes singing, dance, and percussion. This type of music was introduced into Cuba by the Yoruba people, who were brought from Africa as slaves during the colonial period. They settled all over Cuba, but were concentrated mainly in Havana, Matanzas, and the Las Villas provinces. The Yoruba were known as Lucumís. Their musical instruments are the *batá* drums, the *abwes*, also called *chekerés* or *güiros*, and *bembé* drums, as well as *iyesá* drums, a variety of timbrels, *agogós* (bells), *atcherés* (a kind of maraca), whistles, and percussion instruments. The solo vocalist, the *akpwón*, is the lead singer to whom the chorus responds (León, *Música folklórica cubana*, 21–26). Yoruba singers originally sang in the Lucumí language, but with time they have also assimilated Spanish words.

yuka drums. Instruments used by various groups of Congo origin and brought to Cuba during colonial times. The word *yuka* is Bantú, and means "to beat" or "to drum." *Yukas* are preferably made from the hollow trunk of the avocado tree. The leather is nailed to one end, and the player hits the drumhead of the slanted body with both hands. The largest of these drums is a *caja*; the medium-sized a *mula*, because it is beaten at a constant rhythm recalling the trotting of the animal; the smallest a *cachimbo*, a term allusive to its small size. The *yuka* drums are accompanied by *palos*, on a *guagua* or on the drum body, and also by a percussive piece of iron. The rhythms on the drum body are played with one bare hand and with a hard mallet in the other. The player wears two small maracas (*nkembí*), made of gourd or metal, on his wrists. *Yuka* drums are used to accompany a dance called *yuka*, performed by a couple standing apart facing each other, moving with very short steps like short, quick taps, alternating toe and heel. This dance represents a stylized conquest: the man chases the woman, and she avoids him (León, *Del canto y el tiempo*, 67).

Yumuri. *See* Valle, Moises.

Z

Zaballa, Miguel. Guitarist and *trova* singer. Born 1886, Havana; died 17 December 1965. Zaballa performed second voice in the orchestra he was part of. During the 1920s, he set up in a popular duo with Floro Zorrilla. They both performed in theaters and movie theaters in the Cuban capital and on tours of the island. They also made records that sold in the United States, the Dominican Republic, Haiti, Puerto Rico, and Mexico. He later sang in duos with Antonio Machín, Pepe Luis, and others. In 1924 he joined the Sexteto Colín as a guitarist. In 1927 he joined Don Azpiazu's orchestra and sang alongside Machín at the Casino Nacional. In 1929 he founded the Conjunto Zaballa, in which he also conducted, played guitar, and sang.

(Los) Zafiros. Vocal quartet founded in 1962. They sang in different popular genres, including Cuban *canción*, rumba, conga, calypso, *bossa nova*, and even doo-wop. In structure, the instrumentalists alternated with each other while the backup singers maintained the rhythm. The members were Ignacio Elejalde, Miguel Galban, Eduardo "El Chino" Hernandez, and Leoncio "Kike" Morua. The quartet was influenced by American doowop groups of the day, but its repertoire was undoubtedly Cuban. It was particularly popular during the 1960s. A new generation of young singers is currently following their line. The electric guitarist, Miguel Galban, had a distinctive playing style. He enjoyed a new success after performing on records by members of the Buena Vista Social Club and has subsequently toured with bass player Cachaito. Galban has recorded a solo album, which was produced by the American guitarist Ry Cooder.

Zamora, Jorge. Composer. Born 19 April 1918, Havana. Zamora was also a guitarist and member of the *fílin* movement. He is author of such pieces as "Derroche de felicidad" and "Enséñame" (*canciones*); "La basura" and "Señor Juez" (*cha-cha-chá*); "Qué bueno está el ambiente" (mambo); and "Bomboro quiñá" (*son*). He is a television and movie actor and has lived in Mexico since the 1940s.

zapateo cubano. Dance style from the Cuban countryside, derived from the *zapateo andaluz* (a tap dance from Andalusia in Spain). It is also related to different Latin American *zapateos*. There is documentary evidence of the existence of the Cuban *zapateo* by the beginning of the seventeenth century. The dance follows the same principles as the *punto guajiro*: the partners dance separately, and as its name suggests (the word *zapateo* derives from the Spanish word *zapato*, "shoe"), the dancers have to constantly tap with their heels while keeping the rhythm. The man performs the most difficult steps, with his arms crossed at the back. Some experienced dancers put knives into their shoes in imitation of a cock's spurs, adding a real danger to the performance of the steps. As they dance, the women flirt with their skirts and follow the rhythm with their feet. The Cuban *zapateo* was popular during the second half of the nineteenth century and began to fade in the first decades of the twentieth century. It was danced mainly at country parties and fairs, in small towns, and at *bufo* shows. Today the dance has practically disappeared.

zarzuela. Cuban operetta. Although its origins stretch back to the seventeenth century, it was not until the second half of the nineteenth century that the *zarzuela* reached its peak of popularity in Spain. Under the influence of the Spanish version, the Cuban *zarzuela* emerged in the twentieth century. In 1927 a lyrical period reigned at the Regina Theater in Havana, as works by Cuban authors were staged there and became very popular. In 1931 a successful *zarzuela* company, managed by Agustín Rodríguez (with Gonzalo Roig's musical collaboration), mounted a season at the Martí Theater. They performed there for many years. The most important Cuban *zarzuela* composers and their works include: Eliseo Grenet with *La virgen morena*, *El submarino cubano*, and *Niña Rita* (with Ernesto Lecuona and lyrics by Aurelio Riancho and Antonio Castell), which launched the singer Rita Montaner; Ernesto Lecuona with *El cafetal*, *María la O*, *El batey*, *Lola Cruz* (with script by Gustavo Sánchez Galarraga), *Cuando la Habana era inglesa*, *La plaza de la catedral*, *Rosa la china*, and *Niña Rita* (with Eliseo Grenet); Gonzalo Roig with *La hija del sol*, *El clarín*, *La Habana de noche*, and, above all, the immortal *Cecilia Valdés* (with a script by Agustín Rodríguez and Rodrigo Prats, who also wrote *Soledad*, *María Belén Chacón*, *Amalia Batista*, *Guamá*, *La Habana que vuelve*, *La perla del caribe* and *El mayoral*). The Cuban *zarzuela* reflected the country's social and historic problems at the time and displayed them within the frame of Cuban musical expression.

Zayas, Alberto. Rumba composer and singer. Born 14 February 1908, Matanzas; died 1983, Guanabacoa. When he was one year old, Zayas's family moved to Havana. At the age of fifteen, he started singing and became a member of the Septeto Habanero and other *son* bands. He directed a folk group that made recordings and performed in theaters and on radio. He toured outside Cuba with the Cuban Folkloric Group. He is the author of such *guaguancós* as "Tindé aró," "Ya no tengo amigos," "Oye mi rumba," "A la rumba no le temas," and "El vive bien." Along with Fernando Ortiz, he disseminated information and gave lectures about Cuban folklore.

Zerquera, Orquesta de Pablo. Wind orchestra that played at many festivities in Havana in the 1920s. It was conducted by the cornetist Pablo Zerquera and composed of Rogelio Solís (double bass); Eleno Herrera (trombone); Jesús Goicochea (ophicleide); Francisco Morales and Isaac Fernández (violins); Eduardo Goicochea Arrieta and Avelino Sis Gutiérrez (clarinets); Jesús Delgado (*güiro*); and Santiago Sandoval (timbales).

Zerquera, Pablo. Cornetist and conductor. Born 1 June 1886, Sagua la Grande; died 1966, Havana. As a young man, Zerquera moved to Havana to study music with Professor Avelino Ceballos. He was a cornetist in the *orquesta típica* Orquesta de Valenzuela, and later launched his own *danzón* band, which played until the 1920s.

Zertucha, Casimiro. Violinist. Born 1880, Havana; died 1950. When Zertucha was a child, his family moved to Bejucal. At the age of fifteen, he began studying violin with Juan Mercado, and a year later he entered the National Conservatory, where he studied with Professor Tomás de la Rosa. He won awards for his playing and went to Paris to study with José White and Marsick. He played violin in several concerts in France and conducted a small orchestra at the Riche festivals. In 1914 he returned to Cuba, where he gave concerts and became the bandleader for Albert Falcón's Orquesta de Cámara. He also worked as a teacher for many years.

Zervigón, Eddy. Flutist and bandleader. Born 1 July 1940, Guines. With his brothers Rudy and Kelvin, Eddy Zervigón has lived and worked in New York since 1962. He played in the orchestras of Johnny Pacheco and Ion Pérez. In the 1970s, the three brothers and the singer Roberto Torres founded a *charanga* band called Orquesta Broadway, which was very successful. Their repertoire included Cuban and Caribbean songs, of which Eddy wrote several. In the 1990s he joined the Africando project, which united West African singers with New York–based salsa musicians.

Appendix

A. Musical Instruments

abebe
agogo
anakué
Arará drums
arébe
assongué
atcheré
bandurria
batá drums
binkomé (or biankomé)
bocú
bombo criollo (Creole bass-drum)
bongó
bonkó enchemiyá
botija
cajón
cencerro
chachá
chekeré
claves
conga drum
corneta china
cuchara
ekón
ekué
enkómo
erikundi
flute, aboriginal
fondo
fotuto
galleta
guataca
güiro
hierro
iyesá drums
kinfuiti
kuchi-yeremá
laud
maraca
maraca, aboriginal
marímbula
maruga

mayohuacán
olivas sonoras
opiabá
órgano oriental
paila criolla
quijada
quinto
reja
sanmartín
sartén
tahona
timbal criollo
tingotalango (or tumbadera)
tiple
tres
tumbadora
tumba francesa, tambores de la
viola
yuka drums

B. Music Magazines

Boletín de Música
Conservatorio
Cuba Musical
Filarmónico Mensual
Musicalia
Periódico Musical
Pro-Arte Musical
Revista de Música

C. Orchestras and Bands

Afrocuba, Grupo
Afro-Cuban All Stars
Aguilar, Grupo Campesino de
Aleman, Orquesta
Alfonso, Orquesta de Tata
Aliamen, Orquesta
Almendra, Orquesta
America, Orquesta
Anacaona, Orquesta
Aragon, Orquesta
Arcaño y Sus Maravillas, Orquesta
Aviles, Orquesta
(Los) Bocucos
Bolero, Sexteto

Boloña, Sexteto
Broadway, Orquesta
Buena Vista Social Club
Caney, Conjunto
Casino, Conjunto
Casino de la Playa, Orquesta
Castro, Orquesta Hermanos
Cervantes, Orquesta
Charanga Cubana
Cisneros, Orquesta de Gabriel
Clave y Guaguancó
(La) Concha de Oro, Orquesta
Corbacho, Orquesta de
Cosmopolita, Orquesta
Cuba, Sexteto
Ensueño, Orquesta
Estrellas Cubanas, Orquesta
Estudiantina Oriental
Experimentación Sonora del ICAIC, Grupo de
Failde, Orquesta
(La) Flor de Cuba, Orquesta
Gloria Matancera, Conjunto
González, Orquesta de Félix
González, Orquesta de Neno
González, Orquesta de Nicolas
Gris, Orquesta
Guaracheros de Oriente
Habanero, Sexteto
Havana Chamber Orchestra
Havana Municipal Orchestra
Havana Philharmonic Orchestra
Havana Quartet
Havana Symphony Orchestra
Hermanos Bravo
Ideal, Orquesta
Irakere, Grupo
Jorrín, Orquesta
Jovenes Classicos del Son
Jovenes del Cayo, Conjunto
Karachi, Grupo
Lebatard, Orquesta Hermanos
López, Orquesta de Belisario
Maravillas de Florida, Orquesta
Melodias del 40, Orquesta
Moncada, Grupo
Moré, Banda Gigante de Benny
Muñequitos, Grupo Los
Muñoz, Orquesta de Ernesto
Nacional, Septeto

National Folkloric Ensemble
National Symphony Orchestra
(Los) Naranjos
NG La Banda
Ojeda, Grupo Campesino de
Original de Manzanillo, Orquesta
Palau, Orquesta Hermanos
Peña, Orquesta de Enrique
Puig, Orquesta de Cheo Belén
Puig, Orquesta de Jose Belen
Renovación Musical, Grupo de
Revé, Orquesta
Ritmo Oriental, Orquesta
Riverside, Orquesta
Rodríguez, Conjunto de Arsenio
Rojas, Orquesta de Perico
Romeu, Orquesta
Ruiz, Orquesta de Pedrito
Rumbavana, Conjunto
Saratoga, Conjunto
Sensación, Orquesta
Sierra Maestra, Septeto
(Los) Sobrinos del Juez
Son 14, Conjunto
Sonora Matancera
Sublime, Orquesta
Torroella, Orquesta
Valenzuela, Orquesta
Van Van, Orquesta
Zerquera, Orquesta de Pablo

D. Theaters

Alhambra Theater
Coliseo Theater (later, the Principal)
Diorama Theater
Irijoa Theater (later, the Martí)
Payret Theater
Principal Theater
Reina Theater (later, the Cuba)
Sauto Theater
Tacón Theater (later, the National; currently, the Garcia Lorca)
Villanueva Theater

Works Cited

Acosta, Leonardo. "La música, el cine y la experiencia cubana." *Del tambor al sintetizador*. Havana: Editorial Letras Cubanas, 1983.

Alvarenga, Oneyda. *Música popular Brasileña*. Mexico City: Fondo de Cultura Económica, 1947.

Ardévol, José. *Introducción a Cuba: La música*. Havana: Instituto del Libro, 1969.

Barnet, Miguel. "Pregones Cubanos." *Cuba*, September 1964.

Carpentier, Alejo. *Carteles*, 12 July 1931.

———. *La música en Cuba*. Mexico City: Fondo de Cultura Económica, 1946.

Castellanos, Israel. "Los instrumentos musicales de los afrocubanos." In *Archivos del Folklore* 2, nos. 2 and 4 (1927).

Durán, Gustavo. *Recordings of Latin American Song and Dances: An Annotated and Selected List of Popular and Folk Music*. Washington, D.C.: Music Division, Pan-American Union, 1942.

Fernández de Oviedo, Gonzalo. *Historia general y natural de las Indias*. 2 vols. Madrid, Imprenta de la Real Academia de la Historia, 1851–55.

Giro, Radamés. *Panorama de la música popular cubana*. Havana: Editorial Letras Cubanas, 1998.

González, Jorge Antonio. *La composición operística en Cuba*. Havana: Editorial Letras Cubanas, 1986.

González Freire, Natividad. *Teatro cubano 1927–1961*. Havana: Ministerio de Relacioned Exteriores, 1961.

Gonzalez Rubiera, Vicente ("Guyún"). "Armonia aplicada a la guitarra." Unpublished manuscript.

González Rubiera, Vicente, and Rosendo Ruiz Jr. "Música popular cubana: Una valoración necesaria." Unpublished manuscript.

González Rubiera, Vincente, and Rosendo Ruiz Jr. "Los años trreinta: núcleo central de la trova intermedia." In *Panorama de la música popular cubana*, edited by Radamés Giro. Havana: Editorial Letras Cubanas, 1998.

Grenet, Emilio. "Música cubana: Orientaciones para su conocimiento y estudio." In *Panorama de la música popular cubana*, edited by Radamés Giro. Havana: Editorial Letras Cubanas, 1998.

Grenet, Emilio. *Música popular cubana*. Havana: Carasa y Cía, 1939. Reprinted as "Musica cubana: Orientaciones para sy conocimiento y estudio," in *Panorama de la música popular cubana*, edited by Radamés Giro. Havana: Editorial Letras Cubanas, 1998.

Grenet, Emilio. *Popular Cuban Music*. Havana: Ministry of Education, 1939.

León, Argeliers. *Música folklórica cubana*. Havana: Ediciones del Departamento de Música de la Biblioteca Nacional José Martí, 1964.

———. *Del canto y el tiempo*. Havana: Ediciones del Departamento de Música de la Biblioteca Nacional José Martí, 1964.

Linares, María Teresa. *El sucu-sucu de Isla de Pinos*, 1967.

———. *Viejos cantos afrocubanos* (LP). Vol. 1 of *Antología de la música afrocubana*. LD3325. Havana: EGREM, 1981.

Martínez Furé, Rogelio. "Los iyesás." *La Gaceta de Cuba* (Havana), June 1974.

Morales Patiño, Oswaldo. *Las olivas sonoras en Cuba y en Mexico*. Havana: Grupo Guamá, 1942.

Muguercia, Alberto. "Teodora Ginés: ¿Mito o realidad histórica?" *Revista de la Biblioteca Nacional José Martí* (Havana), no. 3, September/December 1971.

Ortiz, Fernando. *Los instrumentos de la música afrocubana*. 5 vols. Havana: Editora Universitaria, 1952.

Pichardo, Esteban. *Diccionario provincial casi razonado de voces cubanas*. La Habana, 1836.

Rivero de la Calle, José. *Las culturas aborígenes en Cuba*. Havana, 1966.

Ruiz, Rosendo, Jr. "El bolero cubano." In *Panorama de la musica popular cubana*, edited by Radamés Giro. Havana: Editorial Letras Cubanas, 1998.

Sánchez de Fuentes, Eduardo. *El folk-lor en la música cubana*. Havana: Imprenta El Siglo XX, 1923.

"Septeto Nacional." Published by Museo Nacional de la Música for the 50th anniversary of its formation.

Simon, Pedro. "La música cubana en la danza." *Cuba en el Ballet*, September 1971.

Suero, Augusto. "Tonadas trinitarias." *Signos*, 1974.

Urfé, Odilio. *Islas Magazine: Universidad Central de las Villas* 2, no. 1 (September–December 1959).

———. *El danzón*. Havana: CNC, 1965.

Helio Orovio is a historian and musicologist with the Institute of Ethnology and Folklore at the Academy of Sciences
in Cuba. He is the author of *El bolero latino* (Cuba, 1995) and
Música por el Caribe (Cuba, 1994).

Library of Congress Cataloging-in-Publication Data
Orovio, Helio.
[Diccionario de la música cubana. English]
Cuban music from A to Z / Helio Orovio.
1st English-language ed.
Includes bibliographical references.
ISBN 0-8223-3186-1 (alk. paper)
ISBN 0-8223-3212-4 (pbk.: alk. paper)
1. Music—Cuba—Dictionaries.   2. Musicians—Cuba—
Biography—Dictionaries.   I. Title.
ML106.C807613   2003   780'.97291'03pdc22
2003017350